HOW TO
AVOID
PROBATE

HOW TO AVOID PROBATE

by

Norman F. Dacey

CROWN PUBLISHERS, INC., NEW YORK

TABLE OF CONTENTS

PLEASE NOTE THAT ALL WILL AND TRUST FORMS ARE ON PAGES WHICH ARE
PERFORATED FOR EASY REMOVAL FROM THE BOOK

"The current cost of probate administration is nothing more nor less than another 'death tax' levied on the assets of a decedent's estate, yet producing nothing of benefit for the family of the deceased. This drain on an estate is tolerated by the general public only because it has been led to believe that such costs are 'normal' and unavoidable.

"The writer urges that the legal profession give greater consideration to the use of the revocable inter vivos trust as a means of reducing the high cost of dying."

Milton E. Meyer, Jr., in the
Colorado Bar Journal

"One who seeks to find a solution to the problems of dispensing with or shortening the administration of decedents' estates is literally a voice crying in the wilderness."

Prof. Thomas E. Atkinson
(in "Wills" [2d ED 1953])

HOW TO
AVOID
PROBATE

Chapter 1

WHAT IS "PROBATE"?

In every legal jurisdiction in America there exists a special court which concerns itself with the administration of estates. Sometimes called the "orphans", "surrogate" or "chancery" court, its most common name is "probate court".

A properly drawn will should state your wishes as to the disposition of your property and name an "executor" whose duty it will be to see to it that your instructions are carried out. The executor will present your will to the probate court with an inventory of the assets and liabilities of your estate. The court will determine that the document is legal in both form and execution and will "accept" it for probate. Through the medium of a court-ordered legal notice inserted in a local newspaper, your creditors will be notified of your death and given an opportunity to present their claims. The notice will also serve to alert interested parties who may wish to enter a legal objection to the disposition of your estate in accordance with the terms of your will. The court will hear the claims of all such parties and rule upon their validity. If the terms of your will are unclear, the court will "construe" them, deciding officially what you meant.

If you have died intestate—that is, without leaving a valid will—the state will write your will for you. By this is meant that in the absence of a legal and valid will, your estate will be distributed in accordance with the law of the state in which you live. The probate court will appoint an "administrator" whose duties will approximate those of the executor who would have attended to the details of probating your estate if you had left a proper will.

If through illness or senility an individual becomes incompetent to handle his own affairs, relatives or other persons responsible for him may appeal to the probate court to appoint a "conservator" over his assets to protect them against loss. In the case of a minor legally disqualified by reason of his age from acting on his own behalf, the court may appoint a "guardian" to act for him if he owns, or is to receive, property in his own right.

If under the terms of your will, you establish a trust for the benefit of your heirs naming as trustee an individual or a bank, the probate court might be called upon to appoint a successor trustee if the individual trustee dies or the corporate trustee resigns or goes out of business.

While there may be many variations of the above, as well as additional peripheral duties, these are the principal concerns of the probate court. Your legal residence determines the jurisdiction of the probate court. Perhaps you reside in two or more places—you have a home in the country in Connecticut, a town house in New York and a winter home in Florida. The legal profession will bless your memory and the probate judges in all three jurisdictions will lick their chops. Each will make as good a case as he can that you were a legal resident of his bailiwick and will attempt to enfold your estate into the jurisdiction of his court.

Recently, a wealthy New Yorker died leaving a valid will in which he declared himself to be a legal resident of New York City and specifically directed that his will be probated there. Not so, said the probate judge in the small Connecticut town where he'd had a country home. Ruling that the deceased had spent enough time at his country home to be considered a resident of Connecticut, the judge assumed jurisdiction —and that's where the will was probated.

Perhaps there will be no question about your legal residence. Perhaps it can be clearly established. But that property you own in another state—the house in Florida, the retirement site in sunny Arizona, the farm you bought in Vermont—these can be a real nuisance. They will require an "ancillary administration", which simply means that they'll have to be probated where they are. The lawyer who handles the probating of your estate at the place of your legal residence will hire another lawyer at the place where the out-of-state property is physically located. By the time your estate gets through paying for this legal daisy chain, your shade, gloomily peering down from some heavenly point, will be wishing you'd simply rented.

The probate procedure is time-consuming. Not long ago, an up-to-date survey was made of the time involved in probating an estate. In a questionnaire sent to knowledgeable attorneys in all 50 states, inquiry was made as to the time required to clear the average estate through probate in their jurisdictions. They were asked to indicate the most appropriate description from among a wide choice ("less than six months", "six months to one year", "one to two years", etc.). Overwhelmingly, the time indicated was "two to five years". If there is any complication or any contest by the heirs, it can drag on interminably.

It is the general practice to permit a widow to draw a modest allowance from the estate during the course of probate. Other heirs, including children, do not ordinarily have this privilege, however, and none of the heirs—the widow included—has access to the principal until probate is completed.

The probate procedure attracts publicity. Every newspaper has a reporter regularly assigned to cover the probate court. If there is anything unusual about the size of the estate or the nature of the assets, or if the decedent is at all known in the community, his private financial affairs are publicized in the newspapers. That publicity often attracts the attention of unscrupulous persons who prey upon the beneficiaries.

The probate procedure is costly. Recently, in an article in a national magazine, a well-known estate attorney answered questions about probate. Asked to estimate the costs of estate administration, he replied:

> "On small estates of $10,000 to $20,000 they are likely to be, on average, 20%. On medium sized estates of, say $100,000, they probably would be around 10%. On larger estates they would be a smaller percentage."

Avoiding probate does not mean avoiding taxes. Taxes are something else again. What we are talking about avoiding here is the expense, the delay and the publicity of probating. So far as the expense is concerned, a leading legal reference service gives the following estimated costs of estate administration (the figures include lawyers', executors', appraisers', and probate court costs but do not include taxes):

Gross Estate Less Debts, Etc.		Probate and Administration Expenses	
From	To	Amount on Column 1	Rates in Excess
50,000	100,000	4,300	7.8
100,000	200,000	8,200	7.2
200,000	300,000	15,400	6.8
300,000	400,000	22,200	6.5
400,000	500,000	28,700	6.3
500,000	600,000	35,000	6.0
600,000	700,000	41,000	5.9
700,000	800,000	46,900	5.8
800,000	900,000	52,700	5.7
900,000	1,000,000	58,400	5.6
1,000,000	1,500,000	64,000	5.6
1,500,000	2,000,000	92,000	5.6
2,000,000	2,500,000	120,000	5.5
2,500,000	3,000,000	147,550	5.5
3,000,000	3,500,000	175,000	5.4
3,500,000	4,000,000	202,000	5.3
4,000,000	4,500,000	228,500	5.2
4,500,000	5,000,000	254,500	5.1
5,000,000	6,000,000	280,000	5.0
6,000,000	7,000,000	330,000	4.9
7,000,000	8,000,000	379,000	4.8
8,000,000	9,000,000	427,000	4.7
9,000,000	10,000,000	474,000	4.6
10,000,000	-----------	520,000	4.5

Several months after completing his duties and being discharged by the probate court, an executor received a check for three cents from the Internal Revenue Service with a note explaining that it represented a refund of an overpayment resulting from an error in addition which an audit had uncovered on the tax return he had filed. Wanting to be perfectly correct, he stopped in at the probate court and asked what he should do with it. The procedure was simple, he was told. They would re-open the estate, instruct him officially to pay the three cents to a specified heir and then close the estate again. All this was done and a few days later he received his instruction from the court to pay the three cents to the heir. Enclosed with it was the probate court's bill for $8.78 for re-opening the estate. There being no money left in the estate, he had to pay it out of his own pocket.

"Woe unto you, lawyers! For ye have taken away the key of knowledge: Ye entered not in yourselves, and them that were entering in ye hindered."

(Luke XI, 52)

Chapter 2

PROBATE: THE UGLY SIDE

In most areas of this country the probate procedure is a scandal, a form of tribute levied by the legal profession upon the estates of its victims, both living and dead.

The New York Herald-Tribune editorially denounced the probate system in that city where "clubhouse lawyers profit to the extent of $1,000,000 annually in fees, many taken, at a large percentage, from small guardianships where every dollar is needed".

This corrupt system has been a fixture in America for generations. New York's famous reform mayor, Fiorello La Guardia, called the probate court "the most expensive undertaking establishment in the world".

The magazine *Trusts And Estates,* a professional journal in the trust field, editorially condemned the corrupt practices in the probate field, observing that "the public respect for judges and members of the Bar is at stake".

An article in the Journal of the American Bar Association described the Connecticut probate system as "one of the most viciously corrupt systems ever distorted by the inventive minds of the greedy". An article in the Bridgeport Post called the probate system a "gravy train".

The heiress to one of America's great farm machinery fortunes died leaving several children. The Democratic probate judge in the New England town where she'd had her legal residence appointed a political crony as guardian of the children. He milked the estate with scandalous fees approved by his friend on the bench. On the strength of an exposure of the facts, the judge's Republican opponent ousted him in an election—and promptly fired the guardian and appointed one of his own Republican friends to replace him. This example will serve to illustrate the extent to which the estates of children and incompetents are at the mercy of a vicious politico/legal spoils system.

Many probate judges earn more than the governors of their states—indeed, one Connecticut judge has an income 20% greater than that of the Chief Justice in Washington!

The Connecticut Republican Citizens Committee announced that it would delve into the records of the operation of probate courts "to examine the pursuits of the big city bosses—the politics for profit boys—tracing their tentacles through probate court fees".

The probate judge in one Connecticut town, concurrently pursuing his private law practice, appeared before the town zoning commission on behalf of a client. The board acted favorably upon his client's petition. Later, it was discovered that immediately prior to the hearing he had named each of the members of the zoning commission to a juicy appraisership. Here was a brazen example of bribery, the pay-off being not out of his own pocket but out of the pockets of the beneficiaries of the estates which were forced to pass through his court. When those who had opposed the zoning petition took the matter to court, the judge who heard the case ruled that while the affair had a strong odor of impropriety, there was no proof that the zoning commissioners would not have acted favorably upon the petition even without the bribe—and he dismissed the appeal!

Probably no area of the probate procedure is as openly scandalous as the appointment of paid appraisers. A former president of the Connecticut Bar Association has described this as an out-and-out racket. Said he:

> "The court-appointed appraiser is almost always a political henchman whose loyalty in getting votes to help re-elect the probate judge will be strengthened by his gratitude for the fees he will get.
>
> "Instead of being disinterested and concerned with estimating the estate at the fairest possible figure, they place the highest values on the property with which they can get away in order to increase their own fees."

There have been countless instances where appraisers fees have been "kicked back" to the probate judge or to the clerk of the probate court or to the political party controlling the court in that jurisdiction, or to the lawyer handling the estate.

There are some exceptions to this practice of over-valuation. A documentary program recently shown on network television disclosed an instance where a probate judge, a court-appointed administrator, and two court-appointed appraisers conspired to inventory at $30,000 the real estate in a trust of which two children were the sole beneficiaries. They then formed a dummy corporation which bought the real estate from the administrator at that price—and promptly re-sold it for $240,000!

When you die, a probate judge will appoint two complete strangers to appraise your estate. The political boss of your town may have called the judge and said: "You remember old Joe Green, don't you, over in the 5th district? Joe's out of a job and has had a lot of hard luck lately. He needs a little help. Give him an appraisership." Two such "old Joe Greens" will be appointed as appraisers of your estate.

The executor whom you have appointed in your will, helpless before the legal mumbo-jumbo with which the probate process has been surrounded, will hire a lawyer to do the job. The lawyer will telephone a broker and obtain quotations on the stocks and bonds you've left. A friend of the lawyer in the real estate business will drive by your house and provide the lawyer with a rough estimate of its value. The lawyer will list these figures in an "appraisal". The two court-appointed "Joe Greens" will be called in and asked to sign their names at the bottom of the appraisal. Each will then be handed a check which will represent a chunk of your estate. Neither person did any work of any kind to earn the fee paid him. Perhaps your estate is small and it will be all that your widow and children can do to get by on what has been left to them. That is of no consequence. Before your family gets a penny, the probate racketeers will have exacted their legal tribute.

In a closed-session speech to the Connecticut probate assembly, a powerful "union" of probate judges, a member from one of the larger districts acknowledged that 90% of the persons appointed as appraisers do no work at all.

Why isn't this disgraceful system ended, you ask? Because to end it would require legislative action—and the state legislatures of America are controlled by lawyer-members who have a vested interest in continuing the system exactly as it is. They see to it that non-lawyer legislators get occasional appraiserships to keep them happy—and silent.

Why don't crusading newspapermen disclose the facts? In 90% of American communities, there is but one newspaper. A check of the probate court records will disclose that juicy appraiserships go regularly to two or three key men on the newspaper. They see to it that nobody bites the hand that is feeding them.

So-called "special guardianships" are another shock-ing aspect of the probate racket. These "special guardians", invariably lawyers, bleed the estates of minors of huge amounts annually. A probate court clerk in Chicago appointed 691 such guardians in a nine-month period. Forty percent of the guardianships went to four of his friends. One of them got 76 guardianships in that period—about two a week.

The New York World-Telegram recently called for an end to the "judicial gravy" which marks the appointment in that state of lawyers as guardians, referees and committees for minors and incompetents. Scoring the fantastically high fees extorted for little or no work done, the newspaper decried the "milk and bilk scandal" and called for public disclosure of the appointments and the fees involved. Branding the present custom as a "covert hocus-pocus system" the editorial demanded to know why judges and lawyers should object to such disclosure—unless they have something to hide.

The foreign-born proprietor of a small grocery store recently sought my advice. He'd won $95,000 in the Irish Sweepstakes. Since the ticket was for himself "and family", the winnings were split. The lawyer he employed to help him send for the money not only charged him $5,000, but had himself appointed special guardian of the grocer's children. The bewildered man hounded the probate judge for eighteen months until the latter finally removed the special guardian—for which stroke of his pen the judge charged the grocer $1,000. When the latter complained to the Grievance Committee of the Bar Association, he was told to be quiet or the lawyer and the probate judge would sue him for every cent he had.

A trust officer reported: "The special guardian's fee seldom has any relationship to the value of the services rendered. In one case, a special guardian—a former city official—came in one Friday at noon. He said: 'Let's see these four securities the estate has. If you have those, I'll assume you have the rest and besides I want to make the first race at Jamaica.' At the most he was here twenty minutes and he asked for and got a special guardian's fee of $6,000."

Said another New York trust officer: "Just don't die in Brooklyn or in Nassau or Suffolk Counties and leave money to children under twenty-one. Those special guardians out there will rip through your estate like a small tornado."

The president of the Boston Bar Association deplored the "unfortunate, if not down-right unethical, situations developing in many counties. The public is being deprived of the integrity and impartiality of the probate system to which it is entitled".

One lawyer to whom I protested the inequity of the probate system wanted to know what I was making a fuss about. "It's a dead man's money, isn't it?" he shrugged.

Professor William J. Pierce, Director of the Legislative Research Center at the University of Michigan Law

School, has decried the corrupt practices in the probate system. Said he:

> "The vast majority of lawyers and judges in the United States recognize the need for basic reform in our probate court. But few lawyers and fewer judges are willing or have the courage to speak out. That means that it's going to be up to the public to make the start. The way to begin is for each community to take a good, long look at what goes on in the local probate court. Sooner or later some of your own family's money will be involved. It's time we found out just what part of the billions going through those courts sticks to the fingers of politicians and court appointees. Then we must find a way to put an end to this legal extortion."

A common practice is for lawyers drawing wills to name themselves as trustees of the estates upon the testators' death. However expert they may be at the law, most lawyers simply are not competent enough at investing to assume such responsibility. However clumsy they may be at investment, though, the wills they draw provide them with a life annuity in the form of a trustee fee.

The practice of most lawyers tends to orbit around a specific bank. Every client who seeks to set up a bank trust will be directed to that particular bank by the lawyer drawing his will. A "gentleman's agreement" requires the bank to whom the executorship and trust are thus directed to reciprocate by hiring the lawyer who drew the will to probate the estate.

There are a lot of people to be paid off. The Connecticut League of Women Voters has pointed out that "the present system provides for a multitude of fees which are paid piecemeal at so many different stages that it tends to create a vested interest in complicated procedures".

John Crosby, writing in the New York Herald-Tribune, observed:

> "Justice is not a simple thing, but it is certainly not as complicated, as tortuous, as technical, as expensive, and as time-wasting as American courts make it. It's time for the entire legal profession to examine its own ethics. It seems to me that the American Bar Association has substituted public relations for ethics. They repeat the words ethics, legal ethics, the ethics of the legal profession the same way that advertising people repeat a simple slogan again and again. If you hear it often enough it must be true."

Recently, Thomas Collins wrote in his widely-syndicated column, "The Golden Years":

> "If you are retired, and have a little property and expect to bequeath it quietly to your heirs some day, you had better be prepared to do some twirling in your grave. Because the lawyers and the government have things balled up good.
>
> "I have known for some time that it was a complicated business to die while owning property. But this week I sat in on the reading of a will in a lawyer's office. Just like in the movies. And it wasn't just complicated. It was unbelievable.
>
> "It seemed a simple estate. The man had three children and his will stated he wanted it divided equally among them after special bequests of $2,500 to old friends. This also seemed simple enough. But then the lawyer folded up the will and in effect told the children to come back in two years and he'd try to have them some money. There was no funny stuff involved and the lawyer was a fine one. This is just the way things are in some states and in some circumstances.
>
> "The lawyer estimated that it would take 18 months to get the will probated and the appraisal made. After that would come liquidation of the property, payment of the taxes and finally distribution of money to the children.
>
> "Paperwork, judges, lawyers, affidavits, appraisals and time, time, time. So much time, in fact, that when the children at last cash in, the grave will be cold, the weeds sprouting—and they will be getting their money not from Papa but from a complex of tax men, lawyers and courts.
>
> "My best advice on the matter is just not to die."
>
> "The dependents must thank a judge, a court, a lawyer, a politician, a bank or somebody for letting them have the money. The claim of lawyers that all this is necessary to protect a man's estate is not enough.
>
> "Most people die without wills. It seems to me that the legal profession cannot shrug its shoulders and say people should know all this. Many people now retiring never finished high school. They don't know what they don't know. Since the lawyers in the main have written the laws and since they and the government are the ones who have made our tax and inheritance laws so complicated, there must be some responsibility on their part to let people know what legal traps lie in front of them.
>
> "In my mail are many letters from people who say they don't trust lawyers. This is an old cliche. But again, it seems that it's something that should be taken care of by lawyers. And not just to make more fees for themselves. People are hurt more than lawyers when people don't trust them."

Under the conditions here described, it remains for each individual to search diligently for some way to avoid probate.

Grateful acknowledgment is made to Murray Teigh Bloom for background material appearing in this chapter.

"The first thing we do, let's kill all the lawyers."
William Shakespeare
(Henry VI, Part II)

Chapter 3

WAYS OF AVOIDING PROBATE

There are three kinds of property which can pass to your heirs at your death without going through the probate procedure. They are:

(1) Life insurance payable to a named beneficiary
(2) Property jointly-owned "with right of survivorship"
(3) Property held in an inter vivos or "living" trust

Life insurance policies payable to a named beneficiary are exempt from probate. If your policy is payable to your estate, it will be subject to probate. I know a lawyer who consistently advises his clients to make their insurance policies payable to their estates, the proceeds to be distributed in accordance with their wills. Like most of his colleagues, he derives a substantial part of his income from seeing the estates of deceased clients through probate. He fattens up the probatable estate of a client in every way possible, including dumping his life insurance into it unnecessarily. One widow complained to me that he had even inventoried her late husband's two fountain pens.

The circumstances when it may be advisable to make life insurance payable to one's estate are relatively rare and the practice should be avoided, particularly in view of the fact that in most states life insurance payable to a named beneficiary is wholly or partially exempt from state inheritance taxes, an advantage denied policies payable to the insured's estate.

Many people use joint ownership as a substitute for a will. While it is true that it avoids the delay, expense and publicity of probate, it frequently creates more problems than it solves.

In the first place, not *all* jointly owned property is probate-exempt. If the deed under which a husband and wife own a home jointly is an old one, they may be "tenants in common". If the husband dies first, his share of the house does not automatically pass to his spouse—its disposition is determined by his will. If he has left no will (and many people who use joint ownership don't bother making a will), his share will be dis-

tributed in accordance with the laws of the state in which he lives.

In many states, for example, if a childless, married man dies intestate (leaving no valid will) the first $5,000 of his estate goes to his widow. The balance of his estate she will share equally with her husband's parents. In the case of a couple with children, the widow will get one-third of his estate and the children will inherit the remaining two-thirds. If their joint ownership of their family residence is as "tenants in common", his share will go to his wife and children in those proportions. The children will then own part of the home and that makes a pretty messy title. If they are minors, the children cannot "sign off" in favor of their mother. Someone will have to apply to the probate court to be appointed their guardian. The guardian can then act for the children. The obvious guardian would be their mother but in such circumstances the propriety of the mother's acting as guardian to turn the children's property over to herself might well be questioned. All of this would be avoided by:

(a) Having husband and wife hold the property under a survivorship deed which would provide that upon the death of one, the property would revert in its entirety to the survivor, or,
(b) Making certain that each of the parties has made a valid will leaving his or her interest in the property to the other.

Under the survivorship deed arrangement, there will be no probating; if it passes under a will, the latter will have to be probated.

Make sure that the deed under which you hold title to your home reads "John and Mary Smith, *or the survivor of them.*" If it doesn't, execute and file a new quit claim deed by which you deed the property to yourselves or the survivor of you. (In some states, the practice of joint owners quit-claiming a piece of property directly to themselves in survivorship is questioned. In such cases, they simply quit-claim the property to a third person who immediately quit-claims it back to them in survivorship.)

Most estate planners recommend joint ownership of the family home but caution against similar holding of other property. Many people have joint checking or savings accounts in banks. It is not uncommon for banks to block such accounts upon the death of one of the co-owners. It would be a good idea for the survivor to go to the bank promptly, withdraw the money and transfer it to a new account in his or her name. Ask your bank to write you a letter stating what its policy is in this respect, so you'll be fore-warned.

In some states, safe deposit boxes of deceased persons can be opened only by a representative of the probate court or a state inheritance tax appraiser. In Illinois, such state appraisers were accused of looting deposit boxes of $40,000 in cash and securities over a period of only a few months.

In states having such requirements on safe deposit boxes, it may be desirable for husband and wife to have two boxes. His property is deposited in her box and her property in his box. Under this arrangement, when the deceased husband's deposit box is opened, no property belonging to him is to be found—it's all in his wife's box, to which she has ready, unquestioned access.

Before you enter into joint ownership, consider the cases of the following:

MR. SMITH, a widower with two children, re-married. The second Mrs. Smith proved a fine mother to the children. Mr. Smith registered his securities in their joint names, knowing that his wife would see that the children were provided for. Vacationing together, their car rolled off a ferry and both were drowned. The law said that in the "common disaster", Mr. Smith died first, his securities reverting to his wife as co-owner. Unfortunately Mrs. Smith hadn't made a will. By law, her estate went to her only surviving blood relative, a cousin whom she heartily disliked. None of Mr. Smith's estate went to his children—to whom she was not related except as stepmother.

MR. LITTLE thought that he had eliminated problems from his joint ownership by making certain that his wife had an appropriate will. Unfortunately, his wife's will was successfully contested after they were both gone and Mr. Little's plans were frustrated.

MR. JONES registered his securities jointly with his wife who later was in and out of sanitariums during periods of mental illness. Many securities which should have been disposed of remained in his portfolio simply because he couldn't sell without her approval and he disliked initiating formal proceedings to have her declared incompetent.

MR. GREEN registered his securities jointly with his wife, thus making her a gift of one-half of their value. He was penalized when a subsequent tax examination disclosed that he had failed to file an appropriate gift tax return. (The only property which Uncle Sam will let you place in joint ownership with your spouse without having to file a gift tax return is your residence).

MR. BROWN, like Mr. Green, made his wife a gift of securities by registering her as joint owner. When they realized the gift tax implications, Mrs. Brown hurriedly turned the jointly-owned property back to her husband. When a subsequent tax examination revealed the facts, a gift tax was assessed for Mr. Brown's "gift" to his wife—and another for her "gift" back to him.

MR. CARTER placed his securities in joint names. When he died, the tax people insisted that Mrs. Carter present documentary proof that she had provided half of the money to purchase the securities. When she could not, they taxed the whole lot as part of Mr. Carter's estate. On the other hand, MR. WILSON registered his security holdings similarly in joint names. When Mrs. Wilson died, 50% of the property was considered a part of her estate and Mr. Wilson paid a tax to get his own property back. (The stories of Mr. Carter and Mr. Wilson illustrate the fact that joint ownership creates a 150% tax liability—the property is 100% taxable if the husband dies and 50% taxable if the wife dies.)

MR. JAMISON placed his securities in joint ownership with his wife, intending that she should have the lifetime use of his estate but that upon her death it would revert to his two children. At his death, his property was automatically turned over to her as the surviving joint owner. A few years later she remarried. Her second husband was a well-meaning but impractical man who led his trusting spouse into unsound financial schemes. When she died, there was nothing left for the two Jamison children. In this instance, joint ownership was a poor substitute for a trust.

MR. ARMITAGE was forced into a disastrous marital settlement simply because it was the only way he could regain control of securities which, in an earlier, happier day, he had registered in joint names.

MR. ADAMS owned his securities jointly with his wife. Upon his death, his entire estate went to her. Upon her subsequent death, the same securities passed, together with her own personally-owned securities, to their children. Mr. Adams' securities were taxed fully at his death and again upon his wife's death. If, instead of registering his securities jointly, he had left them in trust, one-half to his wife and one-half to his children with his wife enjoying the lifetime income from both halves, he would have avoided completely the second estate tax on the half designated for the children. In this case, joint ownership resulted in double taxation and a needless waste of many thousands of dollars.

MR. THOMPSON, thinking to avoid probate, placed some property in joint ownership with his brother. When the latter became the defendant in a legal action in which substantial damages were sought, his half interest in Mr. Thompson's property was attached, effectively preventing Mr. Thompson from disposing of it.

Many persons put securities in joint ownership in order to obtain a doubled $100 exemption on dividends received. As a professional estate planner, I recommend against this procedure. I don't think that the small tax benefit thus gained offsets the disadvantages which joint ownership not infrequently produces.

Conclusion:

(1) Avoid making life insurance proceeds payable to your estate.

(2) Except for your family residence, avoid joint ownership. In the case of your residence, make sure it's held under a survivorship deed.

Chapter 4

THE INTER VIVOS OR "LIVING" TRUST

It is likely to be a long time before there is adequate probate reform in America. Don't be discouraged, though. You need not be the system's victim. There exists a magic key to probate exemption, a legal wonder drug which will give you permanent immunity from the racket.

The magic key is the inter vivos or "living" trust, a financial bridge from one generation to another.

There are two principal types of trusts. The most common, the "testamentary" trust, is so-called because it is established under the provisions of your "last will and testament". You might, for example, direct the executor under your will to turn the net proceeds of your estate over to a local trust company which would invest the money and distribute income and principal in accordance with the instructions contained in your will. This "testamentary" trust would not become effective until your will had passed through probate—with all of the delay, expense and publicity which ordinarily attaches to the probate procedure.

A testamentary trust serves a very useful purpose when heirs are inexperienced or likely to be imprudent or profligate in their handling of the funds they are to receive. Large inheritances frequently fail to provide the lifetime security which the testators intended. Indeed, instances abound where sudden wealth has unhappily affected the lives of the beneficiaries. It almost always is better to leave an estate in the care of a responsible trustee. One way of doing this—the traditional way—has been a "testamentary trust" established under a will.

Our concern here, though, is with avoiding probate and a testamentary trust does not avoid probate. As we have already noted, it cannot come into being until *after* the probate process is completed.

The second, and far less well-known type of trust is the inter vivos or "living" trust. Few laymen know about a living trust. Indeed, only a small proportion of attorneys know about it or understand its use. At least half of the attorneys who *do* know of it will either deny that knowledge or strongly advise against its use. The inter vivos trust, you see, is exempt from probate. Most attorneys derive a substantial proportion of their income from seeing the estates of deceased clients through probate. Seriously, now, do you expect them to tell you how to avoid probate? I would put the proportion of attorneys who know about and recommend the inter vivos trust at less than 1%.

When you set up a living trust you create it now, while you are here, not through the instrumentality of your will after you've gone. In effect, you say: "I hereby declare that I hold this property in trust for the benefit of so-and-so, I appoint John Smith as successor trustee and I direct that at my death the sucessor trustee shall dispose of the property as follows, etc."

An inter vivos trust can be either *revocable* (you can cancel it or alter its terms) or *irrevocable* (you cannot change it). Let's talk about the revocable inter vivos trust. Such a trust offers no tax advantages. On the other hand, it offers no disadvantage—all of the estate and income tax savings obtainable through a skillfully drawn testamentary trust are equally available in a well-drawn living trust.

There are many persons whose faculties or judgment are not so impaired as to justify an adjudication of incompetency but who nevertheless would be benefited if relieved of the details of handling investments or a business which age or ill health may make burdensome. The living trust offers an excellent solution.

By setting up a trust during his lifetime with someone else as trustee, a person has an opportunity to observe the efficiency of the individual or institution whom he has named as trustee—it has been described as "an opportunity to see one's will in action".

If the laws of the state of his residence are not to an individual's liking, he can avoid them by setting up a living trust with a trustee institution in another state whose statutes he finds more palatable.

The exemption from probate accorded a properly drawn and executed revocable trust in virtually all jurisdictions materially reduces, if it does not in fact completely eliminate the likelihood of successful attack by disgruntled persons. Contested wills are an everyday occurrence and estates do not always go to those whom the testator has named to receive them. In the first place, the legal necessity for advertising the fact of a will's having been presented for probate invites the interest and attention of those who may feel that they have a legal basis for contesting the testamentary distribution. An inter vivos trust is distinguished by its privacy—parties likely to protest may not even learn of the settlor's death until long afterward when the transference of the property is a fait accompli. In a word, the publicity of probate invites attack upon a will; the privacy of an inter vivos trust discourages it.

I know of no instances of successful attack by a third party upon the legality or validity of a living trust. Of course, such a trust should not be used to deprive a spouse or creditors of sums to which they might rightfully be entitled. (In one historic case, a widow contested the validity of an inter vivos trust established by her late husband six years before their marriage. The court denied her claim of "widow's rights" and held the trust to be inviolate.)

We have already noted that during the long-drawn-out probate procedure, the court will allow a limited payment of support to a widow. Children and other beneficiaries are not so entitled, however, and the death of a breadwinner frequently results in an interruption of income which works a hardship upon beneficiaries. In the case of an inter vivos trust, the trustee or successor trustee needs only a certification of the death of the settlor to fully activate the trust's income provisions in the interests of the heirs. There is no delay whatsoever. This assurance of uninterrupted income and access to the principal within the terms of the trust can be extremely important to a family beset by the uncertainties and financial problems ordinarily attending the death of the breadwinner.

This advantage of the living trust is particularly important when there is a business to be run or liquidated on favorable terms. The trustee can take action swiftly, without waiting for the ponderous machinery of probate to grind out an approval.

Frequently a great deal of undesirable publicity attaches to the probate of an estate. An inventory of what you own and what you owe, and who is to get what, is a matter of public record. When a business interest is involved, competitors may gain important information from such records, information which can adversely affect efforts to sell the business.

The inter vivos trust eliminates these disadvantages. It is a boon to those who seek privacy. Unlike a will, its terms are not disclosed to a probate court, and its assets and the identity of the persons to receive them are closely-guarded secrets. If you resent the piece in the newspaper telling your business, this is the way to avoid it.

Not infrequently the individual drawing a will simply leaves "my estate" without actually inventorying it. The settlor under an inter vivos trust is called upon to list the trust assets. In the process of making such an inventory he is likely to become more conscious of the weak spots in his financial affairs. Scattered assets are more likely to be assembled. His attention is attracted to special problems attaching to certain assets. Not infrequently, he undertakes to resolve problems himself which might otherwise have been left to the executor of his will. Unsuitable or deteriorating investments are thus removed from the estate by the one person better qualified than the executor to correct the unsatisfactory conditions which may prevail.

In my view, however, the greatest advantage of the living trust lies in its saving of expenses. We noted earlier a quotation from an estate planning attorney who reported that administrative expenses on small estates of $10,000 to $20,000 are likely to be, on average, 20%. On medium-sized estates of, say, $100,000 they probably would be around 10%. On larger estates, they would be a smaller percentage.

This is an important proportion of your total estate. This is what the inter vivos trust can save you.

Let me emphasize again that we are not speaking here of taxes. At least, not taxes legally imposed by your government. Rather, it is a private tax, imposed by one group of citizens upon another, a form of tribute privately levied by the legal profession.

In the view of some lawyers, any attempt to pass property other than under a will amounts to a criminal conspiracy, yet the Colorado Supreme Court has ruled:—

> "If an owner of property can dispose of it inter vivos and thereby render a will unnecessary for accomplishment of his practical purposes, he has a right to do so."
> "The motive in making such a transfer may be to obtain the practical advantages of a will without the necessity of making one, but the motive is immaterial."

If the inter vivos trust can, in fact, accomplish the wonderful end of avoiding probate, why is it not used more frequently? Milton E. Meyer, Jr., distinguished Colorado attorney, writing in the legal journal jointly sponsored by the Denver Bar Association, The Colorado Bar Association and the University of Colorado College of Law, ascribes it to:—

> "1. Unfamiliarity with the potentialities of the living trust on the part of many attorneys and financial advisors.
> "2. An unwillingness on the part of some clients, even after adequate explanation, to depart from patterns they consider familiar.
> "3. An over-zealous preoccupation among some lawyers and some representatives of corporate

fiduciaries with the perpetuation of the application to decedents' estates of tradition-hallowed, time-honored, but overly protective and elaborate judicial machinery, which application has the incidental effect of providing very handsome legal and executors' fees for the same lawyers and corporate fiduciaries for work that frequently is quite routine, if time consuming, in nature.

"The point last made will be vehemently denied by many attorneys and trust officers. A number of 'legal' arguments will be brought to bear for the purpose of demonstrating the dignity of and necessity for the formal administration of estates. There will, perhaps, even be vague references to 'illegality', 'sham', 'fraud' and the like directed at efforts to by-pass probate through use of the living trust."

The late Prof. Thomas E. Atkinson, in his authoritative "Wills" (2nd ed. 1953) wrote:—

"In more than half of the cases in which people leave some property, it has been found possible to avoid administration."

After citing the expense, delays and inconvenience of administration as being the causes for attempts to dispense with probate, he concluded:—

"The popular demand for probate reform is largely inarticulate, but it is nonetheless real as shown by the efforts to shun the probate courts. Yet one who seeks to find a solution to the problems of dispensing with or shortening the administration of estates is literally a voice crying in the wilderness."

Commenting upon the likely reasons for the lack of support for such efforts from members of the Bar and from corporate fiduciaries, Mr. Meyer ascribed it to the thinking described in paragraph 3 of his quotation reported above—that is, to the interest in continuing the "very handsome legal and executors' fees" which the present system begets.

In some states, inheritance taxes are required to be computed upon the basis of appraisals made by persons appointed under the infamous probate court system. It has been established that 90% of such appraisers perform no actual service for the fee they receive. It is the obligation of every American to pay the taxes for which he is liable. There is no obligation, however, to pay tribute to persons who actually perform no service. Heirs should be instructed to compute carefully any taxes due (if necessary, retaining the services of an accountant to assist in such computation) and transmit a check for such taxes to the appropriate state authority with an appropriate tax return, including an inventory.

They should not permit themselves to be bullied into submitting to an unconstitutional demand that they pay for services not rendered by court-appointed appraisers who are in most instances incompetent and unqualified to perform such services.

Remember, the racket persists only because it hasn't occurred to the public to call a halt to this looting of estates.

Property held in trust for another is not subject to attachment by persons having a legal claim against the individual serving as trustee. The trusteeship must be a valid one evidenced by a written instrument, and title to the property must actually be vested in the trustee. In most jurisdictions, then, the inter vivos trust offers an important "bonus" advantage—exemption from attachment.

Chapter 5

AVOIDING PROBATE OF YOUR HOME

In Chapter 3 we discussed the tax and other disadvantages of joint ownership and we observed that the only property which might safely be placed in joint ownership without possible gift tax liability was a domicile to be held jointly by husband and wife. We noted that this was one exception to our rule that joint ownership should be avoided. It is worth another warning that you should make absolutely certain that such property is held under a *survivorship* deed.

But what about the individual who for one reason or another does not desire to establish joint ownership with his spouse? What about the widow to whom the domicile has passed as the surviving joint owner under a survivorship deed? What can such persons do to avoid probate?

The inter vivos trust offers a simple solution. The property owner executes a "declaration of trust" which sets forth that he is holding the property "in trust" for the use and benefit of the beneficiary after the property owner's death.

He can, if he wishes, declare in the instrument that he is holding the property in trust for two or more persons whom he names. If, for example, he states that he is holding the property in trust for "John Smith and Mary Jones, in equal shares, or the survivor of them", the property will pass at his death to the two persons named. If one of these beneficiaries is not living at the time of his death, the property will revert in its entirety to the surviving beneficiary. If one of several beneficiaries dies, the property will pass to the surviving beneficiaries in equal shares.

If, on the other hand, he declares that he is holding the property in trust for "John Smith and Mary Jones, in equal shares, *per stirpes*," and one such beneficiary be not surviving, the deceased beneficiary's share will go to that beneficiary's "issue"—that is, his natural (not adopted) children.

It is essential that a successor trustee be named whose job it will be to turn the property over to the beneficiary or beneficiaries. The simplest arrangement, if one person has been named as beneficiary, is to name that same person as successor trustee. If two or more beneficiaries are named to share equally, it is suggested that the one first mentioned be named as successor trustee.

The declaration of trust completed, the property-owner next executes a quit-claim deed transferring title to the property from himself as an individual to himself as trustee (i.e. from "John Smith" to "John Smith, Trustee under Declaration of Trust dated _____.") Both the quit-claim deed and the declaration of trust should then be filed with the town clerk's or other municipal office where real estate transfers in the community are customarily recorded.

Upon the death of the property-owner, the successor trustee establishes his authority simply by filing a copy of the death certificate with the office where the previous documents had been recorded. If he is the sole beneficiary, he executes a quit-claim deed in his capacity as successor trustee, turning the property over to himself as beneficiary. If there are two or more beneficiaries and the property is to be sold, he attends to such sale, distributes the proceeds and the trust is terminated—all without any probating.

Bear in mind that we are speaking here of a *revocable* trust. The property-owner can cancel it at any time or amend it—to change the beneficiary, for example. The existence of the trust does not alter in the slightest degree the right and privilege of the property-owner to sell or otherwise dispose of the property in any way he chooses during his lifetime.

Because the trust is revocable, the transfer of title incidental to its establishment involves no gift and thus no gift tax liability. For the same reason, it does not remove the property from the estate of the owner for estate or inheritance tax purposes.

On the following pages will be found copies of various declarations of trust and of a quit claim deed which will be suitable for use in connection with the arrangements just described.

DECLARATION OF TRUST
FOR NAMING
ONE BENEFICIARY
TO RECEIVE
REAL ESTATE

Instructions:

On the following pages will be found duplicate copies of a declaration of trust (DT-1) which will be suitable for use where it is desired simply to name some one person to receive real estate upon the death of the property owner

Cross out *"city"* or *"town"*, leaving the appropriate designation of your community. If your house has no street number, cross out *"(and known as)"*.

Enter the description of your property as it appears in the warranty deed or quit claim deed under which you acquired it.

Note that under this instrument, not only your house but also its entire contents—including your personal effects—will pass to the beneficiary named without going through probate. If you do not wish to include your furniture and personal effects in the trust, cross out *"and all furniture, fixtures and real and personal property situated therein"* and initial it.

Enter the name of the beneficiary in the appropriate place in Paragraph 1.

Whenever there is any possibility of a minor child receiving the property, make certain that you name an adult who can act as trustee for the child. The name of that adult should be inserted in Paragraph 5 of the instrument shown here. Avoid naming as trustee a person not likely to survive until the child has reached age 21.

When completed in the manner shown on the reverse side hereof, one copy of the declaration of trust and one copy of the quit claim deed (see Page 41) should be filed with the town clerk's or other municipal office where real estate transfers in your community are customarily recorded. The remaining copies of both instruments may be retained for reference purposes.

NOTE:

The instruments which follow (DT-1, DT-2, DT-3, DT-4 and QCD) are not for use with jointly-held real estate. For instruments suitable for use with the latter, refer to Page 332.

Declaration of Trust

..............................of the

WHEREAS, I, __John J. Smith__, County of __Fairfax__, State of __Connecticut__

~~City~~/Town of __Jonesville__

am the owner of certain real property located at (and known as) __525 Main Street__, State of __Connecticut__

in the said ~~City~~/Town of __Jonesville__

which property is described more fully in the Deed conveying it from __Henry B. Green__

to __John J. Smith__, as "that certain piece or parcel of land with buildings thereon

standing, located in said __Jonesville__, being

the rear portions of Lots #34 and 35, on Map of Building Lots of George Spooner, said map being dated May 3, 1952, and filed for record in the office of the Town Clerk, Jonesville, Connecticut, in Book 5, Page 16, of said Maps. Said parcel of land is more particularly described as:

Beginning at a point on the south line of Lot #34, on said map, 73.5 feet East of the East line of Park Avenue --- running thence North along land of James E. Beach, 100 feet to a point on the North line of Lot #35 on said map, 70.44 feet East of the East line of Cornwall Street, thence East along land of the said James E. Beach (being Lot #51 on said map) 55 feet --- thence South along land of Thomas Cook (being Lot #56 on said map) 100 feet to the aforesaid North line of Bartram Street --- thence West to the point of beginning.

NOW, THEREFORE, KNOW ALL MEN BY THESE PRESENTS, that I do hereby acknowledge and declare that I hold and will hold said real property and all right, title and interest in and to said property and all furniture, fixtures and real and personal property situated therein, IN TRUST

1. For the use and benefit of

(Name) __Mary A. Smith   (my niece)__ City __Jonesville__ State __Connecticut__

(Address) __750 Porter Street__ Number Street

Upon my death, unless the beneficiary shall predecease me or unless we both shall die as a result of a common accident or disaster, my Successor Trustee is hereby directed forthwith to transfer said property and all right, title and interest in and to said property unto the beneficiary absolutely and thereby terminate this trust; provided, however, that if the beneficiary attains the age of twenty-one years, minor, the Successor Trustee shall hold the trust assets in continuing trust until such beneficiary attains the specific trust property herein During such period of continuing trust the Successor Trustee, in his absolute discretion, may retain the specific trust property herein described if he believes it in the best interest of the beneficiary so to do, or he may sell or otherwise dispose of such specific trust

.......................iary. Shou.......

.........tion, and in.............event, I reserve ....and the ....operty shall revert to .

re........designate such new beneficiary, this trust shall terminate upon my d........

5. In the event of my death or legal incapacity, I hereby nominate and appoint as Successor Trustee hereunder whosoever shall at that time be beneficiary hereunder, unless such beneficiary be a minor or legally incapacitated in which event I hereby nominate and appoint

(Name) __Henry P. Adams__ City __Jonesville__ State __Connecticut__

(Address) __125__ Number __Barnum Street__ Street

to be Successor Trustee.

6. This Declaration of Trust shall extend to and be binding upon the heirs, executors, administrators and assigns of the undersigned and upon the Successors to the Trustee.

7. The Trustee and his successors shall serve without bond.

8. This Declaration of Trust shall be construed and enforced in accordance with the laws of the State of __Connecticut__

WHEREAS, I,_____of the

City/Town of_____, County of_____, State of_____

am the owner of certain real property located at (and known as)_____

in the said City/Town of_____, State of_____

which property is described more fully in the Deed conveying it from_____

to_____, as "that certain piece or parcel of land with buildings thereon

standing, located in said_____, being

NOW, THEREFORE, KNOW ALL MEN BY THESE PRESENTS, that I do hereby acknowledge and declare that I hold and will hold said real property and all right, title and interest in and to said property and all furniture, fixtures and real and personal property situated therein, IN TRUST

1. For the use and benefit of

(Name)_____

(Address)_____
          Number   Street   City   State

Upon my death, unless the beneficiary shall predecease me or unless we both shall die as a result of a common accident or disaster, my Successor Trustee is hereby directed forthwith to transfer said property and all right, title and interest in and to said property unto the beneficiary absolutely and thereby terminate this trust; provided, however, that if the beneficiary hereunder shall then be a minor, the Successor Trustee shall hold the trust assets in continuing trust until such beneficiary attains the age of twenty-one years. During such period of continuing trust the Successor Trustee, in his absolute discretion, may retain the specific trust property herein described if he believes it in the best interest of the beneficiary so to do, or he may sell or otherwise dispose of such specific trust property, investing and reinvesting the proceeds as he may deem appropriate. If the specific trust property shall be productive of income or if it be sold or otherwise disposed of, the Successor Trustee may apply or expend any or all of the income or principal directly for the maintenance, education and support of the minor beneficiary without the intervention of any guardian and without application to any court. Such payments of income or principal may be made to the parents of such minor or to the person with whom the minor is living without any liability upon the Successor Trustee to see to the application thereof. If such minor survives me but dies before attaining the age of twenty-one years, at his or her death the Successor Trustee shall deliver, pay over, transfer and distribute the trust property to such minor's personal representatives, absolutely.

2. I reserve unto myself the power and right (1) to place a mortgage or other lien upon the property, (2) to collect any rental or other income which may accrue from the trust property and, in my sole discretion as trustee, either to accumulate such income as an addition to the trust assets being held hereunder or pay such income to myself as an individual.

3. I reserve unto myself the power and right at any time during my lifetime to amend or revoke in whole or in part the trust hereby created without the necessity of obtaining the consent of the beneficiary and without giving notice to the beneficiary. The sale or other disposition by me of the whole or any part of the property held hereunder shall constitute as to such whole or part a revocation of this trust.

4. The death during my lifetime, or in a common accident or disaster with me, of the beneficiary designated hereunder shall revoke such designation, and in the former event, I reserve the right to designate a new beneficiary. Should I for any reason fail to designate such new beneficiary, this trust shall terminate upon my death and the trust property shall revert to my estate.

5. In the event of my death or legal incapacity, I hereby nominate and appoint as Successor Trustee hereunder whosoever shall at that time be beneficiary hereunder, unless such beneficiary be a minor or legally incapacitated in which event I hereby nominate and appoint

(Name)_____

(Address)_____
       Number   Street   City   State

to be Successor Trustee.

6. This Declaration of Trust shall extend to and be binding upon the heirs, executors, administrators and assigns of the undersigned and upon the Successors to the Trustee.

7. The Trustee and his successors shall serve without bond.

8. This Declaration of Trust shall be construed and enforced in accordance with the laws of the State of

_____.

IN WITNESS WHEREOF I have hereunto set my hand and seal this_____

day of_____ 19_____.

        (sign here)_____L.S.

Witness: (1)_____   Witness: (2)_____

State of_____ }
                             ss: _____
County of_____ }

On the_____day of_____, nineteen hundred and_____,

before me came_____,

known to me to be the individual described in, and who executed the foregoing instrument, and ___he acknowledged

that ___he executed the same, and in due form of law acknowledged the foregoing instrument to be_____free act and deed and desired the same might be recorded as such.

    (Notary Seal)   _____
                                      Notary Public

Declaration of Trust

WHEREAS, I,_____of the

City/Town of_____, County of_____, State of_____

am the owner of certain real property located at (and known as)_____

in the said City/Town of_____, State of_____

which property is described more fully in the Deed conveying it from_____

to_____, as "that certain piece or parcel of land with buildings thereon

standing, located in said_____, being

NOW, THEREFORE, KNOW ALL MEN BY THESE PRESENTS, that I do hereby acknowledge and declare that I hold and will hold said real property and all right, title and interest in and to said property and all furniture, fixtures and real and personal property situated therein, IN TRUST

1. For the use and benefit of

(Name)_____   _____

(Address)_____   _____

      Number   Street   City   State

Upon my death, unless the beneficiary shall predecease me or unless we both shall die as a result of a common accident or disaster, my Successor Trustee is hereby directed forthwith to transfer said property and all right, title and interest in and to said property unto the beneficiary absolutely and thereby terminate this trust; provided, however, that if the beneficiary hereunder shall then be a minor, the Successor Trustee shall hold the trust assets in continuing trust until such beneficiary attains the age of twenty-one years. During such period of continuing trust the Successor Trustee, in his absolute discretion, may retain the specific trust property herein described if he believes it in the best interest of the beneficiary so to do, or he may sell or otherwise dispose of such specific trust property, investing and reinvesting the proceeds as he may deem appropriate. If the specific trust property shall be productive of income or if it be sold or otherwise disposed of, the Successor Trustee may apply or expend any or all of the income or principal directly for the maintenance, education and support of the minor beneficiary without the intervention of any guardian and without application to any court. Such payments of income or principal may be made to the parents of such minor or to the person with whom the minor is living without any liability upon the Successor Trustee to see to the application thereof. If such minor survives me but dies before attaining the age of twenty-one years, at his or her death the Successor Trustee shall deliver, pay over, transfer and distribute the trust property to such minor's personal representatives, absolutely.

2. I reserve unto myself the power and right (1) to place a mortgage or other lien upon the property, (2) to collect any rental or other income which may accrue from the trust property and, in my sole discretion as trustee, either to accumulate such income as an addition to the trust assets being held hereunder or pay such income to myself as an individual.

3. I reserve unto myself the power and right at any time during my lifetime to amend or revoke in whole or in part the trust hereby created without the necessity of obtaining the consent of the beneficiary and without giving notice to the beneficiary. The sale or other disposition by me of the whole or any part of the property held hereunder shall constitute as to such whole or part a revocation of this trust.

4. The death during my lifetime, or in a common accident or disaster with me, of the beneficiary designated hereunder shall revoke such designation, and in the former event, I reserve the right to designate a new beneficiary. Should I for any reason fail to designate such new beneficiary, this trust shall terminate upon my death and the trust property shall revert to my estate.

5. In the event of my death or legal incapacity, I hereby nominate and appoint as Successor Trustee hereunder whosoever shall at that time be beneficiary hereunder, unless such beneficiary be a minor or legally incapacitated in which event I hereby nominate and appoint

(Name)_____

(Address)_____
           Number   Street   City   State

to be Successor Trustee.

6. This Declaration of Trust shall extend to and be binding upon the heirs, executors, administrators and assigns of the undersigned and upon the Successors to the Trustee.

7. The Trustee and his successors shall serve without bond.

8. This Declaration of Trust shall be construed and enforced in accordance with the laws of the State of

_____.

IN WITNESS WHEREOF I have hereunto set my hand and seal this_____

day of_____ 19_____.

(sign here)_____L.S.

Witness: (1)_____   Witness: (2)_____

State of_____
                       ss: _____
County of_____

On the_____day of_____, nineteen hundred and_____,

before me came_____,

known to me to be the individual described in, and who executed the foregoing instrument, and __he acknowledged

that __he executed the same, and in due form of law acknowledged the foregoing instrument to be_____free act and deed and desired the same might be recorded as such.

(Notary Seal)   _____
                                    Notary Public

DECLARATION OF TRUST
FOR NAMING
ONE PRIMARY BENEFICIARY
AND
ONE CONTINGENT BENEFICIARY
TO RECEIVE
REAL ESTATE

Instructions:

On the following pages will be found duplicate copies of a declaration of trust (DT-2) which will be suitable for use where it is desired to name *one* person as primary beneficiary, with some *one* other person as contingent beneficiary to receive the property if the primary beneficiary does not survive.

Cross out *"city"* or *"town"*, leaving the appropriate designation of your community. If your house has no street number, cross out *"(and known as)"*.

Enter the description of your property as it appears in the warranty deed or quit claim deed under which you acquired it.

Note that under this instrument, not only your house but also its entire contents—including your personal effects—will pass to the beneficiary named without going through probate. If you do not wish to include your furniture and personal effects in the trust, cross out *"and all furniture, fixtures and real and personal property situated therein"* and initial it.

Enter the names of the beneficiaries in the appropriate places in Paragraph 1.

Whenever there is any possibility of a minor child receiving the property, make certain that you name an adult who can act as trustee for him. The name of that adult should be inserted in Paragraph 5 of the instrument shown here. Avoid naming as trustee a person not likely to survive until the child has reached age 21.

When completed in the manner shown on the reverse side hereof, one copy of the declaration of trust and one copy of the quit claim deed (see Page 41) should be filed in the town clerk's or other municipal office where real estate transfers in your community are customarily recorded. The remaining copies of both instruments may be retained for reference.

Declaration of Trust

_____ of the

WHEREAS, I, __John J. Smith_____, State of __Connecticut__,

~~City~~/Town of __Jonesville__, County of __Fairfax__, __525 Main Street__

am the owner of certain real property located at (and known as) _____, State of __Connecticut__

in the said ~~City~~/Town of __Jonesville__ __Henry B. Green__

which property is described more fully in the Deed conveying it from _____ as "that certain piece or parcel of land with buildings thereon

to __John J. Smith__, being

standing, located in said __Jonesville__

the rear portions of Lots #34 and 35, on Map of Building Lots of George Spooner, said map being dated May 3, 1952, and filed for record in the office of the Town Clerk, Jonesville, Connecticut, in Book 5, Page 16, of said Maps. Said parcel of land is more particularly described as:

Beginning at a point on the south line of Lot #34, on said map, 73.5 feet East of the East line of Park Avenue --- running thence North along land of James E. Beach 100 feet to a point on the North line of Lot #35 on said map, 70.44 feet East of the East line of Cornwall Street, thence East along land of the said James E. Beach (being Lot #51 on said map) 55 feet --- thence South along land of Thomas Cook (being Lot #56 on said map) 100 feet to the aforesaid North line of Bartram Street --- thence West to the point of beginning.

NOW, THEREFORE, KNOW ALL MEN BY THESE PRESENTS, that I do hereby acknowledge and declare that I hold and will hold said real property and all right, title and interest in and to said property and all furniture, fixtures and real and personal property situated therein IN TRUST

1. For the use and benefit of

(Name) __Mary A. Smith__ (my niece) __Jonesville__ __Connecticut__

(Address) __750__ __Porter Street__

Number   Street   City   State

or, if such beneficiary be not surviving, for the use and benefit of

(Name) __William B. Connors__ (my nephew) __Jonesville,__ __Connecticut__

(Address) __250__ __County Street__

Number   Street   City   State

Upon my death, unless the beneficiaries shall predecease me or unless we shall die as a result of a common accident, my Successor Trustee is hereby directed forthwith to transfer said property and all right, title and interest in and to said property unto the beneficiary

... in a common accident or disas... ... a new beneficiary. ... for any reason fail death a... ... in the former event, I reserve the right to desi... ... the trust propery shall revert to my estate. to designate such new beneficiary, this trust shall terminate upon my death and ...evoke such designation...

5. In the event of my death or legal incapacity, I hereby nominate and appoint as Successor Trustee hereunder, unless such beneficiary be a minor or legally incapacitated in whosoever shall at that time be beneficiary hereunder, unless such beneficiary which event I hereby nominate and appoint

(Name) __Henry P. Adams__ __Jonesville__ __Connecticut__

(Address) __125__ __Barnum Street__

Number   Street   City   State

to be Successor Trustee.

6. This Declaration of Trust shall extend to and be binding upon the heirs, executors, administrators and assigns of the undersigned and upon the Successors to the Trustee.

7. The Trustee and his successors shall serve without bond.

8. This Declaration of Trust shall be construed and enforced in accordance with the laws of the State of __Connecticut__.

WHEREAS, I,_____of the

City/Town of_____, County of_____, State of_____,

am the owner of certain real property located at (and known as) _____

in the said City/Town of_____, State of_____

which property is described more fully in the Deed conveying it from_____

to_____ as "that certain piece or parcel of land with buildings thereon

standing, located in said_____, being

NOW, THEREFORE, KNOW ALL MEN BY THESE PRESENTS, that I do hereby acknowledge and declare that I hold and will hold said real property and all right, title and interest in and to said property and all furniture, fixtures and real and personal property situated therein IN TRUST

1. For the use and benefit of

(Name)_____

(Address)_____

| Number | Street | City | State |

or, if such beneficiary be not surviving, for the use and benefit of

(Name)_____

(Address)_____

| Number | Street | City | State |

Upon my death, unless the beneficiaries shall predecease me or unless we shall die as a result of a common accident, my Successor Trustee is hereby directed forthwith to transfer said property and all right, title and interest in and to said property unto the beneficiary absolutely and thereby terminate this trust; provided, however, that if the beneficiary hereunder shall then be a minor, the Successor Trustee shall hold the trust assets in continuing trust until such beneficiary attains the age of twenty-one years. During such period of continuing trust the Successor Trustee, in his absolute discretion, may retain the specific trust property herein described if he believes it in the best interest of the beneficiary so to do, or he may sell or otherwise dispose of such specific trust property, investing and reinvesting the proceeds as he may deem appropriate. If the specific trust property shall be productive of income or if it be sold or otherwise disposed of, the Successor Trustee may apply or expend any or all of the income or principal directly for the maintenance, education, and support of the minor beneficiary without the intervention of any guardian and without application to any court. Such payments of income or principal may be made to the parents of such minor or to the person with whom the minor is living without any liability upon the Successor Trustee to see to the application thereof. If any such minor survives me but dies before attaining the age of twenty-one years, at his or her death the Successor Trustee shall deliver, pay over, transfer and distribute the trust property to such minor's personal representatives, absolutely.

2. I reserve unto myself the power and right (1) to place a mortgage or other lien upon the property, (2) to collect any rental or other income which may accrue from the trust property and, in my sole discretion as trustee, either to accumulate such income as an addition to the trust assets being held hereunder or pay such income to myself as an individual.

3. I reserve unto myself the power and right at any time during my lifetime to amend or revoke in whole or in part the trust hereby created without the necessity of obtaining the consent of the beneficiaries and without giving notice to the beneficiaries. The sale or other disposition by me of the whole or any part of the property held hereunder shall constitute as to such whole or part a revocation of this trust.

4. The death during my lifetime, or in a common accident or disaster with me, of both of the beneficiaries designated hereunder shall revoke such designation, and in the former event, I reserve the right to designate a new beneficiary. Should I for any reason fail to designate such new beneficiary, this trust shall terminate upon my death and the trust property shall revert to my estate.

5. In the event of my death or legal incapacity, I hereby nominate and appoint as Successor Trustee hereunder whosoever shall at that time be beneficiary hereunder, unless such beneficiary be a minor or legally incapacitated in which event I hereby nominate and appoint

(Name)_____

(Address)_____

| | | | |
| Number | Street | City | State |

to be Successor Trustee.

6. This Declaration of Trust shall extend to and be binding upon the heirs, executors, administrators and assigns of the undersigned and upon the Successors to the Trustee.

7. The Trustee and his successors shall serve without bond.

8. This Declaration of Trust shall be construed and enforced in accordance with the laws of the State of

_____.

IN WITNESS WHEREOF I have hereunto set my hand and seal this_____day of

_____ 19____.

(sign here)_____L.S.

Witness: (1)_____   Witness: (2)_____

State of_____
}ss: _____
County of_____

On the_____day of_____, nineteen hundred and_____,

before me came_____
known to me to be the individual described in, and who executed the foregoing instrument, and ___he acknowledged that ___he executed the same, and in due form of law acknowledged the foregoing instrument to be _____ free act and deed and desired the same might be recorded as such.

(Notary Seal)   _____
                                    Notary Public

Declaration of Trust

WHEREAS, I,_____of the

City/Town of_____, County of_____, State of_____,

am the owner of certain real property located at (and known as) _____

in the said City/Town of_____, State of_____

which property is described more fully in the Deed conveying it from_____

to_____ as "that certain piece or parcel of land with buildings thereon

standing, located in said_____, being

NOW, THEREFORE, KNOW ALL MEN BY THESE PRESENTS, that I do hereby acknowledge and declare that I hold and will hold said real property and all right, title and interest in and to said property and all furniture, fixtures and real and personal property situated therein IN TRUST

1. For the use and benefit of

(Name)_____

(Address)_____
        Number   Street   City   State

or, if such beneficiary be not surviving, for the use and benefit of

(Name)_____

(Address)_____
        Number   Street   City   State

Upon my death, unless the beneficiaries shall predecease me or unless we shall die as a result of a common accident, my Successor Trustee is hereby directed forthwith to transfer said property and all right, title and interest in and to said property unto the beneficiary absolutely and thereby terminate this trust; provided, however, that if the beneficiary hereunder shall then be a minor, the Successor Trustee shall hold the trust assets in continuing trust until such beneficiary attains the age of twenty-one years. During such period of continuing trust the Successor Trustee, in his absolute discretion, may retain the specific trust property herein described if he believes it in the best interest of the beneficiary so to do, or he may sell or otherwise dispose of such specific trust property, investing and reinvesting the proceeds as he may deem appropriate. If the specific trust property shall be productive of income or if it be sold or otherwise disposed of, the Successor Trustee may apply or expend any or all of the income or principal directly for the maintenance, education, and support of the minor beneficiary without the intervention of any guardian and without application to any court. Such payments of income or principal may be made to the parents of such minor or to the person with whom the minor is living without any liability upon the Successor Trustee to see to the application thereof. If any such minor survives me but dies before attaining the age of twenty-one years, at his or her death the Successor Trustee shall deliver, pay over, transfer and distribute the trust property to such minor's personal representatives, absolutely.

2. I reserve unto myself the power and right (1) to place a mortgage or other lien upon the property, (2) to collect any rental or other income which may accrue from the trust property and, in my sole discretion as trustee, either to accumulate such income as an addition to the trust assets being held hereunder or pay such income to myself as an individual.

3. I reserve unto myself the power and right at any time during my lifetime to amend or revoke in whole or in part the trust hereby created without the necessity of obtaining the consent of the beneficiaries and without giving notice to the beneficiaries. The sale or other disposition by me of the whole or any part of the property held hereunder shall constitute as to such whole or part a revocation of this trust.

4. The death during my lifetime, or in a common accident or disaster with me, of both of the beneficiaries designated hereunder shall revoke such designation, and in the former event, I reserve the right to designate a new beneficiary. Should I for any reason fail to designate such new beneficiary, this trust shall terminate upon my death and the trust propery shall revert to my estate.

5. In the event of my death or legal incapacity, I hereby nominate and appoint as Successor Trustee hereunder whosoever shall at that time be beneficiary hereunder, unless such beneficiary be a minor or legally incapacitated in which event I hereby nominate and appoint

(Name)_____

(Address)_____
              Number   Street   City   State
to be Successor Trustee.

6. This Declaration of Trust shall extend to and be binding upon the heirs, executors, administrators and assigns of the undersigned and upon the Successors to the Trustee.

7. The Trustee and his successors shall serve without bond.

8. This Declaration of Trust shall be construed and enforced in accordance with the laws of the State of

_____.

IN WITNESS WHEREOF I have hereunto set my hand and seal this_____day of

_____ 19_____.

(sign here)_____L.S.

Witness: (1)_____   Witness: (2)_____

State of_____
                       } ss: _____
County of_____

On the_____day of_____, nineteen hundred and_____,

before me came_____
known to me to be the individual described in, and who executed the foregoing instrument, and __he acknowledged that __he executed the same, and in due form of law acknowledged the foregoing instrument to be _____ free act and deed and desired the same might be recorded as such.

(Notary Seal)   _____
                                             Notary Public

DECLARATION OF TRUST
FOR NAMING
TWO OR MORE BENEFICIARIES
SHARING EQUALLY
TO RECEIVE
REAL ESTATE

Instructions:

On the following pages will be found duplicate copies of a declaration of trust (DT-3) which will be suitable for use where it is desired to name two or more persons to share equally upon the death of the property owner.

Cross out *"city"* or *"town"*, leaving the appropriate designation of your community. If your house has no street number, cross out *"(and known as)"*.

Enter the description of your property as it appears in the warranty deed or quit claim deed under which you acquired it.

Note that under this instrument, not only your house but also its entire contents—including your personal effects—will pass to the beneficiaries named without going through probate. If you do not wish to include your furniture and personal effects in the trust, cross out *"and all furniture, fixtures and real and personal property situated therein"* and initial it.

Note that the instrument specifies that the named beneficiaries are to receive *"in equal shares, or the survivor of them/per stirpes"*.

Now, think carefully: If you have named your three brothers with the understanding that if one brother predeceases you, *his* children are to receive *his* share, cross out *"or the survivor of them"* and initial it. If that is not what you want—if, for example, you prefer that the share of your deceased brother be divided by your two surviving brothers, cross out *"per stirpes"* and initial it. Remember, you *must* cross out *"or the survivor of them"* or *"per stirpes"*—one or the other.

In Paragraph 1, enter the *number* of *persons* you are naming (to discourage unauthorized additions to the list) and then insert their names. The one whose name appears *first* will be the successor trustee responsible for seeing to the distribution of the trust property.

Whenever there is any possibility of a minor child receiving any portion of the property, make certain that you name an adult who can act as trustee for him. The name of that adult should be inserted in Paragraph 5 of the instrument shown here. Avoid naming as trustee a person not likely to survive until the child has reached age 21.

When completed in the manner shown on the reverse side hereof, one copy of the declaration of trust and one copy of the quit claim deed (see Page 41) should be filed with the town clerk's or other municipal office where real estate transactions in your community are customarily recorded. The remaining copies of both instruments may be retained for reference.

Declaration of Trust

WHEREAS, I, **John J. Smith** _____ of the ~~City~~/Town of **Jonesville**, County of **Fairfax**, State of **Connecticut**,

am the owner of certain real property located at (and known as) **525 Main Street**

in the said ~~City~~/Town of **Jonesville**, State of **Connecticut**

which property is described more fully in the Deed conveying it from **Henry B. Green**

to **John J. Smith**, as "that certain piece or parcel of land with buildings thereon

standing, located in said **Jonesville**, being

the rear portions of Lots #34 and 35, on Map of Building Lots of George Spooner, said map being dated May 3, 1952, and filed for record in the office of the Town Clerk, Jonesville, Connecticut, in Book 5, Page 16, of said Maps. Said parcel of land is more particularly described as:

Beginning at a point on the south line of Lot #34, on said map, 73.5 feet East of the East line of Park Avenue --- running thence North along land of James E. Beach, 100 feet to a point on the North line of Lot #35 on said map, 70.44 feet East of the East line of Cornwall Street, thence East along land of the said James E. Beach (being Lot #51 on said map) 55 feet --- thence South along land of Thomas Cook (being Lot #56 on said map) 100 feet to the aforesaid North line of Bartram Street --- thence West to the point of beginning.

NOW, THEREFORE, KNOW ALL MEN BY THESE PRESENTS, that I do hereby acknowledge and declare that I hold and will hold said real property and all right and title and interest in and to said property and all furniture, fixtures and real and personal property situated therein IN TRUST

1. For the use and benefit of the following **three** persons, in equal shares, or the survivor of them/~~per nurnose~~ _J.S._

Thomas B. Smith	(my brother)
William R. Smith	(my brother)
Charles M. Smith	(my brother)

Upon my death, unless all the beneficiaries shall predecease me or unless we all shall die as a result of a common accident or disaster, my Successor Trustee is hereby directed forthwith to transfer said property and all right, title and interest in and to said property unto the beneficiaries absolutely ...... hereby terminate this trust; _provided_, however, that if any beneficiary hereunder shall then be a minor.

...... incapacity, ... at, in wh... ...ent I hereb... ...eneficiary ... and appoint as

...eficiary be a minor or legal... ...ecessor Trustee hereunder the beneficiary whose name appears second above. If such beneficiary named second above shall be a minor or legally incompetent, then I nominate and appoint as Successor Trustee hereunder:

Henry P. Adams   **Jonesville**   **Connecticut**

(Name)   City   State

(Address)   **125**   **Barnum Street**

       Number   Street

6. This Declaration of Trust shall extend to and be binding upon the heirs, executors, administrators and assigns of the undersigned and upon the Successors to the Trustee.

7. The Trustee and his successors shall serve without bond.

8. This Declaration of Trust shall be construed and enforced in accordance with the laws of the State of

Connecticut

WHEREAS, I,_____of the

City/Town of_____, County of_____, State of_____,

am the owner of certain real property located at (and known as)_____

in the said City/Town of_____, State of_____

which property is described more fully in the Deed conveying it from_____

to_____, as "that certain piece or parcel of land with buildings thereon

standing, located in said_____, being

NOW, THEREFORE, KNOW ALL MEN BY THESE PRESENTS, that I do hereby acknowledge and declare that I hold and will hold said real property and all right, title and interest in and to said property and all furniture, fixtures and real and personal property situated therein IN TRUST

1. For the use and benefit of the following_____persons, in equal shares, or the survivor of them/per stirpes:

Upon my death, unless all the beneficiaries shall predecease me or unless we all shall die as a result of a common accident or disaster, my Successor Trustee is hereby directed forthwith to transfer said property and all right, title and interest in and to said property unto the beneficiaries absolutely and thereby terminate this trust; provided, however, that if any beneficiary hereunder shall then be a minor, the Successor Trustee shall hold the trust assets in continuing trust until such beneficiary attains the age of twenty-one years. During such period of continuing trust the Successor Trustee, in his absolute discretion, may retain the specific trust property herein described if he believes it in the best interest of the beneficiary so to do, or he may sell or otherwise dispose of such specific trust property, investing and reinvesting the proceeds as he may deem appropriate. If the specific trust property shall be productive of income or if it be sold or otherwise disposed of, the Successor Trustee may apply or expend any or all of the income or principal directly for the maintenance, education and support of the minor beneficiary without the intervention of any guardian and without application to any court. Such payments of income or principal may be made to the parents of such minor or to the person with whom the minor is living without any liability upon the Successor Trustee to see to the application thereof. If any such minor survives me but dies before the age of twenty-one years, at his or her death the Successor Trustee shall deliver, pay over, transfer and distribute the trust property being held for such minor to said minor's personal representatives, absolutely.

2. I reserve unto myself the power and right (1) to place a mortgage or other lien upon the property, (2) to collect any rental or other income which may accrue from the trust property and, in my sole discretion as trustee, either to accumulate such income as an addition to the trust assets being held hereunder or pay such income to myself as an individual.

3. I reserve unto myself the power and right at any time during my lifetime to amend or revoke in whole or in part the trust hereby created without the necessity of obtaining the consent of any beneficiary and without giving notice to any beneficiary. The sale or other disposition by me of the whole or any part of the property held hereunder shall constitute as to such whole or part a revocation of this trust.

4. The death during my lifetime, or in a common accident or disaster with me, of all of the beneficiaries designated hereunder shall revoke such designation, and in the former event, I reserve the right to designate new beneficiaries. Should I for any reason fail to designate such new beneficiaries, this trust shall terminate upon my death and the trust property shall revert to my estate.

5. In the event of my death or legal incapacity, I hereby nominate and appoint as Successor Trustee hereunder the beneficiary first above named, unless such beneficiary be a minor or legally incompetent, in which event I hereby nominate and appoint as Successor Trustee hereunder the beneficiary whose name appears second above. If such beneficiary named second above shall be a minor or legally incompetent, then I nominate and appoint as Successor Trustee hereunder:

(Name)_____

(Address)_____

      Number   Street   City   State

6. This Declaration of Trust shall extend to and be binding upon the heirs, executors, administrators and assigns of the undersigned and upon the Successors to the Trustee.

7. The Trustee and his successors shall serve without bond.

8. This Declaration of Trust shall be construed and enforced in accordance with the laws of the State of _____

_____.

IN WITNESS WHEREOF I have hereunto set my hand and seal this_____day of

_____ 19_____.

(sign here)_____L.S.

Witness: (1)_____

Witness: (2)_____.

State of_____

County of_____ } ss: _____

On the_____day of_____, nineteen hundred and_____,

before me came_____
known to me to be the individual described in, and who executed the foregoing instrument, and ___he acknowledged that ___he executed the same, and in due form of law acknowledge the foregoing instrument to be _____ free act and deed and desired the same might be recorded as such.

    (Notary Seal)   _____

                                            Notary Public

WHEREAS, I,_____of the

City/Town of_____, County of_____, State of_____,

am the owner of certain real property located at (and known as)_____

in the said City/Town of_____, State of_____

which property is described more fully in the Deed conveying it from_____

to_____, as "that certain piece or parcel of land with buildings thereon

standing, located in said_____, being

NOW, THEREFORE, KNOW ALL MEN BY THESE PRESENTS, that I do hereby acknowledge and declare that I hold and will hold said real property and all right, title and interest in and to said property and all furniture, fixtures and real and personal property situated therein IN TRUST

1. For the use and benefit of the following_____persons, in equal shares, or the survivor of them/per stirpes:

Upon my death, unless all the beneficiaries shall predecease me or unless we all shall die as a result of a common accident or disaster, my Successor Trustee is hereby directed forthwith to transfer said property and all right, title and interest in and to said property unto the beneficiaries absolutely and thereby terminate this trust; provided, however, that if any beneficiary hereunder shall then be a minor, the Successor Trustee shall hold the trust assets in continuing trust until such beneficiary attains the age of twenty-one years. During such period of continuing trust the Successor Trustee, in his absolute discretion, may retain the specific trust property herein described if he believes it in the best interest of the beneficiary so to do, or he may sell or otherwise dispose of such specific trust property, investing and reinvesting the proceeds as he may deem appropriate. If the specific trust property shall be productive of income or if it be sold or otherwise disposed of, the Successor Trustee may apply or expend any or all of the income or principal directly for the maintenance, education and support of the minor beneficiary without the intervention of any guardian and without application to any court. Such payments of income or principal may be made to the parents of such minor or to the person with whom the minor is living without any liability upon the Successor Trustee to see to the application thereof. If any such minor survives me but dies before the age of twenty-one years, at his or her death the Successor Trustee shall deliver, pay over, transfer and distribute the trust property being held for such minor to said minor's personal representatives, absolutely.

2. I reserve unto myself the power and right (1) to place a mortgage or other lien upon the property, (2) to collect any rental or other income which may accrue from the trust property and, in my sole discretion as trustee, either to accumulate such income as an addition to the trust assets being held hereunder or pay such income to myself as an individual.

3. I reserve unto myself the power and right at any time during my lifetime to amend or revoke in whole or in part the trust hereby created without the necessity of obtaining the consent of any beneficiary and without giving notice to any beneficiary. The sale or other disposition by me of the whole or any part of the property held hereunder shall constitute as to such whole or part a revocation of this trust.

4. The death during my lifetime, or in a common accident or disaster with me, of all of the beneficiaries designated hereunder shall revoke such designation, and in the former event, I reserve the right to designate new beneficiaries. Should I for any reason fail to designate such new beneficiaries, this trust shall terminate upon my death and the trust property shall revert to my estate.

5. In the event of my death or legal incapacity, I hereby nominate and appoint as Successor Trustee hereunder the beneficiary first above named, unless such beneficiary be a minor or legally incompetent, in which event I hereby nominate and appoint as Successor Trustee hereunder the beneficiary whose name appears second above. If such beneficiary named second above shall be a minor or legally incompetent, then I nominate and appoint as Successor Trustee hereunder:

(Name)_____

(Address)_____

      Number   Street   City   State

6. This Declaration of Trust shall extend to and be binding upon the heirs, executors, administrators and assigns of the undersigned and upon the Successors to the Trustee.

7. The Trustee and his successors shall serve without bond.

8. This Declaration of Trust shall be construed and enforced in accordance with the laws of the State of _____

_____.

IN WITNESS WHEREOF I have hereunto set my hand and seal this_____day of

_____ 19_____.

                             *(sign here)*_____L.S.

Witness: (1)_____

Witness: (2)_____

State of_____⎫
                           ⎬ ss: _____
County of_____⎭

On the_____day of_____, nineteen hundred and_____,

before me came_____
known to me to be the individual described in, and who executed the foregoing instrument, and __he acknowledged that __he executed the same, and in due form of law acknowledge the foregoing instrument to be _____ free act and deed and desired the same might be recorded as such.

(Notary Seal)   _____

                                                 Notary Public

```
┌─────────────────────────────────────────┐
│          DECLARATION OF TRUST            │
│               FOR NAMING                 │
│        ONE PRIMARY BENEFICIARY           │
│                 WITH                     │
│    YOUR CHILDREN, SHARING EQUALLY,       │
│     AS CONTINGENT BENEFICIARIES          │
│               TO RECEIVE                 │
│              REAL ESTATE                 │
└─────────────────────────────────────────┘
```

Instructions:

On the following pages will be found duplicate copies of a declaration of trust (DT-4) which will be suitable for use where it is desired to name one person (ordinarily, one's spouse) as primary beneficiary, with one's children as contingent beneficiaries to receive the real estate if the primary beneficiary does not survive you.

Cross out *"city"* or *"town"*, leaving the appropriate designation of your community. If your house has no street number, cross out *"(and known as)"*.

Enter the description of your property as it appears in the warranty deed or quit claim deed under which you acquired it.

Note that under this instrument, not only your house but also its entire contents—including your personal effects—will pass to the beneficiary named without going through probate. If you do *not* wish to include your furniture and personal effects in the trust, cross out *"and all furniture, fixtures and real and personal property situated therein"* and initial it.

Enter the name of the primary beneficiary in the appropriate place in Paragraph 1. Note that the instrument first refers to your children as *"natural not/or adopted"*. Now, decide: If you have an adopted child and you wish to *include* him, cross out the word *"not"* in the phrase *"natural not/ or adopted"* and initial it. If you wish to *exclude* your adopted child, cross out the word *"or"* in the same phrase and initial it. Remember, you <u>must</u> cross out *"not"* or *"or"*—one or the other. If you have no adopted child, cross out *"not"*.

Note next that the instrument specifies that your children are to receive *"in equal shares, or the survivor of them/per stirpes"*. Now, think carefully: If it is your wish that if one of your children does not survive you, his share will revert to *his* children in equal shares, cross out *"or the survivor of them"* and initial it. If that is *not* what you want—if, for example, you prefer that the share of any child of yours who predeceases you shall revert to your other surviving children in equal shares, cross out *"per stirpes"* and initial it. Remember, you <u>must</u> cross out *"or the survivor of them"* or *"per stirpes"*—one or the other.

Whenever there is any possibility of a minor child receiving any portion of the property, make certain that you name an adult who can act as trustee for him. The name of that adult should be inserted in Paragraph 5 of the instrument shown here. Avoid naming as trustee a person not likely to survive until the child has reached age 21.

When completed in the manner shown on the reverse side hereof, one copy of the declaration of trust and one copy of the quit claim deed (see Page 41) should be filed with the town clerk's or other municipal office where real estate transactions in your community are customarily recorded. The remaining copies of both instruments may be retained for reference.

shall be productive of income or if it be sold or otherwise disposed of, the Successor Trustee may apply or expend any or all of the income or principal directly for the maintenance, education and support of the minor beneficiary without the intervention of any guardian and without application to any court. Such payments of income or principal may be made to the parents of such minor or to the person with whom the minor is living without any liability upon the Successor Trustee to see to the application thereof. If any such minor survives me but dies before the age of twenty-one years, at his or her death the Successor Trustee shall deliver, pay over, transfer and distribute the trust property being held for such minor to said minor's personal representatives, absolutely.

2. I reserve unto myself the power and right (1) to place a mortgage or other lien upon the property, (2) to collect any rental or other income which may accrue from the trust property and, in my sole discretion as trustee, either to accumulate such income as an addition to the trust assets being held hereunder or pay such income to myself as an individual.

3. I reserve unto myself the power and right at any time during my lifetime to amend or revoke in whole or in part the trust hereby created without the necessity of obtaining the consent of the beneficiaries and without giving notice to the beneficiaries. The sale or other disposition by me of the whole or any part of the property held hereunder shall constitute as to such whole or part a revocation of this trust.

4. The death during my lifetime, or in a common accident or disaster with me, of all the beneficiaries designated hereunder shall revoke such designation, and in the former event, I reserve the right to designate a new beneficiary. Should I for any reason fail to designate such new beneficiary, this trust shall terminate upon my death and the trust property shall revert to my estate.

5. In the event of my death or legal incapacity, I hereby nominate and appoint as Successor Trustee hereunder the First Beneficiary, and upon his or her failure or ceasing to act, then I nominate and appoint

(Name)_____

(Address)_____
          Number   Street   City   State

as Successor Trustee, and upon his or her failure or ceasing to act or should I for any reason fail to designate the person above intended to be nominated, then I nominate and appoint as such Successor Trustee hereunder whosoever shall qualify as executor, administrator, or guardian, as the case may be, of my estate.

6. This Declaration of Trust shall extend to and be binding upon the heirs, executors, administrators and assigns of the undersigned and upon the Successors to the Trustee.

7. The Trustee and his successors shall serve without bond.

8. This Declaration of Trust shall be construed and enforced in accordance with the laws of the State of

_____.

IN WITNESS WHEREOF I have hereunto set my hand and seal this _____day of

_____ 19_____.

(sign here)_____L.S.

Witness: (1)_____

Witness: (2)_____

STATE OF_____ }
                             ss: _____

COUNTY OF_____ }

On the_____day of_____, nineteen hundred and_____,

before me came_____,
known to me to be the individual described in, and who executed the foregoing instrument, and ___he acknowledged that ___he executed the same, and in due form of law acknowledge the foregoing instrument to be _____ free act and deed and desired the same might be recorded as such.

(Notary Seal)   _____
                                            Notary Public

Declaration of Trust

WHEREAS, I,_____of the

City/Town of_____County of_____State of_____,

am the owner of certain real property located at (and known as)_____

in the said City/Town of_____, State of_____,

which property is described more fully in the Deed conveying it from_____

to_____, as "that certain piece or parcel of land with buildings thereon

standing, located in said_____, being

NOW, THEREFORE, KNOW ALL MEN BY THESE PRESENTS, that I do hereby acknowledge and declare that I hold and will hold said real property and all right and title and interest in and to said property and all furniture, fixtures and real and personal property situated therein IN TRUST

   1. For the use and benefit of

(Name)_____

(Address)_____

           Number   Street   City   State

(hereinafter referred to as the "First Beneficiary") and upon his or her death prior to the termination of the trust, for the use and benefit of my children, natural not/or adopted, in equal shares or the survivor of them, per stirpes. Upon my death, unless all of the beneficiaries shall predecease me or unless we all shall die as a result of a common accident or disaster, my Successor Trustee is hereby directed forthwith to transfer said property and all right, title and interest in and to said property unto the beneficiary or beneficiaries absolutely and thereby terminate this trust; provided, however, that if any beneficiary hereunder shall then be a minor, the Successor Trustee shall hold the trust assets in continuing trust until such beneficiary attains the age of twenty-one years. During such period of continuing trust the Successor Trustee, in his absolute discretion, may retain the specific trust property herein described if he believes it in the best interest of the beneficiary so to do, or he may sell or otherwise dispose of such specific trust property, investing and reinvesting the proceeds as he may deem appropriate. If the specific trust property shall be productive of income or if it be sold or otherwise disposed of, the Successor Trustee may apply or expend any or all of the income or principal directly for the maintenance, education and support of the minor beneficiary without the intervention of any guardian and without application to any court. Such payments of income or principal may be made to the parents of such minor or to the person with whom the minor is living without any liability upon the Successor Trustee to see to the application thereof. If any such minor survives me but dies before the age of twenty-one years, at his or her death the Successor Trustee shall deliver, pay over, transfer and distribute the trust property being held for such minor to said minor's personal representatives, absolutely.

2. I reserve unto myself the power and right (1) to place a mortgage or other lien upon the property, (2) to collect any rental or other income which may accrue from the trust property and, in my sole discretion as trustee, either to accumulate such income as an addition to the trust assets being held hereunder or pay such income to myself as an individual.

3. I reserve unto myself the power and right at any time during my lifetime to amend or revoke in whole or in part the trust hereby created without the necessity of obtaining the consent of the beneficiaries and without giving notice to the beneficiaries. The sale or other disposition by me of the whole or any part of the property held hereunder shall constitute as to such whole or part a revocation of this trust.

4. The death during my lifetime, or in a common accident or disaster with me, of all the beneficiaries designated hereunder shall revoke such designation, and in the former event, I reserve the right to designate a new beneficiary. Should I for any reason fail to designate such new beneficiary, this trust shall terminate upon my death and the trust property shall revert to my estate.

5. In the event of my death or legal incapacity, I hereby nominate and appoint as Successor Trustee hereunder the First Beneficiary, and upon his or her failure or ceasing to act, then I nominate and appoint

(Name)_____

(Address)_____
           Number   Street   City   State

as Successor Trustee, and upon his or her failure or ceasing to act or should I for any reason fail to designate the person above intended to be nominated, then I nominate and appoint as such Successor Trustee hereunder whosoever shall qualify as executor, administrator, or guardian, as the case may be, of my estate.

6. This Declaration of Trust shall extend to and be binding upon the heirs, executors, administrators and assigns of the undersigned and upon the Successors to the Trustee.

7. The Trustee and his successors shall serve without bond.

8. This Declaration of Trust shall be construed and enforced in accordance with the laws of the State of

_____.

IN WITNESS WHEREOF I have hereunto set my hand and seal this _____day of

_____ 19_____.

(sign here)_____L.S.

Witness: (1)_____

Witness: (2)_____

STATE OF_____⎫
                              ss: _____
COUNTY OF_____⎭

On the_____day of_____, nineteen hundred and_____,

before me came_____,
known to me to be the individual described in, and who executed the foregoing instrument, and ___he acknowledged that ___he executed the same, and in due form of law acknowledge the foregoing instrument to be _____ free act and deed and desired the same might be recorded as such.

(Notary Seal)   _____
                                                  Notary Public

CHAPTER 5, APPENDIX E

QUIT CLAIM DEED

Instructions:

One or the other of two legal documents is ordinarily used to transfer title to real estate— a warranty deed or a quit claim deed.

When you buy a house, the owner gives you a warranty deed by which he "warrants" or guarantees that the house is his to sell. With that deed, you can hold him responsible if someone else turns up with a valid claim to ownership of the property.

If he gave you a quit claim deed, he would be providing no guarantee at all that he actually owned the property. He'd be saying: "Whatever title or claim I may have to this property I am turning over to you."

When you buy a house, then, you're not satisfied with a quit claim deed; you insist upon being given a warranty deed. The quit claim deed is used when property is being transferred from one member of a family to another, with no financial consideration being involved, or when one of two co-owners, not necessarily related, wishes to transfer his interest in the property to the other co-owner with or without a financial consideration being involved. They know each other and they know that they own the property between them, and there is no need for the retiring co-owner to "warrant" to the other that he owns one-half of the property.

In connection with the transfer of the title to your real estate from yourself as an individual to yourself as trustee, as explained in Chapter 5, a quit claim deed will be found on Page 43 which will adequately serve your purpose.

Enter your name and the date of the Declaration of Trust (DT-1, DT-2, DT-3 or DT-4) which you have executed. In the large space provided, enter the description of the property as it appears in the Declaration of Trust. Finally, sign the instrument in the presence of two witnesses and before a notary, and file it with the town clerk's or other office where property transfers in your community are customarily recorded. After it is recorded, it will be returned to you.

SPECIAL NOTE

To residents of Alabama, Alaska, Arkansas, Delaware, District of Columbia, Florida, Georgia, Hawaii, Illinois, Kansas, Kentucky, Louisiana, Maryland, Michigan, Minnesota, Montana, New Hampshire, New Jersey, North Carolina, Ohio, Oregon, Pennsylvania, Puerto Rico, Rhode Island, South Carolina, Tennessee, Utah, Vermont, West Virginia, Wisconsin, and residents of New York married before September 1, 1930:

Also, residents of the Canadian provinces of Manitoba, New Brunswick, Nova Scotia, Ontario, Prince Edward Island and Quebec:

Under the law, your spouse has a legal claim upon your property in the event of your death, that right being called "dower" in the case of a widow and "curtesy" in the case of a widower.

If you are married and you have executed one of the Declarations of Trust provided in Chapter 5 (DT-1, DT-2, DT-3 or DT-4) naming as beneficiary a person *other than your spouse,* your spouse must join with you in signing the quit claim deed. A space for such signature is provided immediately beneath the line on which you sign as "releasor."

QUIT CLAIM DEED

To all People to whom these Presents shall come, Greetings;

KNOW YE, THAT I,

John J. Smith

(Name) _____

in conformity with the terms of a certain Declaration of Trust executed by me under date of _____

June 20,1965 _____, do by these presents release and forever Quit-Claim to myself as Trustee under the terms of such Declaration of Trust, and to my successors as Trustee under the terms of such Declaration of Trust, all right, title, interest, claim and demand whatsoever which I as Releasor have or ought to have in or to the property located at:

102 Bartram Street, Jonesville, Connecticut, being the rear portions of Lots #34 and 35, on Map of Building Lots of George Spooner, said map being dated May 3, 1952, and filed for record in the office of the Town Clerk, Jonesville, Connecticut, in Book 5, Page 16, of said Maps. Said parcel of land is more particularly described as:

Beginning at a point on the south line of Lot #34, on said map, 73.5 feet East of the East line of Park Avenue --- running thence North along land of James E. Beach, 100 feet to a point on the North line of Lot #35 on said map, 70.44 feet East of the East line of Cornwall Street, thence East along land of the said James E. Beach (being Lot #51 on said map) 55 feet --- thence South along land of Thomas Cook (being Lot #56 on said map) 100 feet to the aforesaid North line of Bartram Street --- thence west to the point of beginning.

To Have and to Hold the premises, with all the appurtenances, as such Trustee forever; and I declare and agree that neither I as an individual nor my heirs or assigns shall have or make any claim or demand upon such property.

In Witness Whereof,

Signed, sealed and delivered in presence of two witnesses:

Arthur Jones

Mary Grey

John J. Smith L.S.
Releasor

The undersigned legal spouse of the above releasor hereby waives all dower or curtesy rights to the hereinabove described property.

_____ L.S.
Spouse

STATE OF *Connecticut*
COUNTY OF *Fairfield* } ss. *Jonesville*

Personally appeared before me this *tenth* day of *February*

19*66*, *John J. Smith* signers and sealers of the foregoing instrument, and acknowledged the same to be *his* free act and deed.

George P. Brown
Notary Public

(Notary Seal)

Attest: _____ Clerk

Received for record _____ Date _____ at _____ Time

The consideration for this transfer is less than One Dollar.

QUIT CLAIM DEED

To all People to whom these Presents shall come, Greetings;

KNOW YE, THAT I,

(Name) _____

in conformity with the terms of a certain Declaration of Trust executed by me under date of_____

_____, do by these presents release and forever Quit-Claim to myself as Trustee under the terms of such Declaration of Trust, and to my successors as Trustee under the terms of such Declaration of Trust, all right, title, interest, claim and demand whatsoever which I as Releasor have or ought to have in or to the property located at:

To Have and to Hold the premises, with all the appurtenances, as such Trustee forever; and I declare and agree that neither I as an individual nor my heirs or assigns shall have or make any claim or demand upon such property.

In Witness Whereof,

Signed, sealed and delivered in presence of

two witnesses:

_____L.S.
Releasor

The undersigned legal spouse of the above releasor hereby waives all dower or curtesy rights to the hereinabove described property.

_____
_____L.S.
Spouse

STATE OF_____ } ss. _____
COUNTY OF_____ }

Personally appeared before me this_____day of_____
19____, _____, known to me to be the signer and sealer of the foregoing instrument, and acknowledged the same to be_____free act and deed.

(Notary Seal)   _____
                                                          Notary Public

Received for record_____at_____Attest:_____
                                Date   Time   Clerk

3

Quit Claim Deed

From

_____

To

_____
, Trustee

Received for record _____ 19____.

At _____
    Time

and recorded in Vol._____

on Page_____of the

Land Records by

_____
Authorized Official

44

QUIT CLAIM DEED

To all People to whom these Presents shall come, Greetings;

KNOW YE, THAT I,

(Name) _____

in conformity with the terms of a certain Declaration of Trust executed by me under date of_____

_____, do by these presents release and forever Quit-Claim to myself as Trustee under the terms of such Declaration of Trust, and to my successors as Trustee under the terms of such Declaration of Trust, all right, title, interest, claim and demand whatsoever which I as Releasor have or ought to have in or to the property located at:

To Have and to Hold the premises, with all the appurtenances, as such Trustee forever; and I declare and agree that neither I as an individual nor my heirs or assigns shall have or make any claim or demand upon such property.

In Witness Whereof,

Signed, sealed and delivered in presence of two witnesses:

_____

_____

_____L.S.

Releasor

The undersigned legal spouse of the above releasor hereby waives all dower or curtesy rights to the hereinabove described property.

_____L.S.

Spouse

STATE OF_____ } ss. _____

COUNTY OF_____ }

Personally appeared before me this_____day of_____

19_____, _____,

signer and sealer of the foregoing instrument, and acknowledged the same to be_____free act and deed.

(Notary Seal) _____

Notary Public

Received for record_____at_____Attest:_____

Date   Time   Clerk

The consideration for this transfer is less than One Dollar.

45

Quit Claim Deed

From

_____

To

_____ , Trustee

Received for record _____ 19____.

At _____
    Time

and recorded in Vol. _____

on Page _____ of the

Land Records by

_____
Authorized Official

" 'If the law supposes that,' said Mr. Bumble, 'the law
is an ass, an idiot.' "

Charles Dickens

Chapter 6

AVOIDING PROBATE OF
CHECKING AND SAVINGS ACCOUNTS

Checking and savings bank accounts ordinarily are registered in one of five principal ways:

(1) In the name of the individual owner
(2) In the names of two persons jointly on a "one *or* the other" basis
(3) In the name of one individual as trustee for another
(4) In the name of one individual as guardian for another
(5) In the name of one individual as custodian for another.

Before we address ourselves to the first type, which represents our principal interest here, let us briefly consider the other four. No. 2, joint registration, is a very common form, particularly with husband and wife. It is importantly different from joint registration of securities—the latter is always "John Smith *and* Mary Smith", never John Smith *or* Mary Smith". Jointly registered securities therefore require the action of both parties to effect a sale or process a dividend payment. In the case of a joint bank account, either party may act alone in connection with the account.

Jointly-held bank accounts have one very important drawback mentioned in an earlier chapter. Many banks will block such an account upon receipt of notification of the death of one of the joint owners. A client of my firm suffered a severe heart attack and was hospitalized. His wife reported a need for extra funds for hospital bills, etc., and we quickly arranged a $10,000 partial withdrawal from his trust account with us. The check was drawn in his name and his wife deposited it in their joint checking account. He died the following day. Not only would the bank not let her draw any of the $10,000, but it also declined to honor the checks which she had hurriedly drawn the previous day in payment of pressing bills. This practice of blocking accounts is not universal. It would be well to ask your bank to write you a letter stating that it will *not* block your jointly-owned account upon the death of one of the joint-owners. Failing this,

the survivor should hustle down and transfer any balance into a new account in his name. A bereaved person is frequently in no frame of mind to hurry down to a bank to transfer funds. In such circumstances, a third party should be dispatched with a check if it be a checking account, or with the simple authorization for payment to a third party which generally is illustrated in every savings bank book.

The third common form of registration—as trustee for another—also involves conditions peculiar to bank accounts, conditions which differ from those attending trustee registration of securities. If you register common stock in your name as trustee, there must be a written trust instrument in existence. The stock's transfer agent may not require you to display the written instrument when you *buy* the stock, but it will almost certainly demand to see it when you want to sell it.

Savings bank accounts require no such written instrument. Savings accounts in *commercial banks* are a different story; they generally want a copy of a proper trust instrument on file if you wish to make withdrawals.

With a trustee registration, many banks will deliver up the proceeds to the beneficiary if the trustee's death certificate is presented, provided the beneficiary has reached the age of reason. If John Smith opens a savings account for his 15-year-old son and dies, in most cases the bank will deliver the money to the son. If the child is quite young, the bank will probably ask that someone obtain probate court appointment as guardian. Remember those "special guardianships" we discussed earlier?

Guardians are appointed by the probate court. For example, a child might be awarded a court or insurance company settlement for injuries suffered in an accident. The probate court would appoint a guardian (probably, but not necessarily, a parent) who would receive and hold the money for the minor. In his capacity as guardian, he could open a bank account. If he died, the court would be called upon to appoint a new guardian who would have access to the money upon presentation to the bank of his credentials from the probate court.

A parent wishing simply to make a cash gift to a child might deposit it in a bank account which he holds as "custodian".

None of these accounts (2 through 5) is subject to probate. The joint account is exempt because there is a surviving co-owner. The others are exempt because the funds are actually not the property of the deceased but rather belong to the beneficiary.

No claim is made here that the conditions and circumstances described represent iron-clad and inflexible law in effect everywhere. There are exceptions to almost every rule and there are bound to be areas where local custom or the policy of an institution differs from that described here. What I am trying to do is alert you to some of the pitfalls which may cause you trouble. Knowing of them, the reader can make careful inquiry to discover what ground rules apply in his own area.

* * *

Like other forms of property, the individually-registered savings or checking account will fall within the jurisdiction of the probate court—if you let it. You can avoid it by using the same "magic key" to probate exemption, the inter vivos trust.

CHAPTER **6**, APPENDIX **A**

> # DECLARATION OF TRUST
> FOR NAMING
> # ONE BENEFICIARY
> TO RECEIVE
> # A BANK ACCOUNT

Instructions:

On the following pages will be found duplicate copies of a declaration of trust (DT-5) which will be suitable for use in connection with the inter vivos trust arrangement suggested in Chapter 6 where it is desired simply to name some one person to receive a checking or savings account upon the death of the owner.

Cross out *"city"* or *"town"*, leaving the appropriate designation of your community. Next, cross out *"checking"* or *"savings"*, leaving the appropriate designation of the bank account, and initial it.

Enter the name of the beneficiary in the appropriate place in Paragraph 1.

Whenever there is any possibility of a minor child receiving the property, make certain that you name an adult who can act as trustee for the child. The name of that adult should be inserted in Paragraph 6 of the instrument shown here. Avoid naming as trustee a person not likely to survive until the child has reached age 21.

When completed in the manner shown on the reverse side hereof, one copy of the declaration of trust should be filed with the bank where the account is maintained. The duplicate may be retained for reference purposes.

Declaration of Trust

of the

WHEREAS, I, **John J. Smith** , State of **Connecticut** ,

City/Town of **Jonesville** , County of **Fairfax** , am the owner of a ~~checking~~/savings account in the **Jonesville Savings Bank**
(Name of Bank)

located in the City/Town of **Jonesville** , State of **Connecticut** .

NOW, THEREFORE, KNOW ALL MEN BY THESE PRESENTS, that I do hereby acknowledge and declare that I hold and will hold said bank account and all right, title and interest in and to said account IN TRUST

1. For the use and benefit of:

(Name) **Mary A. Smith (my niece)** **Jonesville** **Connecticut** .
City State

(Address) **750** **Porter Street**
Number Street

Upon my death, unless the beneficiary shall predecease me or unless we both shall die as a result of a common accident or disaster, my Successor Trustee is hereby directed forthwith to transfer said bank account and all right, title and interest in and to said account unto the beneficiary absolutely and thereby terminate this trust; *provided, however*, that if the beneficiary hereunder shall then be a minor, the Successor Trustee shall hold the trust assets in continuing trust until such beneficiary attains the age of twenty-one years. During such period of continuing trust, the Successor Trustee, in his absolute discretion, may retain the specific bank account herein described if he believes it in the best interest of the beneficiary so to do, or he may terminate it, investing and reinvesting the proceeds as he may deem appropriate. Prior to the date upon which such minor beneficiary attains the age of twenty-one years, the Successor Trustee may apply or expend any or all of the interest or principal directly for the maintenance, education and support of the minor beneficiary without the intervention of any guardian and without application to any court. Such payments of interest or principal may be made to the parents of such minor or to the person with whom the minor is living without any liability upon the Successor Trustee or upon the bank to see to the application thereof. If such minor survives me but dies before attaining the age of twenty-one years, at his or her death the Successor Trustee shall deliver, pay over, transfer and distribute the trust property to such minor's personal representatives, absolutely.

2. This Trust is created with the express understanding that the bank at which the account is maintained shall be under no liability whatsoever to see to the proper administration of the Trust. On the contrary, upon the transfer of the right, title and interest in and to such account by any trustee hereunder, said bank shall conclusively treat the transferee as the sole owner of said account. As and if I shall elect from time to time to cause interest payments on said account to be distributed rather than compounded, the bank shall be fully authorized to pay such interest direct to me individually unless there shall have been filed with it written notice of my death or incapacity satisfactory to it. Until the bank shall receive from some person interested in this trust, written notice of any death or other event upon which the right to receive may depend, the bank shall incur no liability for payments made in good faith to persons whose interests shall have been affected by such event. The bank shall be protected in acting upon any notice or other instrument or document believed by it to be genuine and to have been signed or presented by the proper party or parties.

3. I reserve unto myself the power and right to collect any interest or other income which may accrue from the trust property and, in my sole discretion as Trustee, either to accumulate such interest or income as an addition to the trust assets being held hereunder or pay such interest or income to myself as an individual.

4. I reserve unto myself the power and right at any time during my lifetime to amend or revoke in whole or in part the Trust hereby created without the necessity of obtaining the consent of the beneficiary and without giving notice to the beneficiary. The withdrawal by me of the whole or any part of the bank account held hereunder shall constitute as to such whole or part a revocation of this Trust.

5. The death during my lifetime, or in a common accident or disaster with me, of the beneficiary designated hereunder shall revoke such designation, and in the former event, I reserve the right to designate a new beneficiary. Should I for [...] reason fail to [...] [...] new be[...] property shall revert to my estate.

6. In the event of my death or legal incapacity. I hereby nominate and appoint as Successor Trustee hereunder whosoever shall at that time be beneficiary hereunder, unless such beneficiary be a minor or legally incapacitated in which event I hereby nominate and appoint

(Name) **Henry P. Adams** **Jonesville** **Connecticut** , of
City State

(Address) **125** **Barnum Street**
Number Street

to be Successor Trustee.

7. This Declaration of Trust shall extend to and be binding upon the heirs, executors, administrators and assigns of the undersigned and upon the Successors to the Trustee.

8. The Trustee and his successors shall serve without bond.

9. This Declaration of Trust shall be construed and enforced in accordance with the laws of the State of **Connecticut**

Declaration of Trust

WHEREAS, I,_____of the

City/Town of_____, County of_____, State of_____,

am the owner of a checking/savings account in the_____

(Name of Bank)

located in the City/Town of_____, State of_____.

NOW, THEREFORE, KNOW ALL MEN BY THESE PRESENTS, that I do hereby acknowledge and declare that I hold and will hold said bank account and all right, title and interest in and to said account IN TRUST

1. For the use and benefit of:

(Name)_____, of

(Address)_____.

Number   Street   City   State

Upon my death, unless the beneficiary shall predecease me or unless we both shall die as a result of a common accident or disaster, my Successor Trustee is hereby directed forthwith to transfer said bank account and all right, title and interest in and to said account unto the beneficiary absolutely and thereby terminate this trust; *provided,* however, that if the beneficiary hereunder shall then be a minor, the Successor Trustee shall hold the trust assets in continuing trust until such beneficiary attains the age of twenty-one years. During such period of continuing trust, the Successor Trustee, in his absolute discretion, may retain the specific bank account herein described if he believes it in the best interest of the beneficiary so to do, or he may terminate it, investing and reinvesting the proceeds as he may deem appropriate. Prior to the date upon which such minor beneficiary attains the age of twenty-one years, the Successor Trustee may apply or expend any or all of the interest or principal directly for the maintenance, education and support of the minor beneficiary without the intervention of any guardian and without application to any court. Such payments of interest or principal may be made to the parents of such minor or to the person with whom the minor is living without any liability upon the Successor Trustee or upon the bank to see to the application thereof. If such minor survives me but dies before attaining the age of twenty-one years, at his or her death the Successor Trustee shall deliver, pay over, transfer and distribute the trust property to such minor's personal representatives, absolutely.

2. This Trust is created with the express understanding that the bank at which the account is maintained shall be under no liability whatsoever to see to the proper administration of the Trust. On the contrary, upon the transfer of the right, title and interest in and to such account by any trustee hereunder, said bank shall conclusively treat the transferee as the sole owner of said account. As and if I shall elect from time to time to cause interest payments on said account to be distributed rather than compounded, the bank shall be fully authorized to pay such interest direct to me individually unless there shall have been filed with it written notice of my death or incapacity satisfactory to it. Until the bank shall receive from some person interested in this trust, written notice of any death or other event upon which the right to receive may depend, the bank shall incur no liability for payments made in good faith to persons whose interests shall have been affected by such event. The bank shall be protected in acting upon any notice or other instrument or document believed by it to be genuine and to have been signed or presented by the proper party or parties.

3. I reserve unto myself the power and right to collect any interest or other income which may accrue from the trust property and, in my sole discretion as Trustee, either to accumulate such interest or income as an addition to the trust assets being held hereunder or pay such interest or income to myself as an individual.

4. I reserve unto myself the power and right at any time during my lifetime to amend or revoke in whole or in part the Trust hereby created without the necessity of obtaining the consent of the beneficiary and without giving notice to the beneficiary. The withdrawal by me of the whole or any part of the bank account held hereunder shall constitute as to such whole or part a revocation of this Trust.

5. The death during my lifetime, or in a common accident or disaster with me, of the beneficiary designated hereunder shall revoke such designation, and in the former event, I reserve the right to designate a new beneficiary.

Should I for any reason fail to designate such new beneficiary, this Trust shall terminate upon my death and the trust property shall revert to my estate.

6. In the event of my death or legal incapacity, I hereby nominate and appoint as Successor Trustee hereunder whosoever shall at that time be beneficiary hereunder, unless such beneficiary be a minor or legally incapacitated in which event I hereby nominate and appoint

(Name)_____, of

(Address)_____

          Number   Street   City   State

to be Successor Trustee.

7. This Declaration of Trust shall extend to and be binding upon the heirs, executors, administrators and assigns of the undersigned and upon the Successors to the Trustee.

8. The Trustee and his successors shall serve without bond.

9. This Declaration of Trust shall be construed and enforced in accordance with the laws of the State of

_____.

IN WITNESS WHEREOF I have hereunto set my hand and seal this_____day of_____, 19___.

(sign here)_____L.S.

Witness: (1)_____

Witness: (2)_____

STATE OF_____⎱
                             ⎰ ss: _____
COUNTY OF_____⎰

On the_____day of_____, nineteen hundred and_____,

before me came_____,

known to me to be the individual described in, and who executed the foregoing instrument, and _____ acknowledged

that _____ executed the same, and in due form of law acknowledged the foregoing instrument to be _____ free act and deed and desired the same might be recorded as such.

(Notary Seal)   _____

                                                 Notary Public

Declaration of Trust

WHEREAS, I,_____of the

City/Town of_____, County of_____, State of_____,

am the owner of a checking/savings account in the_____
(Name of Bank)

located in the City/Town of_____, State of_____.

NOW, THEREFORE, KNOW ALL MEN BY THESE PRESENTS, that I do hereby acknowledge and declare that I hold and will hold said bank account and all right, title and interest in and to said account IN TRUST

1. For the use and benefit of:

(Name)_____, of

(Address)_____.
| Number | Street | City | State |

Upon my death, unless the beneficiary shall predecease me or unless we both shall die as a result of a common accident or disaster, my Successor Trustee is hereby directed forthwith to transfer said bank account and all right, title and interest in and to said account unto the beneficiary absolutely and thereby terminate this trust; *provided*, however, that if the beneficiary hereunder shall then be a minor, the Successor Trustee shall hold the trust assets in continuing trust until such beneficiary attains the age of twenty-one years. During such period of continuing trust, the Successor Trustee, in his absolute discretion, may retain the specific bank account herein described if he believes it in the best interest of the beneficiary so to do, or he may terminate it, investing and reinvesting the proceeds as he may deem appropriate. Prior to the date upon which such minor beneficiary attains the age of twenty-one years, the Successor Trustee may apply or expend any or all of the interest or principal directly for the maintenance, education and support of the minor beneficiary without the intervention of any guardian and without application to any court. Such payments of interest or principal may be made to the parents of such minor or to the person with whom the minor is living without any liability upon the Successor Trustee or upon the bank to see to the application thereof. If such minor survives me but dies before attaining the age of twenty-one years, at his or her death the Successor Trustee shall deliver, pay over, transfer and distribute the trust property to such minor's personal representatives, absolutely.

2. This Trust is created with the express understanding that the bank at which the account is maintained shall be under no liability whatsoever to see to the proper administration of the Trust. On the contrary, upon the transfer of the right, title and interest in and to such account by any trustee hereunder, said bank shall conclusively treat the transferee as the sole owner of said account. As and if I shall elect from time to time to cause interest payments on said account to be distributed rather than compounded, the bank shall be fully authorized to pay such interest direct to me individually unless there shall have been filed with it written notice of my death or incapacity satisfactory to it. Until the bank shall receive from some person interested in this trust, written notice of any death or other event upon which the right to receive may depend, the bank shall incur no liability for payments made in good faith to persons whose interests shall have been affected by such event. The bank shall be protected in acting upon any notice or other instrument or document believed by it to be genuine and to have been signed or presented by the proper party or parties.

3. I reserve unto myself the power and right to collect any interest or other income which may accrue from the trust property and, in my sole discretion as Trustee, either to accumulate such interest or income as an addition to the trust assets being held hereunder or pay such interest or income to myself as an individual.

4. I reserve unto myself the power and right at any time during my lifetime to amend or revoke in whole or in part the Trust hereby created without the necessity of obtaining the consent of the beneficiary and without giving notice to the beneficiary. The withdrawal by me of the whole or any part of the bank account held hereunder shall constitute as to such whole or part a revocation of this Trust.

5. The death during my lifetime, or in a common accident or disaster with me, of the beneficiary designated hereunder shall revoke such designation, and in the former event, I reserve the right to designate a new beneficiary.

Should I for any reason fail to designate such new beneficiary, this Trust shall terminate upon my death and the trust property shall revert to my estate.

6. In the event of my death or legal incapacity, I hereby nominate and appoint as Successor Trustee hereunder whosoever shall at that time be beneficiary hereunder, unless such beneficiary be a minor or legally incapacitated in which event I hereby nominate and appoint

(Name)_____, of

(Address)_____
　　　　　　　Number　　　　　　Street　　　　　　City　　　　　　State
to be Successor Trustee.

7. This Declaration of Trust shall extend to and be binding upon the heirs, executors, administrators and assigns of the undersigned and upon the Successors to the Trustee.

8. The Trustee and his successors shall serve without bond.

9. This Declaration of Trust shall be construed and enforced in accordance with the laws of the State of

_____.

IN WITNESS WHEREOF I have hereunto set my hand and seal this_____day of_____, 19___.

(sign here)_____L.S.

Witness: (1)_____

Witness: (2)_____

STATE OF_____⎫
　　　　　　　　　　　　　　　　　　　⎬ ss: _____
COUNTY OF_____⎭

On the_____day of_____, nineteen hundred and_____,

before me came_____,

known to me to be the individual described in, and who executed the foregoing instrument, and _____ acknowledged

that _____ executed the same, and in due form of law acknowledged the foregoing instrument to be _____ free act and deed and desired the same might be recorded as such.

(Notary Seal)　　　　　　　　　　　　_____
　　　　　　　　　　　　　　　　　　　　　　　Notary Public

DECLARATION OF TRUST
FOR NAMING
ONE PRIMARY BENEFICIARY
AND
ONE CONTINGENT BENEFICIARY
TO RECEIVE
A BANK ACCOUNT

Instructions:

On the following pages will be found duplicate copies of a declaration of trust (DT-6) which will be suitable for use in connection with the inter vivos trust arrangement suggested in Chapter 6 where it is desired to name some *one* person as primary beneficiary with some *one* other person as contingent beneficiary to receive a checking or savings account if the primary beneficiary does not survive.

Cross out *"city"* or *"town"*, leaving the appropriate designation of your community. Next, cross out *"checking"* or *"savings"*, leaving the appropriate designation of the bank account, and initial it.

Enter the names of the beneficiaries in the appropriate place in Paragraph 1.

Whenever there is any possibility of a minor child receiving any portion of the bank account, make certain that you name an adult who can act as trustee for him. The name of that adult should be inserted in Paragraph 6 of the instrument shown here. Avoid naming as trustee a person not likely to survive until the child has reached age 21.

When completed in the manner shown on the reverse side hereof, one copy of the declaration of trust should be filed with the bank where the account is maintained. The duplicate may be retained for reference.

Declaration of Trust

WHEREAS, I, __John J. Smith__, State of __Connecticut__, of the

City/Town of __Jonesville__, County of __Fairfax__

am the owner of a checking/savings account in the __Jonesville Savings Bank__
(Name of Bank)

located in the City/Town of __Jonesville__, State of __Connecticut__

NOW, THEREFORE, KNOW ALL MEN BY THESE PRESENTS, that I do hereby acknowledge and declare that I hold and will hold said bank account and all right, title and interest in and to said account IN TRUST

1. For the use and benefit of:

(Name) __Mary A. Smith   (my niece)__, __Jonesville__, __Connecticut__
City, State

(Address) __750__ __Porter Street__, of
Number, Street

or, if such beneficiary be not surviving, for the use and benefit of:

(Name) __William B. Connors (my nephew)__, __Jonesville__, __Connecticut__
City, State

(Address) __250__ __County Street__
Number, Street

Upon my death, unless both of the beneficiaries shall predecease me or unless we shall die as a result of a common accident or disaster, my Successor Trustee is hereby directed forthwith to transfer said bank account and all right, title and interest in and to said account unto the beneficiary absolutely and thereby terminate this trust; *provided, however,* that if the beneficiary hereunder shall then be a minor, the Successor Trustee shall hold the trust assets in continuing trust until such beneficiary attains the age of twenty-one years. During such period of continuing trust the Successor Trustee, in his absolute discretion, may retain the specific bank account herein described if he believes it in the best interest of the beneficiary so to do, or he may terminate it, investing and reinvesting the proceeds as he may deem appropriate. Prior to the date upon which such minor beneficiary attains the age of twenty-one years, the Successor Trustee may apply or expend any or all of the interest or principal directly for the maintenance, education and support of the minor beneficiary without the intervention of any guardian and without application to any court. Such payments of interest or principal may be made to the parents of such minor or to the person with whom the minor is living without any liability upon the Successor Trustee or upon the bank to see to the application thereof. If such minor survives me but dies before attaining the age of twenty-one years, at his or her death the Successor Trustee shall deliver, pay over, transfer and distribute the trust property to such minor's personal representatives, absolutely.

2. This Trust is created with the express understanding that the bank at which the account is maintained shall be under no liability whatsoever to see to the proper administration of the Trust. On the contrary, upon the transfer of the right, title and interest in and to such account by any trustee hereunder, said bank shall conclusively treat the transferee as the sole owner of said account. As and if I shall elect from time to time to cause interest payments on said account to be distributed rather than compounded, the bank shall be fully authorized to pay such interest direct to me individually unless there shall have been filed with it written notice of my death or incapacity satisfactory to it. Until the bank shall receive from some person interested in this trust, written notice of any death or other event upon which the right to receive may depend, the bank shall incur no liability for payments made in good faith to persons whose interests shall have been affected by such event. The bank shall be protected in acting upon any notice or other instrument or document believed by it to be genuine and to have been signed or presented by the proper party or parties.

3. I reserve unto myself the power and right to collect any interest or other income which may accrue from the trust property and, in my sole discretion as Trustee, either to accumulate such interest or income as an addition to the trust assets being held hereunder or pay such interest or income to myself as an individual. ~~~~~~~~~

beneficiary ~~~~~~ iaries. Should I for ~~ y rea ~ fail to designate such new benefic ~ y, this Trust shall terminate upon my death and the trust property shall revert to my estate.

6. In the event of my death or legal incapacity, I hereby nominate and appoint as Successor Trustee hereunder whosoever shall at that time be beneficiary hereunder, unless such beneficiary be a minor or legally incapacitated in which event I hereby nominate and appoint

(Name) __Henry P. Adams__, __Jonesville__, __Connecticut__
City, State

(Address) __125__ __Barnum Street__
Number, Street

to be Successor Trustee.

7. This Declaration of Trust shall extend to and be binding upon the heirs, executors, administrators and assigns of the undersigned and upon the Successors to the Trustee.

8. The Trustee and his successors shall serve without bond.

9. This Declaration of Trust shall be construed and enforced in accordance with the laws of the State of __Connecticut__

Declaration of Trust

WHEREAS, I,_____of the

City/Town of_____, County of_____, State of_____,

am the owner of a checking/savings account in the_____

(Name of Bank)

located in the City/Town of_____, State of_____.

NOW, THEREFORE, KNOW ALL MEN BY THESE PRESENTS, that I do hereby acknowledge and declare that I hold and will hold said bank account and all right, title and interest in and to said account IN TRUST

   1. For the use and benefit of:

(Name)_____, of

(Address)_____

        Number   Street   City   State

or, if such beneficiary be not surviving, for the use and benefit of:

(Name)_____, of

(Address)_____.

        Number   Street   City   State

Upon my death, unless both of the beneficiaries shall predecease me or unless we shall die as a result of a common accident or disaster, my Successor Trustee is hereby directed forthwith to transfer said bank account and all right, title and interest in and to said account unto the beneficiary absolutely and thereby terminate this trust; *provided,* however, that if the beneficiary hereunder shall then be a minor, the Successor Trustee shall hold the trust assets in continuing trust until such beneficiary attains the age of twenty-one years. During such period of continuing trust the Successor Trustee, in his absolute discretion, may retain the specific bank account herein described if he believes it in the best interest of the beneficiary so to do, or he may terminate it, investing and reinvesting the proceeds as he may deem appropriate. Prior to the date upon which such minor beneficiary attains the age of twenty-one years, the Successor Trustee may apply or expend any or all of the interest or principal directly for the maintenance, education and support of the minor beneficiary without the intervention of any guardian and without application to any court. Such payments of interest or principal may be made to the parents of such minor or to the person with whom the minor is living without any liability upon the Successor Trustee or upon the bank to see to the application thereof. If such minor survives me but dies before attaining the age of twenty-one years, at his or her death the Successor Trustee shall deliver, pay over, transfer and distribute the trust property to such minor's personal representatives, absolutely.

    2. This Trust is created with the express understanding that the bank at which the account is maintained shall be under no liability whatsoever to see to the proper administration of the Trust. On the contrary, upon the transfer of the right, title and interest in and to such account by any trustee hereunder, said bank shall conclusively treat the transferee as the sole owner of said account. As and if I shall elect from time to time to cause interest payments on said account to be distributed rather than compounded, the bank shall be fully authorized to pay such interest direct to me individually unless there shall have been filed with it written notice of my death or incapacity satisfactory to it. Until the bank shall receive from some person interested in this trust, written notice of any death or other event upon which the right to receive may depend, the bank shall incur no liability for payments made in good faith to persons whose interests shall have been affected by such event. The bank shall be protected in acting upon any notice or other instrument or document believed by it to be genuine and to have been signed or presented by the proper party or parties.

    3. I reserve unto myself the power and right to collect any interest or other income which may accrue from the trust property and, in my sole discretion as Trustee, either to accumulate such interest or income as an addition to the trust assets being held hereunder or pay such interest or income to myself as an individual.

4. I reserve unto myself the power and right at any time during my lifetime to amend or revoke in whole or in part the Trust hereby created without the necessity of obtaining the consent of the beneficiary and without giving notice to the beneficiary. The withdrawal by me of the whole or any part of the bank account held hereunder shall constitute as to such whole or part a revocation of this Trust.

5. The death during my lifetime or in a common accident or disaster with me, of both of the beneficiaries designated hereunder shall revoke such designation, and in the former event, I reserve the right to designate a new beneficiary or beneficiaries. Should I for any reason fail to designate such new beneficiary, this Trust shall terminate upon my death and the trust property shall revert to my estate.

6. In the event of my death or legal incapacity, I hereby nominate and appoint as Successor Trustee hereunder whosoever shall at that time be beneficiary hereunder, unless such beneficiary be a minor or legally incapacitated in which event I hereby nominate and appoint

(Name)_____, of

(Address)_____

| Number | Street | City | State |

to be Successor Trustee.

7. This Declaration of Trust shall extend to and be binding upon the heirs, executors, administrators and assigns of the undersigned and upon the Successors to the Trustee.

8. The Trustee and his successors shall serve without bond.

9. This Declaration of Trust shall be construed and enforced in accordance with the laws of the State of

_____.

IN WITNESS WHEREOF I have hereunto set my hand and seal this_____day of_____, 19___.

(sign here)_____L.S.

Witness: (1)_____

Witness: (2)_____

STATE OF_____
⎫
ss: _____
COUNTY OF_____
⎭

On the_____day of_____, nineteen hundred and_____,

before me came_____,

known to me to be the individual described in, and who executed the foregoing instrument, and _____ acknowledged

that _____ executed the same, and in due form of law acknowledged the foregoing instrument to be _____ free act and deed and desired the same might be recorded as such.

(Notary Seal)

_____
Notary Public

WHEREAS, I,_____of the

City/Town of_____, County of_____, State of_____,

am the owner of a checking/savings account in the_____
(Name of Bank)

located in the City/Town of_____, State of_____.

NOW, THEREFORE, KNOW ALL MEN BY THESE PRESENTS, that I do hereby acknowledge and declare that I hold and will hold said bank account and all right, title and interest in and to said account IN TRUST

1. For the use and benefit of:

(Name)_____, of

(Address)_____
             Number   Street   City   State

or, if such beneficiary be not surviving, for the use and benefit of:

(Name)_____, of

(Address)_____
             Number   Street   City   State

Upon my death, unless both of the beneficiaries shall predecease me or unless we shall die as a result of a common accident or disaster, my Successor Trustee is hereby directed forthwith to transfer said bank account and all right, title and interest in and to said account unto the beneficiary absolutely and thereby terminate this trust; *provided,* however, that if the beneficiary hereunder shall then be a minor, the Successor Trustee shall hold the trust assets in continuing trust until such beneficiary attains the age of twenty-one years. During such period of continuing trust the Successor Trustee, in his absolute discretion, may retain the specific bank account herein described if he believes it in the best interest of the beneficiary so to do, or he may terminate it, investing and reinvesting the proceeds as he may deem appropriate. Prior to the date upon which such minor beneficiary attains the age of twenty-one years, the Successor Trustee may apply or expend any or all of the interest or principal directly for the maintenance, education and support of the minor beneficiary without the intervention of any guardian and without application to any court. Such payments of interest or principal may be made to the parents of such minor or to the person with whom the minor is living without any liability upon the Successor Trustee or upon the bank to see to the application thereof. If such minor survives me but dies before attaining the age of twenty-one years, at his or her death the Successor Trustee shall deliver, pay over, transfer and distribute the trust property to such minor's personal representatives, absolutely.

2. This Trust is created with the express understanding that the bank at which the account is maintained shall be under no liability whatsoever to see to the proper administration of the Trust. On the contrary, upon the transfer of the right, title and interest in and to such account by any trustee hereunder, said bank shall conclusively treat the transferee as the sole owner of said account. As and if I shall elect from time to time to cause interest payments on said account to be distributed rather than compounded, the bank shall be fully authorized to pay such interest direct to me individually unless there shall have been filed with it written notice of my death or incapacity satisfactory to it. Until the bank shall receive from some person interested in this trust, written notice of any death or other event upon which the right to receive may depend, the bank shall incur no liability for payments made in good faith to persons whose interests shall have been affected by such event. The bank shall be protected in acting upon any notice or other instrument or document believed by it to be genuine and to have been signed or presented by the proper party or parties.

3. I reserve unto myself the power and right to collect any interest or other income which may accrue from the trust property and, in my sole discretion as Trustee, either to accumulate such interest or income as an addition to the trust assets being held hereunder or pay such interest or income to myself as an individual.

4. I reserve unto myself the power and right at any time during my lifetime to amend or revoke in whole or in part the Trust hereby created without the necessity of obtaining the consent of the beneficiary and without giving notice to the beneficiary. The withdrawal by me of the whole or any part of the bank account held hereunder shall constitute as to such whole or part a revocation of this Trust.

5. The death during my lifetime or in a common accident or disaster with me, of both of the beneficiaries designated hereunder shall revoke such designation, and in the former event, I reserve the right to designate a new beneficiary or beneficiaries. Should I for any reason fail to designate such new beneficiary, this Trust shall terminate upon my death and the trust property shall revert to my estate.

6. In the event of my death or legal incapacity, I hereby nominate and appoint as Successor Trustee hereunder whosoever shall at that time be beneficiary hereunder, unless such beneficiary be a minor or legally incapacitated in which event I hereby nominate and appoint

(Name)_____, of

(Address)_____

            Number   Street   City   State

to be Successor Trustee.

7. This Declaration of Trust shall extend to and be binding upon the heirs, executors, administrators and assigns of the undersigned and upon the Successors to the Trustee.

8. The Trustee and his successors shall serve without bond.

9. This Declaration of Trust shall be construed and enforced in accordance with the laws of the State of

_____.

IN WITNESS WHEREOF I have hereunto set my hand and seal this_____day of_____, 19___.

(sign here) _____L.S.

Witness: (1)_____

Witness: (2)_____

STATE OF_____

COUNTY OF_____ } ss: _____

On the_____day of_____, nineteen hundred and_____,

before me came_____,

known to me to be the individual described in, and who executed the foregoing instrument, and _____ acknowledged

that _____ executed the same, and in due form of law acknowledged the foregoing instrument to be _____ free act and deed and desired the same might be recorded as such.

(Notary Seal)   _____

                                            Notary Public

DECLARATION OF TRUST
FOR NAMING
**TWO OR MORE BENEFICIARIES
SHARING EQUALLY**
TO RECEIVE
A BANK ACCOUNT

Instructions:

On the following pages will be found duplicate copies of a declaration of trust (DT-7) which will be suitable for use in connection with the inter vivos trust arrangement suggested in Chapter 6 where it is desired to name two or more persons to share a checking or savings account equally upon the death of the owner.

Cross out *"city" or "town"*, leaving the appropriate designation of your community. Next, cross out *"checking" or "savings"*, leaving the appropriate designation of the bank account, and initial it.

In Paragraph 1, indicate the *number* of *persons* you are naming (to discourage unauthorized additions to the list) and then insert their names. The one whose name appears *first* will be the successor trustee responsible for seeing to the distribution of the trust property.

Note that the instrument specifies that the named beneficiaries are to receive "in equal shares, or the survivor of them/*per stirpes*". Now, think carefully: If you have named your three brothers with the understanding that if one brother predeceases you, *his* children will take *his* share, cross out "or the survivor of them" and initial it. If that is *not* what you want—if, for example, you prefer that the share of your deceased brother be divided by your two surviving brothers, cross out *"per stirpes"* and initial it. Remember, you <u>must</u> cross out either *"or the survivor of them"* or *"per stirpes"* —one or the other.

Whenever there is any possibility of a minor child receiving any portion of the bank account, make certain that you name an adult who can act as trustee for him. The name of that adult should be inserted in Paragraph 6 of the instrument shown here. Avoid naming as trustee a person not likely to survive until the child has reached age 21.

When completed in the manner shown on the reverse side hereof, one copy of the declaration of trust should be filed with the bank where the account is maintained. The duplicate may be retained for reference.

Declaration of Trust

of the

WHEREAS, I __John J. Smith__ , State of __Connecticut__

City/Town of __Jonesville__ , County of __Fairfax__

am the owner of a checking/savings account in the __Jonesville National Bank__

(Name of Bank)

located in the City/Town of __Jonesville__ , State of __Connecticut__

NOW, THEREFORE, KNOW ALL MEN BY THESE PRESENTS, that I do hereby acknowledge and declare that I hold and will hold said bank account and all right, title and interest in and to said account IN TRUST

1. For the use and benefit of the following __three__ persons, in equal shares, or the survivor of them/per stirpes:

_J.J.S._

Thomas B. Smith	(my brother)
William R. Smith	(my brother)
Charles M. Smith	(my brother)

Upon my death, unless all of the beneficiaries shall predecease me or unless we all shall die as a result of a common accident or disaster, my Successor Trustee is hereby directed forthwith to transfer said bank account and all right, title and interest in and to said account unto the beneficiaries absolutely and thereby terminate this Trust; _provided_, however, that if any beneficiary hereunder shall then be a minor, the Successor Trustee shall hold the trust assets in continuing trust until such beneficiary attains the age of twenty-one years. During such period of continuing trust the Successor Trustee, in his absolute discretion, may retain the specific bank account herein described if he believes it in the best interest of the beneficiary so to do, or he may terminate it, investing and reinvesting the proceeds as he may deem appropriate. The Successor Trustee may apply or expend any or all of the income or principal directly for the maintenance, education and support of the minor beneficiary without the intervention of any guardian and without application to any court. Such payments of income or principal may be made to the parents of such minor or to the person with whom the minor is living without any liability upon the Successor Trustee to see to the application thereof. If any such minor survives me but dies before attaining the age of twenty-one years, at his or her death the Successor Trustee shall deliver, pay over, transfer and distribute the trust property being held for such minor to said minor's personal representatives, absolutely.

2. This Trust is created with the express understanding that the bank at which the account is maintained shall be under no liability whatsoever to see to its proper administration, and upon the transfer of the right, title and interest in and to such account by any trustee hereunder, said bank shall conclusively treat the transferee as the sole owner of said account. As and if I shall elect from time to time to cause interest payments on said account to be distributed rather than compounded, the bank shall be fully authorized to pay such interest direct to me individually unless there shall have been filed with it written notice of my death or incapacity satisfactory to it. Until the bank shall receive from some person interested in this Trust, written notice of any death or other event upon which the right to receive may depend, the bank shall incur no liability for payments made in good faith to persons whose interests shall have been affected by such event. The bank shall be protected in acting upon any notice or other instrument or document believed by it to be genuine and to have been signed or presented by the proper party or parties.

3. I reserve unto myself the power and right to collect any interest or other income which may accrue from the trust property and, in my sole discretion as Trustee, either to accumulate such income as an addition to the trust assets being held hereunder or pay such income to myself as an individual.

the right to

beneficiaries. Should I for any ... fail to designate such new beneficiaries, this Trust shall terminate upon death and the trust property shall revert to my estate.

6. In the event of my death or legal incapacity, I hereby nominate and appoint as Successor Trustee hereunder the beneficiary first above named, unless such beneficiary be a minor or legally incompetent, in which event I hereby nominate and appoint as Successor Trustee hereunder the beneficiary whose name appears second above. If such beneficiary named second above shall be a minor or legally incompetent, then I nominate and appoint

__Henry P. Adams__ , of __Jonesville__ __Connecticut__
(Name) City State

__125__ __Barnum Street__
(Address) Number Street

as Successor Trustee hereunder.

7. This Declaration of Trust shall extend to and be binding upon the heirs, executors, administrators and assigns of the undersigned and upon the Successors to the Trustee.

8. The Trustee and his successors shall serve without bond.

9. This Declaration of Trust shall be construed and enforced in accordance with the laws of the State of __Connecticut__

WHEREAS, I_____of the

City/Town of_____, County of_____, State of_____

am the owner of a checking/savings account in the_____
                                                                (Name of Bank)
located in the City/Town of_____, State of_____,

   NOW, THEREFORE, KNOW ALL MEN BY THESE PRESENTS, that I do hereby acknowledge and declare that I hold and will hold said bank account and all right, title and interest in and to said account IN TRUST

   1. For the use and benefit of the following _____ persons, in equal shares, or the survivor of them/per stirpes:

Upon my death, unless all of the beneficiaries shall predecease me or unless we all shall die as a result of a common accident or disaster, my Successor Trustee is hereby directed forthwith to transfer said bank account and all right, title and interest in and to said account unto the beneficiaries absolutely and thereby terminate this Trust; *provided,* however, that if any beneficiary hereunder shall then be a minor, the Successor Trustee shall hold the trust assets in continuing trust until such beneficiary attains the age of twenty-one years. During such period of continuing trust the Successor Trustee, in his absolute discretion, may retain the specific bank account herein described if he believes it in the best interest of the beneficiary so to do, or he may terminate it, investing and reinvesting the proceeds as he may deem appropriate. Prior to the date upon which such minor beneficiary attains the age of twenty-one years, the Successor Trustee may apply or expend any or all of the income or principal directly for the maintenance, education and support of the minor beneficiary without the intervention of any guardian and without application to any court. Such payments of income or principal may be made to the parents of such minor or to the person with whom the minor is living without any liability upon the Successor Trustee to see to the application thereof. If any such minor survives me but dies before attaining the age of twenty-one years, at his or her death the Successor Trustee shall deliver, pay over, transfer and distribute the trust property being held for such minor to said minor's personal representatives, absolutely.

   2. This Trust is created with the express understanding that the bank at which the account is maintained shall be under no liability whatsoever to see to its proper administration, and upon the transfer of the right, title and interest in and to such account by any trustee hereunder, said bank shall conclusively treat the transferee as the sole owner of said account. As and if I shall elect from time to time to cause interest payments on said account to be distributed rather than compounded, the bank shall be fully authorized to pay such interest direct to me individually unless there shall have been filed with it written notice of my death or incapacity satisfactory to it. Until the bank shall receive from some person interested in this Trust, written notice of any death or other event upon which the right to receive may depend, the bank shall incur no liability for payments made in good faith to persons whose interests shall have been affected by such event. The bank shall be protected in acting upon any notice or other instrument or document believed by it to be genuine and to have been signed or presented by the proper party or parties.

   3. I reserve unto myself the power and right to collect any interest or other income which may accrue from the trust property and, in my sole discretion as Trustee, either to accumulate such income as an addition to the trust assets being held hereunder or pay such income to myself as an individual.

4. I reserve unto myself the power and right at any time during my lifetime to amend or revoke in whole or in part the Trust hereby created without the necessity of obtaining the consent of the beneficiaries and without giving notice to the beneficiaries. The withdrawal by me of the whole or any part of the bank account shall constitute as to such whole or part a revocation of this Trust.

5. The death during my lifetime, or in a common accident or disaster with me, of all of the beneficiaries designated hereunder shall revoke such designation, and in the former event, I reserve the right to designate new beneficiaries. Should I for any reason fail to designate such new beneficiaries, this Trust shall terminate upon my death and the trust property shall revert to my estate.

6. In the event of my death or legal incapacity, I hereby nominate and appoint as Successor Trustee hereunder the beneficiary first above named, unless such beneficiary be a minor or legally incompetent, in which event I hereby nominate and appoint as Successor Trustee hereunder the beneficiary whose name appears second above. If such beneficiary named second above shall be a minor or legally incompetent, then I nominate and appoint

(Name)_____, of

(Address)_____
        Number   Street   City   State
as Successor Trustee hereunder.

7. This Declaration of Trust shall extend to and be binding upon the heirs, executors, administrators and assigns of the undersigned and upon the Successors to the Trustee.

8. The Trustee and his successors shall serve without bond.

9. This Declaration of Trust shall be construed and enforced in accordance with the laws of the State of

_____.

IN WITNESS WHEREOF, I have hereunto set my hand and seal this_____day of_____, 19___.

(sign here)_____L.S.

Witness: (1)_____

Witness: (2)_____

STATE OF_____ ⎫
                                   ⎬ ss: _____
COUNTY OF_____ ⎭

On the_____day of_____, nineteen hundred and_____,

before me came_____,

known to me to be the individual described in, and who executed the foregoing instrument, and _____ acknowledged

that _____ executed the same, and in due form of law acknowledged the foregoing instrument to be _____ free act and deed and desired the same might be recorded as such.

(Notary Seal)   _____
                                              Notary Public

Declaration of Trust

WHEREAS, I_____of the

City/Town of_____, County of_____, State of_____

am the owner of a checking/savings account in the_____
(Name of Bank)

located in the City/Town of_____, State of_____,

NOW, THEREFORE, KNOW ALL MEN BY THESE PRESENTS, that I do hereby acknowledge and declare that I hold and will hold said bank account and all right, title and interest in and to said account IN TRUST

1. For the use and benefit of the following _____ persons, in equal shares, or the survivor of them/per stirpes:

Upon my death, unless all of the beneficiaries shall predecease me or unless we all shall die as a result of a common accident or disaster, my Successor Trustee is hereby directed forthwith to transfer said bank account and all right, title and interest in and to said account unto the beneficiaries absolutely and thereby terminate this Trust; *provided,* however, that if any beneficiary hereunder shall then be a minor, the Successor Trustee shall hold the trust assets in continuing trust until such beneficiary attains the age of twenty-one years. During such period of continuing trust the Successor Trustee, in his absolute discretion, may retain the specific bank account herein described if he believes it in the best interest of the beneficiary so to do, or he may terminate it, investing and reinvesting the proceeds as he may deem appropriate. Prior to the date upon·which such minor beneficiary attains the age of twenty-one years, the Successor Trustee may apply or expend any or all of the income or principal directly for the maintenance, education and support of the minor beneficiary without the intervention of any guardian and without application to any court. Such payments of income or principal may be made to the parents of such minor or to the person with whom the minor is living without any liability upon the Successor Trustee to see to the application thereof. If any such minor survives me but dies before attaining the age of twenty-one years, at his or her death the Successor Trustee shall deliver, pay over, transfer and distribute the trust property being held for such minor to said minor's personal representatives, absolutely.

2. This Trust is created with the express understanding that the bank at which the account is maintained shall be under no liability whatsoever to see to its proper administration, and upon the transfer of the right, title and interest in and to such account by any trustee hereunder, said bank shall conclusively treat the transferee as the sole owner of said account. As and if I shall elect from time to time to cause interest payments on said account to be distributed rather than compounded, the bank shall be fully authorized to pay such interest direct to me individually unless there shall have been filed with it written notice of my death or incapacity satisfactory to it. Until the bank shall receive from some person interested in this Trust, written notice of any death or other event upon which the right to receive may depend, the bank shall incur no liability for payments made in good faith to persons whose interests shall have been affected by such event. The bank shall be protected in acting upon any notice or other instrument or document believed by it to be genuine and to have been signed or presented by the proper party or parties.

3. I reserve unto myself the power and right to collect any interest or other income which may accrue from the trust property and, in my sole discretion as Trustee, either to accumulate such income as an addition to the trust assets being held hereunder or pay such income to myself as an individual.

4. I reserve unto myself the power and right at any time during my lifetime to amend or revoke in whole or in part the Trust hereby created without the necessity of obtaining the consent of the beneficiaries and without giving notice to the beneficiaries. The withdrawal by me of the whole or any part of the bank account shall constitute as to such whole or part a revocation of this Trust.

5. The death during my lifetime, or in a common accident or disaster with me, of all of the beneficiaries designated hereunder shall revoke such designation, and in the former event, I reserve the right to designate new beneficiaries. Should I for any reason fail to designate such new beneficiaries, this Trust shall terminate upon my death and the trust property shall revert to my estate.

6. In the event of my death or legal incapacity, I hereby nominate and appoint as Successor Trustee hereunder the beneficiary first above named, unless such beneficiary be a minor or legally incompetent, in which event I hereby nominate and appoint as Successor Trustee hereunder the beneficiary whose name appears second above. If such beneficiary named second above shall be a minor or legally incompetent, then I nominate and appoint

(Name)_____, of

(Address)_____
             Number   Street   City   State
as Successor Trustee hereunder.

7. This Declaration of Trust shall extend to and be binding upon the heirs, executors, administrators and assigns of the undersigned and upon the Successors to the Trustee.

8. The Trustee and his successors shall serve without bond.

9. This Declaration of Trust shall be construed and enforced in accordance with the laws of the State of

_____.

IN WITNESS WHEREOF, I have hereunto set my hand and seal this_____day of_____, 19____.

(sign here)_____L.S.

Witness: (1)_____

Witness: (2)_____

STATE OF_____⎫
                                 ⎬ ss: _____
COUNTY OF_____⎭

On the_____day of_____, nineteen hundred and_____,

before me came_____,

known to me to be the individual described in, and who executed the foregoing instrument, and _____ acknowledged

that _____ executed the same, and in due form of law acknowledged the foregoing instrument to be _____ free act and deed and desired the same might be recorded as such.

(Notary Seal)   _____
                                       Notary Public

DECLARATION OF TRUST
FOR NAMING
**ONE PRIMARY BENEFICIARY WITH
YOUR CHILDREN, SHARING EQUALLY,
AS CONTINGENT BENEFICIARIES**
TO RECEIVE
A BANK ACCOUNT

Instructions:

On the following pages will be found duplicate copies of a declaration of trust (DT-8) which will be suitable for use where it is desired to name one person (ordinarily, one's spouse) as primary beneficiary, with one's children as contingent beneficiaries to receive the bank account if the primary beneficiary does not survive you.

Cross out *"city"* or *"town"*, leaving the appropriate designation of your community. Next, cross out *"checking"* or *"savings"* leaving the appropriate designation of the bank account, and initial it.

Enter the name of the primary beneficiary in the appropriate place in Paragraph 1. Note that the instrument first refers to your children as "natural not/or adopted". Now, decide: If you have an adopted child and you wish to *include* him, cross out the word *"not"* in the phrase *"natural not/or adopted"* and initial it. If you wish to *exclude* your adopted child, cross out the word *"or"* in the same phrase and initial it. Remember, you <u>must</u> cross out *"not"* or *"or"*—one or the other. If you have no adopted child, simply cross out *"not"*.

Note next that the instrument specifies that your children are to receive *"in equal shares, or the survivor of them/per stirpes."* Now, think carefully: If it is your wish that if one of your children does not survive you, his share will revert to *his* children in equal shares, cross out *"or the survivor of them"* and initial it. If that is *not* what you want—if, for example, you prefer that the share of any child of yours who predeceases you shall revert to your other surviving children in equal shares, cross out *"per stirpes"* and initial it. Remember, you <u>must</u> cross out *"or the survivor of them"* or *"per stirpes"*—one or the other.

Whenever there is any possibility of a minor child receiving any portion of the bank account, make certain that you name an adult who can act as trustee for him. The name of that adult should be inserted in Paragraph 6 of the instrument shown here. Avoid naming as trustee a person not likely to survive until the child has reached age 21.

When completed in the manner shown on the reverse side hereof, one copy of the declaration of trust should be filed with the bank. The duplicate may be retained for reference.

Declaration of Trust

WHEREAS, I _____ John J. Smith _____, State of _____ Connecticut _____ of the

City/Town of _____ Jonesville _____, County of _____ Fairfax _____

am the owner of a checking/savings account in the _____ Jonesville National Bank _____,
(Name of Bank)

located in the City/Town of _____ Jonesville _____, State of _____ Connecticut _____,

NOW, THEREFORE, KNOW ALL MEN BY THESE PRESENTS, that I do hereby acknowledge and declare
that I hold and will hold said bank account and all right, title and interest in and to said account IN TRUST

1. For the use and benefit of:

_____ Elizabeth M. Smith _____ (my wife) _____
(Name)

_____ 525 _____ Main Street _____ Jonesville _____ Connecticut _____ State _____
(Address) Number   Street   City

(hereinafter referred to as the "First Beneficiary") and upon his or her death prior to the termination of the trust,
for the use and benefit of my children, natural not/or adopted, in equal shares, or the survivor of them, per stirpes.
Upon my death, unless the beneficiaries shall predecease me or unless we all shall die as a result of a common accident
or disaster, my Successor Trustee is hereby directed forthwith to transfer said bank account and all right, title and
interest in and to said bank account unto the beneficiary or beneficiaries absolutely and thereby terminate this trust;
provided, however, that if any beneficiary hereunder shall then be a minor, the Successor Trustee shall hold the trust
assets in continuing trust until such beneficiary attains the age of twenty-one years. During such period of continuing
trust the Successor Trustee, in his absolute discretion, may retain the specific bank account herein described if he
believes it in the best interest of the beneficiary so to do, or he may terminate it, investing and reinvesting the proceeds
as he may deem appropriate. The Successor Trustee may apply or expend any or all of the income or principal directly
for the maintenance, education and support of the minor beneficiary without the intervention of any guardian and
without application to any court. Such payments of income or principal may be made to the parents of such minor
or to the person with whom the minor is living without any liability upon the Successor Trustee to see to the application
thereof. If any such minor survives me but dies before attaining the age of twenty-one years, at his or her death the
Successor Trustee shall deliver, pay over, transfer and distribute the trust property being held for such minor to said
minor's personal representatives, absolutely.

2. This Trust is created with the express understanding that the bank at which the account is maintained shall
be under no liability whatsoever to see to the proper administration of the trust. On the contrary, upon the transfer
of the right, title and interest in and to such account by any trustee hereunder, said bank shall conclusively treat the
transferee as the sole owner of said account. As and if I shall elect from time to time to cause interest payments on
said account to be distributed rather than compounded, the bank shall be fully authorized to pay such interest direct
to me individually unless there shall have been filed with it written notice of my death or incapacity satisfactory to it.
Until the bank shall receive from some person interested in this Trust, written notice of any death or other event
upon which the right to receive may depend, the bank shall incur no liability for payments made in good faith to
persons whose interests shall have been affected by such event. The bank shall be protected in acting upon any
notice or other instrument or document believed by it to be genuine and to have been signed or presented by the
proper party or parties.

3. I reserve unto myself the power and right to collect any interest or other income which may accrue from
the trust property and, in my sole discretion as Trustee, either to accumulate such interest or income as an addition
to the trust assets being held hereunder or pay such income to myself as an individual.

4. I reserve unto myself the power and right at any time during my lifetime to amend or revoke in whole or in
part the Trust hereby created without the necessity of obtaining the consent of the beneficiaries and without giving
notice to the beneficiaries. The withdrawal by me of the whole or any part of the bank account held hereunder shall
constitute as to such whole or part a revocation of this Trust.

5. ... time, ... revoke such designa... in the for... event, I reser... ...to designate a new
beneficiary or beneficiaries. Should I for any reason fail to designate such new beneficiary, this Trust shall terminate
upon my death and the trust property shall revert to my estate.

6. In the event of my death or legal incapacity, I hereby nominate and appoint as Successor Trustee hereunder
the First Beneficiary, and upon his or her failure or ceasing to act, I nominate and appoint

_____ Henry P. Adams _____ Jonesville _____ Connecticut _____ of
(Name)   City   State

_____ 125 _____ Barnum Street _____
(Address) Number   Street

as Successor Trustee, and upon his or her failure or ceasing to act or should I for any reason fail to designate the
person above intended to be nominated, then I nominate and appoint as such Successor Trustee hereunder whosoever
shall qualify as executor, administrator or guardian, as the case may be, of my estate.

7. This Declaration of Trust shall extend to and be binding upon the heirs, executors, administrators and assigns
of the undersigned and upon the Successors to the Trustee.

8. The Trustee and his successors shall serve without bond.

9. This Declaration of Trust shall be construed and enforced in accordance with the laws of the State of
Connecticut

WHEREAS, I _____ of the

City/Town of_____, County of_____, State of_____,

am the owner of a checking/savings account in the_____
(Name of Bank)

located in the City/Town of_____, State of_____,

NOW, THEREFORE, KNOW ALL MEN BY THESE PRESENTS, that I do hereby acknowledge and declare that I hold and will hold said bank account and all right, title and interest in and to said account IN TRUST

1. For the use and benefit of:

(Name)_____ _____, of

(Address)_____

| Number | Street | City | State |

(hereinafter referred to as the "First Beneficiary"), and upon his or her death prior to the termination of the trust, for the use and benefit of my children, natural not/or adopted, in equal shares, or the survivor of them/per stirpes. Upon my death, unless the beneficiaries shall predecease me or unless we all shall die as a result of a common accident or disaster, my Successor Trustee is hereby directed forthwith to transfer said bank account and all right, title and interest in and to said bank account unto the beneficiary or beneficiaries absolutely and thereby terminate this trust; *provided,* however, that if any beneficiary hereunder shall then be a minor, the Successor Trustee shall hold the trust assets in continuing trust until such beneficiary attains the age of twenty-one years. During such period of continuing trust the Successor Trustee, in his absolute discretion, may retain the specific bank account herein described if he believes it in the best interest of the beneficiary so to do, or he may terminate it, investing and reinvesting the proceeds as he may deem appropriate. Prior to the date upon which such minor beneficiary attains the age of twenty-one years, the Successor Trustee may apply or expend any or all of the income or principal directly for the maintenance, education and support of the minor beneficiary without the intervention of any guardian and without application to any court. Such payments of income or principal may be made to the parents of such minor or to the person with whom the minor is living without any liability upon the Successor Trustee to see to the application thereof. If any such minor survives me but dies before attaining the age of twenty-one years, at his or her death the Successor Trustee shall deliver, pay over, transfer and distribute the trust property being held for such minor to said minor's personal representatives, absolutely.

2. This Trust is created with the express understanding that the bank at which the account is maintained shall be under no liability whatsoever to see to the proper administration of the trust. On the contrary, upon the transfer of the right, title and interest in and to such account by any trustee hereunder, said bank shall conclusively treat the transferee as the sole owner of said account. As and if I shall elect from time to time to cause interest payments on said account to be distributed rather than compounded, the bank shall be fully authorized to pay such interest direct to me individually unless there shall have been filed with it written notice of my death or incapacity satisfactory to it. Until the bank shall receive from some person interested in this Trust, written notice of any death or other event upon which the right to receive may depend, the bank shall incur no liability for payments made in good faith to persons whose interests shall have been affected by such event. The bank shall be protected in acting upon any notice or other instrument or document believed by it to be genuine and to have been signed or presented by the proper party or parties.

3. I reserve unto myself the power and right to collect any interest or other income which may accrue from the trust property and, in my sole discretion as Trustee, either to accumulate such interest or income as an addition to the trust assets being held hereunder or pay such income to myself as an individual.

4. I reserve unto myself the power and right at any time during my lifetime to amend or revoke in whole or in part the Trust hereby created without the necessity of obtaining the consent of the beneficiaries and without giving notice to the beneficiaries. The withdrawal by me of the whole or any part of the bank account held hereunder shall constitute as to such whole or part a revocation of this Trust.

5. The death during my lifetime, or in a common accident or disaster with me, of all of the beneficiaries designated hereunder shall revoke such designation, and in the former event, I reserve the right to designate a new beneficiary or beneficiaries. Should I for any reason fail to designate such new beneficiary, this Trust shall terminate upon my death and the trust property shall revert to my estate.

6. In the event of my death or legal incapacity, I hereby nominate and appoint as Successor Trustee hereunder the First Beneficiary, and upon his or her failure or ceasing to act, I nominate and appoint

(Name)_____, of

(Address)_____
          Number   Street   City   State

as Successor Trustee, and upon his or her failure or ceasing to act or should I for any reason fail to designate the person above intended to be nominated, then I nominate and appoint as such Successor Trustee hereunder whosoever shall qualify as executor, administrator or guardian, as the case may be, of my estate.

7. This Declaration of Trust shall extend to and be binding upon the heirs, executors, administrators and assigns of the undersigned and upon the Successors to the Trustee.

8. The Trustee and his successors shall serve without bond.

9. This Declaration of Trust shall be construed and enforced in accordance with the laws of the State of

_____.

IN WITNESS WHEREOF, I have hereunto set my hand and seal this_____day

of_____, 19_____.

(sign here)_____L.S.

Witness: (1)_____

Witness: (2)_____

STATE OF_____

COUNTY OF_____ } ss: _____

On the_____day of_____, nineteen hundred and_____,

before me came_____,
known to me to be the individual described in, and who executed the foregoing instrument, and _____ acknowledged that _____ executed the same, and in due form of law acknowledged the foregoing instrument to be _____ free act and deed and desired the same might be recorded as such.

(Notary Seal)   _____

                                   (Notary Public)

Declaration of Trust

WHEREAS, I_____of the

City/Town of_____, County of_____, State of_____,

am the owner of a checking/savings account in the_____
                                                        (Name of Bank)

located in the City/Town of_____, State of_____,

NOW, THEREFORE, KNOW ALL MEN BY THESE PRESENTS, that I do hereby acknowledge and declare that I hold and will hold said bank account and all right, title and interest in and to said account IN TRUST

1. For the use and benefit of:

(Name)_____, of

(Address)_____
       Number   Street   City   State

(hereinafter referred to as the "First Beneficiary"), and upon his or her death prior to the termination of the trust, for the use and benefit of my children, natural not/or adopted, in equal shares, or the survivor of them/per stirpes. Upon my death, unless the beneficiaries shall predecease me or unless we all shall die as a result of a common accident or disaster, my Successor Trustee is hereby directed forthwith to transfer said bank account and all right, title and interest in and to said bank account unto the beneficiary or beneficiaries absolutely and thereby terminate this trust; *provided,* however, that if any beneficiary hereunder shall then be a minor, the Successor Trustee shall hold the trust assets in continuing trust until such beneficiary attains the age of twenty-one years. During such period of continuing trust the Successor Trustee, in his absolute discretion, may retain the specific bank account herein described if he believes it in the best interest of the beneficiary so to do, or he may terminate it, investing and reinvesting the proceeds as he may deem appropriate. Prior to the date upon which such minor beneficiary attains the age of twenty-one years, the Successor Trustee may apply or expend any or all of the income or principal directly for the maintenance, education and support of the minor beneficiary without the intervention of any guardian and without application to any court. Such payments of income or principal may be made to the parents of such minor or to the person with whom the minor is living without any liability upon the Successor Trustee to see to the application thereof. If any such minor survives me but dies before attaining the age of twenty-one years, at his or her death the Successor Trustee shall deliver, pay over, transfer and distribute the trust property being held for such minor to said minor's personal representatives, absolutely.

2. This Trust is created with the express understanding that the bank at which the account is maintained shall be under no liability whatsoever to see to the proper administration of the trust. On the contrary, upon the transfer of the right, title and interest in and to such account by any trustee hereunder, said bank shall conclusively treat the transferee as the sole owner of said account. As and if I shall elect from time to time to cause interest payments on said account to be distributed rather than compounded, the bank shall be fully authorized to pay such interest direct to me individually unless there shall have been filed with it written notice of my death or incapacity satisfactory to it. Until the bank shall receive from some person interested in this Trust, written notice of any death or other event upon which the right to receive may depend, the bank shall incur no liability for payments made in good faith to persons whose interests shall have been affected by such event. The bank shall be protected in acting upon any notice or other instrument or document believed by it to be genuine and to have been signed or presented by the proper party or parties.

3. I reserve unto myself the power and right to collect any interest or other income which may accrue from the trust property and, in my sole discretion as Trustee, either to accumulate such interest or income as an addition to the trust assets being held hereunder or pay such income to myself as an individual.

4. I reserve unto myself the power and right at any time during my lifetime to amend or revoke in whole or in part the Trust hereby created without the necessity of obtaining the consent of the beneficiaries and without giving notice to the beneficiaries. The withdrawal by me of the whole or any part of the bank account held hereunder shall constitute as to such whole or part a revocation of this Trust.

5. The death during my lifetime, or in a common accident or disaster with me, of all of the beneficiaries designated hereunder shall revoke such designation, and in the former event, I reserve the right to designate a new beneficiary or beneficiaries. Should I for any reason fail to designate such new beneficiary, this Trust shall terminate upon my death and the trust property shall revert to my estate.

6. In the event of my death or legal incapacity, I hereby nominate and appoint as Successor Trustee hereunder the First Beneficiary, and upon his or her failure or ceasing to act, I nominate and appoint

(Name)_____, of

(Address)_____
        Number   Street   City   State

as Successor Trustee, and upon his or her failure or ceasing to act or should I for any reason fail to designate the person above intended to be nominated, then I nominate and appoint as such Successor Trustee hereunder whosoever shall qualify as executor, administrator or guardian, as the case may be, of my estate.

7. This Declaration of Trust shall extend to and be binding upon the heirs, executors, administrators and assigns of the undersigned and upon the Successors to the Trustee.

8. The Trustee and his successors shall serve without bond.

9. This Declaration of Trust shall be construed and enforced in accordance with the laws of the State of

_____.

IN WITNESS WHEREOF, I have hereunto set my hand and seal this_____day

of_____, 19_____.

(sign here)_____L.S.

Witness: (1)_____

Witness: (2)_____

STATE OF_____ ⎫
                                   ⎬ ss: _____

COUNTY OF_____ ⎭

On the_____day of_____, nineteen hundred and_____,

before me came_____,
known to me to be the individual described in, and who executed the foregoing instrument, and _____ acknowledged that _____ executed the same, and in due form of law acknowledged the foregoing instrument to be _____ free act and deed and desired the same might be recorded as such.

(Notary Seal)

_____
(Notary Public)

Chapter 7

AVOIDING PROBATE OF MUTUAL FUND SHARES

Millions of Americans now own mutual fund shares —reflecting, no doubt, a growing realization that as more and more of the wealth of the country has gravitated toward the funds, more and more of the top investment brains have gravitated in the same direction. Certainly the advantages of wide diversification, professional selection and continuous supervision which the funds offer have increasing appeal.

Mutual fund shares are generally purchased in one of two ways—"outright" or under a "contractual plan". When you buy them "outright", you simply purchase, say, one hundred shares of XYZ Fund from a mutual fund dealer. You may also set up something called a "voluntary plan" under which you make a modest initial investment of from $50 to $500 and indicate an intention of adding small amounts (generally $50 or more) on a regular periodic basis. Shares so purchased are generally registered in the usual way typical of any security—and they're subject to probate when you die, just like any other security.

A "contractual plan" is a special way of buying mutual fund shares. Many persons harbor a mistaken belief that it is necessarily a monthly investment plan. It is not. A contractual plan may provide for a single lump sum or for payments on a regular monthly basis over a ten, fifteen or twenty-five-year period. Of the more than three hundred mutual funds, about fifty are available under contractual plans. In my opinion, your selection of a particular mutual fund should be influenced to some extent by its availability for purchase under a contractual plan.

Contractual plans offer many important advantages over outright purchase of shares. In the first place, for many years a special partial tax exemption has applied to the income from such plans. With newly-organized plans, that exemption may be as much as 90% or more of the distributions. On older plans, it gets down to 5-10%. If you own the same mutual fund shares outright, you'll get the same income—but it will be completely taxable. Next, contractual plans provide for automatic reinvestment of all dividends and distributions. On shares purchased "outright" many funds require a minimum holding of $1,500 before they will reinvest dividends automatically—and then they purchase the new shares at the "asked price", which includes a sales charge. Under contractual plans, some of which may be started with an initial monthly payment of as little as $20, all dividends are immediately automatically reinvested, the Investment Company Act of 1940 specifying that such reinvestment shall be at the "net asset value" which includes no sales charge. There can be a substantial saving, then, in the compounding of the earnings over the years.

Moreover, contractual plans also permit partial withdrawals of up to 90% of the value of the account, with subsequent redeposit of sums so withdrawn. No sales charge is involved either way, the investor paying simply a small custodian bank service fee of approximately $2.50.

This partial withdrawal privilege makes possible an interesting tax advantage: an investor who has deposited a lump sum of $10,000 in such a plan, paying an 8½% ($850) sales charge, cannot deduct that sales charge for tax purposes this year. If and when he sells the shares, he can take the $850 into account in computing his long term gain or loss. If he dies still owning the shares, he will have obtained no tax benefit from the fee he paid. If, however, he establishes the $10,000 lump sum contractual plan and immediately makes a partial withdrawal of the permitted 90% of its value, he thereby establishes a short-term capital loss of 90% of his acquisition fee which he can charge off against capital gains this year or against ordinary income if he has no realized capital gains. At the end of thirty days, he re-deposits the sum withdrawn from his contractual plan account and ends up with his investment substantially as it was before except that he has qualified for a very nice tax credit.

While all of these benefits are important, from an estate planning standpoint the most important "extra" that contractual plans offer is probate exemption. Most

73

contractuals invite the investor to execute a simple form of declaration of trust by which an inter vivos trust is created, placing the investment plan outside the jurisdiction of the probate court.

It is extremely important that purchasers of contractual plans be aware that *some* such plans do *not* provide probate exemption. While they do permit the investor to name a beneficiary to whom the account will be delivered at his death, the instrument used is a "designation of beneficiary". No trust relationship is created and the shares are therefore not outside the jurisdiction of the probate court.

On the following pages will be found forms of declaration of trust which may be used to register mutual fund shares in such manner as to avoid probate. These have been submitted to all of the major funds and their custodian banks and have been found acceptable for use in registering shares purchased outright or under voluntary plans. Most of the funds which use the "designation of beneficiary" on their contractual plan will permit the investor to substitute one of these forms in order to obtain the benefits of probate exemption.

In the case of mutual fund shares purchased outright, execute an appropriate form from among those shown on the pages which follow and instruct your investment dealer that the shares are to be registered *"John Smith, Trustee u/d/t dated_____"*. The "u/d/t" is simply an abbreviation for "under declaration of trust". Some fund custodians will re-write your instructions and issue the shares under a registration reading, *"John Smith, Trustee u/a dated_____"*. The *"u/a"* means "under agreement". An agreement involves two or more persons. There isn't any "agreement" here; the instrument is a declaration of trust. If they don't issue the shares correctly, send them back and insist that they do the job over again.

If you are buying, or now own, a contractual plan which uses the "designation of beneficiary" form, substitute for it one of the suggested forms of declaration of trust. Most contractual plan sponsors, even though you execute a declaration of trust, will open your account simply in your name, *"John Smith"*, and not as *"John Smith, Trustee u/d/t dated_____"*. This gives rise to a peculiar inconsistency—if you buy shares of the XYZ Fund outright and execute a declaration of trust, the fund will insist upon adding *"Trustee u/d/t"* after your name. Some of them even want to include the name of the beneficiary you have designated (*"John Smith, Trustee for Mary Smith u/d/t dated_____"*). But if you buy a contractual plan in the very same fund, they supply you with a declaration of trust—and then issue the plan simply to *"John Smith"*.

While we're discussing these technicalities, it is well to note that *insured* contractual plans sometimes present a special problem. Some funds which sell contractuals which use the "designation of beneficiary" form but which allow investors to substitute one of these suggested forms of declaration of trust, will not allow such substitution in the case of an insured plan. For those who may not be familiar with such plans, they contain a provision for the immediate automatic completion of payments in the event of the death of the investor. The sponsor obtains low-cost reducing term insurance coverage, the planholder's life being insured each month for just enough to complete the account. If you set out to invest $18,000 at the rate of $100 each month for fifteen years, and you die after making the first $100 investment, the $17,900 you didn't have time to invest will be deposited in your account immediately in one lump sum. Your beneficiary becomes the owner of the completed account and can withdraw it at will.

One or two funds contend that their company policy or the terms of their insurance coverage preclude insuring a trustee, and they will not issue an insured account if a declaration of trust is to be filed. Since there is a wide variety of excellent funds and plans available, it is suggested that you select one which will accommodate itself agreeably to your estate planning desires.

```
┌─────────────────────────────────────┐
│        DECLARATION OF TRUST         │
│             FOR NAMING              │
│          ONE BENEFICIARY            │
│             TO RECEIVE              │
│        MUTUAL FUND SHARES           │
└─────────────────────────────────────┘
```

Instructions:

On the following pages will be found duplicate copies of a declaration of trust (DT-9) which will be suitable for use in connection with the inter vivos trust arrangement suggested in Chapter 7 where it is desired simply to name some *one* person to receive mutual fund shares upon the death of the owner.

Cross out *"city"* or *"town"*, leaving the appropriate designation of your community.

Enter the name of the beneficiary in the appropriate place in Paragraph 1.

For shares purchased outright:

If you are buying shares outright, enter the name of the fund in the appropriate place in the instrument. Instruct your mutual fund dealer that the shares are to be registered *(Your name), Trustee u/d/t dated _____"*. Some funds will wish to examine the declaration of trust at the time the shares are issued, so execute both original and duplicate and offer one to the dealer to send along with the registration instructions. In any case, if you ever decide to sell the shares, or if you die and the beneficiary requests their transfer, the fund will ask to see the declaration of trust. It is suggested, therefore, that when the share certificate is issued, the signed declaration of trust be permanently stapled to it. If you make subsequent additional purchases of the same fund, it is not necessary to execute a new declaration of trust each time—simply register the shares exactly as you did your first purchase. If you wish to name a different beneficiary on such subsequent purchases, then you *will* need to execute a new declaration of trust. To avoid confusion, never date two instruments the same date.

If you have a "voluntary plan" or "open account", the fund will hold the shares and no certificate will be issued. It is important, then, that you place the original declaration of trust where you can find it readily if you decide to sell your shares or where the beneficiary can find it if you die.

For contractual plans:

If you are buying a contractual plan which does not provide a declaration of trust to designate the beneficiary, in the place in the instrument provided for the name of the fund, enter *"(Name of fund) held in (Name of fund) Investment Plan No. _____"*. Instruct your mutual fund dealer to send the completed instrument along with the plan application. The plan's custodian bank will fill in the number assigned to your account. With a contractual plan, the beneficiary designation—and therefore the probate exemption—is *not effective* unless and until the instrument is permanently filed with the plan's custodian bank. It isn't absolutely necessary that the instrument be filed at the time the plan is applied for; you can send it in later. If you choose this latter course, be sure to ask for acknowledgment of its receipt. Many banks charge a "late filing fee" of $2.50 if the declaration of trust does not accompany the application.

When your plan certificate is issued, staple the executed duplicate declaration of trust into it for your permanent record and for the information of the beneficiary.

* * *

Whenever there is any possibility of a minor child receiving the property, make certain that you name an adult who can act as trustee for the child. The name of that adult should be inserted in Paragraph 7 of the instrument shown here. Avoid naming as trustee a person not likely to survive until the child has reached age 21.

Declaration of Trust

of the

WHEREAS, I, __John J. Smith__ , County of __Fairfax__ , State of __Connecticut__ ,

~~City~~/Town of __Jonesville__

am the owner of certain shares of the capital stock of:

__Ajax Mutual Fund__
(Name of Fund)

NOW, THEREFORE, KNOW ALL MEN BY THESE PRESENTS, that I do hereby acknowledge and declare that I hold and will hold said Shares and all right, title and interest in and to said Shares IN TRUST, for the following uses and purposes:

1. To add, or cause to be added, to the corpus of this Trust all income and distributions which may from time to time be received on the said Shares, by causing the same to be invested in additional shares, or if I shall so elect from time to time to pay said income and distributions or cause the same to be paid to myself during my lifetime.

2. To hold said Shares and all right, title and interest therein for the use and benefit of:

__Mary A. Smith   (my niece)__ , of
(Name)

__750__   __Porter Street__   __Jonesville__   __Connecticut__
(Address) Number   Street   City   State

Upon my death, unless the beneficiary shall predecease me or unless we both shall die as a result of a common accident or disaster, my Successor Trustee is hereby directed forthwith to transfer said Shares and all right, title and interest in and to said Shares unto the beneficiary absolutely and thereby terminate this trust; _provided_, however, that if the beneficiary hereunder shall then be a minor, the Successor Trustee shall hold the trust assets in continuing trust until such beneficiary attains the age of twenty-one years. Prior to that date, the Successor Trustee may apply or expend any or all of the income or principal for the maintenance, education and support of the minor beneficiary without the intervention of any guardian and without application to any court. Such payments of income or principal may be made to the parents of such minor or to the person with whom the minor is living without any liability upon the Successor Trustee to see to the application thereof. If such minor survives me but dies before attaining the age of twenty-one years, at his or her death the Successor Trustee shall deliver, pay over, transfer and distribute the trust property to such minor's personal representatives, absolutely.

3. I reserve the right to register any shares held hereunder in the name of a nominee, which nominee may be myself as an individual. The right, power and authority is hereby conferred upon any Successor Trustee hereunder, at any time during the minority of the beneficiary, to invest and reinvest without limitation or restriction, to sell all or any part of the Shares being held, holding either Shares or the proceeds of the sale thereof until the minor beneficiary attains the age of twenty-one years.

4. This Trust is created upon the express understanding that the issuer or custodian of the Shares hereunder shall be under no liability whatsoever to see to its proper administration, and that upon the transfer of the right, title and interest in and to said Shares by any Trustee hereunder, said issuer or custodian shall conclusively treat the transferee as the sole owner of said Shares. In the event that any shares, cash or other property shall be distributable at any time under the terms of said Shares, the said issuer or custodian is fully authorized to pay, deliver and distribute the same to whosoever shall then be trustee hereunder, and shall be under no liability to see to the proper application thereof, provided, however, that as and if I shall elect from time to time to cause dividends and distributions on said Shares to be distributed, rather than reinvested, the issuer or custodian shall be fully authorized to pay such payments and distributions direct to me individually rather than to me as Trustee hereunder and may continue such payments to it. The issuer or custodian is authorized to make such distributions under a mutual fund systematic withdrawal plan as have been specified by me or by any Successor Trustee acting hereunder. Until the issuer or custodian shall receive from some person interested in this Trust, written notice of any death or other event upon which the right to receive may depend, the issuer or custodian shall incur no liability for payments made in good faith to persons whose interests shall have been affected by such event. The issuer or custodian shall be protected in acting upon any notice or other instrument or document believed by it to be genuine and to have been signed or presented by the proper party or parties.

[...] unto myself [...] upon the revoc[...] [...]mination of this [...] [...]rust for [...] benefit or any person whatsoever.

7. In the case of my death or legal incapacity, I hereby nominate and appoint as Successor Trustee hereunder the Beneficiary unless he or she shall be a minor or otherwise legally incapacitated, in either of which events, I hereby nominate and appoint __Henry P. Adams__ , of

__125__   __Barnum Street__   __Jonesville__   __Connecticut__
(Name)
(Address) Number   Street   City   State

and upon his or her failure to act (or should I for any reason fail to designate the person intended to be nominated), then and in either event I nominate and appoint as such Successor Trustee whosoever shall qualify as Executor or Administrator of my estate, as the case may be.

8. This Declaration of Trust shall extend to and be binding upon the heirs, executors, administrators and assigns of the undersigned and upon the successors to the Trustee.

9. This Declaration of Trust shall be construed and enforced in accordance with the laws of the State of __Connecticut__

WHEREAS, I,_____of the

City/Town of_____, County of_____, State of_____,

am the owner of certain shares of the capital stock of:

_____
(Name of Fund)

NOW, THEREFORE, KNOW ALL MEN BY THESE PRESENTS, that I do hereby acknowledge and declare that I hold and will hold said Shares and all right, title and interest in and to said Shares IN TRUST, for the following uses and purposes:

1. To add, or cause to be added, to the corpus of this Trust all income and distributions which may from time to time be received on the said Shares, by causing the same to be invested in additional shares, or if I shall so elect from time to time to pay said income and distributions or cause the same to be paid to myself during my lifetime.

2. To hold said Shares and all right, title and interest therein for the use and benefit of:

(Name)_____, of

(Address)_____.
     Number   Street   City   State

Upon my death, unless the beneficiary shall predecease me or unless we both shall die as a result of a common accident or disaster, my Successor Trustee is hereby directed forthwith to transfer said Shares and all right, title and interest in and to said Shares unto the beneficiary absolutely and thereby terminate this trust; *provided,* however, that if the beneficiary hereunder shall then be a minor, the Successor Trustee shall hold the trust assets in continuing trust until such beneficiary attains the age of twenty-one years. Prior to that date, the Successor Trustee may apply or expend any or all of the income or principal for the maintenance, education and support of the minor beneficiary without the intervention of any guardian and without application to any court. Such payments of income or principal may be made to the parents of such minor or to the person with whom the minor is living without any liability upon the Successor Trustee to see to the application thereof. If such minor survives me but dies before attaining the age of twenty-one years, at his or her death the Successor Trustee shall deliver, pay over, transfer and distribute the trust property to such minor's personal representatives, absolutely.

3. I reserve the right to register any shares held hereunder in the name of a nominee, which nominee may be myself as an individual, or to pledge the shares as collateral for a loan. The right, power and authority is hereby conferred upon any Successor Trustee hereunder, at any time during the minority of the beneficiary, to invest and reinvest without limitation or restriction, to sell all or any part of the Shares being held, holding either Shares or the proceeds of the sale thereof until the minor beneficiary attains the age of twenty-one years.

4. This Trust is created upon the express understanding that the issuer or custodian of the Shares hereunder shall be under no liability whatsoever to see to its proper administration, and that upon the transfer of the right, title and interest in and to said Shares by any Trustee hereunder, said issuer or custodian shall conclusively treat the transferee as the sole owner of said Shares. In the event that any shares, cash or other property shall be distributable at any time under the terms of said Shares, the said issuer or custodian is fully authorized to pay, deliver and distribute the same to whosoever shall then be trustee hereunder, and shall be under no liability to see to the proper application thereof, provided, however, that as and if I shall elect from time to time to cause dividends and distributions on said Shares to be distributed, rather than reinvested, the issuer or custodian shall be fully authorized to pay such dividends and distributions direct to me individually rather than to me as Trustee hereunder and may continue such payments to me individually unless there shall have been filed with it written notice of my death or incapacity satisfactory to it. The issuer or custodian is authorized to make such distributions under a mutual fund systematic withdrawal plan as have been specified by me or by any Successor Trustee acting hereunder. Until the issuer or custodian shall receive from some person interested in this Trust, written notice of any death or other event upon which the right to receive may depend, the issuer or custodian shall incur no liability for payments made in good faith to persons whose interests shall have been affected by such event. The issuer or custodian shall be protected in acting upon any notice or other instrument or document believed by it to be genuine and to have been signed or presented by the proper party or parties.

5. The death during my lifetime, or in a common accident or disaster with me, of the beneficiary designated hereunder shall revoke such designation, and in the former event I reserve the right to designate a new beneficiary. Should I for any reason fail to designate such new beneficiary, this trust shall terminate upon my death and the trust property shall revert to my estate.

6. I hereby reserve unto myself the power and right at any time during my lifetime, before actual distribution to the beneficiary hereunder, to revoke in whole or in part or to amend the Trust hereby created without the necessity of obtaining the consent of the beneficiary and without giving notice to the beneficiary. Any one of the following acts shall be conclusive evidence of such revocation of this Trust:

    (a) The delivery to the issuer or custodian of the Shares by me of written notice that this Trust is revoked in whole or in part;

    (b) The transfer by me of my right, title and interest in and to said Shares;

    (c) The delivery by me to the issuer or custodian of the Shares of written notice of the death of the beneficiary hereunder.

I hereby reserve unto myself the right, upon the revocation or termination of this Trust, to create a new Trust for the benefit of any person whatsoever.

7. In the case of my death or legal incapacity, I hereby nominate and appoint as Successor Trustee hereunder the Beneficiary unless he or she shall be a minor or otherwise legally incapacitated, in either of which events, I hereby nominate and appoint

(Name)_____, of

(Address)_____
            Number   Street   City   State

and upon his or her failure to act (or should I for any reason fail to designate the person intended to be nominated), then and in either event I nominate and appoint as such Successor Trustee whosoever shall qualify as Executor or Administrator of my estate, as the case may be.

8. This Declaration of Trust shall extend to and be binding upon the heirs, executors, administrators and assigns of the undersigned and upon the successors to the Trustee.

9. This Declaration of Trust shall be construed and enforced in accordance with the laws of the State of

_____.

    IN WITNESS WHEREOF I have hereunto set my hand and seal this_____day

of_____, 19_____.

                                    (sign here)_____L.S.

Witness: (1)_____

Witness: (2)_____

STATE OF _____⎱
                                      ss: _____
COUNTY OF _____⎰

    On the_____day of_____, nineteen hundred and_____, before

me came_____known to me to be the individual described in, and who executed

the foregoing instrument, and _____ acknowledged that _____ executed the same; and in due form of law acknowledged the foregoing instrument to be _____ act and deed and desired the same might be recorded as such.

    WITNESS my hand and notarial seal the day and year aforesaid.

                                       _____

(Notary Seal)   Notary Public

Declaration of Trust

WHEREAS, I,_____of the

City/Town of_____, County of_____, State of_____,

am the owner of certain shares of the capital stock of:

_____
(Name of Fund)

NOW, THEREFORE, KNOW ALL MEN BY THESE PRESENTS, that I do hereby acknowledge and declare that I hold and will hold said Shares and all right, title and interest in and to said Shares IN TRUST, for the following uses and purposes:

1. To add, or cause to be added, to the corpus of this Trust all income and distributions which may from time to time be received on the said Shares, by causing the same to be invested in additional shares, or if I shall so elect from time to time to pay said income and distributions or cause the same to be paid to myself during my lifetime.

2. To hold said Shares and all right, title and interest therein for the use and benefit of:

(Name)_____, of

(Address)_____.
       Number   Street   City   State

Upon my death, unless the beneficiary shall predecease me or unless we both shall die as a result of a common accident or disaster, my Successor Trustee is hereby directed forthwith to transfer said Shares and all right, title and interest in and to said Shares unto the beneficiary absolutely and thereby terminate this trust; *provided,* however, that if the beneficiary hereunder shall then be a minor, the Successor Trustee shall hold the trust assets in continuing trust until such beneficiary attains the age of twenty-one years. Prior to that date, the Successor Trustee may apply or expend any or all of the income or principal for the maintenance, education and support of the minor beneficiary without the intervention of any guardian and without application to any court. Such payments of income or principal may be made to the parents of such minor or to the person with whom the minor is living without any liability upon the Successor Trustee to see to the application thereof. If such minor survives me but dies before attaining the age of twenty-one years, at his or her death the Successor Trustee shall deliver, pay over, transfer and distribute the trust property to such minor's personal representatives, absolutely.

3. I reserve the right to register any shares held hereunder in the name of a nominee, which nominee may be myself as an individual, or to pledge the shares as collateral for a loan. The right, power and authority is hereby conferred upon any Successor Trustee hereunder, at any time during the minority of the beneficiary, to invest and reinvest without limitation or restriction, to sell all or any part of the Shares being held, holding either Shares or the proceeds of the sale thereof until the minor beneficiary attains the age of twenty-one years.

4. This Trust is created upon the express understanding that the issuer or custodian of the Shares hereunder shall be under no liability whatsoever to see to its proper administration, and that upon the transfer of the right, title and interest in and to said Shares by any Trustee hereunder, said issuer or custodian shall conclusively treat the transferee as the sole owner of said Shares. In the event that any shares, cash or other property shall be distributable at any time under the terms of said Shares, the said issuer or custodian is fully authorized to pay, deliver and distribute the same to whosoever shall then be trustee hereunder, and shall be under no liability to see to the proper application thereof, provided, however, that as and if I shall elect from time to time to cause dividends and distributions on said Shares to be distributed, rather than reinvested, the issuer or custodian shall be fully authorized to pay such dividends and distributions direct to me individually rather than to me as Trustee hereunder and may continue such payments to me individually unless there shall have been filed with it written notice of my death or incapacity satisfactory to it. The issuer or custodian is authorized to make such distributions under a mutual fund systematic withdrawal plan as have been specified by me or by any Successor Trustee acting hereunder. Until the issuer or custodian shall receive from some person interested in this Trust, written notice of any death or other event upon which the right to receive may depend, the issuer or custodian shall incur no liability for payments made in good faith to persons whose interests shall have been affected by such event. The issuer or custodian shall be protected in acting upon any notice or other instrument or document believed by it to be genuine and to have been signed or presented by the proper party or parties.

5. The death during my lifetime, or in a common accident or disaster with me, of the beneficiary designated hereunder shall revoke such designation, and in the former event I reserve the right to designate a new beneficiary. Should I for any reason fail to designate such new beneficiary, this trust shall terminate upon my death and the trust property shall revert to my estate.

6. I hereby reserve unto myself the power and right at any time during my lifetime, before actual distribution to the beneficiary hereunder, to revoke in whole or in part or to amend the Trust hereby created without the necessity of obtaining the consent of the beneficiary and without giving notice to the beneficiary. Any one of the following acts shall be conclusive evidence of such revocation of this Trust:

   (a) The delivery to the issuer or custodian of the Shares by me of written notice that this Trust is revoked in whole or in part;
   (b) The transfer by me of my right, title and interest in and to said Shares;
   (c) The delivery by me to the issuer or custodian of the Shares of written notice of the death of the beneficiary hereunder.

I hereby reserve unto myself the right, upon the revocation or termination of this Trust, to create a new Trust for the benefit of any person whatsoever.

7. In the case of my death or legal incapacity, I hereby nominate and appoint as Successor Trustee hereunder the Beneficiary unless he or she shall be a minor or otherwise legally incapacitated, in either of which events, I hereby nominate and appoint

(Name)_____, of

(Address)_____

        Number   Street   City   State

and upon his or her failure to act (or should I for any reason fail to designate the person intended to be nominated), then and in either event I nominate and appoint as such Successor Trustee whosoever shall qualify as Executor or Administrator of my estate, as the case may be.

8. This Declaration of Trust shall extend to and be binding upon the heirs, executors, administrators and assigns of the undersigned and upon the successors to the Trustee.

9. This Declaration of Trust shall be construed and enforced in accordance with the laws of the State of

_____.

    IN WITNESS WHEREOF I have hereunto set my hand and seal this_____day

of_____, 19_____.

                              (sign here)_____L.S.

Witness: (1)_____

Witness: (2)_____

STATE OF _____
                         } ss: _____
COUNTY OF _____

    On the_____day of_____, nineteen hundred and_____, before

me came_____known to me to be the individual described in, and who executed

the foregoing instrument, and _____ acknowledged that _____ executed the same; and in due form of law acknowledged the foregoing instrument to be _____ act and deed and desired the same might be recorded as such.

    WITNESS my hand and notarial seal the day and year aforesaid.

_____

(Notary Seal)   Notary Public

```
┌─────────────────────────────────────────┐
│          DECLARATION OF TRUST            │
│                FOR NAMING                │
│        ONE PRIMARY BENEFICIARY           │
│                   AND                    │
│      ONE CONTINGENT BENEFICIARY          │
│                TO RECEIVE                │
│          MUTUAL FUND SHARES              │
└─────────────────────────────────────────┘
```

Instructions:

On the following pages will be found duplicate copies of a declaration of trust (DT-10) which will be suitable for use in connection with the inter vivos trust arrangement suggested in Chapter 7 where it is desired to name some *one* person as primary beneficiary with some *one* other person as contingent beneficiary to receive mutual fund shares if the primary beneficiary does not survive.

Cross out "city" or "town", leaving the appropriate designation of your community.

Enter the names of the beneficiaries in the appropriate places in Paragraph 2.

For shares purchased outright:

If you are buying shares outright, enter the name of the fund in the appropriate place in the instrument. Instruct your mutual fund dealer that the shares are to be registered *"(Your Name) Trustee u/d/t dated _____"*. Some funds will wish to examine the declaration of trust at the time the shares are issued, so execute both original and duplicate and offer one to the dealer to send along with the registration instructions. In any case, if you ever decide to sell the shares, or if you die and the beneficiary requests their transfer, the fund will ask to see the declaration of trust. It is suggested, therefore, that when the share certificate is issued, the signed declaration of trust be permanently stapled to it. If you make subsequent additional purchases of the same fund, it is not necessary to execute a new declaration of trust each time—simply register the shares exactly as you did your first purchase. If you wish to name a different beneficiary on such subsequent purchases, then you *will* need to execute a new declaration of trust. To avoid confusion, never date two instruments the same date.

If you have a "voluntary plan" or "open account", the fund will hold the shares and no certificate will be issued. It is important, then, that you place the original declaration of trust where you can find it readily if you decide to sell your shares or where the beneficiary can find it if you die.

For contractual plans:

If you are buying a contractual plan which does not provide a declaration of trust to designate the beneficiary, in the place in the instrument provided for the name of fund, enter *"(Name of fund) held in (Name of Fund) Investment Plan No._____"*. Instruct your mutual fund dealer to send the completed instrument along with the plan application. The plan's custodian bank will fill in the number assigned to your account. With a contractual plan, the beneficiary designation—and therefore the probate exemption—is *not effective* unless and until it is permanently filed with the plan's custodian bank. It isn't absolutely necessary that the instrument be filed at the time the plan is applied for; you can send it in later. If you choose this latter course, be sure to ask for acknowledgment of its receipt. Many banks charge a "late filing fee" of $2.50 if the declaration of trust does not accompany the application.

When your plan certificate is issued, staple the executed duplicate declaration of trust into it for your permanent record and for the information of the beneficiary.

Whenever there is any possibility of a minor child receiving the property, make certain that you name an adult who can act as trustee for the child. The name of that adult should be inserted in Paragraph 7 of the instrument shown here. Avoid naming as trustee a person not likely to survive until the child has reached age 21.

Declaration of Trust

_____ of the _____

WHEREAS, I, _____ **John J. Smith** _____, County of _____ **Fairfax** _____, State of _____ **Connecticut** _____,

~~City~~/Town of _____ **Jonesville** _____

am the owner of certain shares of the capital stock of:

Ajax Mutual Fund

held in Ajax Mutual Fund Investment Plan No. _____

(Name of Fund)

NOW, THEREFORE, KNOW ALL MEN BY THESE PRESENTS, that I do hereby acknowledge and declare that I hold and will hold said Shares and all right, title and interest in and to said Shares IN TRUST, for the following uses and purposes:

1. To add, or cause to be added, to the corpus of this Trust all income and distributions which may from time to time be received on the said Shares, by causing the same to be invested in additional shares, or if I shall so elect from time to time to pay said income and distributions or cause the same to be paid to myself during my lifetime.

2. To hold said Shares and all right, title and interest therein for the use and benefit of: _____, of

(Name) _____ **Mary A. Smith** (my niece) _____

(Address) _____ **750** _____ **Porter Street** _____ **Jonesville** _____ **Connecticut** _____

Number _____ Street _____ City _____ State

or, if such beneficiary be not surviving, for the use and benefit of

(Name) _____ **William B. Connors** (my nephew) _____ **Jonesville** _____ **Connecticut** _____

(Address) _____ **250** _____ **County Street** _____ City _____ State

Number _____ Street

Upon my death, unless the beneficiaries shall predecease me or unless we shall die as a result of a common accident or disaster, my Successor Trustee is hereby directed forthwith to transfer said Shares and all right, title and interest in and to said Shares unto the beneficiary absolutely and thereby terminate this Trust; provided, however, that if the beneficiary hereunder shall then be a minor, the Successor Trustee shall hold the trust assets in continuing trust until such beneficiary attains the age of twenty-one years. Prior to that date, the Successor Trustee may apply or expend any or all of the income or principal for the maintenance, education and support of the minor beneficiary without the intervention of any guardian and without application to any court. Such payments of income or principal may be made to the parents of such minor or to the person with whom the minor is living without any liability upon the Successor Trustee to see to the application thereof. If such minor survives me but dies before attaining the age of twenty-one years, at his or her death the Successor Trustee shall deliver, pay over, transfer and distribute the trust property to such minor's personal representatives, absolutely.

3. I reserve the right to register any shares held hereunder in the name of a nominee, which nominee may be myself as an individual. The right, power and authority is hereby conferred upon any Successor Trustee hereunder, at any time during the minority of the beneficiary, to invest and reinvest without limitation or restriction, to sell all or any part of the Shares being held, holding either Shares or the proceeds of the sale thereof until the minor beneficiary attains the age of twenty-one years.

4. This Trust is created upon the express understanding that the issuer or custodian of the Shares hereunder shall be under no liability whatsoever to see to its proper administration, and that upon the transfer of the right, title and interest in and to said Shares by any Trustee hereunder, said issuer or custodian shall conclusively treat the transferee as the sole owner of said Shares. In the event that any shares, cash or other property shall be distributable at any time under the terms of said hereunder, and shall be under no liability to see to the proper application thereof, provided, rather than reinvested, the issuer or custodian shall be fully authorized to pay such dividends and distributions on said Shares to be distributed, provided, however, that as and if I shall elect from time to time to cause dividends and distributions to pay such payments to me individually unless there shall have been filed with it written notice Trustee hereunder and may continue such payments to me individually rather than to me as of my death or incapacity satisfactory to it. The issuer or custodian is authorized to make such distributions under a mutual fund systematic withdrawal plan as have been specified by me or by any Successor Trustee acting hereunder. Until the issuer or custodian shall receive from some person interested in this Trust, written notice of any death or other event upon which the right to receive may depend, the issuer or custodian shall incur no liability for payments made in good faith to persons whose interests shall have been affected by such event. The issuer or custodian shall be protected in acting upon any notice or other instrument or document believed by it to be genuine and to have been signed or presented by the proper party or parties.

... any person whatso... ...upon the revoca...

7. In the case of my death or legal incapacity, I hereby nominate and appoint as Successor Trustee hereunder whosoever shall at that time be beneficiary unless he or she shall be a minor or otherwise legally incapacitated, in either of which events I hereby nominate and appoint as Successor Trustee: _____, of

(Name) _____ **Henry P. Adams** _____ **Jonesville** _____ **Connecticut** _____

(Address) _____ **125** _____ **Barnum Street** _____ City _____ State

Number _____ Street

and upon his or her failure to act (or should I for any reason fail to designate the person intended to be nominated), then and in either event I nominate and appoint as such Successor Trustee whosoever shall qualify as Executor or Administrator of my estate, as the case may be.

8. This Declaration of Trust shall extend to and be binding upon the heirs, executors, administrators and assigns of the undersigned and upon the successors to the Trustee.

9. This Declaration of Trust shall be construed and enforced in accordance with the laws of the State of

_____ **Connecticut** _____

Declaration of Trust

WHEREAS, I,_____ of the

City/Town of_____, County of_____, State of_____ ,

am the owner of certain shares of the capital stock of:

_____
(Name of Fund)

NOW, THEREFORE, KNOW ALL MEN BY THESE PRESENTS, that I do hereby acknowledge and declare that I hold and will hold said Shares and all right, title and interest in and to said Shares IN TRUST, for the following uses and purposes:

1. To add, or cause to be added, to the corpus of this Trust all income and distributions which may from time to time be received on the said Shares, by causing the same to be invested in additional shares, or if I shall so elect from time to time to pay said income and distributions or cause the same to be paid to myself during my lifetime.

2. To hold said Shares and all right, title and interest therein for the use and benefit of:

(Name)_____ , of

(Address)_____
          Number   Street   City   State

or, if such beneficiary be not surviving, for the use and benefit of

(Name)_____ , of

(Address)_____
          Number   Street   City   State

Upon my death, unless the beneficiaries shall predecease me or unless we shall die as a result of a common accident or disaster, my Successor Trustee is hereby directed forthwith to transfer said Shares and all right, title and interest in and to said Shares unto the beneficiary absolutely and thereby terminate this Trust; provided, however, that if the beneficiary hereunder shall then be a minor, the Successor Trustee shall hold the trust assets in continuing trust until such beneficiary attains the age of twenty-one years. Prior to that date, the Successor Trustee may apply or expend any or all of the income or principal for the maintenance, education and support of the minor beneficiary without the intervention of any guardian and without application to any court. Such payments of income or principal may be made to the parents of such minor or to the person with whom the minor is living without any liability upon the Successor Trustee to see to the application thereof. If such minor survives me but dies before attaining the age of twenty-one years, at his or her death the Successor Trustee shall deliver, pay over, transfer and distribute the trust property to such minor's personal representatives, absolutely.

3. I reserve the right to register any shares held hereunder in the name of a nominee, which nominee may be myself as an individual, or to pledge the shares as collateral for a loan. The right, power and authority is hereby conferred upon any Successor Trustee hereunder, at any time during the minority of the beneficiary, to invest and reinvest without limitation or restriction, to sell all or any part of the Shares being held, holding either Shares or the proceeds of the sale thereof until the minor beneficiary attains the age of twenty-one years.

4. This Trust is created upon the express understanding that the issuer or custodian of the Shares hereunder shall be under no liability whatsoever to see to its proper administration, and that upon the transfer of the right, title and interest in and to said Shares by any Trustee hereunder, said issuer or custodian shall conclusively treat the transferee as the sole owner of said Shares. In the event that any shares, cash or other property shall be distributable at any time under the terms of said Shares, the said issuer or custodian is fully authorized to pay, deliver and distribute the same to whosoever shall then be trustee hereunder, and shall be under no liability to see to the proper application thereof, provided, however, that as and if I shall elect from time to time to cause dividends and distributions on said Shares to be distributed, rather than reinvested, the issuer or custodian shall be fully authorized to pay such dividends and distributions direct to me individually rather than to me as Trustee hereunder and may continue such payments to me individually unless there shall have been filed with it written notice of my death or incapacity satisfactory to it. The issuer or custodian is authorized to make such distributions under a mutual fund systematic withdrawal plan as have been specified by me or by any Successor Trustee acting hereunder. Until the issuer or custodian shall receive from some person interested in this Trust, written notice of any death or other event upon which the right to receive may depend, the issuer or custodian shall incur no liability for payments made in good faith to persons whose interests shall have been affected by such event. The issuer or custodian shall be protected in acting upon any notice or other instrument or document believed by it to be genuine and to have been signed or presented by the proper party or parties.

5. The death during my lifetime, or in a common accident or disaster with me, of any beneficiary designated hereunder shall revoke such designation, and in the former event I reserve the right to designate a new beneficiary. Should I for any reason fail to designate such new beneficiary and should no designated beneficiary be surviving, this Trust shall terminate upon my death and the trust property shall revert to my estate.

6. I hereby reserve unto myself the power and right at any time during my lifetime, before actual distribution to the beneficiary hereunder, to revoke in whole or in part or to amend the Trust hereby created without the necessity of obtaining the consent of the beneficiary and without giving notice to the beneficiary. Any one of the following acts shall be conclusive evidence of such revocation of this Trust:

(a) The delivery to the issuer or custodian of the Shares by me of written notice that this Trust is revoked in whole or in part;

(b) The transfer by me of my right, title and interest in and to said Shares;

(c) The delivery by me to the issuer or custodian of the Shares of written notice of the death of the Beneficiary hereunder.

I hereby reserve unto myself the right, upon the revocation or termination of this Trust, to create a new Trust for the benefit of any person whatsoever.

7. In the case of my death or legal incapacity, I hereby nominate and appoint as Successor Trustee hereunder whosoever shall at that time be beneficiary unless he or she shall be a minor or otherwise legally incapacitated, in either of which events I hereby nominate and appoint as Successor Trustee:

(Name)_____, of

(Address)_____
            Number   Street   City   State

and upon his or her failure to act (or should I for any reason fail to designate the person intended to be nominated), then and in either event I nominate and appoint as such Successor Trustee whosoever shall qualify as Executor or Administrator of my estate, as the case may be.

8. This Declaration of Trust shall extend to and be binding upon the heirs, executors, administrators and assigns of the undersigned and upon the successors to the Trustee.

9. This Declaration of Trust shall be construed and enforced in accordance with the laws of the State of

_____.

IN WITNESS WHEREOF I have hereunto set my hand and seal this_____day

of_____, 19____.

(sign here)_____L.S.

Witness: (1)_____

Witness: (2)_____

STATE OF _____
                                ss: _____

COUNTY OF _____

On the_____day of_____, nineteen hundred and_____,

before me came_____known to me to be the individual described in, and who

executed the foregoing instrument, and_____ acknowledged that _____ executed the same; and in due form of law acknowledged the foregoing instrument to be _____ act and deed and desired the same might be recorded as such.

WITNESS my hand and notarial seal the day and year aforesaid.

(Notary Seal)   _____

                                                  Notary Public

Declaration of Trust

WHEREAS, I,_____of the

City/Town of_____, County of_____, State of_____,

am the owner of certain shares of the capital stock of:

_____
(Name of Fund)

NOW, THEREFORE, KNOW ALL MEN BY THESE PRESENTS, that I do hereby acknowledge and declare that I hold and will hold said Shares and all right, title and interest in and to said Shares IN TRUST, for the following uses and purposes:

1. To add, or cause to be added, to the corpus of this Trust all income and distributions which may from time to time be received on the said Shares, by causing the same to be invested in additional shares, or if I shall so elect from time to time to pay said income and distributions or cause the same to be paid to myself during my lifetime.

2. To hold said Shares and all right, title and interest therein for the use and benefit of:

(Name)_____, of

(Address)_____

| Number | Street | City | State |

or, if such beneficiary be not surviving, for the use and benefit of

(Name)_____, of

(Address)_____

| Number | Street | City | State |

Upon my death, unless the beneficiaries shall predecease me or unless we shall die as a result of a common accident or disaster, my Successor Trustee is hereby directed forthwith to transfer said Shares and all right, title and interest in and to said Shares unto the beneficiary absolutely and thereby terminate this Trust; provided, however, that if the beneficiary hereunder shall then be a minor, the Successor Trustee shall hold the trust assets in continuing trust until such beneficiary attains the age of twenty-one years. Prior to that date, the Successor Trustee may apply or expend any or all of the income or principal for the maintenance, education and support of the minor beneficiary without the intervention of any guardian and without application to any court. Such payments of income or principal may be made to the parents of such minor or to the person with whom the minor is living without any liability upon the Successor Trustee to see to the application thereof. If such minor survives me but dies before attaining the age of twenty-one years, at his or her death the Successor Trustee shall deliver, pay over, transfer and distribute the trust property to such minor's personal representatives, absolutely.

3. I reserve the right to register any shares held hereunder in the name of a nominee, which nominee may be myself as an individual, or to pledge the shares as collateral for a loan. The right, power and authority is hereby conferred upon any Successor Trustee hereunder, at any time during the minority of the beneficiary, to invest and reinvest without limitation or restriction, to sell all or any part of the Shares being held, holding either Shares or the proceeds of the sale thereof until the minor beneficiary attains the age of twenty-one years.

4. This Trust is created upon the express understanding that the issuer or custodian of the Shares hereunder shall be under no liability whatsoever to see to its proper administration, and that upon the transfer of the right, title and interest in and to said Shares by any Trustee hereunder, said issuer or custodian shall conclusively treat the transferee as the sole owner of said Shares. In the event that any shares, cash or other property shall be distributable at any time under the terms of said Shares, the said issuer or custodian is fully authorized to pay, deliver and distribute the same to whosoever shall then be trustee hereunder, and shall be under no liability to see to the proper application thereof, provided, however, that as and if I shall elect from time to time to cause dividends and distributions on said Shares to be distributed, rather than reinvested, the issuer or custodian shall be fully authorized to pay such dividends and distributions direct to me individually rather than to me as Trustee hereunder and may continue such payments to me individually unless there shall have been filed with it written notice of my death or incapacity satisfactory to it. The issuer or custodian is authorized to make such distributions under a mutual fund systematic withdrawal plan as have been specified by me or by any Successor Trustee acting hereunder. Until the issuer or custodian shall receive from some person interested in this Trust, written notice of any death or other event upon which the right to receive may depend, the issuer or custodian shall incur no liability for payments made in good faith to persons whose interests shall have been affected by such event. The issuer or custodian shall be protected in acting upon any notice or other instrument or document believed by it to be genuine and to have been signed or presented by the proper party or parties.

5. The death during my lifetime, or in a common accident or disaster with me, of any beneficiary designated hereunder shall revoke such designation, and in the former event I reserve the right to designate a new beneficiary. Should I for any reason fail to designate such new beneficiary and should no designated beneficiary be surviving, this Trust shall terminate upon my death and the trust property shall revert to my estate.

6. I hereby reserve unto myself the power and right at any time during my lifetime, before actual distribution to the beneficiary hereunder, to revoke in whole or in part or to amend the Trust hereby created without the necessity of obtaining the consent of the beneficiary and without giving notice to the beneficiary. Any one of the following acts shall be conclusive evidence of such revocation of this Trust:

    (a) The delivery to the issuer or custodian of the Shares by me of written notice that this Trust is revoked in whole or in part;

    (b) The transfer by me of my right, title and interest in and to said Shares;

    (c) The delivery by me to the issuer or custodian of the Shares of written notice of the death of the Beneficiary hereunder.

I hereby reserve unto myself the right, upon the revocation or termination of this Trust, to create a new Trust for the benefit of any person whatsoever.

7. In the case of my death or legal incapacity, I hereby nominate and appoint as Successor Trustee hereunder whosoever shall at that time be beneficiary unless he or she shall be a minor or otherwise legally incapacitated, in either of which events I hereby nominate and appoint as Successor Trustee:

(Name)_____, of

(Address)_____

           Number   Street   City   State

and upon his or her failure to act (or should I for any reason fail to designate the person intended to be nominated), then and in either event I nominate and appoint as such Successor Trustee whosoever shall qualify as Executor or Administrator of my estate, as the case may be.

8. This Declaration of Trust shall extend to and be binding upon the heirs, executors, administrators and assigns of the undersigned and upon the successors to the Trustee.

9. This Declaration of Trust shall be construed and enforced in accordance with the laws of the State of

_____.

IN WITNESS WHEREOF I have hereunto set my hand and seal this_____day

of_____, 19_____.

          (sign here)_____L.S.

Witness: (1)_____

Witness: (2)_____

STATE OF _____ }
                       ss: _____
COUNTY OF _____ }

On the_____day of_____, nineteen hundred and_____,

before me came_____known to me to be the individual described in, and who

executed the foregoing instrument, and_____ acknowledged that _____ executed the same; and in due form of law acknowledged the foregoing instrument to be _____ act and deed and desired the same might be recorded as such.

WITNESS my hand and notarial seal the day and year aforesaid.

(Notary Seal)

_____
                  Notary Public

DECLARATION OF TRUST
FOR NAMING
**TWO OR MORE BENEFICIARIES
SHARING EQUALLY**
TO RECEIVE
MUTUAL FUND SHARES

Instructions:

On the following pages will be found duplicate copies of a declaration of trust (DT-11) which will be suitable for use in connection with the inter vivos trust arrangement suggested in Chapter 7 where it is desired to name several persons, sharing equally, to receive mutual fund shares upon the death of the owner.

Cross out "city" or "town", leaving the appropriate designation of your community.

Enter the names of the beneficiaries in the appropriate place in Paragraph 2. Note that the instrument specifies that the named beneficiaries are to receive *"in equal shares, or the survivor of them/per stirpes."* Now, think carefully: If you have named your three brothers with the understanding that if one brother predeceases you, *his* children will take *his* share, cross out *"or the survivor of them"* and initial it. If that is not what you want— if, for example, you prefer that the share of your deceased brother be divided by your two surviving brothers, cross out *"per stirpes"* and initial it. Remember, you must cross out *"or the survivor of them"* or *"per stirpes"*—one or the other.

For shares purchased outright:

If you are buying shares outright, enter the name of the fund in the appropriate place in the instrument. Instruct your mutual fund dealer that the shares are to be registered *(Your Name) Trustee u/d/t dated _____*". Some funds will wish to examine the declaration of trust at the time the shares are issued, so execute both original and duplicate and offer one to the dealer to send along with the registration instructions. In any case, if you ever decide to sell the shares, or if you die and the beneficiary requests their transfer, the fund will ask to see the declaration of trust. It is suggested, therefore, that when the share certificate is issued, the signed declaration of trust be permanently stapled to it. If you make subsequent additional purchases of the same fund, it is not necessary to execute a new declaration of trust each time—simply register the shares exactly as you did your first purchase. If you wish to name a different beneficiary on such subsequent purchases, then you *will* need to execute a new declaration of trust. To avoid confusion, never date two instruments the same date.

If you have a "voluntary plan" or "open account", the fund will hold the shares and no certificate will be issued. It is important, then, that you place the original declaration of trust where you can find it readily if you decide to sell your shares or where the beneficiary can find it if you die.

For contractual plans:

If you are buying a contractual plan which does not use a declaration of trust to designate the beneficiary, in the place in the instrument provided for the name of the fund, enter *"(Name of fund) held in (Name of fund) Investment Plan No._____"*. Instruct your mutual fund dealer to send the completed instrument along with the plan application. The plan's custodian bank will fill in the number assigned to your account. With a contractual plan, the beneficiary designation— and therefore the probate exemption—is *not effective* unless and until the instrument is permanently filed with the plan's custodian bank. It isn't absolutely necessary that the instrument be filed at the time the plan is applied for; you can send it in later. If you choose this latter course, be sure to ask for acknowledgement of its receipt. Many banks charge a "late filing fee" of $2.50 if the declaration of trust does not accompany the application.

When your plan certificate is issued, staple the executed duplicate declaration of trust into it for your permanent record and for the information of the beneficiary.

Whenever there is any possibility of a minor child receiving the property, make certain that you name an adult who can act as trustee for the child. The name of that adult should be inserted in Paragraph 7 of the instrument shown here. Avoid naming as trustee a person not likely to survive until the child has reached age 21.

Declaration of Trust

WHEREAS, I, _____ John J. Smith _____, _____, State of _____ Connecticut _____, of the

City/Town of _____ Jonesville _____, County of _____ Fairfax _____

am the owner of certain shares of the capital stock of:

_____ Ajax Mutual Fund _____

(Name of Fund)

NOW, THEREFORE, KNOW ALL MEN BY THESE PRESENTS, that I do hereby acknowledge and declare that I hold and will hold said Shares and all right, title and interest in and to said Shares IN TRUST, for the following uses and purposes:

1. To add, or cause to be added, to the corpus of this Trust all income and distributions which may from time to time be received on the said Shares, by causing the same to be invested in additional shares, or if I shall so elect from time to time to pay said income and distributions or cause the same to be paid to myself during my lifetime.

2. To hold said Shares and all right, title and interest therein for the use and benefit of the following _____ J.J.S.

_____ three _____ persons, in equal shares, or the survivor of them/

Thomas B. Smith   (my brother)
William R. Smith   (my brother)
Charles M. Smith   (my brother)

Upon my death, unless all of the beneficiaries shall predecease me or unless we shall die as a result of a common accident or disaster, my Successor Trustee is hereby directed forthwith to transfer said Shares and all right, title and interest in and to said Shares unto the beneficiaries absolutely and thereby terminate this trust; provided, however, that if any beneficiary hereunder shall then be a minor, the Successor Trustee shall hold such beneficiary's share of the trust assets in continuing trust until such beneficiary attains the age of twenty-one years. Prior to that date, the Successor Trustee may apply or expend any or all of the income or principal for the maintenance, education and support of the minor beneficiary without the intervention of any guardian and without application to any court. Such payments of income or principal may be made to the parents of such minor or to the person with whom such minor is living without any liability upon the Successor Trustee to see to the application thereof. If such minor survives me but dies before attaining the age of twenty-one years, at his or her death the Successor Trustee shall deliver, pay over, transfer and distribute the trust property to such minor's personal representatives, absolutely.

3. I reserve the right to register any shares held hereunder in the name of a nominee, which nominee may be myself as an individual. The right, power and authority is hereby conferred upon any Successor Trustee hereunder, at any time during the minority of any beneficiary, to invest and reinvest without limitation or restriction, to sell all or any part of the Shares being held, holding either Shares or the proceeds of the sale thereof until the minor beneficiary attains the age of twenty-one years.

4. This Trust is created upon the express understanding that the issuer or custodian of the Shares hereunder shall be under no liability whatsoever to see to its proper administration, and that upon the transfer of the right, title and interest in and to said Shares by any Trustee hereunder, said issuer or custodian shall conclusively treat the transferee as the sole owner of said Shares, the said issuer or custodian is fully authorized to pay, deliver and distribute the same to whosoever shall then be trustee hereunder, and shall be under no liability to see to the proper application thereof, provided, however, that as and if I shall elect from time to time to cause dividends and distributions on said Shares to be distributed, rather than reinvested, the issuer or custodian shall be fully authorized to pay such dividends and distributions direct to me individually rather than to me as Trustee hereunder and may continue such payments to me individually unless there shall have been filed with it written notice of my death or incapacity satisfactory to it. The issuer or custodian is authorized to make such distributions under a mutual fund systematic withdrawal plan as have been specified by me or by any Successor Trustee acting hereunder. Until the issuer ...

I hereby reserve unto ...   ... benefit of any person whatsoever.   ... upon the ... ...ination of this Trust, to create ... ...

7. In the case of my death or legal incapacity, I hereby nominate and appoint as Successor Trustee hereunder the beneficiary first above named unless he or she shall be a minor or otherwise legally incapacitated, in which event I hereby nominate and appoint as Successor Trustee hereunder the beneficiary whose name appears second above. If such beneficiary named second above shall be a minor or legally incompetent, then I nominate and appoint as Successor Trustee:

_____ Henry P. Adams _____, of

(Name) _____ Barnum Street _____ Jonesville _____ Connecticut

(Address) _____ 125 _____ Street _____ City _____ State
         Number

8. This Declaration of Trust shall extend to and be binding upon the heirs, executors, administrators and assigns of the undersigned and upon the successors to the Trustee.

9. This Declaration of Trust shall be construed and enforced in accordance with the laws of the State of _____ Connecticut _____.

WHEREAS, I,_____of the

City/Town of_____, County of_____, State of_____,

am the owner of certain shares of the capital stock of:

_____
(Name of Fund)

NOW, THEREFORE, KNOW ALL MEN BY THESE PRESENTS, that I do hereby acknowledge and declare that I hold and will hold said Shares and all right, title and interest in and to said Shares IN TRUST, for the following uses and purposes:

1. To add, or cause to be added, to the corpus of this Trust all income and distributions which may from time to time be received on the said Shares, by causing the same to be invested in additional shares, or if I shall so elect from time to time to pay said income and distributions or cause the same to be paid to myself during my lifetime.

2. To hold said Shares and all right, title and interest therein for the use and benefit of the following

_____persons, in equal shares, or the survivor of them/per stirpes:

Upon my death, unless all of the beneficiaries shall predecease me or unless we shall die as a result of a common accident or disaster, my Successor Trustee is hereby directed forthwith to transfer said Shares and all right, title and interest in and to said Shares unto the beneficiaries absolutely and thereby terminate this trust; provided, however, that if any beneficiary hereunder shall then be a minor, the Successor Trustee shall hold such beneficiary's share of the trust assets in continuing trust until such beneficiary attains the age of twenty-one years. Prior to that date, the Successor Trustee may apply or expend any or all of the income or principal for the maintenance, education and support of the minor beneficiary without the intervention of any guardian and without application to any court. Such payments of income or principal may be made to the parents of such minor or to the person with whom the minor is living without any liability upon the Successor Trustee to see to the application thereof. If such minor survives me but dies before attaining the age of twenty-one years, at his or her death the Successor Trustee shall deliver, pay over, transfer and distribute the trust property to such minor's personal representatives, absolutely.

3. I reserve the right to register any shares held hereunder in the name of a nominee, which nominee may be myself as an individual, or to pledge the shares as collateral for a loan. The right, power and authority is hereby conferred upon any Successor Trustee hereunder, at any time during the minority of the beneficiary, to invest and reinvest without limitation or restriction, to sell all or any part of the Shares being held, holding either Shares or the proceeds of the sale thereof until the minor beneficiary attains the age of twenty-one years.

4. This Trust is created upon the express understanding that the issuer or custodian of the Shares hereunder shall be under no liability whatsoever to see to its proper administration, and that upon the transfer of the right, title and interest in and to said Shares by any Trustee hereunder, said issuer or custodian shall conclusively treat the transferee as the sole owner of said Shares. In the event that any shares, cash or other property shall be distributable at any time under the terms of said Shares, the said issuer or custodian is fully authorized to pay, deliver and distribute the same to whosoever shall then be trustee hereunder, and shall be under no liability to see to the proper application thereof, provided, however, that as and if I shall elect from time to time to cause dividends and distributions on said Shares to be distributed, rather than reinvested, the issuer or custodian shall be fully authorized to pay such dividends and distributions direct to me individually rather than to me as Trustee hereunder and may continue such payments to me individually unless there shall have been filed with it written notice of my death or incapacity satisfactory to it. The issuer or custodian is authorized to make such distributions under a mutual fund systematic withdrawal plan as have been specified by me or by any Successor Trustee acting hereunder. Until the issuer

or custodian shall receive from some person interested in this Trust, written notice of any death or other event upon which the right to receive may depend, the issuer or custodian shall incur no liability for payments made in good faith to persons whose interests shall have been affected by such event. The issuer or custodian shall be protected in acting upon any notice or other instrument or document believed by it to be genuine and to have been signed or presented by the proper party or parties.

5. The death during my lifetime, or in a common accident or disaster with me, of any beneficiary designated hereunder shall revoke such designation, and in the former event I reserve the right to designate a new beneficiary. Should no designated beneficiary be surviving, this Trust shall terminate upon my death and the trust property shall revert to my estate.

6. I hereby reserve unto myself the power and right at any time during my lifetime, before actual distribution to the beneficiaries hereunder, to revoke in whole or in part or to amend the Trust hereby created without the necessity of obtaining the consent of the beneficiaries and without giving notice to the beneficiaries. Any one of the following acts shall be conclusive evidence of such revocation of this Trust:

    (a) The delivery to the issuer or custodian of the Shares by me of written notice that this Trust is revoked in whole or in part;

    (b) The transfer by me of my right, title and interest in and to said Shares;

    (c) The delivery by me to the issuer or custodian of the Shares of written notice of the death of the Beneficiary hereunder.

I hereby reserve unto myself the right, upon the revocation or termination of this Trust, to create a new Trust for the benefit of any person whatsoever.

7. **In** the case of my death or legal incapacity, I hereby nominate and appoint as Successor Trustee hereunder the beneficiary first above named unless he or she shall be a minor or otherwise legally incapacitated, in which event I hereby nominate and appoint as Successor Trustee hereunder the beneficiary whose name appears second above. If such beneficiary named second above shall be a minor or legally incompetent, then I nominate and appoint as Successor Trustee:

(Name)_____, of

(Address)_____
          Number   Street   City   State

8. **This** Declaration of Trust shall extend to and be binding upon the heirs, executors, administrators and assigns of the undersigned and upon the successors to the Trustee.

9. **This** Declaration of Trust shall be construed and enforced in accordance with the laws of the State of

_____.

IN WITNESS WHEREOF I have hereunto set my hand and seal this_____day

of_____, 19_____.

                     (sign here)_____L.S.

Witness: (1)_____

Witness: (2)_____

STATE OF _____⎫
                          ⎬ ss: _____
COUNTY OF _____⎭

On the_____day of_____, nineteen hundred and_____, before

me came_____known to me to be the individual described in, and who executed

the foregoing instrument, and _____ acknowledged that _____ executed the same; and in due form of law acknowledged the foregoing instrument to be _____ act and deed and desired the same might be recorded as such.

    WITNESS my hand and notarial seal the day and year aforesaid.

(Notary Seal)   _____
                                             Notary Public

WHEREAS, I,_____of the

City/Town of_____, County of_____, State of_____,

am the owner of certain shares of the capital stock of:

_____

(Name of Fund)

NOW, THEREFORE, KNOW ALL MEN BY THESE PRESENTS, that I do hereby acknowledge and declare that I hold and will hold said Shares and all right, title and interest in and to said Shares IN TRUST, for the following uses and purposes:

1. To add, or cause to be added, to the corpus of this Trust all income and distributions which may from time to time be received on the said Shares, by causing the same to be invested in additional shares, or if I shall so elect from time to time to pay said income and distributions or cause the same to be paid to myself during my lifetime.

2. To hold said Shares and all right, title and interest therein for the use and benefit of the following

_____persons, in equal shares, or the survivor of them/per stirpes:

Upon my death, unless all of the beneficiaries shall predecease me or unless we shall die as a result of a common accident or disaster, my Successor Trustee is hereby directed forthwith to transfer said Shares and all right, title and interest in and to said Shares unto the beneficiaries absolutely and thereby terminate this trust; provided, however, that if any beneficiary hereunder shall then be a minor, the Successor Trustee shall hold such beneficiary's share of the trust assets in continuing trust until such beneficiary attains the age of twenty-one years. Prior to that date, the Successor Trustee may apply or expend any or all of the income or principal for the maintenance, education and support of the minor beneficiary without the intervention of any guardian and without application to any court. Such payments of income or principal may be made to the parents of such minor or to the person with whom the minor is living without any liability upon the Successor Trustee to see to the application thereof. If such minor survives me but dies before attaining the age of twenty-one years, at his or her death the Successor Trustee shall deliver, pay over, transfer and distribute the trust property to such minor's personal representatives, absolutely.

3. I reserve the right to register any shares held hereunder in the name of a nominee, which nominee may be myself as an individual, or to pledge the shares as collateral for a loan. The right, power and authority is hereby conferred upon any Successor Trustee hereunder, at any time during the minority of the beneficiary, to invest and reinvest without limitation or restriction, to sell all or any part of the Shares being held, holding either Shares or the proceeds of the sale thereof until the minor beneficiary attains the age of twenty-one years.

4. This Trust is created upon the express understanding that the issuer or custodian of the Shares hereunder shall be under no liability whatsoever to see to its proper administration, and that upon the transfer of the right, title and interest in and to said Shares by any Trustee hereunder, said issuer or custodian shall conclusively treat the transferee as the sole owner of said Shares. In the event that any shares, cash or other property shall be distributable at any time under the terms of said Shares, the said issuer or custodian is fully authorized to pay, deliver and distribute the same to whosoever shall then be trustee hereunder, and shall be under no liability to see to the proper application thereof, provided, however, that as and if I shall elect from time to time to cause dividends and distributions on said Shares to be distributed, rather than reinvested, the issuer or custodian shall be fully authorized to pay such dividends and distributions direct to me individually rather than to me as Trustee hereunder and may continue such payments to me individually unless there shall have been filed with it written notice of my death or incapacity satisfactory to it. The issuer or custodian is authorized to make such distributions under a mutual fund systematic withdrawal plan as have been specified by me or by any Successor Trustee acting hereunder. Until the issuer

or custodian shall receive from some person interested in this Trust, written notice of any death or other event upon which the right to receive may depend, the issuer or custodian shall incur no liability for payments made in good faith to persons whose interests shall have been affected by such event. The issuer or custodian shall be protected in acting upon any notice or other instrument or document believed by it to be genuine and to have been signed or presented by the proper party or parties.

5. The death during my lifetime, or in a common accident or disaster with me, of any beneficiary designated hereunder shall revoke such designation, and in the former event I reserve the right to designate a new beneficiary. Should no designated beneficiary be surviving, this Trust shall terminate upon my death and the trust property shall revert to my estate.

6. I hereby reserve unto myself the power and right at any time during my lifetime, before actual distribution to the beneficiaries hereunder, to revoke in whole or in part or to amend the Trust hereby created without the necessity of obtaining the consent of the beneficiaries and without giving notice to the beneficiaries. Any one of the following acts shall be conclusive evidence of such revocation of this Trust:

    (a) The delivery to the issuer or custodian of the Shares by me of written notice that this Trust is revoked in whole or in part;

    (b) The transfer by me of my right, title and interest in and to said Shares;

    (c) The delivery by me to the issuer or custodian of the Shares of written notice of the death of the Beneficiary hereunder.

I hereby reserve unto myself the right, upon the revocation or termination of this Trust, to create a new Trust for the benefit of any person whatsoever.

7. In the case of my death or legal incapacity, I hereby nominate and appoint as Successor Trustee hereunder the beneficiary first above named unless he or she shall be a minor or otherwise legally incapacitated, in which event I hereby nominate and appoint as Successor Trustee hereunder the beneficiary whose name appears second above. If such beneficiary named second above shall be a minor or legally incompetent, then I nominate and appoint as Successor Trustee:

(Name)_____, of

(Address)_____
           Number   Street   City   State

8. This Declaration of Trust shall extend to and be binding upon the heirs, executors, administrators and assigns of the undersigned and upon the successors to the Trustee.

9. This Declaration of Trust shall be construed and enforced in accordance with the laws of the State of

_____.

IN WITNESS WHEREOF I have hereunto set my hand and seal this_____day

of_____, 19____.

           (sign here)_____L.S.

Witness: (1)_____

Witness: (2)_____

STATE OF _____
                        } ss: _____
COUNTY OF _____

On the_____day of_____, nineteen hundred and_____, before

me came_____known to me to be the individual described in, and who executed

the foregoing instrument, and _____ acknowledged that _____ executed the same; and in due form of law acknowledged the foregoing instrument to be _____ act and deed and desired the same might be recorded as such.

WITNESS my hand and notarial seal the day and year aforesaid.

(Notary Seal)   _____

                                    Notary Public

DECLARATION OF TRUST
FOR NAMING
**ONE PRIMARY BENEFICIARY WITH
YOUR CHILDREN, SHARING EQUALLY,
AS CONTINGENT BENEFICIARIES**
TO RECEIVE
MUTUAL FUND SHARES

Instructions:

On the following pages will be found duplicate copies of a declaration of trust (DT-12) which will be suitable for use in connection with the inter vivos trust arrangement suggested in Chapter 7 where it is desired to name one person (ordinarily, one's spouse) as primary beneficiary, with one's children as contingent beneficiaries to receive mutual fund shares upon the death of the owner.

Cross out *"city"* or *"town"*, leaving the appropriate designation of your community.

Enter the name of the primary beneficiary in the appropriate place in Paragraph 2. Note that the instrument refers to your children as *"natural not/or adopted"*. Now, decide: If you have an adopted child and you wish to *include* him, cross out the word "not" in the phrase *"natural not/or adopted"* and initial it. If you wish to *exclude* your adopted child, cross out the word *"or"* in the same phrase and initial it. Remember, you *must* cross out *"not"* or *"or"*—one or the other. Note next that the instrument specifies that your children are to receive *"in equal shares, or the survivor of them/per stirpes"*. Now, think carefully: If it is your wish that if one of your children does not survive you, his share will revert to *his* children in equal shares, cross out *"or the survivor of them"* and initial it. If that is *not* what you want—if, for example, you prefer that the share of your deceased child be divided among your surviving children, cross out *"per stirpes"* and initial it. Remember, you must cross out *"or the survivor of them"* or *"per stirpes"*—one or the other.

For shares purchased outright:

If you are buying shares outright, enter the name of the fund in the appropriate place in the instrument. Instruct your mutual fund dealer that the shares are to be registered *"(Your Name) Trustee u/d/t dated _____"*. Some funds will wish to examine the declaration of trust at the time the shares are issued, so execute both original and duplicate and offer one to the dealer to

send along with the registration instructions. In any case, if you ever decide to sell the shares, or if you die and the beneficiary requests their transfer, the fund will ask to see the declaration of trust. It is suggested, therefore, that when the share certificate is issued, the signed declaration of trust be permanently stapled to it. If you make subsequent additional purchases of the same fund, it is not necessary to execute a new declaration of trust each time—simply register the shares exactly as you did your first purchase. If you wish to name a different beneficiary on such subsequent purchases, then you *will* need to execute a new declaration of trust. To avoid confusion, never date two instruments the same date.

If you have a "voluntary plan" or "open account", the fund will hold the shares and no certificate will be issued. It is important, then, that you place the original declaration of trust where you can find it readily if you decide to sell your shares or where the beneficiary can find it if you die.

For contractual plans:

If you are buying a contractual plan which does not use a declaration of trust to designate the beneficiary, in the place in the instrument provided for the name of the fund, enter *"(Name of fund) held in (Name of fund) Investment Plan No._____"*. Instruct your mutual fund dealer to send the completed instrument along with the plan application. The plan's custodian bank will fill in the number assigned to your account. With a contractual plan, the beneficiary designation—and therefore the probate exemption—is *not effective* unless and until it is permanently filed with the plan's custodian bank. It isn't absolutely necessary that the instrument be filed at the time the plan is applied for; you can send it in later. If you choose this latter course, be sure to ask for acknowledgement of its receipt. Many banks charge a "late filing fee" of $2.50 if the declaration of trust does not accompany the application.

When your plan certificate is issued, staple the executed duplicate declaration of trust into it for your permanent record and for the information of the beneficiary.

Whenever there is any possibility of a minor child receiving the property, make certain that you name an adult who can act as trustee for the child. The name of that adult should be inserted in Paragraph 7 of the instrument shown here. Avoid naming as trustee a person not likely to survive until the child has reached age 21.

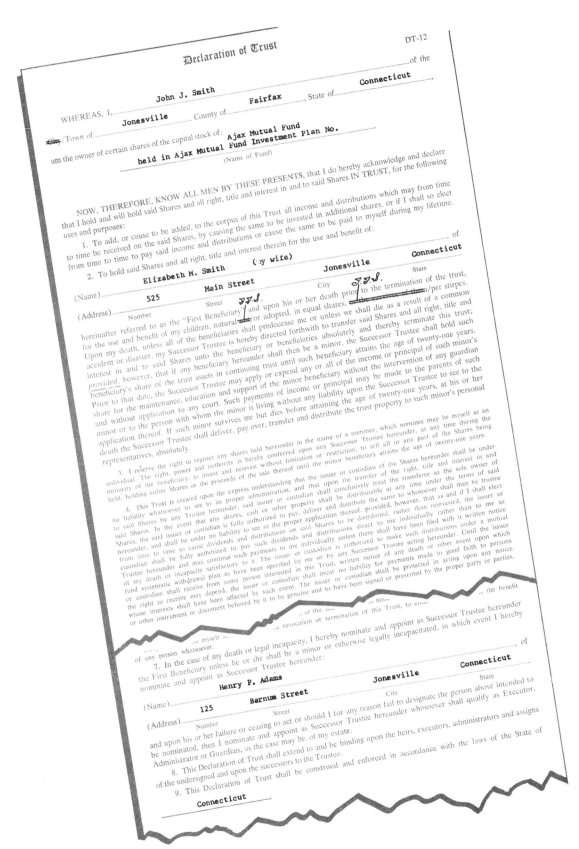

WHEREAS, I,_____of the

City/Town of_____, County of_____, State of_____,

am the owner of certain shares of the capital stock of:

_____

(Name of Fund)

NOW, THEREFORE, KNOW ALL MEN BY THESE PRESENTS, that I do hereby acknowledge and declare that I hold and will hold said Shares and all right, title and interest in and to said Shares IN TRUST, for the following uses and purposes:

1. To add, or cause to be added, to the corpus of this Trust all income and distributions which may from time to time be received on the said Shares, by causing the same to be invested in additional shares, or if I shall so elect from time to time to pay said income and distributions or cause the same to be paid to myself during my lifetime.

2. To hold said Shares and all right, title and interest therein for the use and benefit of:

(Name)_____, of

(Address)_____
　　　　　Number　　　　　Street　　　　　City　　　　　State

(hereinafter referred to as the "First Beneficiary") and upon his or her death prior to the termination of the trust, for the use and benefit of my children, natural not/or adopted, in equal shares, or the survivor of them/per stirpes. Upon my death, unless all of the beneficiaries shall predecease me or unless we shall die as a result of a common accident or disaster, my Successor Trustee is hereby directed forthwith to transfer said Shares and all right, title and interest in and to said Shares unto the beneficiary or beneficiaries absolutely and thereby terminate this trust; *provided,* however, that if any beneficiary hereunder shall then be a minor, the Successor Trustee shall hold such beneficiary's share of the trust assets in continuing trust until such beneficiary attains the age of twenty-one years. Prior to that date, the Successor Trustee may apply or expend any or all of the income or principal of such minor's share for the maintenance, education and support of the minor beneficiary without the intervention of any guardian and without application to any court. Such payments of income or principal may be made to the parents of such minor or to the person with whom the minor is living without any liability upon the Successor Trustee to see to the application thereof. If such minor survives me but dies before attaining the age of twenty-one years, at his or her death the Successor Trustee shall deliver, pay over, transfer and distribute the trust property to such minor's personal representatives, absolutely.

3. I reserve the right to register any shares held hereunder in the name of a nominee, which nominee may be myself as an individual, or to pledge the shares as collateral for a loan. The right, power and authority is hereby conferred upon any Successor Trustee hereunder, at any time during the minority of the beneficiary, to invest and reinvest without limitation or restriction, to sell all or any part of the Shares being held, holding either Shares or the proceeds of the sale thereof until the minor beneficiary attains the age of twenty-one years.

4. This Trust is created upon the express understanding that the issuer or custodian of the Shares hereunder shall be under no liability whatsoever to see to its proper administration, and that upon the transfer of the right, title and interest in and to said Shares by any Trustee hereunder, said issuer or custodian shall conclusively treat the transferee as the sole owner of said Shares. In the event that any shares, cash or other property shall be distributable at any time under the terms of said Shares, the said issuer or custodian is fully authorized to pay, deliver and distribute the same to whosoever shall then be trustee hereunder, and shall be under no liability to see to the proper application thereof, provided, however, that as and if I shall elect from time to time to cause dividends and distributions on said Shares to be distributed, rather than reinvested, the issuer or custodian shall be fully authorized to pay such dividends and distributions direct to me individually rather than to me as Trustee hereunder and may continue such payments to me individually unless there shall have been filed with it written notice of my death or incapacity satisfactory to it. The issuer or custodian is authorized to make such distributions under a mutual fund systematic withdrawal plan as have been specified by me or by any Successor Trustee acting hereunder. Until the issuer or custodian shall receive from some person interested in this Trust, written notice of any death or other event upon which the right to receive may depend, the issuer or custodian shall incur no liability for payments made in good faith to persons whose interests shall have been affected by such event. The issuer or custodian shall be protected in acting upon any notice or other instrument or document believed by it to be genuine and to have been signed or presented by the proper party or parties.

5. The death during my lifetime, or in a common accident or disaster with me, of any beneficiary designated hereunder shall revoke such designation, and in the former event I reserve the right to designate a new beneficiary. Should no designated beneficiary be surviving, this Trust shall terminate upon my death and the trust property shall revert to my estate.

6. I hereby reserve unto myself the power and right at any time during my lifetime, before actual distribution to the beneficiaries hereunder, to revoke in whole or in part or to amend the Trust hereby created without the necessity of obtaining the consent of the beneficiaries and without giving notice to the beneficiaries. Any one of the following acts shall be conclusive evidence of such revocation of this Trust:

   (a) The delivery to the issuer or custodian of the Shares by me of written notice that this Trust is revoked in whole or in part;

   (b) The transfer by me of my right, title and interest in and to said Shares;

   (c) The delivery by me to the issuer or custodian of the Shares of written notice of the death of the Beneficiary hereunder.

I hereby reserve unto myself the right, upon the revocation or termination of this Trust, to create a new Trust for the benefit of any person whatsoever.

7. **In the case of my death or legal incapacity, I hereby nominate and appoint as Successor Trustee hereunder** the First Beneficiary unless he or she shall be a minor or otherwise legally incapacitated, in which event I hereby nominate and appoint as Successor Trustee hereunder:

(Name)_____, of

(Address)_____

         Number   Street   City   State

and upon his or her failure or ceasing to act or should I for any reason fail to designate the person above intended to be nominated, then I nominate and appoint as Successor Trustee hereunder whosoever shall qualify as Executor, Administrator or Guardian, as the case may be, of my estate.

8. This Declaration of Trust shall extend to and be binding upon the heirs, executors, administrators and assigns of the undersigned and upon the successors to the Trustee.

9. This Declaration of Trust shall be construed and enforced in accordance with the laws of the State of

_____.

IN WITNESS WHEREOF I have hereunto set my hand and seal this_____day

of_____, 19_____.

(sign here)_____L.S.

Witness: (1)_____

Witness: (2)_____

STATE OF _____ }
                                    ss: _____

COUNTY OF _____ }

On the_____day of_____, nineteen hundred and_____, before

me came_____known to me to be the individual described in, and who executed

the foregoing instrument, and _____ acknowledged that _____ executed the same; and in due form of law

acknowledged the foregoing instrument to be _____ act and deed and desired the same might be recorded as such.

WITNESS my hand and notarial seal the day and year aforesaid.

(Notary Seal)

_____
                                     Notary Public

Declaration of Trust

WHEREAS, I,_____of the

City/Town of_____, County of_____, State of_____,

am the owner of certain shares of the capital stock of:

_____

(Name of Fund)

NOW, THEREFORE, KNOW ALL MEN BY THESE PRESENTS, that I do hereby acknowledge and declare that I hold and will hold said Shares and all right, title and interest in and to said Shares IN TRUST, for the following uses and purposes:

1. To add, or cause to be added, to the corpus of this Trust all income and distributions which may from time to time be received on the said Shares, by causing the same to be invested in additional shares, or if I shall so elect from time to time to pay said income and distributions or cause the same to be paid to myself during my lifetime.

2. To hold said Shares and all right, title and interest therein for the use and benefit of:

(Name)_____, of

(Address)_____
          Number   Street   City   State

(hereinafter referred to as the "First Beneficiary") and upon his or her death prior to the termination of the trust, for the use and benefit of my children, natural not/or adopted, in equal shares, or the survivor of them/per stirpes. Upon my death, unless all of the beneficiaries shall predecease me or unless we shall die as a result of a common accident or disaster, my Successor Trustee is hereby directed forthwith to transfer said Shares and all right, title and interest in and to said Shares unto the beneficiary or beneficiaries absolutely and thereby terminate this trust; *provided,* however, that if any beneficiary hereunder shall then be a minor, the Successor Trustee shall hold such beneficiary's share of the trust assets in continuing trust until such beneficiary attains the age of twenty-one years. Prior to that date, the Successor Trustee may apply or expend any or all of the income or principal of such minor's share for the maintenance, education and support of the minor beneficiary without the intervention of any guardian and without application to any court. Such payments of income or principal may be made to the parents of such minor or to the person with whom the minor is living without any liability upon the Successor Trustee to see to the application thereof. If such minor survives me but dies before attaining the age of twenty-one years, at his or her death the Successor Trustee shall deliver, pay over, transfer and distribute the trust property to such minor's personal representatives, absolutely.

3. I reserve the right to register any shares held hereunder in the name of a nominee, which nominee may be myself as an individual, or to pledge the shares as collateral for a loan. The right, power and authority is hereby conferred upon any Successor Trustee hereunder, at any time during the minority of the beneficiary, to invest and reinvest without limitation or restriction, to sell all or any part of the Shares being held, holding either Shares or the proceeds of the sale thereof until the minor beneficiary attains the age of twenty-one years.

4. This Trust is created upon the express understanding that the issuer or custodian of the Shares hereunder shall be under no liability whatsoever to see to its proper administration, and that upon the transfer of the right, title and interest in and to said Shares by any Trustee hereunder, said issuer or custodian shall conclusively treat the transferee as the sole owner of said Shares. In the event that any shares, cash or other property shall be distributable at any time under the terms of said Shares, the said issuer or custodian is fully authorized to pay, deliver and distribute the same to whosoever shall then be trustee hereunder, and shall be under no liability to see to the proper application thereof, provided, however, that as and if I shall elect from time to time to cause dividends and distributions on said Shares to be distributed, rather than reinvested, the issuer or custodian shall be fully authorized to pay such dividends and distributions direct to me individually rather than to me as Trustee hereunder and may continue such payments to me individually unless there shall have been filed with it written notice of my death or incapacity satisfactory to it. The issuer or custodian is authorized to make such distributions under a mutual fund systematic withdrawal plan as have been specified by me or by any Successor Trustee acting hereunder. Until the issuer or custodian shall receive from some person interested in this Trust, written notice of any death or other event upon which the right to receive may depend, the issuer or custodian shall incur no liability for payments made in good faith to persons whose interests shall have been affected by such event. The issuer or custodian shall be protected in acting upon any notice or other instrument or document believed by it to be genuine and to have been signed or presented by the proper party or parties.

5. The death during my lifetime, or in a common accident or disaster with me, of any beneficiary designated hereunder shall revoke such designation, and in the former event I reserve the right to designate a new beneficiary. Should no designated beneficiary be surviving, this Trust shall terminate upon my death and the trust property shall revert to my estate.

6. I hereby reserve unto myself the power and right at any time during my lifetime, before actual distribution to the beneficiaries hereunder, to revoke in whole or in part or to amend the Trust hereby created without the necessity of obtaining the consent of the beneficiaries and without giving notice to the beneficiaries. Any one of the following acts shall be conclusive evidence of such revocation of this Trust:

    (a) The delivery to the issuer or custodian of the Shares by me of written notice that this Trust is revoked in whole or in part;

    (b) The transfer by me of my right, title and interest in and to said Shares;

    (c) The delivery by me to the issuer or custodian of the Shares of written notice of the death of the Beneficiary hereunder.

I hereby reserve unto myself the right, upon the revocation or termination of this Trust, to create a new Trust for the benefit of any person whatsoever.

7. In the case of my death or legal incapacity, I hereby nominate and appoint as Successor Trustee hereunder the First Beneficiary unless he or she shall be a minor or otherwise legally incapacitated, in which event I hereby nominate and appoint as Successor Trustee hereunder:

(Name)_____, of

(Address)_____

          Number   Street   City   State

and upon his or her failure or ceasing to act or should I for any reason fail to designate the person above intended to be nominated, then I nominate and appoint as Successor Trustee hereunder whosoever shall qualify as Executor, Administrator or Guardian, as the case may be, of my estate.

8. This Declaration of Trust shall extend to and be binding upon the heirs, executors, administrators and assigns of the undersigned and upon the successors to the Trustee.

9. This Declaration of Trust shall be construed and enforced in accordance with the laws of the State of

_____.

     IN WITNESS WHEREOF I have hereunto set my hand and seal this_____day

of_____, 19_____.

                    (sign here)_____L.S.

Witness: (1)_____

Witness: (2)_____

STATE OF _____

COUNTY OF _____ } ss: _____

     On the_____day of_____, nineteen hundred and_____, before

me came_____known to me to be the individual described in, and who executed

the foregoing instrument, and _____ acknowledged that _____ executed the same; and in due form of law

acknowledged the foregoing instrument to be _____ act and deed and desired the same might be recorded as such.

     WITNESS my hand and notarial seal the day and year aforesaid.

(Notary Seal)

                    _____

                            Notary Public

Chapter 8

AVOIDING PROBATE OF SECURITIES

We have observed earlier that many persons seek to avoid probate of the securities they own by registering them in joint names. Some of the pitfalls of such joint ownership as a solution to the problem of probate avoidance have already been noted. It is important that those who use it understand clearly that while it does establish beyond question to whom the property is to pass at death, it does not assure that it will pass to the surviving co-owner without having been subject to the jurisdiction of the probate court. Many issuers of stock or transfer agents insist upon "clearance" in the form of documents from the probate court indicating the court's knowledge of and lack of objection to the proposed transfer of the property to the surviving co-owner.

All of this presupposes a registration of "John Smith and Mary Smith, as joint tenants with the right of survivorship but not as tenants in common." You'll remember that when we talked about joint ownership of a home a while back, we stressed the importance of making certain that the instrument under which such joint ownership is established is a *survivorship* deed, and we pointed out that if it was not a survivorship deed, the deceased's share of the property would not revert to the survivor but would be distributed to his heirs in accordance with the terms of his will. Lacking a valid will, its distribution would be determined by the laws of the state in which he lived.

A similar form of joint ownership exists with respect to securities. It is called "tenancy in common". Let's illustrate the kind of problem it can create in security ownership: John Smith registers his securities jointly with his wife under a "tenancy in common" registration. He dies leaving three minor children and no will.

The one-half of the securities represented by his wife's joint ownership continues to be her property. Her intestate husband's half of the property passes under the laws of the state which decree that one-third of his share will go to his widow and two-thirds to his children collectively. The net result: The widow now owns two-thirds of the stock and the children one-third. Unless there is some very special circumstance justifying tenancy in common, it should be avoided. Few brokers or others responsible for securities registration would deliberately initiate such a form of ownership. It is worth making certain that you don't have it, though.

To avoid these headaches let us turn once again to that legal "wonder drug", the inter vivos trust, which is readily adaptable for use in connection with the registration of securities. By executing a relatively simple declaration of trust, the owner of securities may thereby not only clearly establish who is to receive such securities upon his death but he can also insure that they will pass to that beneficiary without having become subject to the jurisdiction of the probate court.

We are speaking, again, of a revocable trust, one which may be altered or cancelled completely at any time. The securities will remain a part of your taxable estate so far as both income and death taxes are concerned. Their registration under the declaration of trust will not alter in the slightest degree your right to do with them as you wish during your lifetime. In a word, you have nothing to lose, no possible disadvantage—and everything to gain by placing your securities holdings beyond the reach of the probate court.

On the following pages will be found several trust instruments which should prove useful in implementing the suggestions made here.

DECLARATION OF TRUST
FOR NAMING
ONE BENEFICIARY
TO RECEIVE
STOCKS

Instructions:

On the following pages will be found duplicate copies of a declaration of trust (DT-13) which will be suitable for use in connection with the inter vivos trust arrangement suggested in Chapter 8 where it is desired simply to name some *one* person to receive corporate stock upon the death of the owner.

Cross out *"city"* or *"town"*, leaving the appropriate designation of your community.

Enter the name of the corporation whose stock is involved in the space provided near the top, and the name of the beneficiary in the appropriate place in Paragraph 1.

Instruct your broker to register the shares *"(Your Name), Trustee u/d/t dated_____"*. It will not be necessary to file the declaration of trust with the company or its transfer agent at the time you purchase the stock. However, if and when you sell it at some future date, the transfer agent will most certainly require that you display the instrument. In the circumstances, the safest thing to do is to staple it to the stock certificate when the latter is issued.

Whenever there is any possibility of a minor child receiving the property, make certain that you name an adult who can act as trustee for the child. The name of that adult should be inserted in Paragraph 6 of the instrument shown here. Avoid naming as trustee a person not likely to survive until the child has reached age 21.

NOTE:

The instruments which follow are for use with individual stocks. For instruments to use with brokerage accounts, refer to Page 361.

Declaration of Trust

_____ of the _____

WHEREAS, I, _____ **John J. Smith** _____, County of _____ **Fairfax** _____, State of _____ **Connecticut** _____,

~~City~~/Town of _____ **Jonesville** _____

am the owner of certain shares of the capital stock of:

The Ajax Tool & Die Corporation

(Name of Corporation)

NOW, THEREFORE, KNOW ALL MEN BY THESE PRESENTS, that I do hereby acknowledge and declare that I hold and will hold said Shares and all right, title and interest in and to said Shares IN TRUST for the following uses and purposes:

1. To hold said Shares and all right, title and interest therein for the use and benefit of: _____, of

(Name) _____ **Mary A. Smith** _____ **(my niece)** _____ **Jonesville** _____ **Connecticut** _____
                                                                        City   State

(Address) _____ **750** _____ **Porter Street** _____
              Number   Street

Upon my death, unless the beneficiary shall predecease me or unless we shall die as a result of a common accident or disaster, my Successor Trustee is hereby directed forthwith to transfer said Shares and all right, title and interest in and to said Shares unto the beneficiary absolutely and thereby terminate this trust; _provided_, how-ever, that if the beneficiary hereunder shall then be a minor, the Successor Trustee shall hold the trust assets in continuing trust until such beneficiary attains the age of twenty-one years. Prior to that date, the Successor Trustee may apply or expend any or all of the income or principal for the maintenance, education and support of the minor beneficiary without the intervention of any guardian and without application to any court. Such payments of income or principal may be made to the parents of such minor or to the person with whom the minor is living without any liability upon the Successor Trustee to see to the application thereof. If such minor survives me but dies before attaining the age of twenty-one years, at his or her death the Successor Trustee shall deliver, pay over, transfer and distribute the trust property to such minor's personal representatives, absolutely.

2. I reserve the right to register any shares held hereunder in the name of a nominee, which nominee may be myself as an individual. The right, power and authority is hereby conferred upon any Successor Trustee hereunder, at any time during the minority of the beneficiary, to invest and reinvest the proceeds of the sale thereof until the minor bene-ficiary attains the age of twenty-one years.

3. This Trust is created upon the express understanding that the issuer or transfer agent of the Shares hereunder shall be under no liability whatsoever to see to its proper administration, and that upon the transfer of the right, title and interest in and to said Shares by any Trustee hereunder, said issuer or transfer agent shall conclusively treat the transferee as the sole owner of said Shares. In the event that any shares, cash or other property shall be distributable at any time under the terms of said Shares, the said issuer or transfer agent is fully authorized to pay, deliver and distribute the same to whosoever shall then be Trustee hereunder, and shall be under no liability to see to the proper application thereof. Until the issuer or transfer agent shall receive from some person interested in this Trust, written notice of any death or other event upon which the right to receive may depend, the issuer or transfer agent shall incur no liability for payments made in good faith to persons whose interests shall have been affected by such event. The issuer or transfer agent shall be protected in acting upon any notice or other instrument or document believed by it to be genuine and to have been signed or presented by the proper party or parties.

4. The death during my lifetime, or in a common accident or disaster with me, of the beneficiary designated hereunder shall revoke such designation, and in the former event I reserve the right to designate a new beneficiary. Should I for any reason fail to designate such new beneficiary and should no designated beneficiary be surviving, this Trust shall terminate upon my death and the trust property shall revert to my estate.

5. I hereby reserve unto myself the power and right at any time during my lifetime, before actual distribution to the beneficiary hereunder, to revoke in whole or in part or to amend the Trust hereby created without the necessity

I hereby reserve ... in _____ revocation or termination of this Trust, to create a ...
the benefit of any person whatsover.

6. In the case of my death or legal incapacity, I hereby nominate and appoint as Successor Trustee hereunder whosoever shall at that time be beneficiary unless he or she shall be a minor or otherwise legally incapacitated, in either of which events I hereby nominate and appoint as Successor Trustee: _____, of

(Name) _____ **Henry P. Adams** _____ **Barnum Street** _____ **Jonesville** _____ **Connecticut** _____
                                                                          City   State

(Address) _____ **125** _____
              Number   Street

and upon his or her failure to act (or should I for any reason fail to designate the person intended to be nominated), then and in either event I nominate and appoint as such Successor Trustee whosoever shall qualify as Executor or Administrator of my estate, as the case may be.

7. This Declaration of Trust shall extend to and be binding upon the heirs, executors, administrators and assigns of the undersigned and upon the successors to the Trustee.

8. This Declaration of Trust shall be construed and enforced in accordance with the laws of the State of **Connecticut** _____

Declaration of Trust

WHEREAS, I,_____of the

City/Town of_____, County of_____, State of_____,

am the owner of certain shares of the capital stock of:

_____
(Name of Corporation)

NOW, THEREFORE, KNOW ALL MEN BY THESE PRESENTS, that I do hereby acknowledge and declare that I hold and will hold said Shares and all right, title and interest in and to said Shares IN TRUST for the following uses and purposes:

1. To hold said Shares and all right, title and interest therein for the use and benefit of:

(Name)_____, of

(Address)_____
      Number   Street   City   State

Upon my death, unless the beneficiary shall predecease me or unless we shall die as a result of a common accident or disaster, my Successor Trustee is hereby directed forthwith to transfer said Shares and all right, title and interest in and to said Shares unto the beneficiary absolutely and thereby terminate this trust; *provided,* however, that if the beneficiary hereunder shall then be a minor, the Successor Trustee shall hold the trust assets in continuing trust until such beneficiary attains the age of twenty-one years. Prior to that date, the Successor Trustee may apply or expend any or all of the income or principal for the maintenance, education and support of the minor beneficiary without the intervention of any guardian and without application to any court. Such payments of income or principal may be made to the parents of such minor or to the person with whom the minor is living without any liability upon the Successor Trustee to see to the application thereof. If such minor survives me but dies before attaining the age of twenty-one years, at his or her death the Successor Trustee shall deliver, pay over, transfer and distribute the trust property to such minor's personal representatives, absolutely.

2. I reserve the right to register any shares held hereunder in the name of a nominee, which nominee may be myself as an individual, or to pledge the shares as collateral for a loan. The right, power and authority is hereby conferred upon any Successor Trustee hereunder, at any time during the minority of the beneficiary, to invest and reinvest without limitation or restriction, to sell all or any part of the Shares being held, holding either Shares or the proceeds of the sale thereof until the minor beneficiary attains the age of twenty-one years.

3. This Trust is created upon the express understanding that the issuer or transfer agent of the Shares hereunder shall be under no liability whatsoever to see to its proper administration, and that upon the transfer of the right, title and interest in and to said Shares by any Trustee hereunder, said issuer or transfer agent shall conclusively treat the transferee as the sole owner of said Shares. In the event that any shares, cash or other property shall be distributable at any time under the terms of said Shares, the said issuer or transfer agent is fully authorized to pay, deliver and distribute the same to whosoever shall then be Trustee hereunder, and shall be under no liability to see to the proper application thereof. Until the issuer or transfer agent shall receive from some person interested in this Trust, written notice of any death or other event upon which the right to receive may depend, the issuer or transfer agent shall incur no liability for payments made in good faith to persons whose interests shall have been affected by such event. The issuer or transfer agent shall be protected in acting upon any notice or other instrument or document believed by it to be genuine and to have been signed or presented by the proper party or parties.

4. The death during my lifetime, or in a common accident or disaster with me, of the beneficiary designated hereunder shall revoke such designation, and in the former event I reserve the right to designate a new beneficiary. Should I for any reason fail to designate such new beneficiary and should no designated beneficiary be surviving, this Trust shall terminate upon my death and the trust property shall revert to my estate.

5. I hereby reserve unto myself the power and right at any time during my lifetime, before actual distribution to the beneficiary hereunder, to revoke in whole or in part or to amend the Trust hereby created without the necessity

of obtaining the consent of the beneficiary and without giving notice to the beneficiary. Any one of the following acts shall be conclusive evidence of such revocation of this Trust:

(a) The delivery to the issuer or transfer agent of the Shares by me of written notice that this Trust is revoked in whole or in part;

(b) The transfer by me of my right, title and interest in and to said Shares;

(c) The delivery by me to the issuer or transfer agent of the Shares of written notice of the death of the beneficiary hereunder.

I hereby reserve unto myself the right, upon the revocation or termination of this Trust, to create a new Trust for the benefit of any person whatsoever.

6. In the case of my death or legal incapacity, I hereby nominate and appoint as Successor Trustee hereunder whosoever shall at that time be beneficiary unless he or she shall be a minor or otherwise legally incapacitated, in either of which events I hereby nominate and appoint as Successor Trustee:

(Name)____, of

(Address)____

Number Street City State

and upon his or her failure to act (or should I for any reason fail to designate the person intended to be nominated), then and in either event I nominate and appoint as such Successor Trustee whosoever shall qualify as Executor or Administrator of my estate, as the case may be.

7. This Declaration of Trust shall extend to and be binding upon the heirs, executors, administrators and assigns of the undersigned and upon the successors to the Trustee.

8. This Declaration of Trust shall be construed and enforced in accordance with the laws of the State of

________________________.

IN WITNESS WHEREOF, I have hereunto set my hand and seal this________________day

of________________________, 19____.

(sign here)________________________L.S.

Witness: (1)________________________________

Witness: (2)________________________________

STATE OF ________________________ }
COUNTY OF ________________________ } ss: ________________________

On the________________day of____________, nineteen hundred and________________, before me came________________________, known to me to be the individual described in, and who executed the foregoing instrument, and________acknowledged that________executed the same; and in due form of law acknowledged the foregoing instrument to be________free act and deed and desired the same might be recorded as such.

WITNESS my hand and notarial seal the day and year aforesaid.

(Notary Seal) ________________________________

Notary Public

Declaration of Trust

WHEREAS, I,_____of the

City/Town of_____, County of_____, State of_____,

am the owner of certain shares of the capital stock of:

_____
(Name of Corporation)

NOW, THEREFORE, KNOW ALL MEN BY THESE PRESENTS, that I do hereby acknowledge and declare that I hold and will hold said Shares and all right, title and interest in and to said Shares IN TRUST for the following uses and purposes:

1. To hold said Shares and all right, title and interest therein for the use and benefit of:

(Name)_____, of

(Address)_____
        Number   Street   City   State

Upon my death, unless the beneficiary shall predecease me or unless we shall die as a result of a common accident or disaster, my Successor Trustee is hereby directed forthwith to transfer said Shares and all right, title and interest in and to said Shares unto the beneficiary absolutely and thereby terminate this trust; _provided,_ however, that if the beneficiary hereunder shall then be a minor, the Successor Trustee shall hold the trust assets in continuing trust until such beneficiary attains the age of twenty-one years. Prior to that date, the Successor Trustee may apply or expend any or all of the income or principal for the maintenance, education and support of the minor beneficiary without the intervention of any guardian and without application to any court. Such payments of income or principal may be made to the parents of such minor or to the person with whom the minor is living without any liability upon the Successor Trustee to see to the application thereof. If such minor survives me but dies before attaining the age of twenty-one years, at his or her death the Successor Trustee shall deliver, pay over, transfer and distribute the trust property to such minor's personal representatives, absolutely.

2. I reserve the right to register any shares held hereunder in the name of a nominee, which nominee may be myself as an individual, or to pledge the shares as collateral for a loan. The right, power and authority is hereby conferred upon any Successor Trustee hereunder, at any time during the minority of the beneficiary, to invest and reinvest without limitation or restriction, to sell all or any part of the Shares being held, holding either Shares or the proceeds of the sale thereof until the minor beneficiary attains the age of twenty-one years.

3. This Trust is created upon the express understanding that the issuer or transfer agent of the Shares hereunder shall be under no liability whatsoever to see to its proper administration, and that upon the transfer of the right, title and interest in and to said Shares by any Trustee hereunder, said issuer or transfer agent shall conclusively treat the transferee as the sole owner of said Shares. In the event that any shares, cash or other property shall be distributable at any time under the terms of said Shares, the said issuer or transfer agent is fully authorized to pay, deliver and distribute the same to whosoever shall then be Trustee hereunder, and shall be under no liability to see to the proper application thereof. Until the issuer or transfer agent shall receive from some person interested in this Trust, written notice of any death or other event upon which the right to receive may depend, the issuer or transfer agent shall incur no liability for payments made in good faith to persons whose interests shall have been affected by such event. The issuer or transfer agent shall be protected in acting upon any notice or other instrument or document believed by it to be genuine and to have been signed or presented by the proper party or parties.

4. The death during my lifetime, or in a common accident or disaster with me, of the beneficiary designated hereunder shall revoke such designation, and in the former event I reserve the right to designate a new beneficiary. Should I for any reason fail to designate such new beneficiary and should no designated beneficiary be surviving, this Trust shall terminate upon my death and the trust property shall revert to my estate.

5. I hereby reserve unto myself the power and right at any time during my lifetime, before actual distribution to the beneficiary hereunder, to revoke in whole or in part or to amend the Trust hereby created without the necessity

of obtaining the consent of the beneficiary and without giving notice to the beneficiary. Any one of the following acts shall be conclusive evidence of such revocation of this Trust:

> (a) The delivery to the issuer or transfer agent of the Shares by me of written notice that this Trust is revoked in whole or in part;
>
> (b) The transfer by me of my right, title and interest in and to said Shares;
>
> (c) The delivery by me to the issuer or transfer agent of the Shares of written notice of the death of the beneficiary hereunder.

I hereby reserve unto myself the right, upon the revocation or termination of this Trust, to create a new Trust for the benefit of any person whatsover.

6. In the case of my death or legal incapacity, I hereby nominate and appoint as Successor Trustee hereunder whosoever shall at that time be beneficiary unless he or she shall be a minor or otherwise legally incapacitated, in either of which events I hereby nominate and appoint as Successor Trustee:

(Name)_____, of

(Address)_____

| Number | Street | City | State |

and upon his or her failure to act (or should I for any reason fail to designate the person intended to be nominated), then and in either event I nominate and appoint as such Successor Trustee whosoever shall qualify as Executor or Administrator of my estate, as the case may be.

7. This Declaration of Trust shall extend to and be binding upon the heirs, executors, administrators and assigns of the undersigned and upon the successors to the Trustee.

8. This Declaration of Trust shall be construed and enforced in accordance with the laws of the State of

_____.

IN WITNESS WHEREOF, I have hereunto set my hand and seal this_____day

of_____, 19____.

(sign here)_____L.S.

Witness: (1)_____

Witness: (2)_____

STATE OF_____

COUNTY OF_____ } ss: _____

On the_____day of_____, nineteen hundred and_____, before

me came_____, known to me to be the individual described in, and who executed

the foregoing instrument, and_____acknowledged that_____executed the same; and in due form of law

acknowledged the foregoing instrument to be_____free act and deed and desired the same might be recorded as such.

WITNESS my hand and notarial seal the day and year aforesaid.

(Notary Seal)   _____

                                          Notary Public

DECLARATION OF TRUST
FOR NAMING
ONE PRIMARY BENEFICIARY
AND
ONE CONTINGENT BENEFICIARY
TO RECEIVE
STOCKS

Instructions:

On the following pages will be found duplicate copies of a declaration of trust (DT-14) which will be suitable for use in connection with the inter vivos trust arrangement suggested in Chapter 8 where it is desired to name some *one* person as primary beneficiary, with some *one* other person as contingent beneficiary to receive corporate stocks if the primary beneficiary does not survive.

Cross out *"city"* or *"town"*, leaving the appropriate designation of your community.

Enter the name of the corporation whose stock is involved in the space provided near the top, and the names of the beneficiaries in the appropriate places in Paragraph 1.

Instruct your broker to register the shares *"(Your Name), Trustee u/d/t dated_____"*. It will not be necessary to file the declaration of trust with the company or its transfer agent at the time you purchase the stock. However, if and when you decide to sell it at some future date, the transfer agent will most certainly require that you display the instrument. In the circumstances, the safest thing to do is to staple it to the stock certificate when the latter is issued.

Whenever there is any possibility of a minor child receiving the property, make certain that you name an adult who can act as trustee for the child. The name of that adult should be inserted in Paragraph 6 of the instrument shown here. Avoid naming as trustee a person not likely to survive until the child has reached age 21.

Declaration of Trust

of the

WHEREAS, I, __John J. Smith__,

~~City~~/Town of __Jonesville__, County of __Fairfax__, State of __Connecticut__,

am the owner of certain shares of the capital stock of:

__The Ajax Tool & Die Corporation__

(Name of Corporation)

NOW, THEREFORE, KNOW ALL MEN BY THESE PRESENTS, that I do hereby acknowledge and declare that I hold and will hold said Shares and all right, title and interest in and to said Shares IN TRUST for the following uses and purposes:

1. To hold said Shares and all right, title and interest therein for the use and benefit of:

(Name) __Mary A. Smith__ __(my niece)__ __Jonesville__ __Connecticut__, of
City State

(Address) __750__ __Porter Street__
Number Street

or, if he or she be not surviving, for the use and benefit of

(Name) __William B. Connors__ __(my nephew)__ __Jonesville__ __Connecticut__, of
City State

(Address) __250__ __County Street__
Number Street

Upon my death, unless the beneficiaries shall predecease me or unless we shall die as a result of a common accident or disaster, my Successor Trustee is hereby directed forthwith to transfer said Shares and all right, title and interest in and to said Shares unto the beneficiary absolutely and thereby terminate this trust; *provided*, however, that if the beneficiary hereunder shall then be a minor, the Successor Trustee shall hold the trust assets in continuing trust until such beneficiary attains the age of twenty-one years. Prior to that date, the Successor Trustee may apply or expend any or all of the income or principal for the maintenance, education and support of the minor beneficiary without the intervention of any guardian and without application to any court. Such payments of income or principal may be made to the parents of such minor or to the person with whom the minor is living without any liability upon the Successor Trustee to see to the application thereof. If such minor survives me but dies before attaining the age of twenty-one years, at his or her death the Successor Trustee shall deliver, pay over, transfer and distribute the trust property to such minor's personal representatives, absolutely.

2. I reserve the right to register any shares held hereunder in the name of a nominee, which nominee may be myself as an individual. The right, power and authority is hereby conferred upon any Successor Trustee hereunder, at any time during the minority of the beneficiary, to invest and reinvest without limitation or restriction, to sell all or any part of the Shares being held, holding either Shares or the proceeds of the sale thereof until the minor beneficiary attains the age of twenty-one years.

3. This Trust is created upon the express understanding that the issuer or transfer agent of the Shares hereunder shall be under no liability whatsoever to see to its proper administration, and that upon the transfer of the right, title and interest in and to said Shares by any Trustee hereunder, said issuer or transfer agent shall conclusively treat the transferee as the sole owner of said Shares. In the event that any shares, cash or other property shall be distributable at any time under the terms of said Shares, the said issuer or transfer agent is fully authorized to pay, deliver and distribute the same to whosoever shall then be Trustee hereunder, and shall be under no liability to see to the proper application thereof. Until the issuer or transfer agent shall receive from some person interested in this Trust, written notice of any death or other event upon which the right to receive may depend, the issuer or transfer agent shall incur no liability for payments made in good faith to persons whose interests shall have been affected by such event. The issuer or transfer agent shall be protected in acting upon any notice or other instrument or document believed by it to be genuine and to have been signed or presented by the proper party or parties.

4. The death during my lifetime, or in a common accident or disaster with me, of any beneficiary designated hereunder shall revoke such designation, and in the former event I reserve the right to designate a new beneficiary. Should I for any reason fail to designate such new beneficiary and should no designated beneficiary be surviving, this Trust shall terminate upon my death and the trust property shall revert to my estate.

... the right, upo... ...cation or termination o... ...to create a new ... ...nefit of ... ...here... any person whatsoever.

6. In the case of my death or legal incapacity, I hereby nominate and appoint as Successor Trustee hereunder whosoever shall at that time be beneficiary unless he or she shall be a minor or otherwise legally incapacitated, in either of which events I hereby nominate and appoint as Successor Trustee:

(Name) __Henry P. Adams__ __Jonesville__ __Connecticut__, of
City State

(Address) __125__ __Barnum Street__
Number Street

and upon his or her failure to act (or should I for any reason fail to designate the person intended to be nominated), then and in either event I nominate and appoint as such Successor Trustee whosoever shall qualify as Executor or Administrator of my estate, as the case may be.

7. This Declaration of Trust shall extend to and be binding upon the heirs, executors, administrators and assigns of the undersigned and upon the successors to the Trustee.

8. This Declaration of Trust shall be construed and enforced in accordance with the laws of the State of __Connecticut__.

Declaration of Trust

WHEREAS, I,_____of the

City/Town of_____, County of_____, State of_____,

am the owner of certain shares of the capital stock of:

_____

(Name of Corporation)

NOW, THEREFORE, KNOW ALL MEN BY THESE PRESENTS, that I do hereby acknowledge and declare that I hold and will hold said Shares and all right, title and interest in and to said Shares IN TRUST for the following uses and purposes:

1. To hold said Shares and all right, title and interest therein for the use and benefit of:

(Name)_____, of

(Address)_____

     Number   Street   City   State

or, if he or she be not surviving, for the use and benefit of

(Name)_____, of

(Address)_____

     Number   Street   City   State

Upon my death, unless the beneficiaries shall predecease me or unless we shall die as a result of a common accident or disaster, my Successor Trustee is hereby directed forthwith to transfer said Shares and all right, title and interest in and to said Shares unto the beneficiary absolutely and thereby terminate this trust; *provided,* however, that if the beneficiary hereunder shall then be a minor, the Successor Trustee shall hold the trust assets in continuing trust until such beneficiary attains the age of twenty-one years. Prior to that date, the Successor Trustee may apply or expend any or all of the income or principal for the maintenance, education and support of the minor beneficiary without the intervention of any guardian and without application to any court. Such payments of income or principal may be made to the parents of such minor or to the person with whom the minor is living without any liability upon the Successor Trustee to see to the application thereof. If such minor survives me but dies before attaining the age of twenty-one years, at his or her death the Successor Trustee shall deliver, pay over, transfer and distribute the trust property to such minor's personal representatives, absolutely.

2. I reserve the right to register any shares held hereunder in the name of a nominee, which nominee may be myself as an individual, or to pledge the shares as collateral for a loan. The right, power and authority is hereby conferred upon any Successor Trustee hereunder, at any time during the minority of the beneficiary, to invest and reinvest without limitation or restriction, to sell all or any part of the Shares being held, holding either Shares or the proceeds of the sale thereof until the minor beneficiary attains the age of twenty-one years.

3. This Trust is created upon the express understanding that the issuer or transfer agent of the Shares hereunder shall be under no liability whatsoever to see to its proper administration, and that upon the transfer of the right, title and interest in and to said Shares by any Trustee hereunder, said issuer or transfer agent shall conclusively treat the transferee as the sole owner of said Shares. In the event that any shares, cash or other property shall be distributable at any time under the terms of said Shares, the said issuer or transfer agent is fully authorized to pay, deliver and distribute the same to whosoever shall then be Trustee hereunder, and shall be under no liability to see to the proper application thereof. Until the issuer or transfer agent shall receive from some person interested in this Trust, written notice of any death or other event upon which the right to receive may depend, the issuer or transfer agent shall incur no liability for payments made in good faith to persons whose interests shall have been affected by such event. The issuer or transfer agent shall be protected in acting upon any notice or other instrument or document believed by it to be genuine and to have been signed or presented by the proper party or parties.

4. The death during my lifetime, or in a common accident or disaster with me, of any beneficiary designated hereunder shall revoke such designation, and in the former event I reserve the right to designate a new beneficiary. Should I for any reason fail to designate such new beneficiary and should no designated beneficiary be surviving, this Trust shall terminate upon my death and the trust property shall revert to my estate.

5. I hereby reserve unto myself the power and right at any time during my lifetime, before actual distribution to the beneficiary hereunder, to revoke in whole or in part or to amend the Trust hereby created without the necessity of obtaining the consent of either beneficiary and without giving notice to either beneficiary. Any one of the following acts shall be conclusive evidence of such revocation of this Trust:

    (a) The delivery to the issuer or transfer agent of the Shares by me of written notice that this Trust is revoked in whole or in part;

    (b) The transfer by me of my right, title and interest in and to said Shares;

    (c) The delivery by me to the issuer or transfer agent of the Shares of written notice of the death of the beneficiary hereunder.

I hereby reserve unto myself the right, upon the revocation or termination of this Trust, to create a new Trust for the benefit of any person whatsoever.

6. In the case of my death or legal incapacity, I hereby nominate and appoint as Successor Trustee hereunder whosoever shall at that time be beneficiary unless he or she shall be a minor or otherwise legally incapacitated, in either of which events I hereby nominate and appoint as Successor Trustee:

(Name)_____, of

(Address)_____
          Number   Street   City   State

and upon his or her failure to act (or should I for any reason fail to designate the person intended to be nominated), then and in either event I nominate and appoint as such Successor Trustee whosoever shall qualify as Executor or Administrator of my estate, as the case may be.

7. This Declaration of Trust shall extend to and be binding upon the heirs, executors, administrators and assigns of the undersigned and upon the successors to the Trustee.

8. This Declaration of Trust shall be construed and enforced in accordance with the laws of the State of

_____.

IN WITNESS WHEREOF I have hereunto set my hand and seal this_____day

of_____, 19_____.

(sign here)_____L.S.

Witness: (1)_____

Witness: (2)_____

STATE OF _____
                       }ss: _____
COUNTY OF _____

On the_____day of_____, nineteen hundred and_____, before

me came_____known to me to be the individual described in, and who executed

the foregoing instrument, and_____acknowledged that_____executed the same; and in due form of law

acknowledged the foregoing instrument to be_____act and deed and desired the same might be recorded as such.

WITNESS my hand and notarial seal the day and year aforesaid.

(Notary Seal)   _____
                                     Notary Public

Declaration of Trust

WHEREAS, I,_____of the

City/Town of_____, County of_____, State of_____,

am the owner of certain shares of the capital stock of:

_____

(Name of Corporation)

NOW, THEREFORE, KNOW ALL MEN BY THESE PRESENTS, that I do hereby acknowledge and declare that I hold and will hold said Shares and all right, title and interest in and to said Shares IN TRUST for the following uses and purposes:

1. To hold said Shares and all right, title and interest therein for the use and benefit of:

(Name)_____, of

(Address)_____
          Number   Street   City   State

or, if he or she be not surviving, for the use and benefit of

(Name)_____, of

(Address)_____
          Number   Street   City   State

Upon my death, unless the beneficiaries shall predecease me or unless we shall die as a result of a common accident or disaster, my Successor Trustee is hereby directed forthwith to transfer said Shares and all right, title and interest in and to said Shares unto the beneficiary absolutely and thereby terminate this trust; *provided,* however, that if the beneficiary hereunder shall then be a minor, the Successor Trustee shall hold the trust assets in continuing trust until such beneficiary attains the age of twenty-one years. Prior to that date, the Successor Trustee may apply or expend any or all of the income or principal for the maintenance, education and support of the minor beneficiary without the intervention of any guardian and without application to any court. Such payments of income or principal may be made to the parents of such minor or to the person with whom the minor is living without any liability upon the Successor Trustee to see to the application thereof. If such minor survives me but dies before attaining the age of twenty-one years, at his or her death the Successor Trustee shall deliver, pay over, transfer and distribute the trust property to such minor's personal representatives, absolutely.

2. I reserve the right to register any shares held hereunder in the name of a nominee, which nominee may be myself as an individual, or to pledge the shares as collateral for a loan. The right, power and authority is hereby conferred upon any Successor Trustee hereunder, at any time during the minority of the beneficiary, to invest and reinvest without limitation or restriction, to sell all or any part of the Shares being held, holding either Shares or the proceeds of the sale thereof until the minor beneficiary attains the age of twenty-one years.

3. This Trust is created upon the express understanding that the issuer or transfer agent of the Shares hereunder shall be under no liability whatsoever to see to its proper administration, and that upon the transfer of the right, title and interest in and to said Shares by any Trustee hereunder, said issuer or transfer agent shall conclusively treat the transferee as the sole owner of said Shares. In the event that any shares, cash or other property shall be distributable at any time under the terms of said Shares, the said issuer or transfer agent is fully authorized to pay, deliver and distribute the same to whosoever shall then be Trustee hereunder, and shall be under no liability to see to the proper application thereof. Until the issuer or transfer agent shall receive from some person interested in this Trust, written notice of any death or other event upon which the right to receive may depend, the issuer or transfer agent shall incur no liability for payments made in good faith to persons whose interests shall have been affected by such event. The issuer or transfer agent shall be protected in acting upon any notice or other instrument or document believed by it to be genuine and to have been signed or presented by the proper party or parties.

4. The death during my lifetime, or in a common accident or disaster with me, of any beneficiary designated hereunder shall revoke such designation, and in the former event I reserve the right to designate a new beneficiary. Should I for any reason fail to designate such new beneficiary and should no designated beneficiary be surviving, this Trust shall terminate upon my death and the trust property shall revert to my estate.

5. I hereby reserve unto myself the power and right at any time during my lifetime, before actual distribution to the beneficiary hereunder, to revoke in whole or in part or to amend the Trust hereby created without the necessity of obtaining the consent of either beneficiary and without giving notice to either beneficiary. Any one of the following acts shall be conclusive evidence of such revocation of this Trust:

    (a) The delivery to the issuer or transfer agent of the Shares by me of written notice that this Trust is revoked in whole or in part;

    (b) The transfer by me of my right, title and interest in and to said Shares;

    (c) The delivery by me to the issuer or transfer agent of the Shares of written notice of the death of the beneficiary hereunder.

I hereby reserve unto myself the right, upon the revocation or termination of this Trust, to create a new Trust for the benefit of any person whatsoever.

6. In the case of my death or legal incapacity, I hereby nominate and appoint as Successor Trustee hereunder whosoever shall at that time be beneficiary unless he or she shall be a minor or otherwise legally incapacitated, in either of which events I hereby nominate and appoint as Successor Trustee:

(Name)_____, of

(Address)_____

            Number   Street   City   State

and upon his or her failure to act (or should I for any reason fail to designate the person intended to be nominated), then and in either event I nominate and appoint as such Successor Trustee whosoever shall qualify as Executor or Administrator of my estate, as the case may be.

7. This Declaration of Trust shall extend to and be binding upon the heirs, executors, administrators and assigns of the undersigned and upon the successors to the Trustee.

8. This Declaration of Trust shall be construed and enforced in accordance with the laws of the State of

_____.

    IN WITNESS WHEREOF I have hereunto set my hand and seal this_____day

of_____, 19_____.

                             (sign here)_____L.S.

Witness: (1)_____

Witness: (2)_____

STATE OF _____ ⎫
                                    ⎬ ss: _____
COUNTY OF _____ ⎭

    On the_____day of_____, nineteen hundred and_____, before

me came_____known to me to be the individual described in, and who executed

the foregoing instrument, and_____acknowledged that_____executed the same; and in due form of law

acknowledged the foregoing instrument to be_____act and deed and desired the same might be recorded as such.

    WITNESS my hand and notarial seal the day and year aforesaid.

    (Notary Seal)   _____
                                              Notary Public

DECLARATION OF TRUST
FOR NAMING
TWO OR MORE BENEFICIARIES, SHARING EQUALLY
TO RECEIVE
STOCKS

Instructions:

On the following pages will be found duplicate copies of a declaration of trust (DT-15) which will be suitable for use in connection with the inter vivos trust arrangement suggested in Chapter 8 where it is desired to name several persons, sharing equally, to receive corporate stocks upon the death of the owner.

Cross out *"city"* or *"town"*, leaving the appropriate designation of your community.

Enter the name of the corporation whose stock is involved in the space provided near the top.

In Paragraph 1, indicate the *number* of *persons* you are naming (to discourage unauthorized additions to the list) and then insert their names. The one whose name appears *first* will be the successor trustee responsible for seeing to the distribution of the trust property.

Note that the instrument specifies that the named beneficiaries are to receive *"in equal shares, or the survivor of them/per stirpes"*. Now, think carefully: If you have named your three brothers with the understanding that if one brother predeceases you, his children will take *his* share, cross out *"or the survivor of them"* and initial it. If that is *not* what you want—if, for example, you prefer that the share of your deceased brother be divided by your two surviving brothers, cross out *"per stirpes"* and initial it. Remember, you <u>must</u> cross out *"or the survivor of them"* or *"per stirpes"* —one or the other.

Instruct your broker to register the shares *"(Your Name), Trustee u/d/t dated_____"*. It will not be necessary to file the declaration of trust with the company or its transfer agent at the time you purchase the stock. However, if and when you decide to sell it at some future date, the transfer agent will most certainly require that you display the instrument. If you die, the beneficiary will be required to produce it in order to obtain possession of the stock. In the circumstances, the safest thing to do is to staple it to the stock certificate when the latter is issued.

Whenever there is any possibility of a minor child receiving any portion of the stock owned, make certain that you name an adult who can act as trustee for him. The name of that adult should be inserted in Paragraph 6 of the instrument shown here. Avoid naming as trustee a person not likely to survive until the child has reached age 21.

Declaration of Trust

of the

WHEREAS, I, **John J. Smith**, State of **Connecticut**,

~~City~~ Town of **Jonesville**, County of **Fairfax**

am the owner of certain shares of the capital stock of:

The Ajax Tool & Die Corporation

(Name of Corporation)

NOW, THEREFORE, KNOW ALL MEN BY THESE PRESENTS, that I do hereby acknowledge and declare that I hold and will hold said Shares and all right, title and interest in and to said Shares IN TRUST for the following uses and purposes:

1. To hold said Shares and all right, title and interest therein for the use and benefit of the following **three** persons, in equal shares, or the survivor of them/ *J.J.S.*

Thomas B. Smith	**(my brother)**
William R. Smith	**(my brother)**
Charles M. Smith	**(my brother)**

Upon my death, unless all of the beneficiaries shall predecease me or unless we shall die as a result of a common accident or disaster, my Successor Trustee is hereby directed forthwith to transfer said Shares and all right, title and interest in and to said Shares unto the beneficiaries absolutely and thereby terminate this trust; *provided*, however, that if any beneficiary hereunder shall then be a minor, the Successor Trustee shall hold such minor's share of the trust assets in continuing trust until such beneficiary attains the age of twenty-one years. Prior to that date, the Successor Trustee may apply or expend any or all of the income or principal of such minor's share for the maintenance, education and support of the minor beneficiary without the intervention of any guardian and without application to any court. Such payments of income or principal may be made to the parents of such minor or to the person with whom the minor is living without any liability upon the Successor Trustee to see to the application thereof. If such minor survives me but dies before attaining the age of twenty-one years, at his or her death the Successor Trustee shall deliver, pay over, transfer and distribute the trust property to such minor's personal representatives, absolutely.

2. I reserve the right to register any shares held hereunder in the name of a nominee, which nominee may be myself as an individual. The right, power and authority is hereby conferred upon any Successor Trustee hereunder, at any time during the minority of the beneficiary, to invest and reinvest without limitation or restriction, to sell all or any part of the Shares being held, holding either Shares or the proceeds of the sale thereof until the minor beneficiary attains the age of twenty-one years.

3. This Trust is created upon the express understanding that the issuer or transfer agent of the Shares hereunder shall be under no liability whatsoever to see to its proper administration, and that upon the transfer of the right, title and interest in and to said Shares by any Trustee hereunder, said issuer or transfer agent shall conclusively treat the transferee as the sole owner of said Shares. In the event that any shares, cash or other property shall be distributable at any time under the terms of said Shares, the said issuer or transfer agent is fully authorized to pay, deliver and distribute the same to whosoever shall then be Trustee hereunder, and shall be under no liability to see to the proper application thereof. Until the issuer or transfer agent shall receive from some person interested in this Trust, written notice of any death or other event upon which the right to receive may depend, the issuer or transfer agent shall incur no liability for payments made in good faith to persons whose interests shall have been affected by such event. The issuer or transfer agent shall be protected in acting upon any notice or other instrument or document believed by it to be genuine and to have been signed or presented by the proper party or parties.

(c) The delivery by me to the issuer or transfer agent of the Shares of written ... of the ... y hereunder.

I hereby reserve unto myself the right, upon the revocation or termination of this Trust, to create a new Trust for the benefit of any person whatsoever.

6. In the case of my death or legal incapacity, I hereby nominate and appoint as Successor Trustee hereunder the beneficiary first above named unless he or she shall be a minor or otherwise legally incapacitated, in which event, I hereby nominate and appoint as Successor Trustee hereunder the beneficiary whose name appears second above. If such beneficiary named second above shall be a minor or legally incompetent, then I nominate and appoint as Successor Trustee:

(Name) **Henry P. Adams** **Jonesville** **Connecticut**

City State

(Address) **125** **Barnum Street**

Number Street

7. This Declaration of Trust shall extend to and be binding upon the heirs, executors, administrators and assigns of the undersigned and upon the successors to the Trustee.

8. This Declaration of Trust shall be construed and enforced in accordance with the laws of the State of **Connecticut**.

WHEREAS, I,_____of the

City/Town of_____, County of_____, State of_____,

am the owner of certain shares of the capital stock of:

_____
(Name of Corporation)

NOW, THEREFORE, KNOW ALL MEN BY THESE PRESENTS, that I do hereby acknowledge and declare that I hold and will hold said Shares and all right, title and interest in and to said Shares IN TRUST for the following uses and purposes:

1. To hold said Shares and all right, title and interest therein for the use and benefit of the following

_____persons, in equal shares, or the survivor of them/per stirpes.

Upon my death, unless all of the beneficiaries shall predecease me or unless we shall die as a result of a common accident or disaster, my Successor Trustee is hereby directed forthwith to transfer said Shares and all right, title and interest in and to said Shares unto the beneficiaries absolutely and thereby terminate this trust; *provided,* however, that if any beneficiary hereunder shall then be a minor, the Successor Trustee shall hold such beneficiary's share of the trust assets in continuing trust until such beneficiary attains the age of twenty-one years. Prior to that date, the Successor Trustee may apply or expend any or all of the income or principal of such minor's share for the maintenance, education and support of the minor beneficiary without the intervention of any guardian and without application to any court. Such payments of income or principal may be made to the parents of such minor or to the person with whom the minor is living without any liability upon the Successor Trustee to see to the application thereof. If such minor survives me but dies before attaining the age of twenty-one years, at his or her death the Successor Trustee shall deliver, pay over, transfer and distribute the trust property to such minor's personal representatives, absolutely.

2. I reserve the right to register any shares held hereunder in the name of a nominee, which nominee may be myself as an individual, or to pledge the shares as collateral for a loan. The right, power and authority is hereby conferred upon any Successor Trustee hereunder, at any time during the minority of the beneficiary, to invest and reinvest without limitation or restriction, to sell all or any part of the Shares being held, holding either Shares or the proceeds of the sale thereof until the minor beneficiary attains the age of twenty-one years.

3. This Trust is created upon the express understanding that the issuer or transfer agent of the Shares hereunder shall be under no liability whatsoever to see to its proper administration, and that upon the transfer of the right, title and interest in and to said Shares by any Trustee hereunder, said issuer or transfer agent shall conclusively treat the transferee as the sole owner of said Shares. In the event that any shares, cash or other property shall be distributable at any time under the terms of said Shares, the said issuer or transfer agent is fully authorized to pay, deliver and distribute the same to whosoever shall then be Trustee hereunder, and shall be under no liability to see to the proper application thereof. Until the issuer or transfer agent shall receive from some person interested in this Trust, written notice of any death or other event upon which the right to receive may depend, the issuer or transfer agent shall incur no liability for payments made in good faith to persons whose interests shall have been affected by such event. The issuer or transfer agent shall be protected in acting upon any notice or other instrument or document believed by it to be genuine and to have been signed or presented by the proper party or parties.

4. The death during my lifetime, or in a common accident or disaster with me, of any beneficiary designated hereunder shall revoke such designation, and in the former event I reserve the right to designate a new beneficiary. Should no designated beneficiary be surviving, this Trust shall terminate upon my death and the trust property shall revert to my estate.

5. I hereby reserve unto myself the power and right at any time during my lifetime, before actual distribution to the beneficiaries hereunder, to revoke in whole or in part or to amend the Trust hereby created without the necessity of obtaining the consent of the beneficiaries and without giving notice to the beneficiaries. Any one of the following acts shall be conclusive evidence of such revocation of this Trust:

    (a) The delivery to the issuer or transfer agent of the Shares by me of written notice that this Trust is revoked in whole or in part;

    (b) The transfer by me of my right, title and interest in and to said Shares;

    (c) The delivery by me to the issuer or transfer agent of the Shares of written notice of the death of the beneficiary hereunder.

I hereby reserve unto myself the right, upon the revocation or termination of this Trust, to create a new Trust for the benefit of any person whatsoever.

6. In the case of my death or legal incapacity, I hereby nominate and appoint as Successor Trustee hereunder the beneficiary first above named unless he or she shall be a minor or otherwise legally incapacitated, in which event, I hereby nominate and appoint as Successor Trustee hereunder the beneficiary whose name appears second above. If such beneficiary named second above shall be a minor or legally incompetent, then I nominate and appoint as Successor Trustee:

(Name)_____, of

(Address)_____
          Number   Street   City   State

7. This Declaration of Trust shall extend to and be binding upon the heirs, executors, administrators and assigns of the undersigned and upon the successors to the Trustee.

8. This Declaration of Trust shall be construed and enforced in accordance with the laws of the State of

_____.

IN WITNESS WHEREOF I have hereunto set my hand and seal this_____day

of_____, 19____.

                         (sign here)_____L.S.

Witness: (1)_____

Witness: (2)_____

STATE OF _____ ⎫
                          ⎬ ss: _____
COUNTY OF _____ ⎭

On the_____day of_____, nineteen hundred and_____, before

me came_____known to me to be the individual described in, and who executed

the foregoing instrument,_____acknowledged that_____executed the same; and in due form of law

acknowledged the foregoing instrument to be_____act and deed and desired the same might be recorded as such.

    WITNESS my hand and notarial seal the day and year aforesaid.

(Notary Seal)   _____
                                            Notary Public

Declaration of Trust

WHEREAS, I,_____of the

City/Town of_____, County of_____, State of_____,

am the owner of certain shares of the capital stock of:

_____

(Name of Corporation)

NOW, THEREFORE, KNOW ALL MEN BY THESE PRESENTS, that I do hereby acknowledge and declare that I hold and will hold said Shares and all right, title and interest in and to said Shares IN TRUST for the following uses and purposes:

1. To hold said Shares and all right, title and interest therein for the use and benefit of the following

_____persons, in equal shares, or the survivor of them/per stirpes.

Upon my death, unless all of the beneficiaries shall predecease me or unless we shall die as a result of a common accident or disaster, my Successor Trustee is hereby directed forthwith to transfer said Shares and all right, title and interest in and to said Shares unto the beneficiaries absolutely and thereby terminate this trust; *provided,* however, that if any beneficiary hereunder shall then be a minor, the Successor Trustee shall hold such beneficiary's share of the trust assets in continuing trust until such beneficiary attains the age of twenty-one years. Prior to that date, the Successor Trustee may apply or expend any or all of the income or principal of such minor's share for the maintenance, education and support of the minor beneficiary without the intervention of any guardian and without application to any court. Such payments of income or principal may be made to the parents of such minor or to the person with whom the minor is living without any liability upon the Successor Trustee to see to the application thereof. If such minor survives me but dies before attaining the age of twenty-one years, at his or her death the Successor Trustee shall deliver, pay over, transfer and distribute the trust property to such minor's personal representatives, absolutely.

2. I reserve the right to register any shares held hereunder in the name of a nominee, which nominee may be myself as an individual, or to pledge the shares as collateral for a loan. The right, power and authority is hereby conferred upon any Successor Trustee hereunder, at any time during the minority of the beneficiary, to invest and reinvest without limitation or restriction, to sell all or any part of the Shares being held, holding either Shares or the proceeds of the sale thereof until the minor beneficiary attains the age of twenty-one years.

3. This Trust is created upon the express understanding that the issuer or transfer agent of the Shares hereunder shall be under no liability whatsoever to see to its proper administration, and that upon the transfer of the right, title and interest in and to said Shares by any Trustee hereunder, said issuer or transfer agent shall conclusively treat the transferee as the sole owner of said Shares. In the event that any shares, cash or other property shall be distributable at any time under the terms of said Shares, the said issuer or transfer agent is fully authorized to pay, deliver and distribute the same to whosoever shall then be Trustee hereunder, and shall be under no liability to see to the proper application thereof. Until the issuer or transfer agent shall receive from some person interested in this Trust, written notice of any death or other event upon which the right to receive may depend, the issuer or transfer agent shall incur no liability for payments made in good faith to persons whose interests shall have been affected by such event. The issuer or transfer agent shall be protected in acting upon any notice or other instrument or document believed by it to be genuine and to have been signed or presented by the proper party or parties.

4. The death during my lifetime, or in a common accident or disaster with me, of any beneficiary designated hereunder shall revoke such designation, and in the former event I reserve the right to designate a new beneficiary. Should no designated beneficiary be surviving, this Trust shall terminate upon my death and the trust property shall revert to my estate.

5. I hereby reserve unto myself the power and right at any time during my lifetime, before actual distribution to the beneficiaries hereunder, to revoke in whole or in part or to amend the Trust hereby created without the necessity of obtaining the consent of the beneficiaries and without giving notice to the beneficiaries. Any one of the following acts shall be conclusive evidence of such revocation of this Trust:

    (a) The delivery to the issuer or transfer agent of the Shares by me of written notice that this Trust is revoked in whole or in part;

    (b) The transfer by me of my right, title and interest in and to said Shares;

    (c) The delivery by me to the issuer or transfer agent of the Shares of written notice of the death of the beneficiary hereunder.

I hereby reserve unto myself the right, upon the revocation or termination of this Trust, to create a new Trust for the benefit of any person whatsoever.

6. In the case of my death or legal incapacity, I hereby nominate and appoint as Successor Trustee hereunder the beneficiary first above named unless he or she shall be a minor or otherwise legally incapacitated, in which event, I hereby nominate and appoint as Successor Trustee hereunder the beneficiary whose name appears second above. If such beneficiary named second above shall be a minor or legally incompetent, then I nominate and appoint as Successor Trustee:

(Name)_____, of

(Address)_____

     Number   Street   City   State

7. This Declaration of Trust shall extend to and be binding upon the heirs, executors, administrators and assigns of the undersigned and upon the successors to the Trustee.

8. This Declaration of Trust shall be construed and enforced in accordance with the laws of the State of

_____.

IN WITNESS WHEREOF I have hereunto set my hand and seal this_____day

of_____, 19____.

(sign here)_____L.S.

Witness: (1)_____

Witness: (2)_____

STATE OF _____

                         } ss: _____

COUNTY OF _____

On the_____day of_____, nineteen hundred and_____, before

me came_____known to me to be the individual described in, and who executed

the foregoing instrument,_____acknowledged that_____executed the same; and in due form of law

acknowledged the foregoing instrument to be_____act and deed and desired the same might be recorded as such.

WITNESS my hand and notarial seal the day and year aforesaid.

(Notary Seal)   _____

                                        Notary Public

```
┌─────────────────────────────────────────────┐
│                                             │
│         DECLARATION  OF  TRUST              │
│                 FOR NAMING                  │
│      ONE PRIMARY BENEFICIARY WITH           │
│    YOUR CHILDREN, SHARING EQUALLY,          │
│     AS  CONTINGENT  BENEFICIARIES           │
│                TO RECEIVE                    │
│                 STOCKS                      │
│                                             │
└─────────────────────────────────────────────┘
```

Instructions:

On the following pages will be found duplicate copies of a declaration of trust (DT-16) which will be suitable for use in connection with the inter vivos trust arrangement suggested in Chapter 8 where it is desired to name one person (ordinarily, one's spouse) as primary beneficiary, with one's children as contingent beneficiaries to receive corporate stocks upon the death of the owner.

Cross out *"city"* or *"town"*, leaving the appropriate designation of your community.

Enter the name of the corporation whose stock is involved in the space provided near the top.

Enter the name of the primary beneficiary in the appropriate place in Paragraph 1. Note that the instrument refers to your children as *"natural not/or adopted"*. Now, decide: If you have an adopted child and you wish to *include* him, cross out the word *"not"* in the phrase *"natural not/or adopted"* and initial it. If you wish to *exclude* your adopted child, cross out the word *"or"* in the same phrase and initial it. Remember, you <u>must</u> cross out *"not"* or *"or"*—one or the other.

Note next that the instrument specifies that your children are to receive *"in equal shares, or the survivor of them/per stirpes"*. Now, think carefully: If it is your wish that if one of your children does not survive you, his share will revert to *his* children in equal shares, cross out *"or the survivor of them"* and initial it. If that is *not* what you want—if, for example, you prefer that the share of your deceased child be divided among your surviving children, cross out *"per stirpes"* and initial it. Remember, you <u>must</u> cross out *"or the survivor of them"* or *"per stirpes"*—one or the other.

Instruct your broker to register the shares *"(Your Name), Trustee u/d/t dated_____"*. It will not be necessary to file the declaration of trust with the company or its transfer agent at the time you purchase the stock. However, if and when you decide to sell it at some future date, the transfer agent will most certainly require that you display the instrument. If you die, the beneficiary will be required to produce it in order to obtain possession of the stock. In the circumstances, the safest thing to do is to staple it to the stock certificate when the latter is issued.

Whenever there is any possibility of a minor child receiving any portion of the stock owned, make certain that you name an adult who can act as trustee for him. The name of that adult should be inserted in Paragraph 6 of the instrument shown here. Avoid naming as trustee a person not likely to survive until the child reaches age 21.

Declaration of Trust

WHEREAS, I, _____John J. Smith_____ of the

City/Town of ____Jonesville____, County of ____Fairfax____, State of ____Connecticut____,

am the owner of certain shares of the capital stock of:

The Ajax Tool & Die Corporation

(Name of Corporation)

NOW, THEREFORE, KNOW ALL MEN BY THESE PRESENTS, that I do hereby acknowledge and declare that I hold and will hold said Shares and all right, title and interest in and to said Shares IN TRUST, for the following uses and purposes:

1. To hold said Shares and all right, title and interest therein for the use and benefit of:

(Name) ____Elizabeth M. Smith____ (my wife) ____Jonesville____ ____Connecticut____
                                                          City   State

(Address) ____525____ ____Main Street____   *J.J.S.*
          Number   Street

hereinafter referred to as the "First Beneficiary" and upon his or her death prior to the termination of the trust, for the use and benefit of my children, natural and/or adopted, in equal shares, or the survivor of them, per stirpes. Upon my death, unless all of the beneficiaries shall predecease me or unless we shall die as a result of a common accident or disaster, my Successor Trustee is hereby directed forthwith to transfer said Shares and all right, title and interest in and to said Shares unto the beneficiary or beneficiaries absolutely and thereby terminate this trust; *provided,* however, that if any beneficiary hereunder shall then be a minor, the Successor Trustee shall hold such beneficiary's share of the trust assets in continuing trust until such beneficiary attains the age of twenty-one years. Prior to that date, the Successor Trustee may apply or expend any or all of the income or principal of such minor's share for the maintenance, education and support of the minor beneficiary without the intervention of any guardian and without application to any court. Such payments of income or principal may be made to the parents of such minor or to the person with whom the minor is living without any liability upon the Successor Trustee to see to the application thereof. If such minor survives me but dies before attaining the age of twenty-one years, at his or her death the Successor Trustee shall deliver, pay over, transfer and distribute the trust property to such minor's personal representatives, absolutely.

2. I reserve the right to register any shares held hereunder in the name of a nominee, which nominee may be myself as an individual. The right, power and authority is hereby conferred upon any Successor Trustee hereunder, at any time during the minority of the beneficiary, to invest and reinvest without limitation or restriction, to sell all or any part of the Shares being held, holding either Shares or the proceeds of the sale thereof until the minor beneficiary attains the age of twenty-one years.

3. This Trust is created upon the express understanding that the issuer or transfer agent of the Shares hereunder shall be under no liability whatsoever to see to its proper administration, and that upon the transfer of the right, title and interest in and to said Shares by any Trustee hereunder, said issuer or transfer agent shall conclusively treat the transferee as the sole owner of said Shares. In the event that any shares, cash or other property shall be distributable at any time under the terms of said Shares, the said issuer or transfer agent is fully authorized to pay, deliver and distribute the same to whosoever shall then be Trustee hereunder, and shall be under no liability to see to the proper application thereof. Until the issuer or transfer agent shall receive from some person interested in this Trust, written notice of any death or other event upon which the right to receive may depend, the issuer or transfer agent shall incur no liability for payments made in good faith to persons whose interests shall have been affected by such event. The issuer or transfer agent shall be protected in acting upon any notice or other instrument or document believed by it to be genuine and to have been signed or presented by the proper party or parties.

4. The death during my lifetime, or in a common accident or disaster with me, of any beneficiary designated hereunder shall revoke such designation, and in the former event I reserve the right to designate a new beneficiary. Should no designated beneficiary be surviving, this Trust shall terminate upon my death and the trust property shall revert to my estate.

5. I hereby reserve unto myself the power and right at any time during my lifetime, before actual distribution to the beneficiaries hereunder, to revoke in whole or in part or to amend the Trust hereby created without the necessity of obtaining the consent of

_____ ...der.

... to myself the right upon the revocation or termination of this Trust, to create a new Trust for the benefit of any person whatsoever.

6. In the case of my death or legal incapacity, I hereby nominate and appoint as Successor Trustee hereunder the First Beneficiary unless he or she shall be a minor or otherwise legally incapacitated, in which event I hereby nominate and appoint as Successor Trustee hereunder:

(Name) ____Henry P. Adams____ ____Jonesville____ ____Connecticut____
                                        City   State

(Address) ____125____ ____Barnum Street____
          Number   Street

and upon his or her failure or ceasing to act or should I for any reason fail to designate the person above intended to be nominated, then I nominate and appoint as Successor Trustee hereunder whosoever shall qualify as Executor, Administrator or Guardian, as the case may be, of my estate.

7. This Declaration of Trust shall extend to and be binding upon the heirs, executors, administrators and assigns of the undersigned and upon the successors to the Trustee.

8. This Declaration of Trust shall be construed and enforced in accordance with the laws of the State of **Connecticut**

WHEREAS, I, _____of the

City/Town of_____, County of_____, State of_____,

am the owner of certain shares of the capital stock of:

_____

(Name of Corporation)

NOW, THEREFORE, KNOW ALL MEN BY THESE PRESENTS, that I do hereby acknowledge and declare that I hold and will hold said Shares and all right, title and interest in and to said Shares IN TRUST, for the following uses and purposes:

1. To hold said Shares and all right, title and interest therein for the use and benefit of:

(Name)_____, of

(Address)_____
        Number   Street   City   State

(hereinafter referred to as the "First Beneficiary") and upon his or her death prior to the termination of the trust, for the use and benefit of my children, natural not/or adopted, in equal shares, or the survivor of them/per stirpes. Upon my death, unless all of the beneficiaries shall predecease me or unless we shall die as a result of a common accident or disaster, my Successor Trustee is hereby directed forthwith to transfer said Shares and all right, title and interest in and to said Shares unto the beneficiary or beneficiaries absolutely and thereby terminate this trust; *provided,* however, that if any beneficiary hereunder shall then be a minor, the Successor Trustee shall hold such beneficiary's share of the trust assets in continuing trust until such beneficiary attains the age of twenty-one years. Prior to that date, the Successor Trustee may apply or expend any or all of the income or principal of such minor's share for the maintenance, education and support of the minor beneficiary without the intervention of any guardian and without application to any court. Such payments of income or principal may be made to the parents of such minor or to the person with whom the minor is living without any liability upon the Successor Trustee to see to the application thereof. If such minor survives me but dies before attaining the age of twenty-one years, at his or her death the Successor Trustee shall deliver, pay over, transfer and distribute the trust property to such minor's personal representatives, absolutely.

2. I reserve the right to register any shares held hereunder in the name of a nominee, which nominee may be myself as an individual, or to pledge the shares as collateral for a loan. The right, power and authority is hereby conferred upon any Successor Trustee hereunder, at any time during the minority of the beneficiary, to invest and reinvest without limitation or restriction, to sell all or any part of the Shares being held, holding either Shares or the proceeds of the sale thereof until the minor beneficiary attains the age of twenty-one years.

3. This Trust is created upon the express understanding that the issuer or transfer agent of the Shares hereunder shall be under no liability whatsoever to see to its proper administration, and that upon the transfer of the right, title and interest in and to said Shares by any Trustee hereunder, said issuer or transfer agent shall conclusively treat the transferee as the sole owner of said Shares. In the event that any shares, cash or other property shall be distributable at any time under the terms of said Shares, the said issuer or transfer agent is fully authorized to pay, deliver and distribute the same to whosoever shall then be Trustee hereunder, and shall be under no liability to see to the proper application thereof. Until the issuer or transfer agent shall receive from some person interested in this Trust, written notice of any death or other event upon which the right to receive may depend, the issuer or transfer agent shall incur no liability for payments made in good faith to persons whose interests shall have been affected by such event. The issuer or transfer agent shall be protected in acting upon any notice or other instrument or document believed by it to be genuine and to have been signed or presented by the proper party or parties.

4. The death during my lifetime, or in a common accident or disaster with me, of any beneficiary designated hereunder shall revoke such designation, and in the former event I reserve the right to designate a new beneficiary. Should no designated beneficiary be surviving, this Trust shall terminate upon my death and the trust property shall revert to my estate.

5. I hereby reserve unto myself the power and right at any time during my lifetime, before actual distribution to the beneficiaries hereunder, to revoke in whole or in part or to amend the Trust hereby created without the necessity of obtaining the consent of

the beneficiaries and without giving notice to the beneficiaries. Any one of the following acts shall be conclusive evidence of such revocation of this Trust:

    (a) The delivery to the issuer or transfer agent of the Shares by me of written notice that this Trust is revoked in whole or in part;

    (b) The transfer by me of my right, title and interest in and to said Shares;

    (c) The delivery by me to the issuer or transfer agent of the Shares of written notice of the death of the beneficiary hereunder.

I hereby reserve unto myself the right, upon the revocation or termination of this Trust, to create a new Trust for the benefit of any person whatsoever.

    6. In the case of my death or legal incapacity, I hereby nominate and appoint as Successor Trustee hereunder the First Beneficiary unless he or she shall be a minor or otherwise legally incapacitated, in which event I hereby nominate and appoint as Successor Trustee hereunder:

(Name)_____, of

(Address)_____
          Number   Street   City   State

and upon his or her failure or ceasing to act or should I for any reason fail to designate the person above intended to be nominated, then I nominate and appoint as Successor Trustee hereunder whosoever shall qualify as Executor, Administrator or Guardian, as the case may be, of my estate.

    7. This Declaration of Trust shall extend to and be binding upon the heirs, executors, administrators and assigns of the undersigned and upon the successors to the Trustee.

    8. This Declaration of Trust shall be construed and enforced in accordance with the laws of the State of

_____.

    IN WITNESS WHEREOF I have hereunto set my hand and seal this_____day

of_____, 19____.

                        (sign here)_____L.S.

Witness: (1)_____

Witness: (2)_____

STATE OF _____   }
                                ss: _____
COUNTY OF _____ }

    On the_____day of_____, nineteen hundred and_____, before

me came_____known to me to be the individual described in, and who executed

the foregoing instrument, and_____acknowledged that_____executed the same; and in due form of law

acknowledged the foregoing instrument to be_____act and deed and desired the same might be recorded as such.

    WITNESS my hand and notarial seal the day and year aforesaid.

    (Notary Seal)   _____
                                       Notary Public

WHEREAS, I,_____of the

City/Town of_____, County of_____, State of_____,

am the owner of certain shares of the capital stock of:

_____

(Name of Corporation)

NOW, THEREFORE, KNOW ALL MEN BY THESE PRESENTS, that I do hereby acknowledge and declare that I hold and will hold said Shares and all right, title and interest in and to said Shares IN TRUST, for the following uses and purposes:

1. To hold said Shares and all right, title and interest therein for the use and benefit of:

(Name)_____, of

(Address)_____

Number Street City State

(hereinafter referred to as the "First Beneficiary") and upon his or her death prior to the termination of the trust, for the use and benefit of my children, natural not/or adopted, in equal shares, or the survivor of them/per stirpes. Upon my death, unless all of the beneficiaries shall predecease me or unless we shall die as a result of a common accident or disaster, my Successor Trustee is hereby directed forthwith to transfer said Shares and all right, title and interest in and to said Shares unto the beneficiary or beneficiaries absolutely and thereby terminate this trust; *provided*, however, that if any beneficiary hereunder shall then be a minor, the Successor Trustee shall hold such beneficiary's share of the trust assets in continuing trust until such beneficiary attains the age of twenty-one years. Prior to that date, the Successor Trustee may apply or expend any or all of the income or principal of such minor's share for the maintenance, education and support of the minor beneficiary without the intervention of any guardian and without application to any court. Such payments of income or principal may be made to the parents of such minor or to the person with whom the minor is living without any liability upon the Successor Trustee to see to the application thereof. If such minor survives me but dies before attaining the age of twenty-one years, at his or her death the Successor Trustee shall deliver, pay over, transfer and distribute the trust property to such minor's personal representatives, absolutely.

2. I reserve the right to register any shares held hereunder in the name of a nominee, which nominee may be myself as an individual, or to pledge the shares as collateral for a loan. The right, power and authority is hereby conferred upon any Successor Trustee hereunder, at any time during the minority of the beneficiary, to invest and reinvest without limitation or restriction, to sell all or any part of the Shares being held, holding either Shares or the proceeds of the sale thereof until the minor beneficiary attains the age of twenty-one years.

3. This Trust is created upon the express understanding that the issuer or transfer agent of the Shares hereunder shall be under no liability whatsoever to see to its proper administration, and that upon the transfer of the right, title and interest in and to said Shares by any Trustee hereunder, said issuer or transfer agent shall conclusively treat the transferee as the sole owner of said Shares. In the event that any shares, cash or other property shall be distributable at any time under the terms of said Shares, the said issuer or transfer agent is fully authorized to pay, deliver and distribute the same to whosoever shall then be Trustee hereunder, and shall be under no liability to see to the proper application thereof. Until the issuer or transfer agent shall receive from some person interested in this Trust, written notice of any death or other event upon which the right to receive may depend, the issuer or transfer agent shall incur no liability for payments made in good faith to persons whose interests shall have been affected by such event. The issuer or transfer agent shall be protected in acting upon any notice or other instrument or document believed by it to be genuine and to have been signed or presented by the proper party or parties.

4. The death during my lifetime, or in a common accident or disaster with me, of any beneficiary designated hereunder shall revoke such designation, and in the former event I reserve the right to designate a new beneficiary. Should no designated beneficiary be surviving, this Trust shall terminate upon my death and the trust property shall revert to my estate.

5. I hereby reserve unto myself the power and right at any time during my lifetime, before actual distribution to the beneficiaries hereunder, to revoke in whole or in part or to amend the Trust hereby created without the necessity of obtaining the consent of

the beneficiaries and without giving notice to the beneficiaries. **Any one of the following acts shall be conclusive evidence of** such revocation of this Trust:

(a) The delivery to the issuer or transfer agent of the Shares by me of written notice that this Trust is revoked in whole or in part;

(b) The transfer by me of my right, title and interest in and to said Shares;

(c) The delivery by me to the issuer or transfer agent of the Shares of written notice of the death of the beneficiary hereunder.

I hereby reserve unto myself the right, upon the revocation or termination of this Trust, to create a new Trust for the benefit of any person whatsoever.

6. In the case of my death or legal incapacity, I hereby nominate and appoint as Successor Trustee hereunder the First Beneficiary unless he or she shall be a minor or otherwise legally incapacitated, in which event I hereby nominate and appoint as Successor Trustee hereunder:

(Name)_____, of

(Address)_____
          Number   Street   City   State

and upon his or her failure or ceasing to act or should I for any reason fail to designate the person above intended to be nominated, then I nominate and appoint as Successor Trustee hereunder whosoever shall qualify as Executor, Administrator or Guardian, as the case may be, of my estate.

7. This Declaration of Trust shall extend to and be binding upon the heirs, executors, administrators and assigns of the undersigned and upon the successors to the Trustee.

8. This Declaration of Trust shall be construed and enforced in accordance with the laws of the State of

_____.

IN WITNESS WHEREOF I have hereunto set my hand and seal this_____day

of_____, 19_____.

(sign here)_____L.S.

Witness: (1)_____

Witness: (2)_____

STATE OF _____ } ss: _____

COUNTY OF _____ }

On the_____day of_____, nineteen hundred and_____, before

me came_____known to me to be the individual described in, and who executed

the foregoing instrument, and_____acknowledged that_____executed the same; and in due form of law

acknowledged the foregoing instrument to be_____act and deed and desired the same might be recorded as such.

WITNESS my hand and notarial seal the day and year aforesaid.

(Notary Seal)   _____
                                     Notary Public

Chapter 9

THE CLOSE CORPORATION

The capitalism which is America's trade mark in the world had humble beginnings. Every great corporation, traced back far enough, will be found to be a monument to a single idea in the mind of a single individual—an individual who, when the corporation grows to prosperous maturity and has thousands of shareholders, may become a legend but more likely is forgotten. There is a place for the corporate giants; thank heaven for them.

But it is the countless thousands upon thousands of smaller corporations with stock owned by one man, one family or by a handful of founders, which are the salt of the earth in the industrial and commercial complex that is America.

The death of the owner of a close corporation invariably creates special problems, the first of which is probably death taxes. If it's a successful business, its appraisal for tax purposes may signal the discovery that the business constitutes the whole estate and there are no liquid assets available to pay the death taxes. In such circumstances, many a business has had to be sold. The probate procedure is a public one and when the details of the deceased's ownership of a business are readily available, it can sometimes prejudice the sale of that business by those charged with settling the estate or by the heirs. Information about the business becomes available to competitors.

The period following the death of its principal or sole owner is always a trying one for a business. In some businesses, the owner is the spark plug. Without him, the operations become disorganized. Petty jealousies, carefully hidden while he ruled the roost, erupt and interfere with the smooth running of the company. The customer's personal loyalty to him is no longer a factor upon which the corporation can count. Competitors move in and re-double their efforts to coax customers away.

All in all, it is a difficult time for a business. If, because of the protracted delays which characterize probate administration, the sale of the business drags on interminably, it can be serious, if not fatal. If the stock passes under a will, and the will is contested, the corporation's woes are compounded. Bank loans readily made to the original owner would be more difficult to obtain when the future of the business became doubtful. Existing bank loans may be called. Needed capital would not be available.

In such a situation, the inter vivos trust is a blessing. With such a trust in existence, upon the death of the owner the stock is promptly and quietly transferred to the named beneficiary. If that beneficiary concludes that it is best to sell the business, he can immediately initiate private negotiations without waiting for any action by the probate court, and he can sell the business without having to obtain the probate court's approval. With ownership passing under an inter vivos trust, the sale of the business, if that seemed desirable, could be consumated within a week from the death of the owner. Forced to go through probate, it could not be concluded in less than six months. In that time, beset by uncertainty and with its credit dried up, the business could falter, even fail.

The avoidance of probate is particularly advantageous, then, when the property involved is stock in a close corporation. One of the forms of declaration of trust suggested in Chapter 8 for use in avoiding probate of securities will be found quite suitable for use in obtaining the same exemption for stockholdings in a close corporation.

If the stock is presently registered *"John Smith"*, simply add *"trustee u/d/t dated_____"* after your name, and alter the registration accordingly on the stock record books of the corporation.

Chapter 10

YOUR LIFE INSURANCE

A dismal statistic supplied by the life insurance companies discloses that 60% of all life insurance payable in cash is dissipated within two years. Instances of widows being separated from the estates left them by their husbands are quite common. Compilers of sucker lists offer choice lists of names of women who have been widowed within the past five years. There are many unscrupulous people who use such lists to find beneficiaries upon whom they can prey.

Not all of the money goes to confidence men. Some is just spent or imprudently invested by beneficiaries ill-equipped to care for large sums of money. Most men display a certain confidence in the good sense of their wives. Too many times it is misplaced confidence. I recall reading of the tragic suicide of a woman whose second husband ascribed her sad end to financial worry. Eleven years earlier, her first husband had died leaving her fourteen million dollars. Surely he must have had confidence in her to have turned such a huge sum over to her. Alas, instead of financial security, he bequeathed her a headache, a worry, a job for which she was not qualified. Many a man forgets that as his widow grows older she will be less sharp, less alert to confidence men. Or perhaps he doesn't take into account that the confidence man may be her own son. Precious life insurance proceeds have financed the unsuccessful adventures in business of many a young man whose widowed mother was certain that he could do no wrong.

Our responsibility for providing security for our dependents extends beyond dumping a lot of money into their laps when we die. It includes leaving it in such a fashion that it will provide the continuing financial security they will need, and for as long as they will need it.

Most men leave too little life insurance. Its inadequacy is heightened by the fact that it is not made properly productive for the heirs. As the alternative to leaving insurance to their beneficiaries in cash, they arrange for it to remain with the insurance company

under one or the other of various settlement options which provide for it to be doled out monthly. Meantime, the insurance company puts the money to work, derives a good return, and gives the beneficiary a little bit of interest.

There are four settlement options offered by life insurance companies in connection with payment of the proceeds of life insurance. They are:

1. The entire proceeds paid in cash in one lump sum
2. The proceeds paid to the beneficiary in installments over a period of years
3. The proceeds used to provide a lifetime annuity income to the beneficiary
4. The proceeds left with the company at interest.

Having concluded that the first option is not desirable for their families, many men enter into a plan involving one or the other, or all three, of the other options. Many insurance men are adept at preparing a chart with colored crayons which illustrates the way in which payment of insurance proceeds may be spread over many years through use of some combination of these options. The drawback to these arrangements is that if you deny the beneficiary the right to draw upon the funds when and as she wishes, you also create an inflexible device to pay out money only in accordance with the precise formula you have set, which does not take into account the changing needs and circumstances of the beneficiary.

The simplest way of overcoming this important disadvantage of inflexibility is through a life insurance trust. The trust is an object of your own creation—you mold it to meet the specific needs of your family.

There are two basic ways of setting up a life insurance trust. The first is to create the trust immediately and make it the beneficiary of your life insurance policies. The trust goes into operation as soon as it receives the proceeds of your life insurance after your death.

You can "fund" the trust—that is, you can transfer income-producing property to it, the income to be used to pay the premiums on your policies.

The second way to set up a life insurance trust is by will. Here your estate becomes the beneficiary of the policy. The estate turns the proceeds over to the trust. This plan has important drawbacks. First, if the probate of your will is delayed, so is the operation of the trust. Second, most states tax proceeds of life insurance payable to an estate while exempting at least some portion of proceeds payable to a named beneficiary. Third, as we have observed, probate is something to be avoided at all costs.

Whichever type of life insurance trust you decide upon, you will have broad freedom of action. You may choose a trustee whom you know to be qualified to carry out your instructions. This can be an individual but you should consider that individuals can be away, busy, or ill or die. You'd be better advised to appoint a corporate trustee—your local bank or trust company.

In the trust instrument, you can direct specifically how you want the money to be paid out. Be careful, though. Don't authorize an income of x dollars per month. A few years hence, inflation may make that income inadequate. Relate the income to the amount of principal; if you must be specific, say that the income "shall be not less than." Years ago, Charles Hay-den died and left $55 million, specifying that the beneficiaries were to be paid 6% good years and bad. Gains above that were to be plowed back into the trust in the good years, and could be drawn upon to make up the income deficit during lean years. Many men now use this pattern to provide trust income.

Above all, take advantage of the greatest benefit of the life insurance trust—the opportunity to give the trustee discretion to vary payments in accordance with the needs of your heirs. If you tell an insurance company to pay the proceeds in equal shares to your two daughters, they'll carry out your instructions to the letter. But suppose one of your daughters marries the wealthiest man in town while the other becomes an invalid and spends her life in a wheelchair. It doesn't make sense for the income from your estate to be paid to them equally. You wouldn't do it that way if you were here making the distribution yourself. So give your trustee discretionary power to sprinkle the income where it will do the most good. That's what a trustee is for, to exercise judgment in the application of money to family needs.

The dollars-and-cents advantages of a life insurance trust over settlement options are clearly shown in the chart on the next page, which illustrates two methods of distributing life insurance proceeds: (1) under the most popular life insurance company settlement option and (2) under the insurance trust.

Comparison of Two Methods of Distributing $100,000 Life Insurance Proceeds to a Widow Age 40

1. Under the most popular life insurance settlement option. (Payments for 20 years certain and thereafter for lifetime of primary beneficiary.)

2. Under life insurance trust.

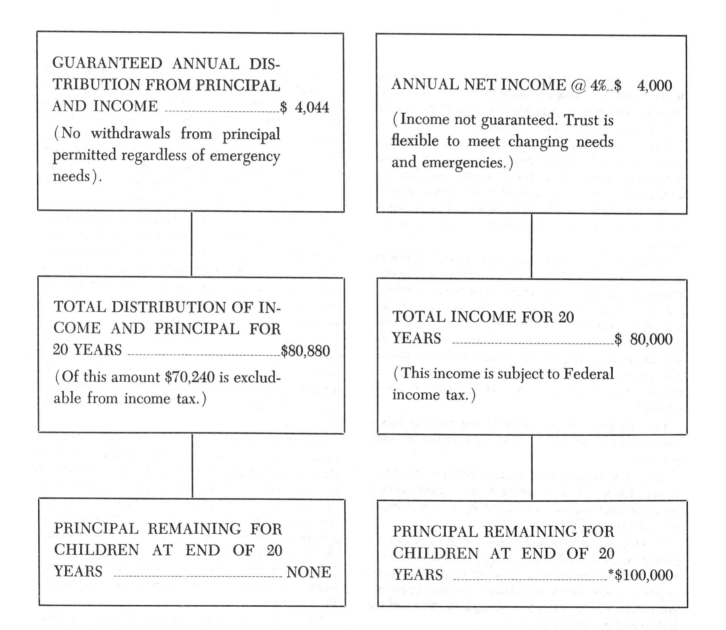

GUARANTEED ANNUAL DISTRIBUTION FROM PRINCIPAL AND INCOME .... $ 4,044 (No withdrawals from principal permitted regardless of emergency needs).	ANNUAL NET INCOME @ 4%..$ 4,000 (Income not guaranteed. Trust is flexible to meet changing needs and emergencies.)
TOTAL DISTRIBUTION OF INCOME AND PRINCIPAL FOR 20 YEARS .... $80,880 (Of this amount $70,240 is excludable from income tax.)	TOTAL INCOME FOR 20 YEARS .... $ 80,000 (This income is subject to Federal income tax.)
PRINCIPAL REMAINING FOR CHILDREN AT END OF 20 YEARS .... NONE	PRINCIPAL REMAINING FOR CHILDREN AT END OF 20 YEARS *$100,000

At a possible sacrifice of $880 income during the 20 years, there is a possible gain of $100,000 through use of the insurance trust for widow and children instead of insurance settlement option.

*Principal invested in all stock and balanced mutual funds for past 20 years showed average appreciation of 125%.

Chapter 11

THE "DACEY TRUST"

Coming into increasingly widespread use is a form of trust which I designed some years ago in recognition of the growing popularity of mutual funds as a medium of investment for entire estates.

The arrangement, which professional and technical services in the legal and trust fields have been kind enough to designate as a "Dacey Trust", combines the services of a local bank as trustee and a mutual fund as investment manager in a plan which embraces one's entire estate, including the proceeds of one's life insurance.

William G. Casey, noted tax attorney and Chairman of the Board of Editors of the Institute of Business Planning, has said: "The Dacey trust offers a unique, practical method of concentrating in one package the investment skill and saving discipline of a mutual fund plan, the mortality protection afforded by a life insurance contract and the experience and discretion of a corporate trustee in making capital available to meet family needs. It offers a fascinating range of possibilities."

Four assumptions contribute to the growing popularity of this device as an effective instrument in estate planning:

1. Bank trusteeship has had one drawback—the occasional instance of poor judgment by a bank lacking adequate trust facilities, or neglect by a large, competent but over-busy bank.

2. This drawback can be substantially reduced by combining the custodial services of the local trust company with the management facilities of completely independent professional investment managers who beyond any question of doubt have both the time and the skill to perform their work well.

3. Such independent management is now relatively easy to find, especially in view of the development of mutual funds with their increasingly-high standards of management performance.

4. In this modern era with its development of the "package" concept, the idea of a new "trust package" which neatly combines a man's entire estate—lifetime investment accumulation, life insurance proceeds and residue of odds and ends of property of which he may die possessed—into a single, tidy, well-managed package obviously strikes a responsive chord in every man wrestling with the problem of how best to preserve his family's financial security after he is gone.

The Dacey trust provides that a local trust company shall have physical possession of the assets. Its duties include safekeeping for those assets and the bookkeeping and accounting incidental to the trust administration. It also maintains personal contact with beneficiaries and exercises discretion with regard to disbursements where authorized to do so.

The Dacey trust is a "dry trust" during the settlor's lifetime—other than providing safekeeping for the settlor's will, trust property and life insurance policies, the bank performs no active service (unless called upon to do so) and therefore receives no compensation during this period.

Investment supervision of the trust should rest with independent investment managers selected by the settlor. There are many investment counsel firms who can provide such investment supervision. Obviously, the more competent the firm, the more accounts it already has with whom your account must compete for the managers' attention. One should choose carefully, bearing in mind that the whole purpose of the search for independent management was to avoid similar competition with other accounts in the trust department of the bank itself.

The remarkable growth of mutual funds in recent years suggests that this practical device for providing investment management service to everyone, regardless of the individual's means, has met a need and done its job well. As more and more of the top-notch investment brains of the country gravitate toward the great aggregations of wealth represented by the mutual funds, it has become easier for the layman to find competent investment management.

Ordinarily, the principal factors in the choice of a trustee bank are faith and hope. Since bank trust accounts are private and confidential, there is usually no means by which one can measure the skill which the trustee bank has demonstrated in performing similar services for others in the past. The record of an isolated, unidentified trust account is not satisfactory—accounts have varying objectives and there are bound to be a few whose objectives, as reflected in their investment policy, coincide with a current economic trend and which therefore look good. Such an account would hardly reflect a true cross section of the bank's accounts generally. By and large, bank investment management must be chosen on the basis of faith in the institution's reputation and hope that it will do a good job.

The use of a mutual fund as the medium of investment in a living trust permits of the selection of management on a much more knowledgeable basis. The comparative performance of all mutual funds is meticulously recorded in standard reference books and it is a simple matter to establish the relative ability of any fund management—to the extent that the record of past performance is indicative of continuing capability.

Mutual funds have a quality of consistency. Having stated their investment objectives, they may not depart from those objectives without individual formal notice to each participant—and such changes are rare. When you select a fund whose objectives coincide with your own, you can be reasonably sure that those objectives will never change. Obviously, neither the trust company nor the mutual fund can guarantee that its stated objectives will be achieved.

The living trust undoubtedly will constitute a major proportion of your assets while you live and, since the trust will include all of your life insurance, it probably will be your family's sole security after you are gone. Management should be selected with great care, then, with due consideration being given to the stated investment objectives of the mutual funds from amongst which you will make your choice. There is risk in all investment, and mutual funds offer no assurance against investment loss. They endeavor to reduce risk through three things—selection, diversification, supervision. The investment of one's entire estate must necessarily differ from the investment of extra dollars. While there are no hard and fast rules and many trust accounts are invested completely in common stocks, it is more customary to have a balanced portfolio of bonds, preferred and common stocks. If one examines the investments of the Carnegie, Rockefeller, Guggenheim and other great endowed foundations, or the large college and university endowment funds, it will be noted that they are invariably balanced funds. It is suggested, then, that a balanced mutual fund will be most suitable for the investment of your living trust. The plan can be very flexible, though—you may choose to invest in a growth-type common stock mutual fund during your lifetime, with instructions to the trustee to switch to a more conservative balanced fund at your death.

Through the use of one of the declarations of trust (DT-9) appearing in Chapter 7, it is possible to so register your mutual fund shares that they will pass into the bank trust account at your death without being subject to the delay, expense and publicity of probate.

Comparative Costs of Six Estate Transfer Methods

In this illustration we will assume the situation of a man with a total estate of $300,000 and we will show how the net value of that estate to his heirs can vary greatly depending upon which of six methods he selects for its distribution and management. In calculating transfer costs, we include Federal estate and gift tax and State tax at the rates which prevail in Connecticut. The variation for residents of other states will not alter the broad picture presented here. Our man is married and has two children, except that in the first transfer method we assume that his wife predeceases him. His wife has no separate estate. Transfer costs include those which apply on the transfer of property upon the death of the husband and his wife, thus showing the total shrinkage in passing the property to the next generation.

% of estate lost
in taxes and
administration costs

43.9%

METHOD A

Entire estate of an unmarried person passes to a sister or a parent (like surviving spouse, assumed to have no separate estate), then property passes to nieces, nephews or grandchildren without benefit of marital deductions. Here we have maximum shrinkage. This can happen where a man is unmarried or his wife predeceases him so that his estate cannot qualify for marital deduction.

26.58%

METHOD B

A man's estate is bequeathed to a trust, with income to his wife for life and property to his children upon her death. Before the 1948 Revenue Act, this was the most economical way to pass an estate. Many wills still run this way and are likely to be obsolete and needlessly costly.

34.85%

METHOD C

All property is willed to a man's wife outright. The wife's will then sends all the property to children. This method qualifies for the marital deduction so that only half the estate is taxed at the husband's death. But, upon the wife's subsequent death, all property is taxed without benefit of marital deduction.

20.56%

METHOD D

A man wills half his property to his wife outright, the other half in trust for his children, possibly with income to his wife for life. Upon his death, half his estate falls subject to tax and all of it to administration costs. Upon his wife's death, the other half of the estate falls subject to tax and administration costs.

17.97%

METHOD E

A man wills his property to two trusts, one trust qualifying for the marital deduction, the other not. This method has the same tax saving value as Method D, but saves administration expense upon the second death and provides the wife with professional management of her property.

12.66%

METHOD F   (THE DACEY TRUST)

Lifetime transfer of all property to a living trust with directions to dispose of property as in Method E, upon deaths of husband and wife. The husband can watch his plan in operation and change the arrangement during his life. It will accomplish maximum savings in taxes and administration costs for his estate.

131

DEED OF TRUST

FOR USE IN ESTABLISHING A

DACEY TRUST

Instructions:

On the following pages will be found duplicate copies of a deed of trust (DT-17) which will be suitable for use in establishing a "Dacey Trust" under which a mutual fund management selected by you during your lifetime will, after your death, supply investment management of a trust account held by a local bank as trustee.

Here are the steps to take:

1. Take the deed of trust to the bank of your choice and invite that institution to accept the trusteeship. The bank will wish to submit your deed to its counsel. Most banks make no charge for the opening of the account, nor do they ordinarily make any annual charge during your lifetime since they have no duties to perform. Some banks prefer to give the trust "active" status by making a nominal charge of $10 annually during the lifetime of the settlor. In most cases, though, the bank's fee begins at your death, and it is a reduced charge (frequently 3% of ordinary income, or about $1.20 per year per $1,000 of trust assets) reflecting the vastly-reduced bookkeeping involved in the holding of a single security, the mutual fund, paying four quarterly dividends, rather than a diversified portfolio with stock rights, stock dividends, splits, etc., and reflecting also the absence of any investment responsibility. If the local bank declines to serve at a reduced rate, seek another trustee. There is no point in paying for services not rendered.

Occasionally, a provincial trust company will assume the attitude that if it is good enough to be trustee, it is good enough to manage the money. I have observed that invariably, these were banks whose investment management services I would hesitate to employ. I suggest that such an attitude forfeits the respect and goodwill of the community. A trust company exists to serve the fiduciary needs of the community—*all* of the fiduciary needs. If, during his lifetime an individual has retained the services of a particular investment management, has come to have complete confidence in that management, and wishes to make certain that it will continue to serve his estate and his heirs when he has gone, he requires a specific fiduciary service which it is the obligation of the local trust company to pro-

vide. Like a small boy who petulantly removes himself and his baseball from a sandlot game because he is not allowed to pitch, the corporate trustee which won't "play" if it cannot manage the money deserves only scorn for a display of financial adolescence.

2. Purchase the mutual fund shares of your choice, registering them *"(Your Name), Trustee under Declaration of Trust dated_____"*, using DT-9 reproduced in Chapter 7. Note that this *declaration* of trust is a separate instrument used only in connection with the registration of the mutual fund shares. It should not be confused with the *deed* of trust mentioned in (1) above. The *declaration* of trust is intended to insure that the mutual fund shares will pass into the bank trust at your death without going through probate. (It may help you differentiate between the functions of the *declaration* and the *deed* if we explain that a declaration involves just one person—he *declares* that he is holding something in trust. A *deed* ordinarily involves more than one person; it is an agreement between the creator of the trust and the trustee, and it spells out the duties and responsibilities of the trustee.)

Note that you should name as *beneficiary* and successor trustee under the *declaration* of trust the same bank you have named as trustee under the *deed* of trust. Each time you purchase additional shares of the mutual fund, have them registered in the same manner and under the same declaration of trust.

3. Advise the companies issuing your life insurance policies that you wish to name the bank to receive the proceeds in its capacity as "Trustee under Deed of Trust dated_____". The companies will supply beneficiary change forms for your signature. Some companies will ask to see a copy of the trust or an excerpt of those provisions in it relating to the insurance.

4. Execute a new will (Will Form W-11 in Chapter 19 is suggested) leaving your house, furniture, automobile, jewelry and other personal effects to your spouse but directing that all other property, including specifically any stocks, bonds or cash, be added to the trust account set up under the deed of trust. As of this writing, this procedure (called "incorporation by reference") is not permitted in a few states. Check this point with the trust officer at your local bank.

It is suggested that you appoint as executor under your will the same bank named as trustee under the deed of trust.

*   *   *

At your death, the trustee bank will collect the proceeds of your life insurance and add them to the mutual fund shares which you have accumulated during your lifetime and which have passed to the trustee automatically at your death. The bank will thereafter collect and disburse the income (and such sums from principal as you have authorized) to your wife during her lifetime. At her death, the income can continue to your children until they are 21, 25, 35 or such other age as you wish the principal to be made available to them—but during this entire period the investment of your combined trust account will be under the constant, day-to-day supervision of the mutual fund management of your choice. Your family will enjoy the traditional safety and security of bank trusteeship with its splendid record going back more than a century and a half. They'll have the convenience of the local trusteeship, with wise counsel available to them on their personal business or financial problems. They won't have the local investment management, though, with its possible limitations.

*   *   *

The following explanatory notes in "layman's language" are keyed to the letters appearing in the margin of the deed of trust (DT-17) which follows immediately thereafter.

A | *It is generally desirable to take advantage of the "marital deduction" allowed when at least half of one's estate is left to one's spouse. There may well be instances, however, where the Settlor's wife has substantial means of her own and it would be disadvantageous to increase her estate by taking advantage of the marital deduction. The taxes ultimately assessed against the combined estates upon her death might far exceed the benefits gained by taking the marital deduction.*

B | *Note that while the Settlor's wife can withdraw the whole marital trust at will, the Trustee is also authorized to disburse portions of the principal on her behalf should she be hospitalized or incompetent and unable to request them herself.*

C | *A trust may qualify for the marital deduction either by giving the Settlor's wife free access to the marital portion or by conferring upon her the right to name who is to receive it at her death. In this case, qualification is made doubly certain by including both provisions. This arrangement enables her to make such distribution of her marital portion of the estate as is appropriate to the family conditions existing at that time, and also permits her to make tax-reducing gifts to heirs while she still lives.*

D | *While in most cases, the income from both the marital and the non-marital portion of the trust will be paid to the Settlor's wife, note that the instrument permits the Trustee in its discretion to withhold the income from the non-marital portion of the trust and add it to the principal. The objective here is to allow the Settlor's wife to draw the income from the marital portion plus sums from principal equal to the income from the non-marital portion which is being accumulated instead of paid to her. This would gradually reduce the marital portion (which would be taxable at her death), and build up the non-marital portion (upon which no further estate tax will have to be paid). That portion of the payments to her which represented a distribution of principal from the marital portion would be completely tax-free. The retained income from the non-marital portion would be taxable to the trust, and it is likely that this splitting of the taxable income would provide a tax saving. Obviously, the Settlor's wife would not request the Trustee's approval of a withdrawal from the non-marital portion of the trust until she had exhausted the marital portion from which withdrawals could be made without asking anyone's approval. The very circumstances which would lead her to request such approval, then, would also serve to indicate the need to impose a little restraint to preserve her remaining security.*

E

While the age at which the Settlor's children are to receive the principal is optional with the Settlor, it is suggested that it be one at which the children will be mature enough to use the money properly. Most Settlors choose age 35, and this is the age designated in the instrument. If you wish to specify another age, cross out 35 wherever it appears in this paragraph, write the preferred figure above it and initial the change. Note that the principal is not wholly withheld from the children until the specified age. In addition to tuition, the Trustee might properly be called upon to pay the cost of opening an office for the Settlor's son who is entering upon the practice of medicine, or assist the Settlor's newly-married daughter with the down payment on a home. The purpose of the trust is not to keep the money from the children but only to encourage them to use it intelligently.

F

Given two daughters, one hopelessly invalided and the other married to a prosperous business man in a high tax bracket, the Settlor would undoubtedly himself choose to apportion a larger share of the income to his less fortunate child. This clause which permits the Trustee to "sprinkle" the income among the surviving beneficiaries according to their needs serves a useful purpose.

G

Increasing numbers of Americans are benefitting from pension, profit-sharing and other plans under which they have a vested interest in the proceeds. This clause permits the inclusion of such proceeds in the trust. Where the procedure is permissible under state law, it also allows the Settlor's wife (or any other person) to add to the trust by will.

H

In this era of multiple plant corporations, executives are subject to frequent geographical shifts. The city in which a man resides at his death may not necessarily be "home" to his family. This provision makes it possible to shift the trust to another more conveniently-located bank if his wife decides to "go back home."

I

In connection with the systematic distribution annually of 6% of the value of the trust, such payments would be accomplished, when ordinary income and capital gain distributions were together insufficient to provide such 6% payment, by liquidating enough of the underlying mutual fund shares to make up the deficit. The value of shares thus liquidated might be more or less than their cost; the trustee bank would in each case compute the gain or loss and advise the income beneficiaries. The Settlor should understand that the suggested 6% payment does not constitute a true "yield" or "income" from or "return" on the investments but rather is an annuity-like payment which may represent in part principal. Naturally, the Settlor should take into account that any invasions of principal necessitated by the inadequacy of the annual ordinary income and capital gains distributions could, if persisted in over a long period of time, ultimately substantially deplete or exhaust the principal, especially in a declining market.

Among other things, this type of income clause is regarded as an ideal hedge against a rising cost of living. In a period of inflated prices, when the beneficiaries' living cost may be assumed to have risen, the designated distribution of 6% of the then value of the trust property will represent a larger total number of dollars and therefore a larger purchasing power. From time to time, the value of the shares and the income they pay may, in the future as in the past, move in the opposite direction from the cost of living trend.

In carrying out the provisions of this section, it is common for the Trustee upon completion of the annual valuation of the trust property, to advise the beneficiary of the figure which constitutes 6% of such value. Thus, on a $100,000 trust, the Trustee would inform the beneficiary that it would pay out $6,000 during the coming year at the rate of $500 per month. This would provide the beneficiary with a regular monthly amount upon the basis of which she could budget her living expenses.

J

It is customary for the Settlor to here designate the mutual fund dealer through whom shares are to be purchased with the proceeds of his life insurance after his death. In most instances, this is the same dealer through whom he purchased shares during his lifetime.

Deed of Trust

Made by and between_____of the

City/Town of_____, County of_____and State of_____

(hereinafter referred to as the "Settlor") and_____ _____

_____located in the City/Town of_____,

County of_____and State of_____(hereinafter referred to as the "Trustee").

WITNESSETH

By this agreement the Settlor desires to create a revocable voluntary living trust consisting of policies of life insurance hereinafter described and of other property which he may add to such trust from time to time, and the Trustee has agreed to accept the same under this agreement.

It is therefore agreed by and between the Settlor and the Trustee as follows:

SECTION A:

With respect to any property except policies of life insurance which now or hereafter may be placed in trust hereunder, the Trustee shall hold, invest and reinvest the same as a trust fund upon the following terms and conditions:

1. During the Settlor's lifetime, pay the income to him in convenient installments or expend or reinvest the same upon his written direction.

2. Upon the Settlor's death, add the trust fund herein created to the trust of the insurance proceeds established by Section B of this agreement and dispose of the same as a part thereof in accordance with the provisions of Section B-1 and B-2.

SECTION B:

The Settlor has delivered to the Trustee certain insurance policies on his life described in Schedule A attached hereto and made a part hereof, in which policies the right to change the beneficiary without consent is specifically reserved to the Settlor during his lifetime; and has executed and delivered or will execute and deliver to the Trustee proper instruments to enable the Trustee to be made the beneficiary under said policies as Trustee under this agreement, which policies and the proceeds thereof as and when received by the Trustee shall be held in trust and disposed of by the Trustee as hereinafter provided. Upon receipt by the Trustee of notice of the death of the Settlor the Trustee shall prepare such proofs of death and other documents as are required to collect the amounts payable upon the death of the Settlor under the terms of the policies then held by it as Trustee and shall present such documents to the companies issuing said policies and for that purpose it shall have full power to execute and deliver such instruments and to institute any action in law or equity as in its judgment may be necessary and proper but the Trustee shall not be required to institute any such action until it shall have been indemnified to its satisfaction against all expenses and liabilities which might be incurred thereby.

The Trustee shall divide the insurance proceeds received by it, together with the then trust fund established by the provisions of Section A, and together with any other property which may be added to this trust before or after the Settlor's death, into two parts. One of said parts, herein termed the "marital share", shall consist of property of a value necessary to utilize to the maximum extent any federal estate tax benefit to the Settlor's estate which may be available from any "marital deduction" allowable in the determination of such tax, after taking into account any other property whether or not passing under this agreement or under the Settlor's Will or otherwise, with respect to which such deduction is allowable and any other deductions or exemptions allowable in the determination of such tax. The other part shall consist of the remainder of the insurance proceeds and the remainder of the trust fund established by the provisions of Section A. In apportioning to the marital and non-marital trusts specific assets previously valued for estate tax purposes, the Trustee shall insure that the two trusts share proportionately in any subsequent appreciation or depreciation in the value of such assets.

1. With respect to the "marital share" so-called, the Trustee shall hold, manage, invest and reinvest the same as a trust fund upon the following terms and conditions: . . .

1

(a) The Trustee shall pay the income (and any other payment authorized by Paragraph 10-A) to the

Settlor's wife,_____, in quarterly or if convenient more frequent payments during her lifetime, together with such sums out of principal as she may request the Trustee in writing to pay to her from time to time and together with such sums out of principal as the Trustee in its sole discretion shall deem necessary for her support or maintenance.

(b) Upon the death of the Settlor's wife, the Trustee shall pay the then trust fund as she shall appoint by her Will and the Settlor hereby confers upon his said wife the sole and unrestricted power to appoint the same by her Will, outright or in further trust, in favor of her estate or in favor of others. To the extent that said power shall not be effectively exercised, the trust fund herein created shall be added to the remaining part and shall be disposed of as hereinafter provided.

(c) If the Settlor and his wife shall die under such circumstances that there is not, in the judgment of the Executor of the Settlor's estate, whose decision shall be conclusive, sufficient evidence to determine readily which of them survived the other, then for the purposes of this trust, the Settlor's wife shall be deemed to have survived him.

2. With respect to the remaining part of the insurance proceeds and trust fund, the Trustee shall hold, invest and reinvest the same as a trust fund upon the following terms and conditions:

(a) If requested by the executor or administrator of the Settlor's estate, the Trustee shall pay or reimburse said executor or administrator for the amount of any ante mortem claim, funeral expense or expense of administration which shall be allowed in connection with the settlement of his estate and which shall be certified to the Trustee by such executor or administrator.

(b) The Trustee shall pay to the proper taxing authority or reimburse the executor or administrator of the Settlor's estate for the amount of any succession, estate, transfer or similar tax, whether state or federal, which shall be imposed lawfully upon the Settlor's taxable estate or upon any beneficiary thereof as the result of the death of the Settlor and which shall be certified to the Trustee by such executor or administrator.

(c) The Trustee shall pay the income (and any other payment authorized by Paragraph 10 A) from the balance of the trust fund remaining in its hands to the Settlor's said wife during her lifetime in quarterly or if convenient more frequent payments or in its sole and absolute discretion withhold and accumulate all or such part of such income (or other payment) as it shall determine and add the same to principal. The Trustee is further authorized to pay to the Settlor's wife or in its discretion expend for her maintenance and support or for the maintenance, support and education of the Settlor's children such sums out of principal as it in its sole discretion may deem proper from time to time for any such purpose.

(d) Upon the death of the Settlor's wife or upon the Settlor's death if she shall not survive the Settlor, the Trustee shall:

(i) If requested by the executor or administrator of the wife's estate, pay or reimburse her estate for the amounts of her funeral expenses and the expenses of her last illness as certified to the Trustee by such executor or administrator.

(ii) Divide the balance of the trust fund into as many equal parts as there shall be children of the Settlor then living and children of the Settlor then deceased leaving issue then living and shall:

(1) Pay one of said parts to the living issue collectively of each such child then deceased in equal shares per stirpes.

(2) Pay one of said parts to each child of the Settlor then living and who shall have become 35 years of age.

(3) Hold, manage, invest and reinvest the remaining parts as one trust fund for the benefit of the children of the Settlor then living and who shall not have become 35 years of age and pay or expend all or none or so much of the income and principal to or for the benefit of each of said children as the Trustee in its sole discretion shall deem proper for their suitable maintenance, support and education until each such child shall become 35 years of age, at which time an equal share of the then principal of the trust fund shall be paid over to such child after making adjustment for the amount by which payments of principal to one child may have exceeded those made to another child. If any such child shall die before becoming 35 years of age, then upon such child's death an equal share of said trust fund after adjustment as aforesaid, shall be paid over to such child's children equally; if there shall be no such children then living such shares shall be added equally to the remaining shares, if any, and held, managed and disposed of as a part thereof; if no such shares remain, such share shall be paid over to the Settlor's issue then living, per stirpes.

(4) Notwithstanding any of the foregoing directions, the share of each living issue of any deceased child of the Settlor, though vested, shall be held in trust and so much of the income and principal as the Trustee shall deem proper shall be paid to or for the benefit of such issue until he or she shall become twenty-one years of age.

SECTION C: ADMINISTRATIVE PROVISIONS

1. Unless directed in accordance with the provisions of Section A-1, the Trustee shall be under no duty to pay any premiums or other charges required to continue the said policies of insurance in force or to procure renewals thereof or otherwise to ascertain that said policies are kept in force.

2. The provisions of Section B shall apply only to such proceeds of said policies as may be due and payable to the Trustee upon the death of the Settlor, and all payments, dividends, surrender values and benefits of any kind which may accrue on any of said policies during the lifetime of the Settlor shall be payable to the Settlor and shall not be collected or disposed of by the Trustee.

3. The Settlor reserves to himself without the consent of said Trustee or of any beneficiary hereunder or of any beneficiary now or hereafter named in any policy now or hereafter deposited hereunder, the right to pledge any of said policies or any other property now or hereafter placed in trust hereunder to secure any loan now existing or hereafter made by any persons, firm or corporation to the Settlor, and further reserves the right to exercise any and all options, elections, rights, and privileges, including the right to borrow on said policies, given to him under the terms of any of said policies, and upon the request of the Settlor the Trustee will execute and deliver such documents as are necessary and proper to permit the Settlor fully to exercise such rights.

4. The Settlor shall have the right at any time during his lifetime to place additional property and/or insurance policies under the terms of the agreement upon delivering such property and/or insurance policies to the Trustee together with a written request that the Trustee place said additional property and policies under this agreement. Upon the delivery of any such additional property and policies and such written request to the Trustee, the Trustee shall issue a receipt therefore to the Settlor. The Settlor shall also have the right to add to the trust fund by an appropriate provision in his Will or to designate the Trustee as beneficiary of any profit-sharing, pension, incentive compensation or other fund in which he may have an interest, and under the terms of which he has the right to name a beneficiary. The Trustee is further authorized to accept additions to this trust from any other source, testamentary or otherwise.

5. The Settlor shall have the right at any time during his lifetime to withdraw from the operation of this agreement any or all property and policies upon his written request delivered to the Trustee and upon delivery to the Trustee of a receipt for the property and/or policies so withdrawn, and upon such withdrawal and thereafter if required, the Trustee shall execute and deliver to the Settlor such instruments as are necessary and proper to release the interest of the Trustee therein.

6. The Settlor shall have the right at any time during his lifetime to terminate this agreement upon giving to the Trustee written notice of such termination, and upon termination the Trustee shall deliver to the Settlor against his written receipt all property and policies then held hereunder and shall execute and deliver to the Settlor such instruments as are necessary and proper to transfer the interest of the Trustee therein to the Settlor.

After the Settlor's death, by mutual agreement between the Beneficiary and the Trustee, the Trustee may resign to be replaced by a successor trustee nominated by the Beneficiary, provided that such successor trustee shall be a bank or trust company authorized by law to exercise fiduciary powers which shall have its principal place of business and be actively engaged in the trust business in the state in which the Beneficiary then legally resides. Such successor trustee having filed its written acceptance with the Trustee, the latter, after finally accounting to the Beneficiary or Beneficiaries, shall deliver all of the trust assets held hereunder to the successor trustee and shall thereafter have no further duties or liabilities with respect thereto.

Should the Settlor's wife, surviving the Settlor, move and establish her domicile in another state, she may request the Trustee to and the Trustee shall resign, *provided* that she shall by written instrument filed with the Trustee name as successor trustee a bank or trust company authorized by law to exercise fiduciary powers which shall have its principal place of business and be actively engaged in the trust business in the state in which she shall have established her domicile. If such nominee shall accept said trust and file its written acceptance with the Trustee, the latter, after finally accounting to the beneficiaries, shall deliver all of the funds held in trust hereunder to the successor trustee and shall thereafter have no further duties or liabilities with respect thereto. All powers and discretions herein conferred upon the Trustee are conferred upon any successor trustee.

7. This agreement may be altered or modified at any time by consent of the Settlor and the Trustee without the consent of any other person.

8. The Trustee shall receive reasonable compensation for its services hereunder but such compensation shall not exceed the amount customarily charged by corporate fiduciaries in the area for similar services.

9. In each year during the Settlor's lifetime that there have been no receipts or disbursements from the trust, the Trustee shall not be required to furnish any statement with respect to the trust property to the Settlor. After the Settlor's death, however, the Trustee shall furnish such an annual statement to his said wife during her lifetime and after the death of both the Settlor and his wife the Trustee shall furnish a similar annual statement with respect to each of the trust funds thereafter administered by it to the respective beneficiaries thereof or to their guardians if they be minors.

10. A. The Trustee is specifically instructed to make all investments and reinvestments of the trust assets (except a reasonable amount of uninvested cash and any real estate which may be added to the trust during the Settlor's lifetime or, subsequently, by reference in his Will, which real estate the Trustee may deem it in the best interests of the beneficiaries to retain), in shares of_____, a registered mutual investment company. Should shares of the said Fund not be available for investment or reinvestment, or should there be a material change in the investment policies or professional standing of such Fund, then the Trustee may substitute for such Fund shares as may then be held or are thereafter to be purchased, the shares of another registered investment fund of good standing. When acting in accordance with the instructions contained herein, the Trustee shall be under no liability for the proper selection or supervision of the investments by the management of the Fund specified or such other fund as may be substituted. In the event that shares of the Fund or of a substitute meeting the requirements of this trust be not available then the Trustee is authorized to invest, reinvest and otherwise manage the assets of the trust in its absolute discretion with due regard to the Settlor's desire to maintain at all times a balanced portfolio of investment securities. As applied to shares of any investment fund held hereunder, the term "income" in this instrument shall be deemed to mean that portion of the distributions made upon such shares held in the trust which has been designated as "ordinary income" as distinguished from "capital gains". Whenever such portion of said distribution as shall be designated "ordinary income" shall be less than 6% of the total principal market value of the trust, then the Trustee is authorized and instructed to add to such distribution from "ordinary income" such portion of any distribution which has been designated as "capital gains" as shall be necessary to cause the total payment to the then income beneficiary or beneficiaries to equal 6% of the total principal market value of the trust. If such distributions from "ordinary income" and "capital gains" shall not together be sufficient to provide the income beneficiary or beneficiaries with a sum equal to 6% per annum of the then current principal market value of the trust, then the Trustee is authorized and instructed to pay said income beneficiary or beneficiaries such amount of the principal of the trust as shall be required to maintain the total annual distribution to such beneficiary or beneficiaries at a minimum of 6% of the then current total principal market value of the trust. Where used herein, "principal market value" shall be deemed to mean the principal market value of the trust shown by the latest regular annual report of the Trustee. Except as provided in the foregoing, "capital gains" distributions shall be considered as principal and added to the corpus of the trust.

B. The Trustee may (a) sell, mortgage, lease, convey, and exchange the whole or any part of the trust funds, whether real or personal without court order and upon such terms as it shall deem best, (b) make any required division or distribution of the trust funds in cash or in kind or in both and at such values as it may fix, (c) apportion Trustee's and attorney's fees between income and principal, (d) register securities in the name of a nominee, (e) compromise claims by or against the trusts and (f) borrow funds for any trust purpose and secure the payment of such loans by the pledge of the whole or any part of the trust funds. The Trustee may make loans to the executors or administrators of the Settlor's estate, whether secured or unsecured, and may purchase and hold any asset of his estate whether or not it shall be considered a prudent trust investment.

11. Until otherwise instructed in writing by the Settlor, the Trustee is specifically authorized and instructed

to obtain such shares as are required to be purchased for the trust through the facilities of_____

_____or their successors so long as such facilities shall be available.

12. This agreement shall be construed and enforced in accordance with the laws of the State of

_____.

IN WITNESS WHEREOF, the said_____, has hereunto and

to a duplicate hereof set his hand and seal and said_____has

caused this instrument to be executed in duplicate by its duly authorized officer(s) as of the_____

_____day of_____, 19____.

Witnessed by:

THE SETTLOR:

_____

_____L.S.

_____

FOR THE TRUSTEE:

_____

_____L.S.

_____

STATE OF_____ }

                   ss:_____

COUNTY OF_____ }

Personally appeared_____, signer

and sealer of the foregoing instrument, who acknowledged the same to be his free act and deed, before me, this

_____day of_____, 19____.

_____

(Notary Seal)   Notary Public

STATE OF_____ }

                   ss:_____

COUNTY OF_____ }

Personally appeared_____, signer

and sealer of the foregoing instrument, and acknowledged the same to be his free act and deed as such officer, and

the free act and deed of said_____

before me, this_____day of_____, 19____.

_____

(Notary Seal)   Notary Public

SCHEDULE A

Deed of Trust

Made by and between_____of the

City/Town of_____, County of_____and State of_____

(hereinafter referred to as the "Settlor") and_____ _____

_____located in the City/Town of_____,

County of_____and State of_____(hereinafter referred to as the "Trustee").

WITNESSETH

By this agreement the Settlor desires to create a revocable voluntary living trust consisting of policies of life insurance hereinafter described and of other property which he may add to such trust from time to time, and the Trustee has agreed to accept the same under this agreement.

It is therefore agreed by and between the Settlor and the Trustee as follows:

SECTION A:

With respect to any property except policies of life insurance which now or hereafter may be placed in trust hereunder, the Trustee shall hold, invest and reinvest the same as a trust fund upon the following terms and conditions:

1. During the Settlor's lifetime, pay the income to him in convenient installments or expend or reinvest the same upon his written direction.

2. Upon the Settlor's death, add the trust fund herein created to the trust of the insurance proceeds established by Section B of this agreement and dispose of the same as a part thereof in accordance with the provisions of Section B-1 and B-2.

SECTION B:

The Settlor has delivered to the Trustee certain insurance policies on his life described in Schedule A attached hereto and made a part hereof, in which policies the right to change the beneficiary without consent is specifically reserved to the Settlor during his lifetime; and has executed and delivered or will execute and deliver to the Trustee proper instruments to enable the Trustee to be made the beneficiary under said policies as Trustee under this agreement, which policies and the proceeds thereof as and when received by the Trustee shall be held in trust and disposed of by the Trustee as hereinafter provided. Upon receipt by the Trustee of notice of the death of the Settlor the Trustee shall prepare such proofs of death and other documents as are required to collect the amounts payable upon the death of the Settlor under the terms of the policies then held by it as Trustee and shall present such documents to the companies issuing said policies and for that purpose it shall have full power to execute and deliver such instruments and to institute any action in law or equity as in its judgment may be necessary and proper but the Trustee shall not be required to institute any such action until it shall have been indemnified to its satisfaction against all expenses and liabilities which might be incurred thereby.

The Trustee shall divide the insurance proceeds received by it, together with the then trust fund established by the provisions of Section A, and together with any other property which may be added to this trust before or after the Settlor's death, into two parts. One of said parts, herein termed the "marital share", shall consist of property of a value necessary to utilize to the maximum extent any federal estate tax benefit to the Settlor's estate which may be available from any "marital deduction" allowable in the determination of such tax, after taking into account any other property whether or not passing under this agreement or under the Settlor's Will or otherwise, with respect to which such deduction is allowable and any other deductions or exemptions allowable in the determination of such tax. The other part shall consist of the remainder of the insurance proceeds and the remainder of the trust fund established by the provisions of Section A. In apportioning to the marital and non-marital trusts specific assets previously valued for estate tax purposes, the Trustee shall insure that the two trusts share proportionately in any subsequent appreciation or depreciation in the value of such assets.

1. With respect to the "marital share" so-called, the Trustee shall hold, manage, invest and reinvest the same as a trust fund upon the following terms and conditions: . . .

1

(a) The Trustee shall pay the income (and any other payment authorized by Paragraph 10-A) to the

Settlor's wife,————————————————————————————————, in quarterly or if convenient more frequent payments during her lifetime, together with such sums out of principal as she may request the Trustee in writing to pay to her from time to time and together with such sums out of principal as the Trustee in its sole discretion shall deem necessary for her support or maintenance.

(b) Upon the death of the Settlor's wife, the Trustee shall pay the then trust fund as she shall appoint by her Will and the Settlor hereby confers upon his said wife the sole and unrestricted power to appoint the same by her Will, outright or in further trust, in favor of her estate or in favor of others. To the extent that said power shall not be effectively exercised, the trust fund herein created shall be added to the remaining part and shall be disposed of as hereinafter provided.

(c) If the Settlor and his wife shall die under such circumstances that there is not, in the judgment of the Executor of the Settlor's estate, whose decision shall be conclusive, sufficient evidence to determine readily which of them survived the other, then for the purposes of this trust, the Settlor's wife shall be deemed to have survived him.

2. With respect to the remaining part of the insurance proceeds and trust fund, the Trustee shall hold, invest and reinvest the same as a trust fund upon the following terms and conditions:

(a) If requested by the executor or administrator of the Settlor's estate, the Trustee shall pay or reimburse said executor or administrator for the amount of any ante mortem claim, funeral expense or expense of administration which shall be allowed in connection with the settlement of his estate and which shall be certified to the Trustee by such executor or administrator.

(b) The Trustee shall pay to the proper taxing authority or reimburse the executor or administrator of the Settlor's estate for the amount of any succession, estate, transfer or similar tax, whether state or federal, which shall be imposed lawfully upon the Settlor's taxable estate or upon any beneficiary thereof as the result of the death of the Settlor and which shall be certified to the Trustee by such executor or administrator.

(c) The Trustee shall pay the income (and any other payment authorized by Paragraph 10 A) from the balance of the trust fund remaining in its hands to the Settlor's said wife during her lifetime in quarterly or if convenient more frequent payments or in its sole and absolute discretion withhold and accumulate all or such part of such income (or other payment) as it shall determine and add the same to principal. The Trustee is further authorized to pay to the Settlor's wife or in its discretion expend for her maintenance and support or for the maintenance, support and education of the Settlor's children such sums out of principal as it in its sole discretion may deem proper from time to time for any such purpose.

(d) Upon the death of the Settlor's wife or upon the Settlor's death if she shall not survive the Settlor, the Trustee shall:

(i) If requested by the executor or administrator of the wife's estate, pay or reimburse her estate for the amounts of her funeral expenses and the expenses of her last illness as certified to the Trustee by such executor or administrator.

(ii) Divide the balance of the trust fund into as many equal parts as there shall be children of the Settlor then living and children of the Settlor then deceased leaving issue then living and shall:

(1) Pay one of said parts to the living issue collectively of each such child then deceased in equal shares per stirpes.

(2) Pay one of said parts to each child of the Settlor then living and who shall have become 35 years of age.

(3) Hold, manage, invest and reinvest the remaining parts as one trust fund for the benefit of the children of the Settlor then living and who shall not have become 35 years of age and pay or expend all or none or so much of the income and principal to or for the benefit of each of said children as the Trustee in its sole discretion shall deem proper for their suitable maintenance, support and education until each such child shall become 35 years of age, at which time an equal share of the then principal of the trust fund shall be paid over to such child after making adjustment for the amount by which payments of principal to one child may have exceeded those made to another child. If any such child shall die before becoming 35 years of age, then upon such child's death an equal share of said trust fund after adjustment as aforesaid, shall be paid over to such child's children equally; if there shall be no such children then living such shares shall be added equally to the remaining shares, if any, and held, managed and disposed of as a part thereof; if no such shares remain, such share shall be paid over to the Settlor's issue then living, per stirpes.

(4) Notwithstanding any of the foregoing directions, the share of each living issue of any deceased child of the Settlor, though vested, shall be held in trust and so much of the income and principal as the Trustee shall deem proper shall be paid to or for the benefit of such issue until he or she shall become twenty-one years of age.

SECTION C: ADMINISTRATIVE PROVISIONS

1. Unless directed in accordance with the provisions of Section A-1, the Trustee shall be under no duty to pay any premiums or other charges required to continue the said policies of insurance in force or to procure renewals thereof or otherwise to ascertain that said policies are kept in force.

2. The provisions of Section B shall apply only to such proceeds of said policies as may be due and payable to the Trustee upon the death of the Settlor, and all payments, dividends, surrender values and benefits of any kind which may accrue on any of said policies during the lifetime of the Settlor shall be payable to the Settlor and shall not be collected or disposed of by the Trustee.

3. The Settlor reserves to himself without the consent of said Trustee or of any beneficiary hereunder or of any beneficiary now or hereafter named in any policy now or hereafter deposited hereunder, the right to pledge any of said policies or any other property now or hereafter placed in trust hereunder to secure any loan now existing or hereafter made by any persons, firm or corporation to the Settlor, and further reserves the right to exercise any and all options, elections, rights, and privileges, including the right to borrow on said policies, given to him under the terms of any of said policies, and upon the request of the Settlor the Trustee will execute and deliver such documents as are necessary and proper to permit the Settlor fully to exercise such rights.

4. The Settlor shall have the right at any time during his lifetime to place additional property and/or insurance policies under the terms of the agreement upon delivering such property and/or insurance policies to the Trustee together with a written request that the Trustee place said additional property and policies under this agreement. Upon the delivery of any such additional property and policies and such written request to the Trustee, the Trustee shall issue a receipt therefore to the Settlor. The Settlor shall also have the right to add to the trust fund by an appropriate provision in his Will or to designate the Trustee as beneficiary of any profit-sharing, pension, incentive compensation or other fund in which he may have an interest, and under the terms of which he has the right to name a beneficiary. The Trustee is further authorized to accept additions to this trust from any other source, testamentary or otherwise.

5. The Settlor shall have the right at any time during his lifetime to withdraw from the operation of this agreement any or all property and policies upon his written request delivered to the Trustee and upon delivery to the Trustee of a receipt for the property and/or policies so withdrawn, and upon such withdrawal and thereafter if required, the Trustee shall execute and deliver to the Settlor such instruments as are necessary and proper to release the interest of the Trustee therein.

6. The Settlor shall have the right at any time during his lifetime to terminate this agreement upon giving to the Trustee written notice of such termination, and upon termination the Trustee shall deliver to the Settlor against his written receipt all property and policies then held hereunder and shall execute and deliver to the Settlor such instruments as are necessary and proper to transfer the interest of the Trustee therein to the Settlor.

After the Settlor's death, by mutual agreement between the Beneficiary and the Trustee, the Trustee may resign to be replaced by a successor trustee nominated by the Beneficiary, provided that such successor trustee shall be a bank or trust company authorized by law to exercise fiduciary powers which shall have its principal place of business and be actively engaged in the trust business in the state in which the Beneficiary then legally resides. Such successor trustee having filed its written acceptance with the Trustee, the latter, after finally accounting to the Beneficiary or Beneficiaries, shall deliver all of the trust assets held hereunder to the successor trustee and shall thereafter have no further duties or liabilities with respect thereto.

Should the Settlor's wife, surviving the Settlor, move and establish her domicile in another state, she may request the Trustee to and the Trustee shall resign, _provided_ that she shall by written instrument filed with the Trustee name as successor trustee a bank or trust company authorized by law to exercise fiduciary powers which shall have its principal place of business and be actively engaged in the trust business in the state in which she shall have established her domicile. If such nominee shall accept said trust and file its written acceptance with the Trustee, the latter, after finally accounting to the beneficiaries, shall deliver all of the funds held in trust hereunder to the successor trustee and shall thereafter have no further duties or liabilities with respect thereto. All powers and discretions herein conferred upon the Trustee are conferred upon any successor trustee.

7. This agreement may be altered or modified at any time by consent of the Settlor and the Trustee without the consent of any other person.

8. The Trustee shall receive reasonable compensation for its services hereunder but such compensation shall not exceed the amount customarily charged by corporate fiduciaries in the area for similar services.

9. In each year during the Settlor's lifetime that there have been no receipts or disbursements from the trust, the Trustee shall not be required to furnish any statement with respect to the trust property to the Settlor. After the Settlor's death, however, the Trustee shall furnish such an annual statement to his said wife during her lifetime and after the death of both the Settlor and his wife the Trustee shall furnish a similar annual statement with respect to each of the trust funds thereafter administered by it to the respective beneficiaries thereof or to their guardians if they be minors.

10. A. The Trustee is specifically instructed to make all investments and reinvestments of the trust assets (except a reasonable amount of uninvested cash and any real estate which may be added to the trust during the Settlor's lifetime or, subsequently, by reference in his Will, which real estate the Trustee may deem it in the best interests of the beneficiaries to retain), in shares of_____, a registered mutual investment company. Should shares of the said Fund not be available for investment or reinvestment, or should there be a material change in the investment policies or professional standing of such Fund, then the Trustee may substitute for such Fund shares as may then be held or are thereafter to be purchased, the shares of another registered investment fund of good standing. When acting in accordance with the instructions contained herein, the Trustee shall be under no liability for the proper selection or supervision of the investments by the management of the Fund specified or such other fund as may be substituted. In the event that shares of the Fund or of a substitute meeting the requirements of this trust be not available then the Trustee is authorized to invest, reinvest and otherwise manage the assets of the trust in its absolute discretion with due regard to the Settlor's desire to maintain at all times a balanced portfolio of investment securities. As applied to shares of any investment fund held hereunder, the term "income" in this instrument shall be deemed to mean that portion of the distributions made upon such shares held in the trust which has been designated as "ordinary income" as distinguished from "capital gains". Whenever such portion of said distribution as shall be designated "ordinary income" shall be less than 6% of the total principal market value of the trust, then the Trustee is authorized and instructed to add to such distribution from "ordinary income" such portion of any distribution which has been designated as "capital gains" as shall be necessary to cause the total payment to the then income beneficiary or beneficiaries to equal 6% of the total principal market value of the trust. If such distributions from "ordinary income" and "capital gains" shall not together be sufficient to provide the income beneficiary or beneficiaries with a sum equal to 6% per annum of the then current principal market value of the trust, then the Trustee is authorized and instructed to pay said income beneficiary or beneficiaries such amount of the principal of the trust as shall be required to maintain the total annual distribution to such beneficiary or beneficiaries at a minimum of 6% of the then current total principal market value of the trust. Where used herein, "principal market value" shall be deemed to mean the principal market value of the trust shown by the latest regular annual report of the Trustee. Except as provided in the foregoing, "capital gains" distributions shall be considered as principal and added to the corpus of the trust.

B. The Trustee may (a) sell, mortgage, lease, convey, and exchange the whole or any part of the trust funds, whether real or personal without court order and upon such terms as it shall deem best, (b) make any required division or distribution of the trust funds in cash or in kind or in both and at such values as it may fix, (c) apportion Trustee's and attorney's fees between income and principal, (d) register securities in the name of a nominee, (e) compromise claims by or against the trusts and (f) borrow funds for any trust purpose and secure the payment of such loans by the pledge of the whole or any part of the trust funds. The Trustee may make loans to the executors or administrators of the Settlor's estate, whether secured or unsecured, and may purchase and hold any asset of his estate whether or not it shall be considered a prudent trust investment.

11. Until otherwise instructed in writing by the Settlor, the Trustee is specifically authorized and instructed

to obtain such shares as are required to be purchased for the trust through the facilities of_____

_____or their successors so long as such facilities shall be available.

12. This agreement shall be construed and enforced in accordance with the laws of the State of

_____.

4

IN WITNESS WHEREOF, the said_____, has hereunto and

to a duplicate hereof set his hand and seal and said_____has

caused this instrument to be executed in duplicate by its duly authorized officer(s) as of the_____

_____day of_____, 19____.

Witnessed by:

THE SETTLOR:

_____

_____L.S.

_____

FOR THE TRUSTEE:

_____

_____L.S.

_____

STATE OF_____⎫

COUNTY OF_____⎭ ss:_____

Personally appeared_____, signer

and sealer of the foregoing instrument, who acknowledged the same to be his free act and deed, before me, this

_____day of_____, 19____.

(Notary Seal)

_____
Notary Public

STATE OF_____⎫

COUNTY OF_____⎭ ss:_____

Personally appeared_____, signer

and sealer of the foregoing instrument, and acknowledged the same to be his free act and deed as such officer, and

the free act and deed of said_____

before me, this_____day of_____, 19____.

(Notary Seal)

_____
Notary Public

SCHEDULE A

Chapter 12

WIFE'S TRUST

The individual with a large amount of life insurance in force on his life may find it desirable to have the policies owned by his spouse, thus exempting the proceeds from federal estate tax at his death. The theory behind the arrangement is simple: Make the policy the property of your wife; they cannot tax your wife's property because you have died.

Obviously, this arrangement serves no useful purpose if your estate is modest and therefore not subject to federal estate tax. The first $60,000 will be tax exempt. In addition, up to one-half of your estate is tax free if you leave it to your spouse—this is called the "marital deduction." Thus, if a man leaves an estate of $120,000 specifying that $60,000 is to go to his wife, that $60,000 is tax free. The remainder of his estate, covered by his $60,000 general exemption, is also tax free.

The practice of having insurance policies owned by one's spouse is most likely to be employed by persons with substantial estates seeking tax relief. It follows that these are quite likely to be the same individuals who, concerned with the preservation of their estates, will choose to set up a "Dacey Trust."

Under the program described in detail in Chapter 11 ("The Dacey Trust"), the insured directs that his policies be payable to his trust account at the bank. If, however, those policies are owned by his wife, he has no authority to direct that the proceeds be paid into his trust account at his death. This does not mean that they cannot be gotten into his trust, though.

The procedure to accomplish this objective is as follows: The wife establishes her own inter vivos trust at the same bank where her husband has established his "Dacey Trust", her trust's assets consisting of the insurance policies on her husband's life owned by her. The trust instrument simply directs the trustee to collect the insurance proceeds at his death, add them to *his* trust account and terminate her account. The husband's life insurance proceeds end up right where he wanted them, in one neat package in *his* trust account, but they have avoided completely the federal estate tax to which they would otherwise have been subject.

For a suitable deed of trust for use in setting up a "wife's trust" see Appendix A immediately following.

DEED OF TRUST

FOR ESTABLISHING A

WIFE'S TRUST

Instructions:

On the following pages will be found duplicate copies of a deed of trust (DT-18) which will be suitable for use where it is desired to implement the arrangement described in Chapter 12 to provide that the proceeds of life insurance policies owned by a spouse on the life of her husband shall pass into his "Dacey Trust" upon his death.

At the top of the first page enter the name of the wife as settlor, and the bank's name as trustee. Cross off "city" or "town", leaving the appropriate designation of your community.

In Paragraph 1, enter the name of the settlor's husband.

When completed, Paragraph 3 should read something like this: "Upon receipt of the proceeds of said insurance policies, the Trustee shall deliver the entire amount to the ABC Trust Company, of the Town of Smithville, County of Fairfax and State of Zenith, as Trustee under the terms of a certain trust instrument executed by the Settlor's husband, John Smith, and said ABC Trust Company as of June 1, 1965, and the Settlor hereby specifically directs and provides that the property received by virtue of this bequest shall be held by said ABC Trust Company, as such Trustee, to be administered and disposed of by it in accordance with Section B thereof".

The Settlor (the insured's wife) and the Trustee bank should each retain one copy of the completed and executed agreement.

The insurance company issuing the policy on the husband's life should then be instructed by the wife in her capacity as owner of the policy to pay the proceeds at his death to the Trustee bank with whom she has entered into this agreement.

Deed of Trust

_____ of the ~~City~~/Town of _____

Made by and between **Elizabeth M. Smith** , County of **Fairfax** (hereinafter referred to as the "Settlor"),

Jonesville

and State of **Connecticut**

and **The First National Bank** , County of **Fairfax**

located in the ~~City~~/Town of **Jonesville** (hereinafter referred to as the "Trustee").

and State of **Connecticut**

WITNESSETH

By this agreement the Settlor desires to create a revocable voluntary living trust consisting of policies of life insurance hereinafter described and of other property which she may add to such trust from time to time, and the Trustee has agreed to accept the same under this agreement.

It is therefore agreed by and between the Settlor and the Trustee as follows:

1. The Settlor has delivered to the Trustee certain insurance policies (described in Schedule A attached hereto and made a part hereof) on the life of her husband, **John J. Smith** , of which policies the Settlor is the absolute owner and in which policies the right to change the beneficiary is specifically reserved to the Settlor during her lifetime. The Settlor has executed proper instruments to name the Trustee to receive the proceeds as beneficiary under such policies, said policies and proceeds to be held in trust and disposed of by the Trustee as hereinafter provided.

2. Upon receipt by the Trustee of notice of the death of the Settlor's said husband, the Trustee shall prepare such proofs of death and other documents as are required to collect the amounts payable upon the death of the Settlor's said husband under the terms of the policies then held by it as Trustee and shall present such documents to the companies issuing said policies and for that purpose it shall have full power to execute and deliver such instruments and to institute any action in law or equity as in its judgment may be necessary and proper but the Trustee shall not be required to institute any such action until it shall have been indemnified to its satisfaction against all expenses and liabilities which might be incurred thereby.

3. Upon receipt of the proceeds of said insurance policies, the Trustee shall deliver the entire amount to **The First National Bank** of the ~~City~~/Town of **Jonesville** , as Trustee

County of **Fairfax** and State of **Connecticut**

under the terms of a certain trust instrument executed by the Settlor's husband, **John J. Smith** as of **June 20, 1965** ,

and said **The First National Bank**

and the Settlor hereby directs and provides that the property received by virtue of this bequest shall be held by

said **The First National Bank** , as Trustee, to be administered and disposed of by it in

accordance with the provisions of Section B thereof.

Upon delivery of the property as above provided, this trust shall terminate forthwith.

1

Deed of Trust

Made by and between_____of the City/Town of

_____, County of_____

and State of_____(hereinafter referred to as the "Settlor")

and_____,

located in the City/Town of_____, County of_____

and State of_____(hereinafter referred to as the "Trustee").

WITNESSETH

By this agreement the Settlor desires to create a revocable voluntary living trust consisting of policies of life insurance hereinafter described and of other property which she may add to such trust from time to time, and the Trustee has agreed to accept the same under this agreement.

It is therefore agreed by and between the Settlor and the Trustee as follows:

1. The Settlor has delivered to the Trustee certain insurance policies (described in Schedule A attached hereto and made a part hereof) on the life of her husband,_____, of which policies the Settlor is the absolute owner and in which policies the right to change the beneficiary is specifically reserved to the Settlor during her lifetime. The Settlor has executed proper instruments to name the Trustee to receive the proceeds as beneficiary under such policies, said policies and proceeds to be held in trust and disposed of by the Trustee as hereinafter provided.

2. Upon receipt by the Trustee of notice of the death of the Settlor's said husband, the Trustee shall prepare such proofs of death and other documents as are required to collect the amounts payable upon the death of the Settlor's said husband under the terms of the policies then held by it as Trustee and shall present such documents to the companies issuing said policies and for that purpose it shall have full power to execute and deliver such instruments and to institute any action in law or equity as in its judgment may be necessary and proper but the Trustee shall not be required to institute any such action until it shall have been indemnified to its satisfaction against all expenses and liabilities which might be incurred thereby.

3. Upon receipt of the proceeds of said insurance policies, the Trustee shall deliver the entire amount to

_____of the City/Town of_____,

County of_____and State of_____, as Trustee

under the terms of a certain trust instrument executed by the Settlor's husband,_____

and said_____ as of_____,

and the Settlor hereby directs and provides that the property received by virtue of this bequest shall be held by

said_____, as Trustee, to be administered and disposed of by it in

accordance with the provisions of Section B thereof.

Upon delivery of the property as above provided, this trust shall terminate forthwith.

1

4. The Trustee shall be under no duty to pay any premiums or other charges required to continue the said policies of insurance in force or to procure renewals thereof or otherwise to ascertain that said policies are kept in force.

The provisions of this trust shall apply only to such proceeds of said policies as may be due and payable to the Trustee upon the death of the Settlor's husband, and all payments, dividends, surrender values and benefits of any kind which may accrue on any of said policies during the lifetime of the Settlor's husband shall be payable to the Settlor and shall not be collected or disposed of by the Trustee.

The Settlor reserves to herself without the consent of said Trustee or of the beneficiary hereunder or of any beneficiary now or hereafter named in any policy now or hereafter deposited hereunder, the right to pledge any of said policies or any other property now or hereafter placed in trust hereunder to secure any loan now existing or hereafter made by any persons, firm or corporation to the Settlor, and further reserves the right to exercise any and all options, elections, rights and privileges, including the right to borrow on said policies, given to her under the terms of any of said policies, and upon the request of the Settlor the Trustee shall execute and deliver such documents as are necessary and proper to permit the Settlor to exercise such rights.

The Settlor shall have the right at any time during her lifetime to place additional insurance policies and/or other property under the terms of the agreement upon delivering such insurance policies and/or property to the Trustee together with a written request that the Trustee place said additional policies and/or property under this agreement. Upon the delivery of any such additional policies and/or property and such written request to the Trustee, the Trustee shall issue a receipt therefore to the Settlor. The Settlor shall also have the right to add to the trust fund by an appropriate provision in her Will.

The Settlor shall have the right at any time during her lifetime to withdraw from the operation of this agreement any or all policies and/or property upon her written request delivered to the Trustee and upon delivery to the Trustee of a receipt for the policies and/or property so withdrawn, and upon such withdrawal and thereafter if required, the Trustee shall execute and deliver to the Settlor such instruments as are necessary and proper to release the interest of the Trustee therein.

The Settlor shall have the right at any time during her lifetime to terminate this agreement upon giving to the Trustee written notice of such termination, and upon termination the Trustee shall deliver to the Settlor against her written receipt all policies and/or property then held hereunder and shall execute and deliver to the Settlor such instruments as are necessary and proper to transfer the interest of the Trustee therein to the Settlor. The death of the Settlor before her husband shall in no way effect the operation of this trust. Title to any insurance policies or other property held hereunder shall thereafter revert irrevocably to the Trustee who will continue to retain possession of them under the same terms and conditions which prevailed during the Settlor's lifetime. Upon the death of the Settlor's husband (the insured under the policies), the Trustee shall proceed in accordance with the provisions of Section 2 and 3 hereinbefore set forth. If at such time there shall be in existance no trust account thereinbefore established by the Settlor's husband, then the Trustee is authorized and instructed to pay the then trust fund to the Settlor's issue in equal shares, per stirpes. If the Settlor shall have died leaving no issue, then the Trustee is authorized and instructed to pay the then trust fund to the Settlor's heirs at law, in equal shares, per stirpes.

5. This agreement may be altered or modified at any time by consent of the Settlor and the Trustee without the consent of any other person.

6. The Trustee shall receive reasonable compensation for its services hereunder but such compensation shall not exceed the amount customarily charged by corporate fiduciaries in the area for similar services.

7. The Trustee may (a) sell, mortgage, lease, convey, or exchange the whole or any part of the trust funds, whether real or personal, without court order and upon such terms at it shall deem best, (b) apportion Trustee's and attorney's fees between income and principal, (c) compromise claims by or against the trust, (d) borrow funds for any trust purpose and secure the payment of such loans by the pledge of the whole or any part of the trust funds, and (e) make loans to the executors or administrators of the Settlor's estate, whether secured or unsecured.

8. This agreement and its terms shall be construed and enforced in accordance with the laws of the

State of_____.

IN WITNESS WHEREOF, the said_____

has hereunto and to a duplicate hereof set her hand and seal and said_____

has caused this instrument to be executed in duplicate by its duly authorized officer as of the_____

day of_____19_____.

Witnessed by:

THE SETTLOR:

_____

_____L.S.

_____

FOR THE TRUSTEE:

_____

_____L.S.

_____

STATE OF_____⎤
⎬ ss:_____
COUNTY OF_____⎦

Personally appeared_____, signer and

sealer of the foregoing Agreement who acknowledged the same to be her free act and deed, before me, this

_____day of_____, 19_____.

(Notary Seal)   _____
                                          Notary Public

STATE OF_____⎤
⎬ ss:_____
COUNTY OF_____⎦

Personally appeared_____, _____
                                                                                          (Title)

of_____, signer and sealer of the

foregoing instrument, and acknowledged the same to be his free act and deed as such officer, and the free act and

deed of said_____

before me, this_____day of_____, 19_____.

(Notary Seal)   _____
                                          Notary Public

SCHEDULE A

Deed of Trust

Made by and between_____of the City/Town of

_____, County of_____

and State of_____(hereinafter referred to as the "Settlor")

and_____,

located in the City/Town of_____, County of_____

and State of_____(hereinafter referred to as the "Trustee").

WITNESSETH

By this agreement the Settlor desires to create a revocable voluntary living trust consisting of policies of life insurance hereinafter described and of other property which she may add to such trust from time to time, and the Trustee has agreed to accept the same under this agreement.

It is therefore agreed by and between the Settlor and the Trustee as follows:

1. The Settlor has delivered to the Trustee certain insurance policies (described in Schedule A attached hereto and made a part hereof) on the life of her husband,_____, of which policies the Settlor is the absolute owner and in which policies the right to change the beneficiary is specifically reserved to the Settlor during her lifetime. The Settlor has executed proper instruments to name the Trustee to receive the proceeds as beneficiary under such policies, said policies and proceeds to be held in trust and disposed of by the Trustee as hereinafter provided.

2. Upon receipt by the Trustee of notice of the death of the Settlor's said husband, the Trustee shall prepare such proofs of death and other documents as are required to collect the amounts payable upon the death of the Settlor's said husband under the terms of the policies then held by it as Trustee and shall present such documents to the companies issuing said policies and for that purpose it shall have full power to execute and deliver such instruments and to institute any action in law or equity as in its judgment may be necessary and proper but the Trustee shall not be required to institute any such action until it shall have been indemnified to its satisfaction against all expenses and liabilities which might be incurred thereby.

3. Upon receipt of the proceeds of said insurance policies, the Trustee shall deliver the entire amount to

_____of the City/Town of_____,

County of_____and State of_____, as Trustee

under the terms of a certain trust instrument executed by the Settlor's husband,_____

and said_____ as of_____,

and the Settlor hereby directs and provides that the property received by virtue of this bequest shall be held by

said_____, as Trustee, to be administered and disposed of by it in accordance with the provisions of Section B thereof.

Upon delivery of the property as above provided, this trust shall terminate forthwith.

4. The Trustee shall be under no duty to pay any premiums or other charges required to continue the said policies of insurance in force or to procure renewals thereof or otherwise to ascertain that said policies are kept in force.

The provisions of this trust shall apply only to such proceeds of said policies as may be due and payable to the Trustee upon the death of the Settlor's husband, and all payments, dividends, surrender values and benefits of any kind which may accrue on any of said policies during the lifetime of the Settlor's husband shall be payable to the Settlor and shall not be collected or disposed of by the Trustee.

The Settlor reserves to herself without the consent of said Trustee or of the beneficiary hereunder or of any beneficiary now or hereafter named in any policy now or hereafter deposited hereunder, the right to pledge any of said policies or any other property now or hereafter placed in trust hereunder to secure any loan now existing or hereafter made by any persons, firm or corporation to the Settlor, and further reserves the right to exercise any and all options, elections, rights and privileges, including the right to borrow on said policies, given to her under the terms of any of said policies, and upon the request of the Settlor the Trustee shall execute and deliver such documents as are necessary and proper to permit the Settlor to exercise such rights.

The Settlor shall have the right at any time during her lifetime to place additional insurance policies and/or other property under the terms of the agreement upon delivering such insurance policies and/or property to the Trustee together with a written request that the Trustee place said additional policies and/or property under this agreement. Upon the delivery of any such additional policies and/or property and such written request to the Trustee, the Trustee shall issue a receipt therefore to the Settlor. The Settlor shall also have the right to add to the trust fund by an appropriate provision in her Will.

The Settlor shall have the right at any time during her lifetime to withdraw from the operation of this agreement any or all policies and/or property upon her written request delivered to the Trustee and upon delivery to the Trustee of a receipt for the policies and/or property so withdrawn, and upon such withdrawal and thereafter if required, the Trustee shall execute and deliver to the Settlor such instruments as are necessary and proper to release the interest of the Trustee therein.

The Settlor shall have the right at any time during her lifetime to terminate this agreement upon giving to the Trustee written notice of such termination, and upon termination the Trustee shall deliver to the Settlor against her written receipt all policies and/or property then held hereunder and shall execute and deliver to the Settlor such instruments as are necessary and proper to transfer the interest of the Trustee therein to the Settlor. The death of the Settlor before her husband shall in no way effect the operation of this trust. Title to any insurance policies or other property held hereunder shall thereafter revert irrevocably to the Trustee who will continue to retain possession of them under the same terms and conditions which prevailed during the Settlor's lifetime. Upon the death of the Settlor's husband (the insured under the policies), the Trustee shall proceed in accordance with the provisions of Section 2 and 3 hereinbefore set forth. If at such time there shall be in existance no trust account thereinbefore established by the Settlor's husband, then the Trustee is authorized and instructed to pay the then trust fund to the Settlor's issue in equal shares, per stirpes. If the Settlor shall have died leaving no issue, then the Trustee is authorized and instructed to pay the then trust fund to the Settlor's heirs at law, in equal shares, per stirpes.

5. This agreement may be altered or modified at any time by consent of the Settlor and the Trustee without the consent of any other person.

6. The Trustee shall receive reasonable compensation for its services hereunder but such compensation shall not exceed the amount customarily charged by corporate fiduciaries in the area for similar services.

7. The Trustee may (a) sell, mortgage, lease, convey, or exchange the whole or any part of the trust funds, whether real or personal, without court order and upon such terms at it shall deem best, (b) apportion Trustee's and attorney's fees between income and principal, (c) compromise claims by or against the trust, (d) borrow funds for any trust purpose and secure the payment of such loans by the pledge of the whole or any part of the trust funds, and (e) make loans to the executors or administrators of the Settlor's estate, whether secured or unsecured.

8. This agreement and its terms shall be construed and enforced in accordance with the laws of the

State of_____.

IN WITNESS WHEREOF, the said_____

has hereunto and to a duplicate hereof set her hand and seal and said_____

has caused this instrument to be executed in duplicate by its duly authorized officer as of the_____

day of_____19_____.

Witnessed by:

THE SETTLOR:

_____

_____L.S.

_____

FOR THE TRUSTEE:

_____

_____L.S.

_____

STATE OF_____ ⎞
                                 ⎟ ss:_____
COUNTY OF_____ ⎠

Personally appeared_____, signer and

sealer of the foregoing Agreement who acknowledged the same to be her free act and deed, before me, this

_____day of_____, 19_____.

(Notary Seal)   _____
                                        Notary Public

STATE OF_____ ⎞
                                 ⎟ ss:_____
COUNTY OF_____ ⎠

Personally appeared_____, _____
                                                              (Title)

of_____, signer and sealer of the

foregoing instrument, and acknowledged the same to be his free act and deed as such officer, and the free act and

deed of said_____

before me, this_____day of_____, 19_____.

(Notary Seal)   _____
                                        Notary Public

SCHEDULE A

_____

_____

_____

_____

_____

_____

_____

_____

_____

_____

_____

_____

_____

_____

_____

_____

_____

_____

_____

_____

_____

SCHEDULE A

Chapter 13

LEAVING MONEY TO CHARITY

There are two ways of leaving money to charity. The first is the old-fashioned way—you simply direct in your Will that a specific sum is to be paid to a specific charity. When you die, your Will will be submitted for probate. Other persons or charities whom you chose not to remember in your Will may find cause for resentment when they read all of the details in the local newspaper. Your creditors will have six months (in some jurisdictions, one year) in which to present their claims. On average, it will take two to five years for your estate to clear probate. If your Will should be successfully contested, your bequest to charity might be cancelled. Lawyers, appraisers, executors and probate court fees will be levied against your estate—including the amount you were bequeathing to charity. Some day, when this involved procedure is concluded, the charity will receive the bequest. There is a good chance that this will be so long after your death that the object of your benevolence may have forgotten who you were.

The other and far more sensible way of leaving money to charity is through the instrumentality of an inter vivos trust of which you yourself may be trustee.

Let's assume, for example, that you own 500 shares of General Motors stock having a present value of $5,000. You've held the stock a long time—its original cost to you was only $2,000. If you were to sell the stock and give the college the $5,000, you would become liable for a long term capital gain tax on the $3,000 profit. Besides, the stock would be gone—and so would the income it was producing for you.

Instead, execute a simple form of *irrevocable* declaration of trust in which you identify the stock and state that you are holding it in trust for your alma mater, Old Siwash College. Reserve the life income to yourself. Re-register the stock in your name as trustee.

Now, continue to enjoy the dividends on your General Motors stock as long as you live. If you wish, you may reserve the income for your own lifetime plus that of your spouse.

You've given the college $5,000. There is no capital gains tax liability, of course, because you didn't liquidate the stock. The college won't receive the money until you die, so this is called "a gift of a future interest"—but it's still a gift and Uncle Sam will let you deduct a substantial proportion of it from your income this year for tax purposes. Expressed as a percentage, that proportion will be approximately the same as your age. Thus, if you're age 60 now and you make your college a "future interest" gift of $5,000 worth of General Motors stock, you may deduct 60% of $5,000, or $3,000, from your income this year as a gift to charity. If you're in a 50% tax bracket, you'll save $1,500 in taxes this year. The net cost to you of your $5,000 gift to charity will be only $3,500, then.

When you make a charitable bequest in your Will, it is deducted from your taxable estate at your death. If you make the bequest via an inter vivos trust, your taxable estate is similarly reduced at your death. Thus, either way you pay no death taxes on the charitable bequest. With the testamentary bequest, however, there is no *current* tax benefit *now* while you are still here. The important *income tax deduction* offered by the inter vivos trust method of making the bequest is extremely valuable. Noting that no citizen should *evade* taxes, the Supreme Court has ruled that it is nevertheless his right and duty to *avoid* all possible taxes—and the inter vivos trust offers a practical means of doing that.

Instead of the two-to-five-year delay in making the testamentary bequest available to the beneficiary after your death, the inter vivos trust can pass the property to that beneficiary 24 hours after you are gone. All that is required is a copy of your death certificate. No lawyers, no executors, no appraisers, no probate court. No delay, no expense, no publicity.

Here is a table which shows the proportion of your "gift of a future interest", dependent upon your age, which you can deduct from your income this year as a gift to charity:

Age	Percent	Age	Percent	Age	Percent
50	48%	59	59%	68	70%
51	49%	60	60%	69	71%
52	50%	61	61%	70	72%
53	51%	62	62%	71	73%
54	52%	63	64%	72	74%
55	54%	64	65%	73	76%
56	55%	65	66%	74	77%
57	56%	66	67%	75	78%
58	57%	67	69%		

If you wish to reserve the income during the lifetime of your spouse as well as during your own lifetime, a somewhat smaller percentage figure will apply, reflecting the fact that the charitable beneficiary will have to wait longer before it receives the principal.

With certain types of charitable beneficiaries, you may deduct from your income as a gift to charity an amount equal to 20% of your adjusted gross annual income. With other beneficiaries, such as churches and colleges, you may deduct up to 30% of your adjusted gross annual income.

Under the trust arrangement, you are entitled to all of the dividends paid by the stock which you have placed in trust. If there are any stock splits, the new stock belongs to the trust and ultimately to the charitable beneficiary, although any dividends paid on such new stock during your lifetime are yours. You may not at any time use any part of the principal, however.

A word of caution, if you are placing mutual fund shares in the trust: in addition to ordinary income dividends, such shares generally pay capital gains distributions which many persons choose to regard as a form of income. You can't do it with your charitable trust, however. All capital gains distributions on mutual funds must be reinvested as additions to the principal. You still get the benefit of them, though—the ordinary income dividends earned by the shares purchased with such reinvested distributions are yours. Under ordinary conditions, this will tend to make the income which you enjoy from the trust edge up over the years as the constantly increasing number of shares held produces more dividends.

Appendix A hereafter provides a declaration of trust which may be used to implement the desirable arrangements just described.

A note about gift taxes:

You may give any number of persons or institutions up to $3,000 each in any calendar year without being required to file a gift tax return or pay a gift tax. This $3,000 amount is called the "annual exclusion." If your spouse joins in the gift by signing the gift tax return, you may give an additional $3,000 to each donee regardless of whether the funds given are partly contributed by your spouse or are in fact all yours. A "gift of a future interest" such as is contemplated by the establishment of the income-reserved charitable trust *does not* qualify for the $3,000 annual exclusion. This does not necessarily mean that you must pay a gift tax when you set up such a trust, for you are also entitled to a "lifetime exemption" of $30,000 and you can charge your gift off against that exemption. It *does* mean that when you set up an income-reserved charitable trust, you must be sure to file a gift tax return regardless of how small the gift may be. If your spouse joins you in the gift, Treasury regulations require that he or she file a *separate* gift tax return, even though you customarily file a *joint* income tax return.

Sound complicated? It isn't. Just re-read the foregoing carefully.

```
┌─────────────────────────────────────────┐
│         DECLARATION OF TRUST            │
│          FOR ESTABLISHING A             │
│          CHARITABLE TRUST               │
│               WITH                      │
│    INCOME RESERVED DURING THE           │
│      LIFE OF THE DONOR ONLY             │
└─────────────────────────────────────────┘
```

Instructions:

On the following pages will be found duplicate copies of a declaration of trust (DT-19) which will be suitable for use where it is desired to establish a charitable trust as described in Chapter 13, with income reserved during the lifetime of the donor only.

Insert the name of the stock or mutual fund and the number of shares in the appropriate place at the top of the instrument.

In Paragraph 2, insert the name of the person whom you wish to have receive any undistributed income at the time of your death.

In Paragraph 3, insert the name of the charitable organization to whom you are making the gift of the property. Be careful, now—don't get these two beneficiaries mixed-up. It is in *Paragraph 3* that you name the charitable beneficiary.

Execute both copies; keep one in your safe deposit box. The other may be retained at home as a reference copy, or you may wish to send it to the charitable beneficiary so that it will be aware of your plans.

Re-register the mutual fund shares *"(Your Name), Trustee u/d/t dated_____."*

Declaration of Trust

WHEREAS, I, _____ of

Address _____
       Number   Street   City   State

am the owner of_____shares of the capital stock of:

_____

(Name of Company or Fund)

NOW, THEREFORE, KNOW ALL MEN BY THESE PRESENTS, that I do hereby declare that I hold and will hold such shares, and all right, title and interest in and to such shares IN TRUST for the following uses and purposes:

1. To pay to myself during my lifetime all dividends which shall be distributed upon such shares, *provided*, that if mutual investment company shares be held hereunder, the term "dividends" shall be taken to mean such payments on the shares as shall be designated by the issuer as "ordinary income". Any and all distributions which shall be designated as "realized profits" or "capital gains" shall be reinvested in additional shares and shall become part of the corpus of the Trust, and no part of such distributions shall be payable to or received by me as an individual.

2. In the event of my death, my Successor Trustee shall pay any undistributed income to which I would be entitled under the terms of this trust to:

(Name) _____, of

(Address) _____
       Number   Street   City   State

If the person named above be not then living, or should I for any reason fail to designate such person, my Successor Trustee shall pay such undistributed income to my estate or to my personal representatives.

3. Upon my death, my Successor Trustee shall transfer the trust property and all right, title and interest in and to such trust property unto:

(Name) _____

(Address) _____
       Number   Street   City   State

and thereby terminate this trust.

4. This Trust is created upon the express understanding that the issuer, custodian or transfer agent of any shares held hereunder shall be under no liability whatsoever to see to its proper administration, and that upon the transfer of the right, title and interest in and to such shares by any trustee hereunder, said issuer, custodian or transfer agent shall conclusively treat the transferee as the sole owner of such shares. In the event that any shares, cash or other property shall be distributable at any time under the terms of said shares, the said issuer, custodian or transfer agent is fully authorized to pay, deliver and distribute the same to whosoever shall then be the trustee hereunder, and shall be under no liability to see to the proper application thereof. The issuer, custodian or transfer agent shall be protected in acting upon any notice or other instrument or document believed by it to be genuine and to have been signed or presented by the proper party or parties.

5. I hereby reserve unto myself the power and right during my lifetime to cause the income from the trust to be directed to a person other than myself or to change the beneficiary designated in Paragraph 2 to receive any income remaining undistributed at the time of my death without notice to such beneficiary.

6. I have been advised of the consequences of establishing an irrevocable trust and I hereby declare that this trust shall be irrevocable by me or by any other person, it being my intention hereby to make an absolute gift of the trust property to the beneficiary named in Paragraph 3 above, with income reserved to myself during my lifetime.

7. In case of my death or legal incapacity, I hereby nominate and appoint as Successor Trustee hereunder the beneficiary named in Paragraph 3.

8. Any Trustee or Successor Trustee hereunder shall serve without bond.

9. This Declaration of Trust shall extend to and be binding upon the heirs, executors, administrators and assigns of the undersigned.

10. This Declaration of Trust shall be construed and enforced in accordance with the laws of the State of

_____.

IN WITNESS WHEREOF I have hereunto set my hand and seal as of the _____

day of _____, 19_____.

(sign here) _____ L.S.

Witness: (1) Name _____

Address _____

Witness: (2) Name _____

Address _____

STATE OF _____ ⎫

COUNTY OF _____ ⎬ ss: _____

On the _____ day of _____, 19_____, before me came

_____ known to me to be the individual described in, and who executed

the foregoing instrument, and _he acknowledged that _he executed the same; and in due form of law acknowledged

the foregoing instrument to be _____ free act and deed and desired the same might be recorded as such.

WITNESS my hand and notarial seal the day and year aforesaid.

(Notary Seal) _____

Notary Public

Declaration of Trust

WHEREAS, I, _____ of

Address _____
      Number   Street   City   State

am the owner of _____ shares of the capital stock of:

_____
(Name of Company or Fund)

NOW, THEREFORE, KNOW ALL MEN BY THESE PRESENTS, that I do hereby declare that I hold and will hold such shares, and all right, title and interest in and to such shares IN TRUST for the following uses and purposes:

1. To pay to myself during my lifetime all dividends which shall be distributed upon such shares, _provided,_ that if mutual investment company shares be held hereunder, the term "dividends" shall be taken to mean such payments on the shares as shall be designated by the issuer as "ordinary income". Any and all distributions which shall be designated as "realized profits" or "capital gains" shall be reinvested in additional shares and shall become part of the corpus of the Trust, and no part of such distributions shall be payable to or received by me as an individual.

2. In the event of my death, my Successor Trustee shall pay any undistributed income to which I would be entitled under the terms of this trust to:

(Name) _____ , of

(Address) _____
      Number   Street   City   State

If the person named above be not then living, or should I for any reason fail to designate such person, my Successor Trustee shall pay such undistributed income to my estate or to my personal representatives.

3. Upon my death, my Successor Trustee shall transfer the trust property and all right, title and interest in and to such trust property unto:

(Name) _____

(Address) _____
      Number   Street   City   State

and thereby terminate this trust.

4. This Trust is created upon the express understanding that the issuer, custodian or transfer agent of any shares held hereunder shall be under no liability whatsoever to see to its proper administration, and that upon the transfer of the right, title and interest in and to such shares by any trustee hereunder, said issuer, custodian or transfer agent shall conclusively treat the transferee as the sole owner of such shares. In the event that any shares, cash or other property shall be distributable at any time under the terms of said shares, the said issuer, custodian or transfer agent is fully authorized to pay, deliver and distribute the same to whosoever shall then be the trustee hereunder, and shall be under no liability to see to the proper application thereof. The issuer, custodian or transfer agent shall be protected in acting upon any notice or other instrument or document believed by it to be genuine and to have been signed or presented by the proper party or parties.

5. I hereby reserve unto myself the power and right during my lifetime to cause the income from the trust to be directed to a person other than myself or to change the beneficiary designated in Paragraph 2 to receive any income remaining undistributed at the time of my death without notice to such beneficiary.

6. I have been advised of the consequences of establishing an irrevocable trust and I hereby declare that this trust shall be irrevocable by me or by any other person, it being my intention hereby to make an absolute gift of the trust property to the beneficiary named in Paragraph 3 above, with income reserved to myself during my lifetime.

1

7. In case of my death or legal incapacity, I hereby nominate and appoint as Successor Trustee hereunder the beneficiary named in Paragraph 3.

8. Any Trustee or Successor Trustee hereunder shall serve without bond.

9. This Declaration of Trust shall extend to and be binding upon the heirs, executors, administrators and assigns of the undersigned.

10. This Declaration of Trust shall be construed and enforced in accordance with the laws of the State of

_____.

IN WITNESS WHEREOF I have hereunto set my hand and seal as of the_____

day of_____, 19____.

(sign here)_____L.S.

Witness: (1) Name_____

Address_____

Witness: (2) Name_____

Address_____

STATE OF_____ }
                                                            ss:_____
COUNTY OF_____ }

On the_____day of_____, 19____, before me came

_____known to me to be the individual described in, and who executed

the foregoing instrument, and _he acknowledged that _he executed the same; and in due form of law acknowledged

the foregoing instrument to be_____free act and deed and desired the same might be recorded as such.

WITNESS my hand and notarial seal the day and year aforesaid.

(Notary Seal)   _____
                                                                    Notary Public

Chapter 14

REDUCING TAXES WITH
A REVERSIONARY TRUST

The living trust has many variations—one, for example, is the "reversionary" trust, so-called because the trust property reverts to the grantor (or "settlor") of the trust after a stated period of time.

Under this arrangement, securities or other property are placed in the care of a trustee with the understanding that the income is to be paid to a third party for a period of not less than ten years. This would be a very valuable arrangement, for example, if one were providing support for an elderly relative. By placing in a reversionary trust securities sufficient to provide the required income, one could have that income paid to—and taxable to—the beneficiary. The dependent beneficiary probably pays little or no taxes, and in any case the income escapes taxation in the settlor's high tax bracket.

Let's illustrate the advantage: John Smith is in a 35% tax bracket, which means that in order to contribute $1,000 to the support of his mother-in-law, he must first earn $1,540. He places in a reversionary trust sufficient securities to produce $1,000 of income, and directs the trustee to pay that income to his mother-in-law. Now, Mr. Smith has to earn only $1,000 (in dividends on the securities in the trust) in order to provide the beneficiary with the needed support. That support is now costing him only two-thirds of what it cost before he set up the reversionary trust. His mother-in-law pays no tax, so the whole becomes tax-free.

If Mr. Smith's mother-in-law dies during the next ten years, the trust will terminate immediately and the securities will come back to him.

A similar arrangement with income payable to a child may prove valuable to you. The income, taxable to the child, might be used to pay for his college education or to provide some other benefit for which you as his parent are not legally responsible. This does not interfere with your continuing to claim the child as a dependent for tax purposes. As long as you are providing the bulk of his support, you may claim him as an exemption regardless of how much income he has in his own right.

Never name more than one beneficiary on a reversionary trust. If you wish to use the arrangement with several children, set up a separate trust for each.

The reversionary trust also makes a handy tax-saving vehicle for making annual donations to charity. Instead of giving your church $1,000 out of what is left of your income after taxes, you might place in a reversionary trust sufficient securities to provide $1,000 of income. The trustee pays the whole income direct to the charitable beneficiary without it having been taxed as a part of your income. Unlike the non-charitable reversionary trust which must run for at least ten years, this type may run for as short a time as two years.

At the end of the trust period or upon termination by reason of the death of the beneficiary, the trust property reverts to the settlor without any taxable gain being realized, even though the securities have appreciated substantially in value—provided they are the same securities he placed in the trust as its inception.

Obviously, there would be little point in placing cash in a reversionary trust. The trustee could deposit it in a savings account and the interest income would be tax-free. But money is a servant and should be productively employed. Its interment in a savings account would be a foolish waste of potential earnings. Nor should you give the trustee cash with instructions to invest it. *You* invest it—and give the securities to the trustee to hold. If you hand the trustee $10,000 in cash and the trustee invests that money in securities which grow to $15,000 in value by the end of the ten years the trust is to run, you'll pay a tax on $5,000 of capital gains when the assets are returned to you. If you buy the securities in the first place, and get back the same property you gave, you will not have realized a profit on it and you will avoid tax liability on the profit until such time as you sell the securities.

You should consider thoughtfully another aspect of the reversionary trust having to do with the nature of the investments which are to underlie it. If you start out with a portfolio of securities which you have placed in the trust, it is hardly likely that it can remain unchanged over a ten-year period. A generation or two ago, one may have been able to "buy a few good stocks and put them away and forget them". In the nervous times in which we live, however, investments must be continuously watched to make certain that they stay good. He who buys a "few good stocks" and puts them away and forgets them may find himself sitting upon either dry rot or a powder keg. If you buy individual securities, then, for the purposes of your reversionary trust, you are first of all giving the trustee the job of being an investment manager. Not uncommonly, a man will name his wife as trustee. Just remember that most wives are not equipped to take on a job of investment management. You could name a corporate trustee but this would mean that you'd pay an annual fee for the bank's services.

Bear in mind, too, that any replacement from time to time of securities in the trust will result in your becoming liable for a tax on any capital gains realized.

Investment company or "mutual fund" shares offer a simple solution to most of this problem. They have built-in management in the form of continuous investment supervision which keeps them good and makes it unnecessary for the trustee to assume management responsibilities. The trustee will not be obliged to sell something because it has ceased to be a good investment, and thus you'll be saved the necessity of paying taxes on capital gains you were required to realize in the course of the weeding-out process.

Mutual fund shares also offer a particularly convenient investment vehicle when young children are the beneficiaries of the trust and the income is being accumulated for their college education. Nearly all funds offer the shareholder the privilege of automatic re-investment of all dividends and distributions. If the trust assets are 1,000 shares of the ABC Fund, the trustee can simply direct the issuer to plow back all the earnings. When the trust terminates, the trustee delivers the original 1,000 shares to the settlor, and any shares that are left represent the compounding of the earnings and belong

to the child. It's all very simple and requires no bookkeeping.

Most reversionary trust instruments spell out the statutory requirement that the non-charitable trust run for at least ten years. However, there is nothing to prevent you from setting up a trust to run for *longer* than ten years. This might be particularly useful if the beneficiary is a young child who will not be ready for college for, say, fifteen years.

The instrument supplied in Appendix A to this chapter conveniently provides that the trust shall be irrevocable for one hundred twenty-one months but may be continued beyond that period if the settlor chooses not to terminate it.

When you execute a reversionary trust instrument, *transfer the trust property to the trustee immediately*. The statutory ten-year period dates not from the time you sign the instrument but from the time you actually transfer the property to the trustee.

Take note, too, of the taxability of the income from the trust. If the income is paid to or disbursed on behalf of the beneficiary, any required tax return is filed by the beneficiary. If the income is accumulated, the tax return is filed by the trust. The beneficiary has a $600 exemption ($1,200 if an elderly person) whereas the trust has only a $100 exemption.

If you appoint your wife as trustee of a reversionary trust the assets of which consist of mutual fund shares, it is suggested that she accept the dividends and distributions in additional shares, which shares she then registers in her name as custodian under the Uniform Gifts to Minors Act or the Model Act (see Chapter 15). Under this arrangement, the income is being accumulated, but not by the trust, and thus it qualifies for the $600 exemption.

While there is no prohibition against your serving as trustee yourself, it is suggested that in the interest of preserving arm's-length dealing, you appoint another person. A husband commonly names his wife as trustee in establishing a reversionary trust for the benefit of his child.

One final word of caution: The reversionary trust is not for "Indian givers". It's irrevocable for ten years. Be realistic—don't place in it assets which you feel there is some chance that you will need to use before the ten years are up.

DEED OF TRUST

FOR ESTABLISHING A

REVERSIONARY TRUST

Instructions:

On the following pages will be found duplicate copies of a deed of trust (DT-20) which will be suitable for use in establishing a reversionary trust.

Enter your name (as "Grantor") and that of the Trustee in the appropriate places at the beginning of the instrument.

Cross off *"city"* or *"town"*, leaving the correct designation of your community.

Enter the name of the beneficiary in Paragraph 1.

In Paragraph 5, space is provided for the naming of an individual to receive the trust property if the Grantor does not survive the trust period. If you do *not* wish to name such an individual, if you prefer to have the property revert to your estate if you die (this arrangement is *not* recommended), write "none" in the space provided for the naming of such beneficiary.

It is important that you enter in Paragraph 10 the name of an adult to serve as successor trustee in the event of the death or incapacity of the trustee.

The trust assets should be listed in Schedule A at the end.

The trust instrument need not be filed anywhere. The original should be retained by the Grantor, the duplicate by the Trustee. It is likely that the Trustee will be called upon to display the instrument at the end of the trust period when the trust is to be terminated and the property returned to the Grantor. The instrument should therefore be carefully preserved.

Deed of Trust

Made this_____day of_____, 19_____,

between_____of the City/Town of

_____, County of_____, State of_____,

(hereinafter called the "Grantor") and_____of the City/Town of

_____, County of_____, State of_____,

(hereinafter called the "Trustee").

1. By this instrument, the Grantor establishes a trust for the benefit of:

(Name) _____

(Address) _____
             Number   Street   City   State

hereinafter called the "Beneficiary".

2. The Grantor herewith assigns, transfers and conveys to the Trustee the property described in Schedule A hereto annexed, receipt of which is hereby acknowledged by the Trustee, which property shall be held by the Trustee in trust for the uses and purposes and upon the terms and conditions hereinafter set forth.

3. The Trustee shall hold, manage, invest and reinvest the trust property, collect the income therefrom and, in such Trustee's absolute discretion, disburse such income to the Beneficiary, or accumulate, apply or expend said income on the Beneficiary's behalf. Where used herein, the term "income" shall include all distributions made on any shares held hereunder, whether designated by the issuers as "ordinary income" or as "capital gains". Upon the termination of this trust, any and all undistributed income shall be paid over and delivered to the Beneficiary, absolutely.

4. If the Beneficiary shall die before the termination of this trust, any and all of the then undistributed income shall be paid over to the Beneficiary's estate or to his personal representatives; *provided* that no portion of such undistributed income shall under any circumstances revert to the Grantor or to the Grantor's estate.

5. Upon the termination of this trust, the trust property shall revert to the Grantor, if he be then living. If he be not then living, the Trustee shall deliver the trust property and all right, title and interest in and to such property unto

(Name) _____, of

(Address) _____
             Number   Street   City   State

if such person be living. If the above-designated Beneficiary be not then living, or if the Grantor has indicated an intention not to designate such a beneficiary by writing "None" in the space above provided for such designation, then upon the termination of this trust subsequent to the death of the Grantor, the trust property shall revert to the Grantor's estate. The Grantor reserves the right during his lifetime, by written notice to the Trustee, to alter the provisions of this paragraph by designating a beneficiary if none has been designated theretofore, or by substituting a new beneficiary for one previously named. Such change of beneficiary may be accomplished without notice to any existing beneficiary.

6. This Trust shall be irrevocable for a period of one hundred and twenty-one (121) months from the date hereof. Thereafter, by written instrument filed with the Trustee, the Grantor may revoke the Trust in whole or in part, and in similar manner may, after the expiration of said period of one hundred and twenty-one (121) months, alter or divert the interests of or change the beneficiary and, with the written consent of the Trustee, amend the Trust without limitation in any respect and cancel or amend any such amendment. If after the expiration of the period of

one hundred and twenty-one (121) months, the Grantor shall die without having exercised the right to revoke the Trust by written notice to the Trustee, then the Trust shall terminate forthwith. Upon the revocation of the Trust as hereinabove provided, the Trustee shall promptly assign, transfer and convey the trust property to the Grantor.

7. The Trustee and any Successor Trustee shall have the following powers in addition to those given them by law, to be exercised in their sole discretion:

(a) To sell, exchange, assign, lease, mortgage, pledge or borrow upon and in any other manner to deal with and dispose of all or any part of the trust property, including the power to sell in order to make distribution hereunder, and to invest the proceeds of any sale or other disposition, liquidation or withdrawal as often as may be necessary in the discretion of the Trustee in securities or real or personal property, as the Trustee may deem fitting and proper or advisable, without being required to make application for more specific authority to any court of law or equity, and without being restricted to securities or property that may be approved by any such court or that may be known as legal investments, including specifically the common and/or preferred stocks of any corporations and the shares of mutual investment companies.

(b) To expend and apply current or accumulated income from the trust property without application to any court and without the interposition of a guardian if the Beneficiary be a minor. Payments of income may be made to the parents of such minor or to the person with whom the minor is living without liability upon the Trustee to see to the proper application thereof.

8. This Trust is created upon the express understanding that no issuer of any securities held hereunder shall be under any liability to see to the proper administration of the Trust and that upon the transfer by the Trustee of the right, title and interest in and to any such securities, said issuer shall conclusively treat the transferee as the sole owner of such securities and shall be under no liability to see to the proper application of the proceeds of such transfer or of any distribution hereunder.

9. No interest nor any part of the interest of any beneficiary hereunder shall be subject in any event to sale, alienation, hypothecation, pledge, transfer or subject to any debt of such beneficiary or any judgment against the beneficiary or process in aid of execution of such judgment.

10. The Trustee and any Successor Trustee hereunder shall serve without bond.

11. In the event of the death, incapacity or failure to act of the Trustee, the Grantor hereby appoints

(Name) _____, of

(Address) _____
        Number   Street   City   State

as Successor Trustee, and in the event such person be not surviving and willing and able to act hereunder, the Grantor reserves the right to appoint another as Successor Trustee. If the Grantor be not then living, in such circumstances there shall be designated as Successor Trustee hereunder whosoever shall qualify as executor or administrator of the estate of the Grantor.

12. The validity, construction and effect of this agreement and of the trust created hereunder and its enforcement shall be determined by the laws of the State of _____.

IN WITNESS WHEREOF, the parties hereto have signed and sealed this instrument as of the date first above written.

_____   _____L.S.
          Witness   Grantor

_____   _____L.S.
          Witness   Trustee

SCHEDULE A

Deed of Trust

Made this _____ day of _____, 19____,

between _____ of the City/Town of

_____, County of _____, State of _____,

(hereinafter called the "Grantor") and _____ of the City/Town of

_____, County of _____, State of _____,

(hereinafter called the "Trustee").

1. By this instrument, the Grantor establishes a trust for the benefit of:

(Name) _____

(Address) _____
           Number   Street   City   State

hereinafter called the "Beneficiary".

2. The Grantor herewith assigns, transfers and conveys to the Trustee the property described in Schedule A hereto annexed, receipt of which is hereby acknowledged by the Trustee, which property shall be held by the Trustee in trust for the uses and purposes and upon the terms and conditions hereinafter set forth.

3. The Trustee shall hold, manage, invest and reinvest the trust property, collect the income therefrom and, in such Trustee's absolute discretion, disburse such income to the Beneficiary, or accumulate, apply or expend said income on the Beneficiary's behalf. Where used herein, the term "income" shall include all distributions made on any shares held hereunder, whether designated by the issuers as "ordinary income" or as "capital gains". Upon the termination of this trust, any and all undistributed income shall be paid over and delivered to the Beneficiary, absolutely.

4. If the Beneficiary shall die before the termination of this trust, any and all of the then undistributed income shall be paid over to the Beneficiary's estate or to his personal representatives; _provided_ that no portion of such undistributed income shall under any circumstances revert to the Grantor or to the Grantor's estate.

5. Upon the termination of this trust, the trust property shall revert to the Grantor, if he be then living. If he be not then living, the Trustee shall deliver the trust property and all right, title and interest in and to such property unto

(Name) _____, of

(Address) _____
           Number   Street   City   State

if such person be living. If the above-designated Beneficiary be not then living, or if the Grantor has indicated an intention not to designate such a beneficiary by writing "None" in the space above provided for such designation, then upon the termination of this trust subsequent to the death of the Grantor, the trust property shall revert to the Grantor's estate. The Grantor reserves the right during his lifetime, by written notice to the Trustee, to alter the provisions of this paragraph by designating a beneficiary if none has been designated theretofore, or by substituting a new beneficiary for one previously named. Such change of beneficiary may be accomplished without notice to any existing beneficiary.

6. This Trust shall be irrevocable for a period of one hundred and twenty-one (121) months from the date hereof. Thereafter, by written instrument filed with the Trustee, the Grantor may revoke the Trust in whole or in part, and in similar manner may, after the expiration of said period of one hundred and twenty-one (121) months, alter or divert the interests of or change the beneficiary and, with the written consent of the Trustee, amend the Trust without limitation in any respect and cancel or amend any such amendment. If after the expiration of the period of

one hundred and twenty-one (121) months, the Grantor shall die without having exercised the right to revoke the Trust by written notice to the Trustee, then the Trust shall terminate forthwith. Upon the revocation of the Trust as hereinabove provided, the Trustee shall promptly assign, transfer and convey the trust property to the Grantor.

7. The Trustee and any Successor Trustee shall have the following powers in addition to those given them by law, to be exercised in their sole discretion:

(a) To sell, exchange, assign, lease, mortgage, pledge or borrow upon and in any other manner to deal with and dispose of all or any part of the trust property, including the power to sell in order to make distribution hereunder, and to invest the proceeds of any sale or other disposition, liquidation or withdrawal as often as may be necessary in the discretion of the Trustee in securities or real or personal property, as the Trustee may deem fitting and proper or advisable, without being required to make application for more specific authority to any court of law or equity, and without being restricted to securities or property that may be approved by any such court or that may be known as legal investments, including specifically the common and/or preferred stocks of any corporations and the shares of mutual investment companies.

(b) To expend and apply current or accumulated income from the trust property without application to any court and without the interposition of a guardian if the Beneficiary be a minor. Payments of income may be made to the parents of such minor or to the person with whom the minor is living without liability upon the Trustee to see to the proper application thereof.

8. This Trust is created upon the express understanding that no issuer of any securities held hereunder shall be under any liability to see to the proper administration of the Trust and that upon the transfer by the Trustee of the right, title and interest in and to any such securities, said issuer shall conclusively treat the transferee as the sole owner of such securities and shall be under no liability to see to the proper application of the proceeds of such transfer or of any distribution hereunder.

9. No interest nor any part of the interest of any beneficiary hereunder shall be subject in any event to sale, alienation, hypothecation, pledge, transfer or subject to any debt of such beneficiary or any judgment against the beneficiary or process in aid of execution of such judgment.

10. The Trustee and any Successor Trustee hereunder shall serve without bond.

11. In the event of the death, incapacity or failure to act of the Trustee, the Grantor hereby appoints

(Name) _____, of

(Address) _____
Number   Street   City   State

as Successor Trustee, and in the event such person be not surviving and willing and able to act hereunder, the Grantor reserves the right to appoint another as Successor Trustee. If the Grantor be not then living, in such circumstances there shall be designated as Successor Trustee hereunder whosoever shall qualify as executor or administrator of the estate of the Grantor.

12. The validity, construction and effect of this agreement and of the trust created hereunder and its enforcement shall be determined by the laws of the State of_____.

IN WITNESS WHEREOF, the parties hereto have signed and sealed this instrument as of the date first above written.

_____   _____L.S.
Witness   Grantor

_____   _____L.S.
Witness   Trustee

2

SCHEDULE A

Chapter 15

MAKING A GIFT TO A MINOR

In our increasingly-affluent society, it has become commonplace for children to own property. The one-time lavish gift of a five dollar gold piece has been supplanted by a one hundred dollar savings bond or an even more substantial gift of mutual fund shares.

Too, as estate taxes have mounted, persons in a position to do so have grown increasingly conscious of the advantages of making lifetime gifts to children or grandchildren.

In our time, then, everybody's richer—including the kids.

Transfer agents and issuers of securities ordinarily are reluctant to register such property in the name of a minor, since a child is under what is called a "legal disability", meaning that those who enter into a contract with him do so at their peril. The child could demand recision of a purchase which had resulted disadvantageously. It is generally necessary, then, for an adult to hold title to property for a child.

When it comes to savings bank accounts, this has presented no special problem, such institutions being quite willing to open trustee accounts in the name of adults for the benefit of children without the formality of a written instrument establishing the fact of the trusteeship.

The registration of securities held for a minor traditionally has been another matter, however, requiring a written trust instrument setting forth the duties and responsibilities of the trustee. The making of a gift of securities to a child thus was something of a cumbersome process requiring the services of an attorney to prepare a suitable instrument. Frequently, this proved a deterrent to the making of gifts.

Happily, under legislation known in most states as the "Uniform Gifts to Minors Act" and in some (Alaska, Colorado, District of Columbia, Georgia, New Jersey, Ohio, Rhode Island and South Carolina) as the "Model Law", there has been developed a type of registration requiring no written instrument. Except in Georgia, the Model Law permits gifts of securities only. The Uniform Act permits gifts of money as well as securities.

Under such legislation, securities may be registered in the name of "John Smith, custodian for Willie Smith, under the Connecticut Uniform Gifts to Minors Act". It is important to understand that this form of registration is not intended for use in connection with the investment of funds *already owned* by the child. Rather, it is permitted only in connection with the making of a current gift.

While there is nothing to prevent a donor from naming himself as custodian, the naming of a third party is strongly recommended for estate tax considerations. Under either the Uniform Act or Model Law registration, the *income* from the investment is taxable to the child. However, if the donor is also the custodian, the property will be taxed as a part of his estate at his death. On the other hand, if a person other than the donor serves as custodian, this estate tax disadvantage is completely avoided. Many donors, having established the arrangement with themselves as custodian without full knowledge of its tax aspects, have sought later to shift the custodianship to a spouse or to some other person, only to discover that this is not easily done. Some few states now permit a custodian to resign his custodianship in favor of another person by means of a written instrument which he executes. Many others, however, require him to formally petition the probate court (from which Heaven preserve us!) for permission to transfer the custodianship.

The moral is simply not to rush blindly into registration under either the Uniform Act or Model Law with less than careful thought. Unless special circumstances dictate otherwise, you should name someone other than yourself as custodian if you are the donor.

Property registered in the name of an adult as custodian for a minor under the Uniform Act must be turned over promptly to the young person when he reaches age 21. There are many donors who feel, especially if the gift is a substantial one, that this is too early an age at which to turn absolute control of the property over to the beneficiary. Also, many donors prefer to place some restrictions on the use of the money during the life of the trust (e.g., they may choose to specify that the income and/or principal be used only to pay for the youngster's college education, etc.). Finally, they may not wish to appoint someone else as custodian. A grandparent, for example, might wish to divest himself of estate tax liability by not serving as custodian of the funds himself but may lack complete confidence in the fiduciary responsibility of the only other likely candidate for the custodianship, the child's parent.

In such circumstances, the use of an irrevocable inter vivos trust is indicated.

In the first place, if he wishes to do so, the donor himself may serve as trustee without fear of estate tax liability. So long as the trust is absolute and irrevocable, the trust property will not be considered a part of his estate at his death.

In the event of the death or resignation of a custodian holding securities under the Uniform Act, court appointment of a successor is required. Not so with the trust—the instrument simply provides that in the event of the death or resignation of the trustee, another person specified as successor trustee is to take over. It is not necessary to apply to the court for instructions or approval.

When there are two or more children in a family, many donors appreciate the opportunity which the trust gives them to direct that if the named beneficiary does not survive until the trust is terminated and the property turned over to him, the property is to revert to the deceased child's brother or sister. Under the custodian arrangement, the property must revert to the child's estate if he dies, thus throwing it into probate.

In making a gift in trust to a minor, it is well to remember that there are two gift tax exemptions available to you. First, you may give any number of persons $3,000 each in any one calendar year—$6,000 if your spouse joins in the gift. Second, in addition to this $3,000 "annual exclusion", you have a $30,000 "lifetime exemption". A gift which continues in trust beyond the beneficiary's 21st birthday does not qualify for the $3,000 annual gift tax exclusion. Thus, if you specify that the beneficiary is not to receive the principal until, say, age 25 or 30, the gift must be charged against your $30,000 lifetime exemption rather than against the annual exclusion. This point should be borne in mind by persons desiring to make gifts to the full limit of the law.

On the pages which follow will be found instructions and a deed of trust which may be suitable for your use in establishing a trust for a minor.

DEED OF TRUST

FOR MAKING

GIFT TO MINOR

Instructions:

On the following pages will be found duplicate copies of a deed of trust (DT-21) which will be suitable for use in making a gift in trust for a minor where someone other than the donor is to be trustee.

Cross out *"city"* or *"town"*, leaving the appropriate designation of your community.

In Paragraph 2, enter the name of the minor to whom you are making the gift. In Paragraph 3, enter first the name of the person or persons whom you wish to have receive the property if the minor does not live until the termination of the trust.

In Paragraph 5, insert the age at which you wish the trust property to be turned over to the beneficiary.

In Paragraph 9, enter the name and address of the person whom you wish to appoint as successor trustee.

The original of the executed instrument should be retained by the Settlor, the duplicate by the Trustee.

When the Trustee makes investments in stocks, bonds or mutual fund shares in accordance with the terms of the trust, such securities should be registered *"Mary Smith, trustee for Willie Smith under deed of trust dated_____"*.

Deed of Trust

THIS AGREEMENT made this_____day of_____,

19_____, by and between_____, of the

Town/City of_____, County of_____ and State of

_____, (hereinafter referred to as the "Settlor") and_____

_____, of the Town/City of_____,

County of_____and State of_____, (hereinafter referred to as the "Trustee").

WITNESSETH

WHEREAS, the Settlor desires now and from time to time in the future to make certain gifts of his own funds to the Trustee; and

WHEREAS, the Trustee is willing to accept and administer such funds as Trustee under the terms of this agreement,

NOW THEREFORE, intending to be legally bound hereby the Settlor and the Trustee do hereby covenant and agree as follows:

1. The Settlor hereby transfers to the Trustee the sum of One Dollar, to be held with subsequent additions and accretions pursuant to the terms hereof and reserves the right and privilege of making further additions from time to time in cash or in such property as the Trustee may agree to accept.

2. The Trustee shall hold the principal of the trust and income accumulated thereon for the use and benefit of

(Name) _____, of

(Address) _____
           Number   Street   City   State
(hereinafter referred to as the "primary beneficiary") until the termination of this trust at which time the Trustee shall assign, transfer or pay over the balance of the principal and all income accrued thereon unto the said beneficiary.

3. In the event of the death of the above-named beneficiary hereunder prior to the termination of the trust as herein provided, the then trust fund shall be payable to the "contingent beneficiary" named below. If two or more persons be named below, the trust fund shall be divided, in equal shares, among them or the survivors of them if they be not all living:

provided that if any of the above-named contingent beneficiaries shall not have attained the age specified in Paragraph 5 hereof, then his (or her) share of the trust shall be held by the Trustee and such portion of the income and principal as the Trustee in his sole discretion shall deem suitable shall be paid to, disbursed or expended on behalf of such beneficiary until he (or she) attains the stated age. If none of the above-named contingent beneficiaries shall survive until the stated age, the then trust fund shall be payable upon the death of the last survivor of them to:

(Name) _____

(Address) _____
           Number   Street   City   State
or to such beneficiary's heirs, executors, administrators or assigns, if such beneficiary be not surviving, except that under no circumstances shall any portion of the trust property revert to the Settlor or to the Settlor's estate.

4. All income and profits from the trust property shall, subject to the provisions of Paragraph 6 (e) hereof, be accumulated and reinvested in accordance with the terms hereof.

5. This trust shall terminate with respect to the primary beneficiary or any contingent beneficiary upon the attainment by that beneficiary of the age of_____years.

6. The Trustee (including any Successor Trustee) shall have the following powers in addition to those given him by law, to be exercised in his sole discretion:

(a) To invest and reinvest the principal and any accumulated income in such securities (including common and preferred stocks, shares of mutual investment companies, and contractual plans for the acquisition of such shares) as the Trustee shall deem proper, without restriction to so-called legal investments.

(b) To add or cause to be added to the principal of this trust all income and distributions which may from time to time be received on such shares held by causing the same to be reinvested in additional shares, or if said Trustee shall so elect from time to time to cause said income and distributions to be distributed without reinvestment.

(c) To elect any option or privilege that may be vested in the owner of such shares (or plans for the acquisition of such shares), including the right to make a partial or a complete withdrawal under the said plans and either to hold the shares or proceeds thereof, in kind or in cash or to reinvest the proceeds as provided in paragraph 6 (d) hereof or to dispose of all or a part of such proceeds as provided in Paragraph 6 (e) hereof.

(d) To sell, exchange, assign, lease, mortgage, pledge or borrow upon and in any other manner to deal with and dispose of all or any part of the trust property, including the power to sell in order to make distribution hereunder, and to invest the proceeds of any sale or other disposition, liquidation or withdrawals as often as may be necessary in the discretion of the Trustee in securities or real or personal property, as the Trustee may deem fitting and proper or advisable, without being required to make application for more specific authority to any court of law or equity, and without being restricted to securities or property that may be approved by such court or that may be known as legal investments including specifically the common and/or preferred stock of any corporations.

(e) To expend or apply the principal of or the current or accumulated income from the trust property without the interposition of a guardian, in or about the education, maintenance and support of the beneficiary, except that no such expenditure or application of principal or income shall be made to provide education, maintenance or support for which a parent shall be legally responsible.

7. This trust is created upon the understanding that the issuer or custodian for the issuer of any securities held hereunder shall be under no liability whatsoever to see to the proper administration of the trust and that upon the transfer of any right, title and interest in and to any shares or plan for the acquisition of any shares or any other trust property, said issuer or custodian for such issuer shall conclusively treat the transferee as the sole owner of such shares, plan or trust property and shall be under no liability to see to the proper application of the proceeds of such transfer, or of any partial or complete withdrawal under any such shares or plan, or of any distribution hereunder.

8. I have been advised of the consequences of creating an irrevocable trust and do hereby declare that the trust created hereby is not revocable by me or any other person.

9. In the event of the death, incapacity or resignation of the Trustee hereunder, I hereby nominate and appoint:

(Name) _____, of

(Address) _____

       Number   Street   City   State

as Successor Trustee, and in the event of his (or her) death, incapacity, resignation or unwillingness to serve, I hereby designate as Successor Trustee whosoever shall qualify as executor or administrator of my estate. No bond shall be required of the Trustee or any Successor Trustee.

IN WITNESS WHEREOF, I have hereunto set my hand and seal this_____day of

_____, 19_____.

_____   _____

       Witness   Settlor

                     Accepted:

_____   _____

       Witness   Trustee

𝔇𝔢𝔢𝔡 𝔬𝔣 𝔗𝔯𝔲𝔰𝔱

THIS AGREEMENT made this_____day of_____,

19_____, by and between_____, of the

Town/City of_____, County of_____ and State of

_____, (hereinafter referred to as the "Settlor") and_____

_____, of the Town/City of_____,

County of_____and State of_____, (hereinafter referred to as the "Trustee").

WITNESSETH

WHEREAS, the Settlor desires now and from time to time in the future to make certain gifts of his own funds
to the Trustee; and

WHEREAS, the Trustee is willing to accept and administer such funds as Trustee under the terms of this
agreement,

NOW THEREFORE, intending to be legally bound hereby the Settlor and the Trustee do hereby covenant
and agree as follows:

1. The Settlor hereby transfers to the Trustee the sum of One Dollar, to be held with subsequent additions and
accretions pursuant to the terms hereof and reserves the right and privilege of making further additions from time
to time in cash or in such property as the Trustee may agree to accept.

2. The Trustee shall hold the principal of the trust and income accumulated thereon for the use and benefit of

(Name) _____, of

(Address) _____

          Number   Street   City   State

(hereinafter referred to as the "primary beneficiary") until the termination of this trust at which time the Trustee
shall assign, transfer or pay over the balance of the principal and all income accrued thereon unto the said beneficiary.

3. In the event of the death of the above-named beneficiary hereunder prior to the termination of the trust as
herein provided, the then trust fund shall be payable to the "contingent beneficiary" named below. If two or more
persons be named below, the trust fund shall be divided, in equal shares, among them or the survivors of them if
they be not all living:

provided that if any of the above-named contingent beneficiaries shall not have attained the age specified in Paragraph 5 hereof, then his (or her) share of the trust shall be held by the Trustee and such portion of the income and
principal as the Trustee in his sole discretion shall deem suitable shall be paid to, disbursed or expended on behalf
of such beneficiary until he (or she) attains the stated age. If none of the above-named contingent beneficiaries shall
survive until the stated age, the then trust fund shall be payable upon the death of the last survivor of them to:

(Name) _____

(Address) _____

          Number   Street   City   State

or to such beneficiary's heirs, executors, administrators or assigns, if such beneficiary be not surviving, except that
under no circumstances shall any portion of the trust property revert to the Settlor or to the Settlor's estate.

4. All income and profits from the trust property shall, subject to the provisions of Paragraph 6 (e) hereof,
be accumulated and reinvested in accordance with the terms hereof.

5. This trust shall terminate with respect to the primary beneficiary or any contingent beneficiary upon the attainment by that beneficiary of the age of_____years.

6. The Trustee (including any Successor Trustee) shall have the following powers in addition to those given him by law, to be exercised in his sole discretion:

(a) To invest and reinvest the principal and any accumulated income in such securities (including common and preferred stocks, shares of mutual investment companies, and contractual plans for the acquisition of such shares) as the Trustee shall deem proper, without restriction to so-called legal investments.

(b) To add or cause to be added to the principal of this trust all income and distributions which may from time to time be received on such shares held by causing the same to be reinvested in additional shares, or if said Trustee shall so elect from time to time to cause said income and distributions to be distributed without reinvestment.

(c) To elect any option or privilege that may be vested in the owner of such shares (or plans for the acquisition of such shares), including the right to make a partial or a complete withdrawal under the said plans and either to hold the shares or proceeds thereof, in kind or in cash or to reinvest the proceeds as provided in paragraph 6 (d) hereof or to dispose of all or a part of such proceeds as provided in Paragraph 6 (e) hereof.

(d) To sell, exchange, assign, lease, mortgage, pledge or borrow upon and in any other manner to deal with and dispose of all or any part of the trust property, including the power to sell in order to make distribution hereunder, and to invest the proceeds of any sale or other disposition, liquidation or withdrawals as often as may be necessary in the discretion of the Trustee in securities or real or personal property, as the Trustee may deem fitting and proper or advisable, without being required to make application for more specific authority to any court of law or equity, and without being restricted to securities or property that may be approved by such court or that may be known as legal investments including specifically the common and/or preferred stock of any corporations.

(e) To expend or apply the principal of or the current or accumulated income from the trust property without the interposition of a guardian, in or about the education, maintenance and support of the beneficiary, except that no such expenditure or application of principal or income shall be made to provide education, maintenance or support for which a parent shall be legally responsible.

7. This trust is created upon the understanding that the issuer or custodian for the issuer of any securities held hereunder shall be under no liability whatsoever to see to the proper administration of the trust and that upon the transfer of any right, title and interest in and to any shares or plan for the acquisition of any shares or any other trust property, said issuer or custodian for such issuer shall conclusively treat the transferee as the sole owner of such shares, plan or trust property and shall be under no liability to see to the proper application of the proceeds of such transfer, or of any partial or complete withdrawal under any such shares or plan, or of any distribution hereunder.

8. I have been advised of the consequences of creating an irrevocable trust and do hereby declare that the trust created hereby is not revocable by me or any other person.

9. In the event of the death, incapacity or resignation of the Trustee hereunder, I hereby nominate and appoint:

(Name) _____, of

(Address) _____
        Number   Street   City   State

as Successor Trustee, and in the event of his (or her) death, incapacity, resignation or unwillingness to serve, I hereby designate as Successor Trustee whosoever shall qualify as executor or administrator of my estate. No bond shall be required of the Trustee or any Successor Trustee.

IN WITNESS WHEREOF, I have hereunto set my hand and seal this_____day of

_____, 19_____.

_____   _____
        Witness   Settlor

                              Accepted:

_____   _____
        Witness   Trustee

2

Chapter 16

AVOIDING PROBATE OF PERSONAL EFFECTS

Many individuals possess personal effects which have intrinsic value and which therefore can become subject to the probate process. A valuable painting, a piece of jewelry, a fur piece, antique furniture—these are typical of the personal possessions which many persons bequeath in their wills while others make no specific provision for their distribution, leaving to the executor or administrator of their estate the ticklish job of apportioning the personal effects amongst the heirs.

Here, then, is another area where the inter vivos trust can serve a useful purpose by making unnecessary the detailed listing in your will of your possessions together with instructions as to who is to receive what after your death.

In a simple declaration of trust, you may identify the specific object or objects and assert that you are holding it or them in trust for a beneficiary whom you name. You may list a number of different objects in the same declaration of trust provided all are to go to the same beneficiary. If you are dividing your possessions amongst several persons, you will need to execute a separate instrument for each person.

It is suggested that in each instrument you appoint the beneficiary as successor trustee. At your death, he simply turns the property over to himself. While it would be possible here to explore endlessly the technical ramifications of this method of distribution, suffice it to say that in 99% of cases, the inter vivos trust provides a simple means of passing personal effects without the delay, expense and publicity of probate.

An instrument suitable for use in this connection will be found on the pages which follow.

DECLARATION OF TRUST

FOR LEAVING

PERSONAL EFFECTS

Instructions:

On the following pages will be found duplicate copies of a declaration of trust (DT-22) which will be suitable for use where it is desired to name some one person to receive specific personal effects.

Cross out *"city"* or *"town"*, leaving the appropriate designation of your community.

In Paragraph 1 insert a description of the property which is sufficiently detailed to insure its accurate identification. Don't just say "my diamond ring"; if you cannot describe it completely and accurately, take it to a jeweler and ask him to dictate a description of it. Don't just leave someone "a sofa"—it's the "antique Empire sofa upholstered in green velvet which I inherited from my Aunt Elizabeth and which stands in the living room of my home". If it's a painting, identify the artist and describe the subject and the frame and indicate the room in your home where it is to be found. If it is jewelry you're leaving, always indicate where it is to be found.

In Paragraph 2 enter the name of the beneficiary to whom you wish the article or object to go at your death. Space is provided for the naming of a primary beneficiary and a contingent beneficiary to receive the property if the primary beneficiary does not survive you. If you wish to leave something valuable to an institution—a museum, for example—there is no need to indicate a contingent beneficiary, and you can simply write "none" in the space provided for such name.

It is suggested that you execute both copies of the instrument, retaining one in your safe deposit box or in the possession of a trusted friend or relative and delivering the duplicate to the person you have named to receive the property. This assures that if the original should be "lost", the second copy will be available to evidence your wishes.

Declaration of Trust

1. WHEREAS, I, _____ John J. Smith _____, County of _____ Fairfax _____ of the City/Town of _____ Jonesville _____ and State of _____ Connecticut _____, am the sole and undisputed owner of the following articles of personal property: One set of six Hitchcock chairs, black, with gold stenciling, in my dining room;
An oil painting, "Harvest Time", by Samuel Bentley, white frame, hanging on the north wall of my study;
An antique highboy, four drawers, cherry wood, in my bedroom.

2. NOW, THEREFORE, KNOW ALL MEN BY THESE PRESENTS, that I do hereby acknowledge and declare that I hold and will hold said articles of personal property, and all right, title and interest in and to said articles IN TRUST for the use and benefit of: _____, of

Mary A. Smith   (my niece)

(Name) _____ Jonesville _____ Connecticut _____
City   State

(Address) _____ 750 Porter Street _____
Number   Street

or, if such person does not survive me, for the use and benefit of: _____, of

William B. Connors (my nephew)

(Name) _____ Jonesville _____ Connecticut _____
City   State

(Address) _____ 250 County Street _____
Number   Street

3. I reserve the right to deliver the trust property to the beneficiary during my lifetime or, in my discretion, to defer such delivery until my death.

4. Upon my death, if the above-described trust property has not theretofore been delivered to the beneficiary, my Successor Trustee is hereby directed forthwith to transfer such property and all right, title and interest in and to such property, unto the beneficiary, to be his (or hers) absolutely and forever.

should I for ...
... property shall

... revoke ... serve the ...
... reason fail to designate such new beneficiar..., this trust shall terminate upon my death a... ... revert to my estate.

7. In the event of my death or legal incapacity, I hereby nominate and appoint as Successor Trustee hereunder, unless such beneficiary be a minor or legally incompetent, in which event I hereby nominate and appoint as Successor Trustee hereunder: _____, of

Henry P. Adams

(Name) _____ Jonesville _____ Connecticut _____
City   State

(Address) _____ 125   Barnum Street _____
Number   Street

8. This Declaration of Trust shall extend to and be binding upon the heirs, executors, administrators and assigns of the undersigned and upon the Successors to the Trustee.

9. The Trustee and his successors shall serve without bond.

10. This Declaration of Trust shall be construed and enforced in accordance with the laws of the State of _____ Connecticut _____.

1. WHEREAS, I, _____,

of the City/Town of_____, County of_____

and State of_____, am the sole and undisputed owner of the following articles of
personal property:

2. NOW, THEREFORE, KNOW ALL MEN BY THESE PRESENTS, that I do hereby acknowledge and
declare that I hold and will hold said articles of personal property, and all right, title and interest in and to said
articles IN TRUST for the use and benefit of:

(Name) _____, of

(Address) _____

         Number   Street   City   State

or, if such person does not survive me, for the use and benefit of:

(Name) _____, of

(Address) _____

         Number   Street   City   State

3. I reserve the right to deliver the trust property to the beneficiary during my lifetime or, in my discretion, to
defer such delivery until my death.

4. Upon my death, if the above-described trust property has not theretofore been delivered to the beneficiary,
my Successor Trustee is hereby directed forthwith to transfer such property and all right, title and interest in and to
such property, unto the beneficiary, to be his (or hers) absolutely and forever.

5. I reserve unto myself the power and right at any time during my lifetime to amend or revoke in whole or in part the trust hereby created without the necessity of obtaining the consent of the beneficiaries and without giving notice to the beneficiaries. The sale or other disposition by me of the whole or any part of the trust property shall constitute as to such whole or part a revocation of this trust.

6. The death during my lifetime of both the primary and the contingent beneficiaries designated hereunder shall revoke such designation, and in such event, I reserve the right to designate new beneficiaries. Should I for any reason fail to designate such new beneficiaries, this trust shall terminate upon my death and the trust property shall revert to my estate.

7. In the event of my death or legal incapacity, I hereby nominate and appoint as Successor Trustee hereunder whosoever shall then be beneficiary hereunder, unless such beneficiary be a minor or legally incompetent, in which event I hereby nominate and appoint as Successor Trustee hereunder:

(Name) _____, of

(Address) _____
             Number   Street   City   State

8. This Declaration of Trust shall extend to and be binding upon the heirs, executors, administrators and assigns of the undersigned and upon the Successors to the Trustee.

9. The Trustee and his successors shall serve without bond.

10. This Declaration of Trust shall be construed and enforced in accordance with the laws of the State of

_____.

IN WITNESS WHEREOF, I have hereunto set my hand and seal this_____day of

_____, 19____.

(sign here)_____L.S.

Witness: (1)_____

Witness: (2)_____

STATE OF_____⎱
                                                                      ⎰ ss:_____
COUNTY OF_____⎱

On the_____day of_____, nineteen hundred

and_____, before me came_____,

known to me to be the individual described in, and who executed the foregoing instrument, and_____acknowledged

that_____executed the same, and in due form of law acknowledged the foregoing instrument to be_____free act

and deed and desired the same might be recorded as such.

(Notary Seal)   _____
                                                                              Notary Public

Declaration of Trust

1. WHEREAS, I, ——————————————————————————————————,

of the City/Town of——————————————, County of——————————

and State of——————————————, am the sole and undisputed owner of the following articles of personal property:

2. NOW, THEREFORE, KNOW ALL MEN BY THESE PRESENTS, that I do hereby acknowledge and declare that I hold and will hold said articles of personal property, and all right, title and interest in and to said articles IN TRUST for the use and benefit of:

(Name) ——————————————————————————, of

(Address) ————————————————————————————
       Number   Street   City   State

or, if such person does not survive me, for the use and benefit of:

(Name) ——————————————————————————, of

(Address) ————————————————————————————
       Number   Street   City   State

3. I reserve the right to deliver the trust property to the beneficiary during my lifetime or, in my discretion, to defer such delivery until my death.

4. Upon my death, if the above-described trust property has not theretofore been delivered to the beneficiary, my Successor Trustee is hereby directed forthwith to transfer such property and all right, title and interest in and to such property, unto the beneficiary, to be his (or hers) absolutely and forever.

1

5. I reserve unto myself the power and right at any time during my lifetime to amend or revoke in whole or in part the trust hereby created without the necessity of obtaining the consent of the beneficiaries and without giving notice to the beneficiaries. The sale or other disposition by me of the whole or any part of the trust property shall constitute as to such whole or part a revocation of this trust.

6. The death during my lifetime of both the primary and the contingent beneficiaries designated hereunder shall revoke such designation, and in such event, I reserve the right to designate new beneficiaries. Should I for any reason fail to designate such new beneficiaries, this trust shall terminate upon my death and the trust property shall revert to my estate.

7. In the event of my death or legal incapacity, I hereby nominate and appoint as Successor Trustee hereunder whosoever shall then be beneficiary hereunder, unless such beneficiary be a minor or legally incompetent, in which event I hereby nominate and appoint as Successor Trustee hereunder:

(Name) _____ , of

(Address) _____
           Number   Street   City   State

8. This Declaration of Trust shall extend to and be binding upon the heirs, executors, administrators and assigns of the undersigned and upon the Successors to the Trustee.

9. The Trustee and his successors shall serve without bond.

10. This Declaration of Trust shall be construed and enforced in accordance with the laws of the State of

_____ .

IN WITNESS WHEREOF, I have hereunto set my hand and seal this_____day of

_____ , 19____ .

(sign here)_____L.S.

Witness: (1)_____

Witness: (2)_____

STATE OF_____⎫
                                     ⎬ ss:_____
COUNTY OF_____⎭

On the_____day of_____ , nineteen hundred

and_____ , before me came_____ ,

known to me to be the individual described in, and who executed the foregoing instrument, and_____acknowledged

that_____executed the same, and in due form of law acknowledged the foregoing instrument to be_____free act

and deed and desired the same might be recorded as such.

(Notary Seal)   _____
                                                Notary Public

Chapter 17

AVOIDING PROBATE OF A SMALL UNINCORPORATED BUSINESS

Helen Woodruff, a widow, is the owner of a small but successful shop selling greeting cards and giftwares.

Although her friend, Martha McEwan, owns no part of the business, she has been a faithful assistant to Mrs. Woodruff in its operation over the years, carrying on efficiently when the proprietress was hospitalized once or twice and during her annual vacations. By any standards, the business is a modest one but it has provided the two ladies with a dignified, comfortable living for more than a decade.

Such an enterprise has very little sale value upon the death of the owner, a fact which Helen Woodruff well recognizes. Liquidation of the business as a part of her estate would be a sad affair, with the stock going for ten cents on the dollar. Besides not wanting to see her little business come to such a dreary end, she feels a certain obligation to her loyal employee, Miss McEwan, whose age would probably preclude her finding other work.

In a word, Helen Woodruff wants to retain complete ownership and control of the business during her lifetime, but upon her death she wants it to go to Martha McEwan with no strings attached, for she realizes that her friend could never raise any appreciable sum of money to buy it from the estate.

If she leaves it to Miss McEwan in her Will, the inevitable delays of the probate procedure may dry up the flow of funds needed for every-day operation of the shop, thus interfering with the successful transition of the business to the new owner.

The answer, of course, is for Helen Woodruff to create an inter vivos trust for the benefit of Martha McEwan. The trust is revocable—if Miss McEwan should predecease her friend, or in the unlikely circumstance of their having an irreparable falling out, Mrs. Woodruff can name a different beneficiary or cancel the trust entirely and throw the business into her estate to be liquidated after her death, with the proceeds being distributed in accordance with the provisions of her Will.

All over America there are to be found endless variations of this situation involving the fate of small businesses operated as proprietorships. In some instances, a loyal employee or co-worker is the likely beneficiary. In other cases, the owner may simply choose to pass the business to a relative. These suggested situations are intended to be merely illustrative of the point that through the use of an inter vivos trust, an unincorporated business or proprietorship may be passed on to another person without the delay, expense and publicity of probate.

DECLARATION OF TRUST

FOR LEAVING

AN UNINCORPORATED BUSINESS

Instructions:

On the following pages will be found duplicate copies of a Declaration of Trust (DT-23) which will be suitable for use in avoiding probate of an unincorporated business, as explained in Chapter 17.

Cross off "city" or "town", leaving the appropriate designation of your community.

In Paragraph 1, enter the location of the business and the name by which it is known.

In Paragraph 2, give a brief description of the nature of the business ("retailing of greeting cards and giftwares", "electrical appliance repair", "retailing of men's wear", "roofing repair and installation", etc.).

In Paragraph 3, enter the name of the primary beneficiary whom you wish to have receive the property at your death, and that of the contingent beneficiary whom you desire to have receive it if the primary beneficiary does not survive you.

To establish beyond question the fact of the trusteeship relationship file one executed copy of the Declaration of Trust with the town clerk's or other office in your community where property transfers are customarily recorded. Once recorded the original will be returned to you. You may wish to give the duplicate executed copy to the primary beneficiary to hold in case your original should be inadvertently "lost" after your death.

Declaration of Trust

1. WHEREAS, I, __Helen Woodruff__, of the City/Town of __Jonesville__, County of __Fairfax__ and State of __Connecticut__, am the sole owner of the unincorporated business located at __150 High Street__ in the City/Town of __Jonesville__ County of __Fairfax__ and State of __Connecticut__, and known as __Fairport Gift Shoppe__ and

_____

2. WHEREAS the principal business of the said __Fairport Gift Shoppe__ is __the retail sale of greeting cards and giftwares__

_____

3. NOW, THEREFORE, KNOW ALL MEN BY THESE PRESENTS, that I do hereby acknowledge and declare that I hold and will hold said business and all right, title and interest in and to said business and all furniture, fixtures, stock in trade, inventory, machinery, vehicles, accounts receivable, prepaid insurance and all other assets of such business, IN TRUST for the use and benefit of:

(Name) __Martha McEwan__, of __Jonesville__ __Connecticut__
                                     City   State

(Address) __350 Grove Street__
           Number   Street

(hereinafter referred to as the "Primary Beneficiary") or, if such primary beneficiary does not survive me, for the use and benefit of:

(Name) __Mary A. Smith (my niece)__, of __Jonesville__ __Connecticut__
                                       City   State

(Address) __750 Porter Street__
           Number   Street

(hereinafter referred to as the "Contingent Beneficiary"). If the word "none" appears in the space provided above for the designation of a contingent beneficiary, then if the primary beneficiary does not survive me, the trust property shall revert to my estate.

8. The Trustee and his successors shall serve without bond.

9. This Declaration of Trust shall be construed and enforced in accordance with the laws of the State of __Connecticut__

1. WHEREAS, I, _____, of the

City/Town of_____, County of_____

and State of_____, am the sole owner of the unincorporated business located

at_____in the City/Town of_____,

County of_____and State of_____,

and known as_____

_____

_____ and

2. WHEREAS the principal business of the said_____

_____

is_____

_____

_____

3. NOW, THEREFORE, KNOW ALL MEN BY THESE PRESENTS, that I do hereby acknowledge and declare that I hold and will hold said business and all right, title and interest in and to said business and all furniture, fixtures, stock in trade, inventory, machinery, vehicles, accounts receivable, prepaid insurance and all other assets of such business, IN TRUST for the use and benefit of:

(Name) _____, of

(Address) _____
           Number   Street   City   State

(hereinafter referred to as the "Primary Beneficiary") or, if such primary beneficiary does not survive me, for the use and benefit of:

(Name) _____, of

(Address) _____
           Number   Street   City   State

(hereinafter referred to as the "Contingent Beneficiary"). If the word "none" appears in the space provided above for the designation of a contingent beneficiary, then if the primary beneficiary does not survive me, the trust property shall revert to my estate.

4. I reserve unto myself the power and right at any time during my lifetime to amend or revoke in whole or in part the trust hereby created without the necessity of obtaining the consent of the beneficiary and without giving notice to the beneficiary. The sale or other disposition by me of the whole or any part of the trust property shall constitute as to such whole or part a revocation of this trust.

5. The death during my lifetime of both of the beneficiaries designated hereunder shall revoke such designation, and in such event, I reserve the right to designate a new beneficiary. Should I for any reason fail to designate such new beneficiary, this trust shall terminate upon my death and the trust property shall revert to my estate.

6. In the event of my death or legal incapacity, I hereby nominate and appoint as Successor Trustee hereunder the Primary Beneficiary and if such Primary Beneficiary shall be deceased or upon his or her failure or ceasing to act, then I nominate and appoint as Successor Trustee the Contingent Beneficiary, and upon his or her failure or ceasing to act or should I for any reason fail to designate the person above intended to be nominated, then I nominate and appoint as such Successor Trustee hereunder whosoever shall qualify as executor, administrator or guardian, as the case may be, of my estate.

7. This Declaration of Trust shall extend to and be binding upon the heirs, executors, administrators and assigns of the undersigned and upon the Successors to the Trustee.

8. The Trustee and his successors shall serve without bond.

9. This Declaration of Trust shall be construed and enforced in accordance with the laws of the State of

_____.

IN WITNESS WHEREOF, I have hereunto set my hand and seal this_____day of

_____, 19____.

(sign here)_____L.S.

Witness: (1)_____

Witness: (2)_____

STATE OF_____ \
                              } ss:_____ \
COUNTY OF_____ /

On the_____day of_____, nineteen hundred

and_____, before me came_____,

known to me to be the individual described in, and who executed the foregoing instrument, and_____acknowledged

that_____executed the same, and in due form of law acknowledged the foregoing instrument to be_____free

act and deed and desired the same might be recorded as such.

_____

(Notary Seal)   Notary Public

Declaration of Trust

1. WHEREAS, I, _____, of the

City/Town of_____, County of_____

and State of_____, am the sole owner of the unincorporated business located

at_____in the City/Town of_____,

County of_____and State of_____,

and known as_____

_____ and

_____

2. WHEREAS the principal business of the said_____

_____

is_____

_____

3. NOW, THEREFORE, KNOW ALL MEN BY THESE PRESENTS, that I do hereby acknowledge and declare that I hold and will hold said business and all right, title and interest in and to said business and all furniture, fixtures, stock in trade, inventory, machinery, vehicles, accounts receivable, prepaid insurance and all other assets of such business, IN TRUST for the use and benefit of:

(Name) _____, of

(Address) _____
      Number   Street   City   State

(hereinafter referred to as the "Primary Beneficiary") or, if such primary beneficiary does not survive me, for the use and benefit of:

(Name) _____, of

(Address) _____
      Number   Street   City   State

(hereinafter referred to as the "Contingent Beneficiary"). If the word "none" appears in the space provided above for the designation of a contingent beneficiary, then if the primary beneficiary does not survive me, the trust property shall revert to my estate.

4. I reserve unto myself the power and right at any time during my lifetime to amend or revoke in whole or in part the trust hereby created without the necessity of obtaining the consent of the beneficiary and without giving notice to the beneficiary. The sale or other disposition by me of the whole or any part of the trust property shall constitute as to such whole or part a revocation of this trust.

1

5. The death during my lifetime of both of the beneficiaries designated hereunder shall revoke such designation, and in such event, I reserve the right to designate a new beneficiary. Should I for any reason fail to designate such new beneficiary, this trust shall terminate upon my death and the trust property shall revert to my estate.

6. In the event of my death or legal incapacity, I hereby nominate and appoint as Successor Trustee hereunder the Primary Beneficiary and if such Primary Beneficiary shall be deceased or upon his or her failure or ceasing to act, then I nominate and appoint as Successor Trustee the Contingent Beneficiary, and upon his or her failure or ceasing to act or should I for any reason fail to designate the person above intended to be nominated, then I nominate and appoint as such Successor Trustee hereunder whosoever shall qualify as executor, administrator or guardian, as the case may be, of my estate.

7. This Declaration of Trust shall extend to and be binding upon the heirs, executors, administrators and assigns of the undersigned and upon the Successors to the Trustee.

8. The Trustee and his successors shall serve without bond.

9. This Declaration of Trust shall be construed and enforced in accordance with the laws of the State of

_____.

IN WITNESS WHEREOF, I have hereunto set my hand and seal this_____day of

_____, 19_____.

(sign here)_____L.S.

Witness: (1)_____

Witness: (2)_____

STATE OF_____⎱

⎰ ss:_____

COUNTY OF_____⎰

On the_____day of_____, nineteen hundred

and_____, before me came_____,

known to me to be the individual described in, and who executed the foregoing instrument, and_____acknowledged

that_____executed the same, and in due form of law acknowledged the foregoing instrument to be_____free

act and deed and desired the same might be recorded as such.

_____

(Notary Seal)   Notary Public

Chapter 18

AVOIDING PROBATE OF YOUR AUTOMOBILE

By now, you've probably concluded that you've taken care of everything and there'll be nothing left to probate. You may have forgotten one thing—your automobile.

Through joint ownership of their home, their bank accounts and their securities, many persons have avoided probate only to have the wife discover, after the death of her husband, that she must either (a) sign her deceased husband's name illegally on the back of the automobile registration certificate, if she wishes to sell the car or simply transfer it into her name, or (b) apply to the probate court for an appointment as administrator which will legally entitle her to transfer title to the vehicle.

A used car frequently has a very limited sale value, and the trouble and expense of going through the probate process in order to dispose of it is way out of proportion to that value. Be careful, then, that you don't force your estate into probate just because of your automobile.

On the back of nearly all automobile registration certificates is a place where you are to sign if you sell the car or turn it in on a new one. Sign it—now. If anything happens to you, your spouse or other family member can take it down to the Motor Vehicle Department and freely transfer it to another name without having to forge any signature or apply to the probate court for "letters testamentary".

Some states now require possession of a title form in connection with ownership of a motor vehicle, which form must be signed and surrendered to the Motor Vehicle Department when the vehicle is being transferred to someone else. If your state is one requiring a title form, make certain that you sign it now as well as the car registration certificate.

Chapter 19

IF YOU CHANGE YOUR MIND . . .

Permanence, alas, is not the hallmark of our modern society. Our homes, our automobiles, our refrigerators —seemingly all of the material things which make up our world—have a built-in obsolescence which dictates constant replacement.

Our financial planning is no exception to the rule. In the nervous age in which we live, in which the weekly visit to the psychoanalyst has become for many a status symbol, the best-laid financial schemes "gang aft a-gley", as Bobbie Burns put it.

Accordingly, having gotten you into this, I now must tell you how to get out of it in the event you change your mind about any of the plans you've made.

* * *

1. YOUR HOME

First, as to the arrangements to exempt your real estate from probate: You executed a declaration of trust (DT-1, DT-2, DT-3 or DT-4) in which you established that you were holding the property in trust for someone else. You filed a copy of that declaration of trust with the town clerk's or other office in your community where real estate transactions are customarily recorded. After filing, the original trust instrument was returned to you. Actually, it was not absolutely necessary that you file the declaration of trust. If you were particularly anxious to preserve the privacy of the transaction, you could withhold such filing. But by filing it in the public records, you made absolutely certain that the existence of the trust and its terms and conditions could be proven. If after your death a copy of the executed instrument could not be found among your effects, or if it were found by someone who had occasion to be displeased by its terms, litigation might ensue to dispute its existence. Filing it was in the nature of an insurance policy against any such happening.

With the declaration of trust, you filed a quit-claim deed by which you, as an individual, deeded the property to yourself as trustee. This *had* to be filed.

If you have changed your mind, observe these instructions:

(a) *If you simply wish to change the beneficiary*:

On the following pages will be found duplicate copies of a simple "Revocation of Trust, DT-1-2-3-4". Complete this instrument. Next, from among the forms (DT-1, DT-2, DT-3 or DT-4) provided in this book for use in connection with the avoidance of probate of real estate, select one which will suitably reflect your changed desires with respect to the beneficiary. If the form which you regard as appropriate has already been used in connection with the establishment of the earlier trust which you are now revoking, you may (a) make a typed copy of the original form, or (b) use the blank provided at the end of this book to send for another copy of the particular declaration of trust you now require. Complete the new form in duplicate in accordance with the instructions given in Chapter 5 and its appendices. Finally, file the revocation and the new declaration of trust with the same town office where you filed the original documents. The original declaration which you are now cancelling should be destroyed. If you insist upon preserving it for your records, make certain that you write across it boldly and *indelibly* "revoked (date)". If you gave the duplicate copy of the original declaration of trust to the beneficiary whom you have now replaced with someone else, or if you simply left it in your safe deposit box or in the keeping of a trusted third party, be certain that you recover and destroy the document so that it cannot be made the basis for any claim after you are gone.

(b) *If you wish to cancel the trust arrangement entirely without naming a new beneficiary:*

Follow the instructions given above with respect to the execution of the revocation. Next, in your capacity as trustee execute a new quit claim deed returning the property to yourself as an individual ("I, John Smith, trustee under Declaration of Trust dated_____ do hereby transfer unto John Smith, all right, title and interest, etc.") File both documents with the town clerk's or other office in your community where real estate transactions are customarily recorded.

* * *

2. YOUR BANK ACCOUNT

As to the arrangements to exempt your bank account from probate: You executed a declaration of trust (DT-5, DT-6, DT-7 or DT-8) in which you established that you were holding the account in trust for someone else. The original of that instrument was delivered to the bank for permanent filing. You retained the duplicate. Here, again, you could simply have advised the bank of the existence of the trust. But upon your death the bank will be called upon to turn the account over to the successor trustee whom you have named. If a copy of the instrument cannot be found among your effects, or has been lost or "mislaid" by a disgruntled non-beneficiary, the bank obviously won't know to whom the account is to be transferred. It was important, then, that you file the original instrument with the bank and get a receipt for it. Now, however, you conclude that you want to leave things differently.

(a) *If you simply want to change the beneficiary:*

From among the forms (DT-5, DT-6, DT-7 or DT-8) provided in Chapter 6 of this book for use in avoiding probate of bank accounts, select one which suitably reflects your changed desires with respect to the beneficiary. If the form which you regard as appropriate has already been used in connection with the establishment of the earlier trust which you are now revoking, you may (a) make a typed copy of the original form with the beneficiary change you desire, or (b) use the blank provided at the end of this book to send for another copy of the particular declaration of trust you now require. Complete the new form in duplicate in accordance with the instructions given in Chapter 6 and its appendices. Take the original to the bank and substitute it for the one in that institution's files. Insist upon the return to you of the old form in order that you may personally destroy it. If you *must* preserve it for your records—which I do *not* recommend—make certain that you write across it boldly and indelibly, "Revoked (date)". If for

any reason the bank cannot readily produce the old form, insist upon being given a letter acknowledging receipt from you of notice of the revocation of the old instrument dated _____and naming _____as beneficiary, as well as the new declaration dated_____ and naming_____ as beneficiary. Staple this letter from the bank to your duplicate copy of the new declaration of trust which you are putting away in safe-keeping.

Note that you have not executed a revocation as you were required to do with your real estate. None is required.

(b) *If you wish to cancel the trust arrangement entirely without naming a new beneficiary:*

Simply go into the bank and request the return of the old declaration of trust. Then, draw the money out of the existing account in your name as trustee and open a new account in your name as an individual.

* * *

3. YOUR MUTUAL FUND SHARES

As to the arrangement to exempt your mutual fund shares purchased outright (as distinguished from those held in a contractual plan) from probate: You executed a declaration of trust (DT-9, DT-10, DT-11 or DT-12) in which you established that you were holding the shares in trust for someone else. If you followed the instructions given in Chapter 7, the original declaration of trust is stapled to your share certificate, if you received a share certificate. If you have had an "open account" or "accumulation plan", the shares have been held for you by the fund's custodian bank. We explained, remember, that some custodian banks will accept the declaration of trust for permanent filing in connection with such accounts, but most will not. You will recall, or your records will show, whether the custodian of the particular fund you own accepted the form for permanent filing or whether you retained it yourself in safekeeping. It is quite possible that you hold a certificate representing your original purchase of shares but that ordinary income dividends and/or capital gains distributions have been accumulating in an "open account".

(a) *If you simply want to change the beneficiary:*

On the following pages will be found duplicate copies of a "Revocation of Trust DT-9-10-11-12". Complete this instrument. Next, from among the forms (DT-9, DT-10, DT-11 or DT-12) provided in Chapter 7 of this book for use in avoiding probate of mutual fund shares, select one which suitably reflects your changed desires with respect to the beneficiary. If the form which you regard as appropriate has already been used in connection with the establishment of the earlier trust which you are now revoking, you may (a) make a typed copy of the original form with the beneficiary change you desire, or (b) use the blank provided at the end of this book to send for another copy of the particular declaration of trust you now require. Complete the new form in duplicate in accordance with the instructions given in Chapter 7 and its appendices, *dating it the same date as the original.* (If you don't, the shares will have to be re-registered and you'll have to pay a transfer tax.) Send both the revocation and the new declaration of trust to the custodian bank of the fund whose shares you hold. If it is a fund which does *not* accept the declaration for permanent filing, direct the bank to make appropriate note in its files of the existence of the revocation and new declaration of trust. Commonly, the custodian bank will photostat the documents for its records and return the originals to you. If it is a fund which *does* accept the instruments for permanent filing, ask for a receipt when you send them the revocation and new declaration of trust.

If you own a contractual plan which provides a form of declaration of trust for naming a beneficiary, the sponsor will have established a procedure for changing the beneficiary. Ordinarily, this will involve the execution of a revocation and new declaration of trust not unlike those provided here. If the contractual plan which you own is one of the few using a so-called "designation of beneficiary" which does not provide probate exemption, and you have followed our suggestion in Chapter 7 and filed instead our declaration of trust form, the procedure to accomplish the change of beneficiary is simple. Execute Revocation DT-9-10-11-12 and a new declaration of trust and send both to your contractual plan's custodian bank with a request that they be filed in place of the existing beneficiary designation and that a receipt be sent you.

(b) *If you wish to cancel the trust arrangement entirely without naming a new beneficiary:*

Execute Revocation DT-9-10-11-12 and send it with your share certificate if the latter is in your possession or with your account number or other identifying data if you have an "open account" or "accumulation account," to the custodian bank together with a letter requesting that the shares be transferred from your name as "trustee u/d/t dated _____"

to your name as an individual. You must sign the back of the certificate and have your signature guaranteed by a national bank or trust company.

If you own a contractual plan, simply execute the revocation and send it to the bank. This will cancel the existing beneficiary designation represented by the earlier declaration of trust, leaving no beneficiary. On such plans, if no beneficiary has been named, the account automatically reverts to your estate.

* * *

4. YOUR SECURITIES

As to the arrangements to exempt stocks and bonds from probate: You executed a declaration of trust (DT-13, DT-14, DT-15 or DT-16) in which you established that you were holding the securities in trust for someone else. I know of no issuers or transfer agents who will accept the declaration of trust for permanent filing, so if you followed the instructions given in Chapter 8, the original declaration of trust is stapled to the stock certificate.

(a) *If you simply wish to change the beneficiary:*

On the following pages will be found duplicate copies of a simple "R e v o c a t i o n of Trust DT-13-14-15-16". Complete this instrument. Next, from among the forms (DT-13, DT-14, DT-15 or DT-16) provided in Chapter 8 of this book for use in avoiding probate of securities, select one which suitably reflects your changed desires with respect to the beneficiary. If the form which you regard as appropriate has already been used in connection with the establishment of the earlier trust which you are now revoking, you may (a) make a typed copy of the original form with the beneficiary change you desire, or (b) use the blank at the end of this book to send for another copy of the particular declaration of trust you now require. Complete the new form in duplicate in accordance with the instructions given in Chapter 8 and its appendices. Detach the old declaration of trust from the stock certificate to which it has been stapled and replace it with the revocation and new declaration of trust. Actually, you could probably get along without the revocation—most stock transfer agents don't ask to see the trust instrument when they issue the shares; it's when you want to get out that they get sticky and demand to see the instrument under which you've been acting as trustee. If the transfer agent hasn't photocopied the original instrument, it won't know whether the one attached to the certificate you produce later at the time of liquidation is the original or one

241

which you have since substituted. Against the possibility that the original was displayed to and photocopied by the transfer agent, take no chances—execute the revocation and staple it to the certificate along with the new declaration of trust.

(b) *If you wish to cancel the trust arrangement entirely without naming a new beneficiary:*

Execute "Revocation DT-13-14-15-16". Next, sign the back of the stock certificate exactly as it is registered on the front and have your signature guaranteed by a national bank or trust company. Finally, send the revocation and the stock certificate to the transfer agent with a letter requesting that the registration be changed from your name as trustee to your name as an individual.

* * *

5. YOUR DACEY TRUST

In establishing a Dacey Trust, you entered into a trust agreement (DT-17) with the bank whom you appointed as trustee. That agreement provided that it might be amended or revoked at any time by written notice to the trustee.

(a) *If you now wish to amend it:*

On the following pages will be found duplicate copies of a suggested "Amendment to Deed of Trust DT-17". Frankly, the "Dacey Trust" instrument is a long one and it is not possible to anticipate what changes you may wish to make in that instrument. Occasionally someone will wish to change the age at which young people are to receive principal. Others may wish to change the mutual fund management which is to be responsible for the investment of the assets after the Settlor's death. The instrument is so drawn that if the Settlor's wife predeceases him, it is not necessary to alter or amend the trust instrument in order that the entire trust shall revert to the surviving children.

In the third paragraph of the amendment, indicate which section and/or paragraph of the instrument you wish to amend. When completed, this paragraph should read something like this:

NOW, THEREFORE, it is agreed by the Settlor and the Trustee that Section B, Paragraph 2 of the said agreement shall cease to be effective as of the date of this Amend-

ment and that the following shall be substituted therefor and thereafter be known as Section B, Paragraph 2 of the Agreement entered into by the parties on March 26, 1964:

Thereafter, insert the revised version of the text with the corrections or amendments you desire. If these are too extensive to fit into the amendment form provided, make a typed copy of the form large enough to contain the changes. At least you know *how* to amend the trust. If the nature and scope of the changes you desire are such as to be beyond your understanding and capacity to re-work the instrument on your own, seek the services of an attorney. If he's worth his salt, it's not more than a twenty-minute job.

Bear one important point in mind:

If you have executed a will (such as W-11 in the section on Wills which appears later in this book) by which you have incorporated the balance of your estate into your Dacey Trust, and you subsequently amend the trust, <u>draw a new will</u>. It can read exactly like the original version except that where it states that the trustee bank is to receive and administer the funds "under the terms of a certain trust executed by me and by said XYZ trust company as of_____", it should add "and amended as of_____". The will should always bear a later date than the trust or amendment to the trust. (Actually you *could* achieve your purpose with a codicil to the old will, but it's a simple will and it's just as easy to draw a new one. That way, you have a will only instead of a will-plus-a-codicil.)

(b) *If you want to revoke the Dacey Trust completely:*

The assets of your Dacey Trust probably consist of life insurance policies, plus mutual fund shares and/or individual securities registered in accordance with the instructions contained in this book so that they will pass into the trust at your death without going through probate. If you wish to cancel your Dacey Trust: (1) Deliver written notice to this effect to the trustee bank; (2) Obtain from the insurance company suitable change of beneficiary forms to enable you to name a new beneficiary to replace the trustee beneficiary; (3) Carry out the procedures described earlier in this chapter for revoking trust arrangements involving mutual fund shares or individual securities.

* * *

6. YOUR "WIFE'S TRUST"

The sole objective of a "Wife's Trust" is to direct the proceeds of an insurance policy on her husband's life into his Dacey Trust upon his death. It would seem that there would be little occasion for the wife to amend such a trust. It is more likely that she might wish to revoke it—obviously if the husband revoked his Dacey Trust, for example, his wife would have to revoke her trust.

There seems little point, then, in attempting to supply here a form of amendment. It should suffice to explain that if you desire to revoke a "Wife's Trust", you should simply give the trustee bank written notice of such revocation and request return of the policy or policies. Concurrently, you should execute appropriate "Change of Beneficiary" forms supplied by the life insurance company to appoint someone beneficiary in the bank's stead.

* * *

7. PERSONAL EFFECTS

Using Declaration of Trust DT-22, you have created a living trust which will cause certain personal effects to pass to a beneficiary whom you have named exempt from probate.

It is suggested that you not attempt to amend such a trust—simply draw a new one. If, for example, you made a trust leaving your Uncle Herman's diamond stickpin to your nephew, Willie—and Willie has turned out to be a perfect blister—just tear up the trust and so far as the stickpin is concerned, Willie's had it. Ordinarily, you don't have to revoke anything. Just destroy the trust instrument and that ends it. Without the trust the property will pass under your will. _One word of caution:_ If you gave Willie a copy of the Declaration of Trust to hold as evidence to prove that the stickpin was to come to him, be _certain_ that you get it back. If he won't return it, or can't find it, or if you just don't want to make an issue of it by asking him for it, then by all means execute a "Revocation of Declaration of Trust D-22", which will officially nullify your earlier designation of Willie to receive the stickpin.

Then, using Declaration of Trust DT-22, create a new trust naming a new beneficiary. If the Form DT-22 in this book has already been used in connection with the establishment of the earlier account which you are now revoking, you may (a) make a typed copy of the original form, or (b) use the blank provided at the end

of this book to send for another copy of the declaration of trust you now require. Complete the new form in accordance with the instructions given in Chapter 16.

In using these arrangements to avoid probate of personal effects, it is essential that the trust instrument and the trust property be in the keeping of a trusted person. Remember, if you leave the trust instrument among your personal effects and it is found by someone who is disgruntled by your disposition of the property via the trust, that person can frustrate your plans simply by destroying the trust instrument. Similarly, it will do you little good to leave a valuable diamond ring to a favorite niece if the ring can be filched from a dresser-top jewel box by family prowlers after you're gone. Probably the best arrangement with jewelry is to (a) name some trusted person as successor trustee under the declaration of trust, and (b) place the jewelry in a safe deposit box to which the successor trustee has access after your death. If you wish, you can give the beneficiary a letter explaining that you have left the jewelry in trust.

* * *

8. YOUR SMALL, UNINCORPORATED BUSINESS

As to the arrangements to exempt your small, unincorporated business from probate: You executed a Declaration of Trust (DT-23) in which you established that you were holding the business in trust for someone else. You filed the original of that Declaration of Trust in the town clerk's or other office in your community where property transfers are customarily recorded. After filing, it was returned to you. The executed duplicate of the Declaration of Trust you either retained or gave to the person whom you named to receive the business at your death.

(a) *If you simply wish to change the beneficiary:*

On the following pages will be found duplicate copies of a simple "Revocation of Trust DT-23". Complete this instrument. Next, execute a new Declaration of Trust DT-23 provided in Chapter 17 of this book for use in avoiding probate of a small, unincorporated business, completing it in accordance with the instructions given in the Appendix to Chapter 17. If this trust form has already been used in connection with the establishment of the earlier trust which you are now revoking, you may (a) make a typed copy of the original form with the beneficiary change you desire, or (b) use the blank at the end of this book to send for another copy of Declaration of Trust DT-23. File both the Revocation and the new Declaration of Trust with the same town office where you filed the original documents. The original Declaration of Trust which you are now cancelling should be destroyed. If you insist upon preserving it for your records— which I do *not* recommend, make certain that you write a c r o s s it boldly and *indelibly,* "revoked (date)". If you gave the duplicate copy of the original Declaration of Trust to the beneficiary whom you have now replaced with someone else, or if you simply left it in your safe deposit box or in the keeping of a trusted third party, be certain that you recover and destroy the document so that it cannot be made the basis for any claim after you are gone.

(b) *If you wish to cancel the trust arrangement entirely without naming a new beneficiary:*

Simply execute "Revocation of Trust DT-23" and file it with the same municipal office where you earlier filed the original Declaration of Trust.

On the pages immediately following will be found these instruments in duplicate:

Revocation of Trust
DT-1-2-3-4

Revocation of Trust
DT-9-10-11-12

Revocation of Trust
DT-13-14-15-16

Revocation of Trust
DT-22

Revocation of Trust
DT-23

Amendment to Deed of Trust
DT-17

Revocation of Trust

This instrument of revocation made this_____day of_____, 19____,

by _____,

WHEREAS, by Declaration of Trust dated_____ 19____, I created

in writing a Revocable Trust as a result of which a beneficial interest in certain real estate accrued to:

_____

_____

_____

_____, and

WHEREAS, by the terms of the said Declaration of Trust, I reserve the full power and right to revoke said Trust at any time without the consent of or notice to any beneficiary of said Trust created by me;

NOW THEREFORE, pursuant to the power and right of revocation aforesaid, I do hereby revoke in its entirety the Trust created by me by the aforesaid Declaration of Trust, to the end that as of the date of this instrument of revocation, I hold the former trust property free and discharged of all the Trust's terms and provisions in said Declaration of Trust contained.

_____L.S.
Signature

Revocation of Trust

This instrument of revocation made this_____day of_____, 19_____,

by _____,

WHEREAS, by Declaration of Trust dated_____ 19_____, I created

in writing a Revocable Trust as a result of which a beneficial interest in certain real estate accrued to:

_____

_____

_____

_____, and

WHEREAS, by the terms of the said Declaration of Trust, I reserve the full power and right to revoke said Trust at any time without the consent of or notice to any beneficiary of said Trust created by me;

NOW THEREFORE, pursuant to the power and right of revocation aforesaid, I do hereby revoke in its entirety the Trust created by me by the aforesaid Declaration of Trust, to the end that as of the date of this instrument of revocation, I hold the former trust property free and discharged of all the Trust's terms and provisions in said Declaration of Trust contained.

_____L.S.
Signature

Revocation of Trust

This instrument of revocation made this_____day of_____, 19_____,

WHEREAS, by Declaration of Trust dated_____ 19_____, I created in writing

a Revocable Trust as a result of which a beneficial interest in certain shares of_____

(Name of Mutual Fund)

accrued to:

_____

_____

_____

_____, and

WHEREAS, by the terms of the said Declaration of Trust, I reserve the full power and right to revoke said Trust at any time without the consent of or notice to any beneficiary of said Trust created by me;

NOW THEREFORE, pursuant to the power and right of revocation aforesaid, I do hereby revoke in its entirety the Trust created by me by the aforesaid Declaration of Trust, to the end that as of the date of this instrument of revocation, I hold the said mutual fund shares free and discharged of all the Trust's terms and provisions in said Declaration of Trust contained.

_____L.S.

Signature

Revocation of Trust

This instrument of revocation made this_____day of_____, 19____,

WHEREAS, by Declaration of Trust dated_____ 19____, I created in writing

a Revocable Trust as a result of which a beneficial interest in certain shares of_____

(Name of Mutual Fund)

accrued to:

_____

_____

_____

_____, and

WHEREAS, by the terms of the said Declaration of Trust, I reserve the full power and right to revoke said Trust at any time without the consent of or notice to any beneficiary of said Trust created by me;

NOW THEREFORE, pursuant to the power and right of revocation aforesaid, I do hereby revoke in its entirety the Trust created by me by the aforesaid Declaration of Trust, to the end that as of the date of this instrument of revocation, I hold the said mutual fund shares free and discharged of all the Trust's terms and provisions in said Declaration of Trust contained.

_____L.S.

Signature

1

Revocation of Trust

This instrument of revocation made this_____day of_____, 19____,

WHEREAS, by Declaration of Trust dated_____ 19____, I created in writing a Revocable Trust as a result of which a beneficial interest in certain shares of stock of

_____accrued to:

(Name of Corporation)

_____

_____

_____

_____, and

WHEREAS, by the terms of the said Declaration of Trust, I reserve the full power and right to revoke said Trust at any time without the consent of or notice to any beneficiary of said Trust created by me;

NOW THEREFORE, pursuant to the power and right of revocation aforesaid, I do hereby revoke in its entirety the Trust created by me by the aforesaid Declaration of Trust, to the end that as of the date of this instrument of revocation, I hold the said shares of stock free and discharged of all the Trust's terms and provisions in said Declaration of Trust contained.

_____L.S.

Signature

3

Revocation of Trust

This instrument of revocation made this_____day of_____, 19_____,

WHEREAS, by Declaration of Trust dated_____ 19_____, I created
in writing a Revocable Trust as a result of which a beneficial interest in certain shares of stock of

_____accrued to:

(Name of Corporation)

_____

_____

_____

_____, and

WHEREAS, by the terms of the said Declaration of Trust, I reserve the full power and right to revoke said Trust at any time without the consent of or notice to any beneficiary of said Trust created by me;

NOW THEREFORE, pursuant to the power and right of revocation aforesaid, I do hereby revoke in its entirety the Trust created by me by the aforesaid Declaration of Trust, to the end that as of the date of this instrument of revocation, I hold the said shares of stock free and discharged of all the Trust's terms and provisions in said Declaration of Trust contained.

_____L.S.

Signature

Revocation of Trust

This instrument of revocation made this_____day of_____, 19_____,

WHEREAS, by Declaration of Trust dated_____ 19_____, I created in writing a Revocable Trust as a result of which a beneficial interest in:

_____

_____

_____

_____

accrued to:

_____

_____

_____, and

WHEREAS, by the terms of the said Declaration of Trust, I reserve the full power and right to revoke said Trust at any time without the consent of or notice to any beneficiary of said Trust created by me;

NOW THEREFORE, pursuant to the power and right of revocation aforesaid, I do hereby revoke in its entirety the Trust created by me by the aforesaid Declaration of Trust, to the end that as of the date of this instrument of revocation, I hold the above-described trust property free and discharged of all the Trust's terms and provisions in said Declaration of Trust contained.

_____
Signature

Revocation of Trust

This instrument of revocation made this_____day of_____, 19_____,

WHEREAS, by Declaration of Trust dated_____ 19_____, I created in writing a Revocable Trust as a result of which a beneficial interest in:

_____

_____

_____

_____

accrued to:

_____

_____

_____, and

WHEREAS, by the terms of the said Declaration of Trust, I reserve the full power and right to revoke said Trust at any time without the consent of or notice to any beneficiary of said Trust created by me;

NOW THEREFORE, pursuant to the power and right of revocation aforesaid, I do hereby revoke in its entirety the Trust created by me by the aforesaid Declaration of Trust, to the end that as of the date of this instrument of revocation, I hold the above-described trust property free and discharged of all the Trust's terms and provisions in said Declaration of Trust contained.

_____
Signature

Revocation of Trust

This instrument of revocation made this_____day of_____, 19_____,

WHEREAS, by Declaration of Trust dated_____ 19_____, I created in writing a Revocable Trust as a result of which a beneficial interest in the unincorporated business known as

_____accrued to:

_____

_____

_____

_____, and

WHEREAS, by the terms of the said Declaration of Trust, I reserve the full power and right to revoke said Trust at any time without the consent of or notice to any beneficiary of said Trust created by me;

NOW THEREFORE, pursuant to the power and right of revocation aforesaid, I do hereby revoke in its entirety the Trust created by me by the aforesaid Declaration of Trust, to the end that as of the date of this instrument of revocation I hold the said unincorporated business free and discharged of all the Trust's terms and provisions in said Declaration of Trust contained.

_____
Signature

Revocation of Trust

This instrument of revocation made this_____day of_____, 19_____,

WHEREAS, by Declaration of Trust dated_____ 19_____, I created in writing a Revocable Trust as a result of which a beneficial interest in the unincorporated business known as

_____accrued to:

_____

_____

_____

_____, and

WHEREAS, by the terms of the said Declaration of Trust, I reserve the full power and right to revoke said Trust at any time without the consent of or notice to any beneficiary of said Trust created by me;

NOW THEREFORE, pursuant to the power and right of revocation aforesaid, I do hereby revoke in its entirety the Trust created by me by the aforesaid Declaration of Trust, to the end that as of the date of this instrument of revocation I hold the said unincorporated business free and discharged of all the Trust's terms and provisions in said Declaration of Trust contained.

_____
Signature

Amendment to Deed of Trust

WHEREAS, under date of_____, an agreement was entered into between_____of the City/Town of _____, County of_____ and State of _____(hereinafter referred to as the "Settlor") and _____, located in the City/Town of _____, County of_____ and State of_____ (hereinafter referred to as the "Trustee"), and

WHEREAS, Section C-7 of the said agreement provides that it may be altered or modified at any time by the Settlor and the Trustee without the consent of any other person,

NOW THEREFORE, it is agreed by the Settlor and the Trustee that Section_____, Paragraph(s)_____ of said agreement shall cease to be effective as of the date of this Amendment and that the following shall be substituted therefor and shall hereafter be known as Section_____, Paragraph(s)_____ of the agreement entered into by the parties on_____:

IN WITNESS WHEREOF, the said_____has

hereunto set his hand and seal and said_____has

set its hand by its officer thereunto duly authorized and to a duplicate hereof, this_____

day of_____ 19_____.

Witnessed by:

The Settlor:

_____

_____(L.S.)

The Trustee:

_____

_____(L.S.)

STATE OF_____

}ss:_____

COUNTY OF_____

Personally appeared_____signer and sealer of the

foregoing Amendment to Deed of Trust, who acknowledged the same to be his free act and deed, before me, this

_____day of_____, 19_____.

_____

Notary Public

STATE OF_____

}ss:_____

COUNTY OF_____

Personally appeared_____by its

duly authorized officer, as Trustee as aforesaid, signer and sealer of the foregoing Amendment to Deed of Trust

and acknowledged that he executed the same in the capacity and for the purposes therein stated and that the

same is his free act and deed and the free act and deed of_____

before me this_____day of_____, 19_____.

_____

Notary Public

Amendment to Deed of Trust

WHEREAS, under date of_____, an agreement was entered into between_____of the City/Town of _____, County of_____ and State of _____(hereinafter referred to as the "Settlor") and _____, located in the City/Town of _____, County of_____ and State of_____ (hereinafter referred to as the "Trustee"), and

WHEREAS, Section C-7 of the said agreement provides that it may be altered or modified at any time by the Settlor and the Trustee without the consent of any other person,

NOW THEREFORE, it is agreed by the Settlor and the Trustee that Section_____, Paragraph(s)_____ of said agreement shall cease to be effective as of the date of this Amendment and that the following shall be substituted therefor and shall hereafter be known as Section_____, Paragraph(s)_____ of the agreement entered into by the parties on_____:

IN WITNESS WHEREOF, the said_____has

hereunto set his hand and seal and said_____has

set its hand by its officer thereunto duly authorized and to a duplicate hereof, this_____

day of_____ 19_____.

Witnessed by:

_____

_____

_____

_____

The Settlor:

_____(L.S.)

The Trustee:

_____(L.S.)

STATE OF_____

COUNTY OF_____

}ss:_____

Personally appeared_____signer and sealer of the

foregoing Amendment to Deed of Trust, who acknowledged the same to be his free act and deed, before me, this

_____day of_____, 19_____.

_____

Notary Public

STATE OF_____

COUNTY OF_____

}ss:_____

Personally appeared_____by its

duly authorized officer, as Trustee as aforesaid, signer and sealer of the foregoing Amendment to Deed of Trust
and acknowledged that he executed the same in the capacity and for the purposes therein stated and that the

same is his free act and deed and the free act and deed of_____

before me this_____day of_____, 19_____.

_____

Notary Public

Chapter 20

YOU'LL STILL NEED A WILL!

If you have read the foregoing chapters thoughtfully, careful selection and execution of one or more of the instruments provided should now make it possible for you to eliminate completely the necessity for probating your estate.

That doesn't mean, however, that you shouldn't have a will. It is not possible to anticipate and thus to exempt from probate every last asset with which you may be endowed at the time of your death. For example, let's suppose that you have carefully inventoried every scrap of property you own and have covered it with an inter vivos trust arrangement excluding it from the jurisdiction of the probate court.

On the way down town tomorrow morning, your car is struck by a skidding truck, causing you fatal injuries. Your estate sues and collects a large financial settlement from the owner of the truck.

What is to become of that settlement? Who is to get it if you have left no will? You will have died "intestate" and the laws of the state in which you live will determine which of your relatives are entitled to share the wealth which your untimely passing has created. The persons whom the law designates as beneficiaries are not necessarily the same ones you might designate. It is important, then, that you have a will just in case there are some loose ends to your estate which you have not anticipated. If everything goes as you planned, and everything you leave is covered by an inter vivos trust, there'll be nothing to probate and your family can simply forget the will. It will be there, however, if it is needed.

Some wills are simple, brief and to the point. Others, like the Mississippi, roll on and on, incorporating a heritage of three centuries or more of ponderous phrases and legalistic mumbo-jumbo. This has come to be accepted practice and I suspect that if the average man were to be offered a will written in simple, straight-forward modern-day English, without the usual complement of "whereas's," "now therefore's" and "know all men by these presents," he'd feel cheated.

To supplement the selection of trust instruments which you have already examined, I have prepared a series of will forms which appear on the pages which follow. From among them, most readers can select an instrument which fits their particular situation and meets their particular needs. I've sprinkled a few "whereas's" and "now, therefore's" here and there to make them look nice and legal and so you won't feel cheated. The instruments, numbered from 1 to 12, are first summarized in a series of explanatory notes which include precise instructions on filling out the form.

You must sign the will in the presence of three witnesses and a notary public. The three witnesses must be adults. They must be "disinterested" persons—that is, they must not benefit in any way from the terms and provisions of your will. They must be together and they must actually *see* you sign the will.

The execution of a will is an extremely serious business. There is an established procedure which must be strictly observed. This is no place for original ideas or short-cuts. Immediately following this section is a "script" covering the signing of a will. Follow it exactly.

If there is something in a will which is not correct, you may cross it out and/or write in a few words to make it correct. Be sure to initial the change. If the alterations are extensive, don't use the will; have it retyped correctly.

The will forms are in duplicate. Only one copy should be signed by you, the witnesses and the notary. This should be put away in a safe place where it will be found by the people you *want* to have find it. If your only heirs at law are your two sisters, and you've left everything to one of them, the other one can get half of your estate after your death by getting to your will first and burning it. Many an unscrupulous relative has shared in an estate illegally by the simple process of finding and destroying a will which cut him off. Make sure *your* will is safe.

The duplicate copy of your will is for handy reference purposes. "Conform" it—that is, type or print in all of the names which are signed to the original.

Do everything slowly, methodically. Make sure you have it right.

PROCEDURE FOR EXECUTING
A WILL

The testator (the person making the will), the three witnesses and the notary assemble. The testator signs the will. The three witnesses each sign the will in two places. The following is then said *aloud:*

Notary: "John Smith, do you identify this document as your Last Will and Testament, do you wish it to be so regarded, and have you signed it of your own free will?"

Testator: "Yes."

Notary: "And have you requested that these persons witness your signature and make an affidavit concerning your execution of this Will?"

Testator: "I have."

Notary: "The witnesses will please raise their right hands. Do each of you individually declare under oath that Mr. Smith has identified this document as his Last Will and Testament and stated that he wished it to be so regarded?"

Witnesses: (in unison) "He has."

Notary: "Has he signed it in your presence, saying that he was doing so of his own free will and did he at that time appear to be of sound mind and legal age and free of undue influence?"

Witnesses: (in unison) "Yes."

Notary: "Have you, in his presence and at his request, and in the presence of each other, affixed your signatures to this document as witnesses, and have you made this affidavit at his request?"

Witnesses: (in unison) "We have."

Notary: "You may put your hands down."

The witnesses' affidavit at the end of the will is then notarized.

<table>
<tr><td>

**WILL FORM
W-1**

</td><td>

HUSBAND'S WILL LEAVING EVERYTHING TO WIFE, OR TO SOME ONE OTHER PERSON IF HIS WIFE DOES NOT SURVIVE HIM

</td></tr>
</table>

Example: John Smith and his wife Mary are childless. Mr. Smith wishes to leave his estate to his wife at his death. If Mrs. Smith does not survive him, though, he wishes his estate to go to his sister.

Procedure: Using Will Form W-1, Mr. Smith:

1. Enters his name and place of residence at the top;

2. Enters his wife's name ("Mary Smith", not "Mrs. John Smith") in Paragraph "Second";

3. Enters his sister's name and address in Paragraph "Third";

4. Enters his wife's name as Executrix in the first sentence of Paragraph "Fourth". In the second sentence of Paragraph "Fourth" he enters the name of an adult to serve as Executor or Executrix if his wife does not survive him. This could be the contingent beneficiary (his sister) if she is not a minor.

5. Signs the document in the presence of three adult, disinterested witnesses and a notary public.

<table>
<tr><td>

**WILL FORM
W-2**

</td><td>

WIFE'S WILL LEAVING EVERYTHING TO HUSBAND, OR TO SOME ONE OTHER PERSON IF HER HUSBAND DOES NOT SURVIVE HER

</td></tr>
</table>

Example: John Smith and his wife Mary are childless. Mrs. Smith wishes to leave her estate to her husband at her death. If Mr. Smith does not survive her, though, she wishes her estate to go to her nephew.

Procedure: Using Will Form W-2, Mrs. Smith:

1. Enters her name and place of residence at the top;

2. Enters her husband's name in Paragraph "Second";

3. Enters her nephew's name and address in Paragraph "Third";

4. Enters her husband's name as Executor in the first sentence of Paragraph "Fourth". In the second sentence of Paragraph "Fourth" she enters the name of an adult to serve as Executor or Executrix if her husband does not survive her. This could be the contingent beneficiary (her nephew) if he is not a minor.

5. Signs the document in the presence of three adult, disinterested witnesses and a notary public.

WILL FORM W-3

HUSBAND'S WILL LEAVING EVERYTHING TO WIFE OR, IF SHE DOES NOT SURVIVE HIM, TO TWO OR MORE OTHER PERSONS WHOSE CHILDREN WILL TAKE THEIR SHARE IF THEY ARE NOT LIVING

Example: John Smith and his wife Mary are childless. Mr. Smith wishes to leave his estate to his wife at his death. If Mrs. Smith does not survive him, though, he wishes his estate to be divided among his three sisters. The share of any sister not then living is to go to that sister's children in equal shares. If the deceased sister has left no children, Mr. Smith wants her share to be divided equally between his two surviving sisters.

Procedure: Using Will Form W-3, Mr. Smith:

1. Enters his name and place of residence at the top;

2. Enters his wife's name in Paragraph "Second";

3. Enters in Paragraph "Third" the *number* of sisters to share his estate if his wife does not survive him, and their names;

4. Enters his wife's name as Executrix in the first sentence of Paragraph "Fourth". In the second sentence of Paragraph "Fourth" he enters the name of the person whom he wishes to have serve as Executor or Executrix if his wife does not survive him;

5. Signs the document in the presence of three adult, disinterested witnesses and a notary public.

WILL FORM W-4

WIFE'S WILL LEAVING EVERYTHING TO HUSBAND OR, IF HE DOES NOT SURVIVE HER, TO TWO OR MORE OTHER PERSONS WHOSE CHILDREN WILL TAKE THEIR SHARE IF THEY ARE NOT LIVING

Example: John and Mary Smith are childless. Mrs. Smith wishes to leave her estate to her husband at her death. If Mr. Smith does not survive her, though, she wishes her estate to be divided among her three nephews. The share of any nephew not then living is to go to that nephew's children in equal shares. If the deceased nephew has left no children, Mrs. Smith wants his share to be divided equally between her two surviving nephews.

Procedure: Using Will Form W-4, Mrs. Smith:

1. Enters her name and place of residence at the top;

2. Enters her husband's name in Paragraph "Second";

3. Enters in Paragraph "Third" the *number* of nephews to share her estate, and their names;

4. Enters her husband's name as Executor in the first sentence in Paragraph "Fourth". In the second sentence of Paragraph "Fourth" she enters the name of the person whom she wishes to have serve as Executor or Executrix if her husband does not survive her;

5. Signs the document in the presence of three adult, disinterested witnesses and a notary public.

HUSBAND'S WILL LEAVING EVERYTHING TO WIFE OR, IF SHE DOES NOT SURVIVE HIM, TO TWO OR MORE OTHER PERSONS SHARING EQUALLY; IF ONE OF SUCH PERSONS DIES, THE SURVIVING PERSONS WILL DIVIDE HIS SHARE

Example: John Smith and his wife Mary are childless. Mr. Smith wishes to leave his estate to his wife at his death. If Mrs. Smith does not survive him, though, he wishes his estate to be divided among his three brothers. The share of any brother who does not survive Mr. Smith is to be divided equally between the surviving brothers.

Procedure: Using Will Form W-5, Mr. Smith:

1. Enters his name and place of residence at the top;

2. Enters his wife's name in Paragraph "Second";

3. Enters in Paragraph "Third" the *number* of brothers to share his estate if his wife does not survive him, and their names;

4. Enters his wife's name as Executrix in the first sentence of Paragraph "Fourth". In the second sentence of Paragraph "Fourth" he enters the name of the person whom he wishes to have serve as Executor or Executrix if his wife does not survive him;

5. Signs the document in the presence of three adult, disinterested witnesses and a notary public.

WIFE'S WILL LEAVING EVERYTHING TO HUSBAND OR, IF HE DOES NOT SURVIVE HER, TO TWO OR MORE OTHER PERSONS SHARING EQUALLY; IF ONE OF SUCH PERSONS DIES, THE SURVIVING PERSONS WILL DIVIDE HIS SHARE.

Example: John Smith and his wife Mary are childless. Mrs. Smith wishes to leave her estate to her husband at her death. If Mr. Smith does not survive her, though, she wishes her estate to be divided among her three nieces. The share of any niece who does not survive Mrs. Smith is to be divided equally between the surviving nieces.

Procedure: Using Will Form W-6, Mrs. Smith:

1. Enters her name and place of residence at the top;

2. Enters her husband's name in Paragraph "Second";

3. Enters in Paragraph "Third" the *number* of nieces to share her estate if her husband does not survive her, and names them;

4. Enters her husband's name as Executor in the first sentence of Paragraph "Fourth". In the second sentence of Paragraph "Fourth" she enters the name of the person whom she wishes to have serve as Executor or Executrix if her husband does not survive her;

5. Signs the document in the presence of three adult, disinterested witnesses and a notary public.

WILL FORM W-7	**WILL LEAVING EVERYTHING TO TWO OR MORE PERSONS TO SHARE EQUALLY; IF ONE OF SUCH PERSONS DIES, HIS CHILDREN WILL TAKE HIS SHARE**

Example: John Smith is unmarried. He wishes to leave his estate to his three sisters at his death. If any sister does not survive him, he wishes the share of that sister to go to her children, in equal shares. If the deceased sister left no children, he wishes her share to be divided equally by his two surviving sisters.

Procedure: Using Will Form W-7, Mr. Smith:

1. Enters his name and place of residence at the top;

2. Enters in Paragraph "Second" the *number* of sisters to share his estate, and their names;

3. Enters in Paragraph "Third" the name of the person whom he wishes to appoint as Executor/Executrix of his estate;

4. Signs the document in the presence of three adult, disinterested witnesses and a notary public.

WILL FORM W-8	**WILL LEAVING EVERYTHING TO THE TWO OR MORE PERSONS TO SHARE EQUALLY; IF ONE OF SUCH PERSONS DIES, THE SURVIVING PERSONS WILL DIVIDE HIS SHARE**

Example: Mary Smith is unmarried. She wishes to leave her estate to three distant relatives at her death. If any such relative does not survive her, she wishes that relative's share to be divided equally between the surviving relatives.

Procedure: Using Will Form W-8, Miss Smith:

1. Enters her name and place of residence at the top;

2. Enters in Paragraph "Second" the *number* of persons to share her estate, and their names *and addresses* (if they are distant relatives, she may be the only one who knows their addresses);

3. Enters in Paragraph "Third" the name of the person whom she wishes to appoint as Executor/Executrix of her estate;

4. Signs the document in the presence of three adult, disinterested witnesses and a notary public.

WILL OF HUSBAND AND FATHER LEAVING EVERYTHING TO HIS WIFE, AND TO HIS CHILDREN IF HIS WIFE DOES NOT SURVIVE HIM

Example: John and Mary Smith have three children. Mr. Smith wishes to leave everything to his wife, and if she does not survive him, he wishes it to go to his children in equal shares. The share of any child who does not survive him is to go to that child's issue, in equal shares. If any child dies leaving no issue, that child's share is to be divided between the surviving children.

Procedure: Using Will Form W-9, Mr. Smith:

1. Enters his name and place of residence at the top;

2. Enters the name of his wife in Paragraph "Second";

3. Enters in Paragraph "Fourth" the name of the person whom he wishes to have serve as guardian of his children if his wife does not survive him;

4. Enters the name of his wife as Executrix in the first sentence of Paragraph "Fifth". In the second sentence of Paragraph "Fifth", he enters the name of the person whom he wishes to have serve as Executor/Executrix if his wife does not survive him.

5. Signs the document in the presence of three adult, disinterested witnesses and a notary public.

WILL OF WIFE AND MOTHER LEAVING EVERYTHING TO HER HUSBAND, AND TO HER CHILDREN IF HER HUSBAND DOES NOT SURVIVE HER

Example: John and Mary Smith have three children. Mrs. Smith wishes to leave everything to her husband, and if he does not survive her, she wishes it to go to her children in equal shares. The share of any child who does not survive her is to go to that child's issue in equal shares. If any child dies leaving no issue, that child's share is to be divided between the surviving children.

Procedure: Using Will Form W-10, Mrs. Smith:

1. Enters her name and place of residence at the top;

2. Enters the name of her husband in Paragraph "Second";

3. Enters in Paragraph "Fourth" the name of the person whom she wishes to have serve as guardian of her children if her husband does not survive her;

4. Enters the name of her husband as Executor in the first sentence of Paragraph "Fifth". In the second sentence of Paragraph "Fifth" she enters the name of the person whom she wishes to have serve as Executor/Executrix if her husband does not survive her;

5. Signs the document in the presence of three adult, disinterested witnesses and a notary public.

WILL FOR INDIVIDUAL WHO HAS ESTABLISHED A DACEY TRUST. INCORPORATES THE BALANCE OF HIS ESTATE INTO THE TRUST

Example: John Smith has established a "Dacey" trust with his local bank. He wishes to leave his personal effects to Mrs. Smith but any stocks, bonds, cash or real estate which he owns at the time of his death are to be added to his trust account at the bank.

Procedure: Using Will Form W-11, Mr. Smith:

1. Enters his name and place of residence at the top;

2. Enters his wife's name in Paragraph "Second";

3. Enters in Paragraph "Third" the name and location of the bank or trust company with whom he has established the "Dacey" trust, and the date of the trust instrument;

4. Enters in Paragraph "Fourth" the name of the person whom he wishes to appoint as guardian of his children (if they be minors) if his wife does not survive him;

5. Enters in Paragraph "Sixth" the name of the bank or trust company as Executor;

6. Signs the document in the presence of three adult, disinterested witnesses and a notary public.

WILL FOR WIFE OF INDIVIDUAL WHO HAS ESTABLISHED A DACEY TRUST. LEAVES EVERYTHING TO HER HUSBAND IF HE SURVIVES HER. IF HE DOES NOT SURVIVE HER, INCORPORATES HER ESTATE INTO HIS DACEY TRUST

Example: John and Mary Smith have three children. Mr. Smith has established a "Dacey" trust with his local bank. Mrs. Smith wishes to leave everything to her husband if he survives her. If he does not survive her, she wishes her personal effects to go to their children, but any stocks, bonds, cash or real estate which she owns at her death are to be added to his "Dacey" trust.

Procedure: Using Will Form W-12, Mrs. Smith:

1. Enters her name and place of residence at the top;

2. Enters her husband's name in Paragraph "Second";

3. Enters in Paragraph "Third" the name of the bank or trust company at which her husband has established his "Dacey" trust, and the date of his agreement with that trustee;

4. Enters her husband's name as Executor in the first sentence of Paragraph "Fourth". In the second sentence of Paragraph "Fourth", she enters the name of her husband's trustee bank as Executor of her estate if her husband does not survive her.

5. Signs the document in the presence of three adult, disinterested witnesses and a notary public.

Last Will and Testament

KNOW ALL MEN BY THESE PRESENTS: That I_____,

of the City/Town of_____, County of_____

and State of_____, being of sound and disposing mind and memory, do make, publish and declare the following to be my LAST WILL AND TESTAMENT, hereby revoking all Wills by me at any time heretofore made.

FIRST: I direct my Executrix, hereinafter named, to pay all my funeral expenses, administration expenses of my estate, including inheritance and succession taxes, state or federal, which may be occasioned by the passage of or succession to any interest in my estate under the terms of this instrument, and all my just debts, excepting mortgage notes secured by mortgages upon real estate.

SECOND: All the rest, residue and remainder of my estate, both real and personal, of whatsoever kind or character, and wheresoever situated, I give, devise and bequeath to my beloved wife:

_____, to be hers absolutely and forever.

THIRD: If my said wife does not survive me, then I give, devise and bequeath such rest, residue and remainder of my estate to:

Name:_____

Address_____

| Number | Street | City | State |

to be his/hers absolutely and forever.

FOURTH: I hereby appoint my wife_____as Executrix of this my LAST WILL AND TESTAMENT. If she does not survive me, then I appoint_____ as Executor/Executrix. I direct that no Executor/Executrix serving hereunder shall be required to post bond.

IN WITNESS WHEREOF, I have hereunto set my hand and seal at_____

this_____day of_____19____.

(sign here)_____L.S.

Signed, sealed, published and declared to be his LAST WILL AND TESTAMENT by the within named Testator in the presence of us, who in his presence and at his request, and in the presence of each other, have hereunto subscribed our names as witnesses:

(1)_____of_____
                                              City   State

(2)_____of_____
                                              City   State

(3)_____of_____
                                              City   State

AFFIDAVIT

STATE OF_____ ⎫
                                        ⎬ ss:_____
COUNTY OF_____ ⎭

Personally appeared (1)_____,

(2)_____and (3)_____,

who being duly sworn, depose and say that they attested the said Will and they subscribed the same at the request and in the presence of the said Testator and in the presence of each other, and the said Testator signed said Will in their presence and acknowledged that he had signed said Will and declared the same to be his LAST WILL AND TESTAMENT and deponents further state that at the time of the execution of said Will the said Testator appeared to be of lawful age and sound mind and memory and there was no evidence of undue influence. The deponents make this affidavit at the request of the Testator.

(1)_____

(2)_____

(3)_____

Subscribed and sworn to before me this_____day of_____19_____.

(Notary Seal)   _____
                                                        Notary Public

Last Will and Testament

KNOW ALL MEN BY THESE PRESENTS: That I_____,

of the City/Town of_____, County of_____

and State of_____, being of sound and disposing mind and memory, do make, publish and declare the following to be my LAST WILL AND TESTAMENT, hereby revoking all Wills by me at any time heretofore made.

FIRST: I direct my Executrix, hereinafter named, to pay all my funeral expenses, administration expenses of my estate, including inheritance and succession taxes, state or federal, which may be occasioned by the passage of or succession to any interest in my estate under the terms of this instrument, and all my just debts, excepting mortgage notes secured by mortgages upon real estate.

SECOND: All the rest, residue and remainder of my estate, both real and personal, of whatso-ever kind or character, and wheresoever situated, I give, devise and bequeath to my beloved wife:

_____, to be hers absolutely and forever.

THIRD: If my said wife does not survive me, then I give, devise and bequeath such rest, residue and remainder of my estate to:

Name_____

Address_____

| Number | Street | City | State |

to be his/hers absolutely and forever.

FOURTH: I hereby appoint my wife_____as Executrix of this my

LAST WILL AND TESTAMENT. If she does not survive me, then I appoint_____ as Executor/Executrix. I direct that no Executor/Executrix serving hereunder shall be required to post bond.

IN WITNESS WHEREOF, I have hereunto set my hand and seal at_____

this_____day of_____19____.

(sign here)_____L.S.

Signed, sealed, published and declared to be his LAST WILL AND TESTAMENT by the within named Testator in the presence of us, who in his presence and at his request, and in the presence of each other, have here-unto subscribed our names as witnesses:

(1)_____of_____

    City   State

(2)_____of_____

    City   State

(3)_____of_____

    City   State

AFFIDAVIT

STATE OF_____ ⎫
                                      ⎬ ss:_____
COUNTY OF_____ ⎭

Personally appeared (1)_____,

(2)_____and (3)_____,

who being duly sworn, depose and say that they attested the said Will and they subscribed the same at the request and in the presence of the said Testator and in the presence of each other, and the said Testator signed said Will in their presence and acknowledged that he had signed said Will and declared the same to be his LAST WILL AND TESTAMENT and deponents further state that at the time of the execution of said Will the said Testator appeared to be of lawful age and sound mind and memory and there was no evidence of undue influence. The deponents make this affidavit at the request of the Testator.

(1)_____

(2)_____

(3)_____

Subscribed and sworn to before me this_____day of_____19____.

(Notary Seal)

_____
Notary Public

Last Will and Testament

KNOW ALL MEN BY THESE PRESENTS: That I_____

of the City/Town of_____, County of_____

and State of_____, being of sound and disposing mind and memory, do make, publish and declare the following to be my LAST WILL AND TESTAMENT, hereby revoking all Wills by me at any time heretofore made.

FIRST: I direct my Executor, hereinafter named, to pay all my funeral expenses, administration expenses of my estate, including inheritance and succession taxes, state or federal, which may be occasioned by the passage of or succession to any interest in my estate under the terms of this instrument, and all my just debts, excepting mortgage notes secured by mortgages upon real estate.

SECOND: All the rest, residue and remainder of my estate, both real and personal, of whatsoever kind or character, and wheresoever situated, I give, devise and bequeath to my beloved husband:

_____, to be his absolutely and forever.

THIRD: If my said husband does not survive me, then I give, devise and bequeath such rest, residue and remainder of my estate to

Name_____

Address_____

| Number | Street | City | State |

to be his/hers absolutely and forever.

FOURTH: I hereby appoint my husband_____as Executor of this my

LAST WILL AND TESTAMENT. If he does not survive me, then I appoint_____ as Executor/Executrix. I direct that no Executor/Executrix serving hereunder shall be required to post bond.

IN WITNESS WHEREOF, I have hereunto set my hand and seal at_____

this_____day of_____19_____.

(sign here) _____L.S.

Signed, sealed, published and declared to be her LAST WILL AND TESTAMENT by the within named Testatrix in the presence of us, who in her presence and at her request, and in the presence of each other, have hereunto subscribed our names as witnesses:

(1)_____of_____

| | City | State |

(2)_____of_____

| | City | State |

(3)_____of_____

| | City | State |

AFFIDAVIT

STATE OF_____ }
                                         ss:_____

COUNTY OF_____ }

    Personally appeared (1)_____,

(2)_____and (3)_____,

who being duly sworn, depose and say that they attested the said Will and they subscribed the same at the request and in the presence of the said Testatrix and in the presence of each other, and the said Testatrix signed said Will in their presence and acknowledged that she had signed said Will and declared the same to be her **LAST WILL AND TESTAMENT** and deponents further state that at the time of the execution of said Will the said Testatrix appeared to be of lawful age and sound mind and memory and there was no evidence of undue influence. The deponents make this affidavit at the request of the Testatrix.

                                        (1)_____

                                        (2)_____

                                        (3)_____

Subscribed and sworn to before me this_____day of_____19_____.

    (Notary Seal)   _____

                                                Notary Public

Last Will and Testament

KNOW ALL MEN BY THESE PRESENTS: That I_____

of the City/Town of_____, County of_____

and State of_____, being of sound and disposing mind and memory, do make, publish and declare the following to be my LAST WILL AND TESTAMENT, hereby revoking all Wills by me at any time heretofore made.

FIRST: I direct my Executor, hereinafter named, to pay all my funeral expenses, administration expenses of my estate, including inheritance and succession taxes, state or federal, which may be occasioned by the passage of or succession to any interest in my estate under the terms of this instrument, and all my just debts, excepting mortgage notes secured by mortgages upon real estate.

SECOND: All the rest, residue and remainder of my estate, both real and personal, of whatsoever kind or character, and wheresoever situated, I give, devise and bequeath to my beloved husband:

_____, to be his absolutely and forever.

THIRD: If my said husband does not survive me, then I give, devise and bequeath such rest, residue and remainder of my estate to

Name_____

Address_____

      Number   Street   City   State

to be his/hers absolutely and forever.

FOURTH: I hereby appoint my husband_____as Executor of this my

LAST WILL AND TESTAMENT. If he does not survive me, then I appoint_____ as Executor/Executrix. I direct that no Executor/Executrix serving hereunder shall be required to post bond.

IN WITNESS WHEREOF, I have hereunto set my hand and seal at_____

this_____day of_____19_____.

(sign here)_____L.S.

Signed, sealed, published and declared to be her LAST WILL AND TESTAMENT by the within named Testatrix in the presence of us, who in her presence and at her request, and in the presence of each other, have hereunto subscribed our names as witnesses:

(1)_____of_____

                City   State

(2)_____of_____

                City   State

(3)_____of_____

                City   State

1

AFFIDAVIT

STATE OF_____ ⎞
                           ⎬ ss:_____
COUNTY OF_____ ⎠

Personally appeared (1)_____,

(2)_____and (3)_____,

who being duly sworn, depose and say that they attested the said Will and they subscribed the same at the request and in the presence of the said Testatrix and in the presence of each other, and the said Testatrix signed said Will in their presence and acknowledged that she had signed said Will and declared the same to be her LAST WILL AND TESTAMENT and deponents further state that at the time of the execution of said Will the said Testatrix appeared to be of lawful age and sound mind and memory and there was no evidence of undue influence. The deponents make this affidavit at the request of the Testatrix.

(1)_____

(2)_____

(3)_____

Subscribed and sworn to before me this_____day of_____19_____.

(Notary Seal)   _____
                                           Notary Public

Last Will and Testament

KNOW ALL MEN BY THESE PRESENTS: That I_____

of the City/Town of_____, County of_____

and State of_____, being of sound and disposing mind and memory, do make, publish and declare the following to be my LAST WILL AND TESTAMENT, hereby revoking all Wills by me at any time heretofore made.

FIRST: I direct my Executrix, hereinafter named, to pay all of my funeral expenses, administration expenses of my estate, including inheritance and succession taxes, state or federal, which may be occasioned by the passage of or succession to any interest in my estate under the terms of this instrument, and all my just debts, excepting mortgage notes secured by mortgages upon real estate.

SECOND: All the rest, residue and remainder of my estate, both real and personal, of whatsoever kind or character, and wheresoever situated, I give, devise and bequeath to my beloved wife:

_____, to be hers absolutely and forever.

THIRD: If my beloved wife does not survive me, I direct that the rest, residue and remainder of my estate

shall be divided into_____equal parts, and I give, devise and bequeath one of such parts to each of the

following_____persons, to be his/hers absolutely and forever:

The share of any person above named who shall not survive me shall revert to such person's issue in equal shares, per stirpes; if such person has died leaving no issue, the part designated above as being for such person shall be divided among the other beneficiaries named above, in equal shares, per stirpes.

FOURTH: I hereby appoint my wife,_____, as Executrix of this my

LAST WILL AND TESTAMENT, if she be living. If she be not living, I appoint_____ as Executor/Executrix. I direct that no Executor or Executrix serving hereunder shall be required to post bond.

IN WITNESS WHEREOF, I have hereunto set my hand and seal at_____,

this_____day of_____19____.

(sign here)_____L.S.

Signed, sealed, published and declared to be his LAST WILL AND TESTAMENT by the within named Testator in the presence of us, who in his presence and at his request, and in the presence of each other, have hereunto subscribed our names as witnesses:

(1)_____of_____

                                                                         City   State

(2)_____of_____

                                                                         City   State

(3)_____of_____

                                                                         City   State

AFFIDAVIT

STATE OF_____⎱

                                        ⎰ ss:_____

COUNTY OF_____⎱

Personally appeared (1)_____,

(2)_____and (3)_____,

who being duly sworn, depose and say that they attested the said Will and they subscribed the same at the request and in the presence of the said Testator and in the presence of each other, and the said Testator signed said Will in their presence and acknowledged that he had signed said Will and declared the same to be his LAST WILL AND TESTAMENT, and deponents further state that at the time of the execution of said Will the said Testator appeared to be of lawful age and sound mind and memory and there was no evidence of undue influence. The deponents make this affidavit at the request of the Testator.

                                     (1)_____

                                     (2)_____

                                     (3)_____

Subscribed and sworn to before me this_____day of_____19____.

(Notary Seal)   _____

                                                      Notary Public

Last Will and Testament

KNOW ALL MEN BY THESE PRESENTS: That I_____

of the City/Town of_____, County of_____

and State of_____, being of sound and disposing mind and memory, do make, publish and declare the following to be my LAST WILL AND TESTAMENT, hereby revoking all Wills by me at any time heretofore made.

FIRST: I direct my Executrix, hereinafter named, to pay all of my funeral expenses, administration expenses of my estate, including inheritance and succession taxes, state or federal, which may be occasioned by the passage of or succession to any interest in my estate under the terms of this instrument, and all my just debts, excepting mortgage notes secured by mortgages upon real estate.

SECOND: All the rest, residue and remainder of my estate, both real and personal, of whatsoever kind or character, and wheresoever situated, I give, devise and bequeath to my beloved wife:

_____, to be hers absolutely and forever.

THIRD: If my beloved wife does not survive me, I direct that the rest, residue and remainder of my estate shall be divided into_____equal parts, and I give, devise and bequeath one of such parts to each of the following_____persons, to be his/hers absolutely and forever:

The share of any person above named who shall not survive me shall revert to such person's issue in equal shares, per stirpes; if such person has died leaving no issue, the part designated above as being for such person shall be divided among the other beneficiaries named above, in equal shares, per stirpes.

FOURTH: I hereby appoint my wife,_____, as Executrix of this my

LAST WILL AND TESTAMENT, if she be living. If she be not living, I appoint_____ as Executor/Executrix. I direct that no Executor or Executrix serving hereunder shall be required to post bond.

IN WITNESS WHEREOF, I have hereunto set my hand and seal at_____,

this_____day of_____19_____.

(sign here)_____L.S.

291

Signed, sealed, published and declared to be his LAST WILL AND TESTAMENT by the within named Testator in the presence of us, who in his presence and at his request, and in the presence of each other, have hereunto subscribed our names as witnesses:

(1)_____of_____
City   State

(2)_____of_____
City   State

(3)_____of_____
City   State

AFFIDAVIT

STATE OF_____ |
COUNTY OF_____ | ss:_____

Personally appeared (1)_____,

(2)_____and (3)_____,

who being duly sworn, depose and say that they attested the said Will and they subscribed the same at the request and in the presence of the said Testator and in the presence of each other, and the said Testator signed said Will in their presence and acknowledged that he had signed said Will and declared the same to be his LAST WILL AND TESTAMENT, and deponents further state that at the time of the execution of said Will the said Testator appeared to be of lawful age and sound mind and memory and there was no evidence of undue influence. The deponents make this affidavit at the request of the Testator.

(1)_____

(2)_____

(3)_____

Subscribed and sworn to before me this_____day of_____19_____.

(Notary Seal)

_____
Notary Public

2

Last Will and Testament

KNOW ALL MEN BY THESE PRESENTS: That I_____

of the City/Town of_____, County of_____

and State of_____, being of sound and disposing mind and memory, do make, publish and declare the following to be my LAST WILL AND TESTAMENT, hereby revoking all Wills by me at any time heretofore made.

FIRST: I direct my Executor, hereinafter named, to pay all of my funeral expenses, administration expenses of my estate, including inheritance and succession taxes, state or federal, which may be occasioned by the passage of or succession to any interest in my estate under the terms of this instrument, and all my just debts, excepting mortgage notes secured by mortgages upon real estate.

SECOND: All the rest, residue and remainder of my estate, both real and personal, of whatsoever kind or character, and wheresoever situated, I give, devise and bequeath to my beloved husband:

_____, to be his absolutely and forever.

THIRD: If my beloved husband does not survive me, I direct that the rest, residue and remainder of my estate shall be divided into_____equal parts, and I give, devise and bequeath one of such parts to each of the following_____persons, to be theirs absolutely and forever:

The share of any person above named who shall not survive me shall revert to such person's issue in equal shares, per stirpes; if such person has died leaving no issue, the part designated above as being for such person shall be divided among the other beneficiaries named above, in equal shares, per stirpes.

FOURTH: I hereby appoint my husband,_____, as Executor of this my

LAST WILL AND TESTAMENT, if he be living. If he be not living, I appoint_____ as Executor/Executrix. I direct that no Executor or Executrix serving hereunder shall be required to post bond.

IN WITNESS WHEREOF, I have hereunto set my hand and seal at_____

this_____day of_____19_____.

(sign here)_____L.S.

Signed, sealed, published and declared to be her LAST WILL AND TESTAMENT by the within named Testatrix in the presence of us, who in her presence and at her request, and in the presence of each other, have hereunto subscribed our names as witnesses:

(1)_____of_____
　　　　　　　　　　　　　　　　　　　　　　　　City　　　　　　　　　State

(2)_____of_____
　　　　　　　　　　　　　　　　　　　　　　　　City　　　　　　　　　State

(3)_____of_____
　　　　　　　　　　　　　　　　　　　　　　　　City　　　　　　　　　State

AFFIDAVIT

STATE OF_____⎫
　　　　　　　　　　　　　　　　　　　　　⎬ ss:_____
COUNTY OF_____⎭

Personally appeared (1)_____,

(2)_____and (3)_____,

who being duly sworn, depose and say that they attested the said Will and they subscribed the same at the request and in the presence of the said Testatrix and in the presence of each other, and the said Testatrix signed said Will in their presence and acknowledged that she had signed said Will and declared the same to be her LAST WILL AND TESTAMENT, and deponents further state that at the time of the execution of said Will the said Testatrix appeared to be of lawful age and sound mind and memory and there was no evidence of undue influence. The deponents make this affidavit at the request of the Testatrix.

(1)_____

(2)_____

(3)_____

Subscribed and sworn to before me this_____day of_____19_____.

(Notary Seal)　　　　　　　　　　_____
　　　　　　　　　　　　　　　　　　　　　　　　Notary Public

Last Will and Testament

KNOW ALL MEN BY THESE PRESENTS: That I_____

of the City/Town of_____, County of_____

and State of_____, being of sound and disposing mind and memory, do make, publish and declare the following to be my LAST WILL AND TESTAMENT, hereby revoking all Wills by me at any time heretofore made.

FIRST: I direct my Executor, hereinafter named, to pay all of my funeral expenses, administration expenses of my estate, including inheritance and succession taxes, state or federal, which may be occasioned by the passage of or succession to any interest in my estate under the terms of this instrument, and all my just debts, excepting mortgage notes secured by mortgages upon real estate.

SECOND: All the rest, residue and remainder of my estate, both real and personal, of whatsoever kind or character, and wheresoever situated, I give, devise and bequeath to my beloved husband:

_____, to be his absolutely and forever.

THIRD: If my beloved husband does not survive me, I direct that the rest, residue and remainder of my

estate shall be divided into_____equal parts, and I give, devise and bequeath one of such parts to each

of the following_____persons, to be theirs absolutely and forever:

The share of any person above named who shall not survive me shall revert to such person's issue in equal shares, per stirpes; if such person has died leaving no issue, the part designated above as being for such person shall be divided among the other beneficiaries named above, in equal shares, per stirpes.

FOURTH: I hereby appoint my husband,_____, as Executor of this my

LAST WILL AND TESTAMENT, if he be living. If he be not living, I appoint_____
as Executor/Executrix. I direct that no Executor or Executrix serving hereunder shall be required to post bond.

IN WITNESS WHEREOF, I have hereunto set my hand and seal at_____

this_____day of_____19_____.

(sign here)_____L.S.

Signed, sealed, published and declared to be her **LAST WILL AND TESTAMENT** by the within named Testatrix in the presence of us, who in her presence and at her request, and in the presence of each other, have here-unto subscribed our names as witnesses:

(1)_____of_____
City   State

(2)_____of_____
City   State

(3)_____of_____
City   State

AFFIDAVIT

STATE OF_____   ⎱ ss:_____

COUNTY OF_____   ⎰

Personally appeared (1)_____,

(2)_____and (3)_____,

who being duly sworn, depose and say that they attested the said Will and they subscribed the same at the request and in the presence of the said Testatrix and in the presence of each other, and the said Testatrix signed said Will in their presence and acknowledged that she had signed said Will and declared the same to be her **LAST WILL AND TESTAMENT**, and deponents further state that at the time of the execution of said Will the said Testatrix appeared to be of lawful age and sound mind and memory and there was no evidence of undue influence. The deponents make this affidavit at the request of the Testatrix.

(1)_____

(2)_____

(3)_____

Subscribed and sworn to before me this_____day of_____19_____.

(Notary Seal)   _____
Notary Public

Last Will and Testament

KNOW ALL MEN BY THESE PRESENTS: That I_____

of the City/Town of_____, County of_____

and State of_____, being of sound and disposing mind and memory, do make, publish and declare the following to be my LAST WILL AND TESTAMENT, hereby revoking all Wills by me at any time heretofore made.

FIRST: I direct my Executrix, hereinafter named, to pay all of my funeral expenses, administration expenses of my estate, including inheritance and succession taxes, state or federal, which may be occasioned by the passage of or succession to any interest in my estate under the terms of this instrument, and all my just debts, excepting mortgage notes secured by mortgages upon real estate.

SECOND: All the rest, residue and remainder of my estate, both real and personal, of whatsoever kind or character, and wheresoever situated, I give, devise and bequeath to my beloved wife:

_____, to be hers absolutely and forever.

THIRD: If my beloved wife does not survive me, I direct that the rest, residue and remainder of my estate shall be divided into_____equal parts, and I give, devise and bequeath one of such parts to each of the following_____persons, to be his/hers absolutely and forever:

The share of any person above named who shall not survive me shall be divided among the other beneficiaries named above, in equal shares.

FOURTH: I hereby appoint my wife,_____, as Executrix of this my

LAST WILL AND TESTAMENT, if she be living. If she be not living, I appoint_____ as Executor/Executrix. I direct that no Executor or Executrix serving hereunder shall be required to post bond.

IN WITNESS WHEREOF, I have hereunto set my hand and seal at_____,

this_____day of_____19_____.

(sign here)_____L.S.

Signed, sealed, published and declared to be his **LAST WILL AND TESTAMENT** by the within named Testator in the presence of us, who in his presence and at his request, and in the presence of each other, have hereunto subscribed our names as witnesses:

(1)_____of_____
                                                      City   State

(2)_____of_____
                                                      City   State

(3)_____of_____
                                                      City   State

AFFIDAVIT

STATE OF_____}
                                    ss:_____

COUNTY OF_____}

Personally appeared (1)_____,

(2)_____and (3)_____,
who being duly sworn, depose and say that they attested the said Will and they subscribed the same at the request and in the presence of the said Testator and in the presence of each other, and the said Testator signed said Will in their presence and acknowledged that he had signed said Will and declared the same to be his **LAST WILL AND TESTAMENT**, and deponents further state that at the time of the execution of said Will the said Testator appeared to be of lawful age and sound mind and memory and there was no evidence of undue influence. The deponents make this affidavit at the request of the Testator.

                             (1)_____

                             (2)_____

                             (3)_____

Subscribed and sworn to before me this_____day of_____19____.

(Notary Seal)   _____
                                            Notary Public

Last Will and Testament

KNOW ALL MEN BY THESE PRESENTS: That I_____

of the City/Town of_____, County of_____

and State of_____, being of sound and disposing mind and memory, do make, publish and declare the following to be my LAST WILL AND TESTAMENT, hereby revoking all Wills by me at any time heretofore made.

FIRST: I direct my Executrix, hereinafter named, to pay all of my funeral expenses, administration expenses of my estate, including inheritance and succession taxes, state or federal, which may be occasioned by the passage of or succession to any interest in my estate under the terms of this instrument, and all my just debts, excepting mortgage notes secured by mortgages upon real estate.

SECOND: All the rest, residue and remainder of my estate, both real and personal, of whatsoever kind or character, and wheresoever situated, I give, devise and bequeath to my beloved wife:

_____, to be hers absolutely and forever.

THIRD: If my beloved wife does not survive me, I direct that the rest, residue and remainder of my estate

shall be divided into_____equal parts, and I give, devise and bequeath one of such parts to each of the

following_____persons, to be his/hers absolutely and forever:

The share of any person above named who shall not survive me shall be divided among the other beneficiaries named above, in equal shares.

FOURTH: I hereby appoint my wife,_____, as Executrix of this my

LAST WILL AND TESTAMENT, if she be living. If she be not living, I appoint_____
as Executor/Executrix. I direct that no Executor or Executrix serving hereunder shall be required to post bond.

IN WITNESS WHEREOF, I have hereunto set my hand and seal at_____,

this_____day of_____19_____.

(sign here)_____L.S.

Signed, sealed, published and declared to be his LAST WILL AND TESTAMENT by the within named Testator in the presence of us, who in his presence and at his request, and in the presence of each other, have hereunto subscribed our names as witnesses:

(1)_____of_____
City   State

(2)_____of_____
City   State

(3)_____of_____
City   State

AFFIDAVIT

STATE OF_____ }
                                  } ss:_____
COUNTY OF_____ }

Personally appeared (1)_____,

(2)_____and (3)_____,
who being duly sworn, depose and say that they attested the said Will and they subscribed the same at the request and in the presence of the said Testator and in the presence of each other, and the said Testator signed said Will in their presence and acknowledged that he had signed said Will and declared the same to be his LAST WILL AND TESTAMENT, and deponents further state that at the time of the execution of said Will the said Testator appeared to be of lawful age and sound mind and memory and there was no evidence of undue influence. The deponents make this affidavit at the request of the Testator.

(1)_____

(2)_____

(3)_____

Subscribed and sworn to before me this_____day of_____19_____.

(Notary Seal)   _____
                                   Notary Public

Last Will and Testament

KNOW ALL MEN BY THESE PRESENTS: That I,_____

of the City/Town of_____, County of_____

and State of_____, being of sound and disposing mind and memory, do make, publish and declare the following to be my LAST WILL AND TESTAMENT, hereby revoking all Wills by me at any time heretofore made.

FIRST: I direct my Executor, hereinafter named, to pay all of my funeral expenses, administration expenses of my estate, including inheritance and succession taxes, state or federal, which may be occasioned by the passage of or succession to any interest in my estate under the terms of this instrument, and all my just debts, excepting mortgage notes secured by mortgages upon real estate.

SECOND: All the rest, residue and remainder of my estate, both real and personal, of whatsoever kind or character, and wheresoever situated, I give, devise and bequeath to my beloved husband:

_____, to be his absolutely and forever.

THIRD: If my beloved husband does not survive me, I direct that the rest, residue and remainder of my estate shall be divided into_____equal parts, and I give, devise and bequeath one of such parts to each of the following_____persons, to be his/hers absolutely and forever:

The share of any person above named who shall not survive me shall be divided among the other beneficiaries named above, in equal shares.

FOURTH: I hereby appoint my husband,_____, as Executor of this my LAST WILL AND TESTAMENT, if he be living. If he be not living, I appoint_____ as Executor/Executrix. I direct that no Executor or Executrix serving hereunder shall be required to post bond.

IN WITNESS WHEREOF, I have hereunto set my hand and seal at_____

this_____day of_____19_____.

(sign here)_____L.S.

1

Signed, sealed, published and declared to be her LAST WILL AND TESTAMENT by the within named Testatrix in the presence of us, who in her presence and at her request, and in the presence of each other, have hereunto subscribed our names as witnesses:

(1)_____of_____
City   State

(2)_____of_____
City   State

(3)_____of_____
City   State

AFFIDAVIT

STATE OF_____ ⎫
                                    ⎬ ss:_____
COUNTY OF_____ ⎭

Personally appeared (1)_____,

(2)_____and (3)_____,
who being duly sworn, depose and say that they attested the said Will and they subscribed the same at the request and in the presence of the said Testatrix and in the presence of each other, and the said Testatrix signed said Will in their presence and acknowledged that she had signed said Will and declared the same to be her LAST WILL AND TESTAMENT, and deponents further state that at the time of the execution of said Will the said Testatrix appeared to be of lawful age and sound mind and memory and there was no evidence of undue influence. The deponents make this affidavit at the request of the Testatrix.

(1)_____

(2)_____

(3)_____

Subscribed and sworn to before me this_____day of_____19____.

(Notary Seal)   _____
Notary Public

Last Will and Testament

KNOW ALL MEN BY THESE PRESENTS: That I,_____

of the City/Town of_____, County of_____

and State of_____, being of sound and disposing mind and memory, do make, publish and declare the following to be my LAST WILL AND TESTAMENT, hereby revoking all Wills by me at any time heretofore made.

FIRST: I direct my Executor, hereinafter named, to pay all of my funeral expenses, administration expenses of my estate, including inheritance and succession taxes, state or federal, which may be occasioned by the passage of or succession to any interest in my estate under the terms of this instrument, and all my just debts, excepting mortgage notes secured by mortgages upon real estate.

SECOND: All the rest, residue and remainder of my estate, both real and personal, of whatsoever kind or character, and wheresoever situated, I give, devise and bequeath to my beloved husband:

_____, to be his absolutely and forever.

THIRD: If my beloved husband does not survive me, I direct that the rest, residue and remainder of my

estate shall be divided into_____equal parts, and I give, devise and bequeath one of such parts to each

of the following_____persons, to be his/hers absolutely and forever:

The share of any person above named who shall not survive me shall be divided among the other beneficiaries named above, in equal shares.

FOURTH: I hereby appoint my husband,_____, as Executor of this my

LAST WILL AND TESTAMENT, if he be living. If he be not living, I appoint_____
as Executor/Executrix. I direct that no Executor or Executrix serving hereunder shall be required to post bond.

IN WITNESS WHEREOF, I have hereunto set my hand and seal at_____

this_____day of_____19_____.

(sign here)_____L.S.

Signed, sealed, published and declared to be her LAST WILL AND TESTAMENT by the within named Testatrix in the presence of us, who in her presence and at her request, and in the presence of each other, have hereunto subscribed our names as witnesses:

(1)_____of_____
                                            City   State

(2)_____of_____
                                            City   State

(3)_____of_____
                                            City   State

AFFIDAVIT

STATE OF_____ ⎫
                                    ⎬ ss:_____
COUNTY OF_____ ⎭

Personally appeared (1)_____,

(2)_____and (3)_____,

who being duly sworn, depose and say that they attested the said Will and they subscribed the same at the request and in the presence of the said Testatrix and in the presence of each other, and the said Testatrix signed said Will in their presence and acknowledged that she had signed said Will and declared the same to be her LAST WILL AND TESTAMENT, and deponents further state that at the time of the execution of said Will the said Testatrix appeared to be of lawful age and sound mind and memory and there was no evidence of undue influence. The deponents make this affidavit at the request of the Testatrix.

                        (1)_____

                        (2)_____

                        (3)_____

Subscribed and sworn to before me this_____day of_____19_____.

(Notary Seal)   _____
                                        Notary Public

Last Will and Testament

KNOW ALL MEN BY THESE PRESENTS: That I_____

of the City/Town of_____, County of_____

and State of_____, being of sound and disposing mind and memory, do make, publish and declare the following to be my LAST WILL AND TESTAMENT, hereby revoking all Wills by me at any time heretofore made.

FIRST: I direct my Executor/Executrix, hereinafter named, to pay all my funeral expenses, administration expenses of my estate, including inheritance and succession taxes, state or federal, which may be occasioned by the passage of or succession to any interest in my estate under the terms of this instrument, and all my just debts, excepting mortgage notes secured by mortgages upon real estate.

SECOND: All the rest, residue and remainder of my estate, both real and personal, of whatsoever kind or character, and wheresoever situated, shall be divided into_____equal parts, and I give, devise and bequeath one such part to each of the following_____persons, to be his/hers absolutely and forever:

The share of any person above named who shall not survive me shall revert to such person's issue in equal shares, per stirpes; if such person has died leaving no issue, the part designated above as being for such person shall be divided among the other beneficiaries named above, in equal shares, per stirpes.

THIRD: I hereby appoint_____as Executor/Executrix of this my LAST WILL AND TESTAMENT and I direct that such person shall serve without bond.

IN WITNESS WHEREOF, I have hereunto set my hand and seal at_____,

this_____day of_____19____.

(**sign** here)_____L.S.

Signed, sealed, published and declared to be his/her LAST WILL AND TESTAMENT by the within named Testator in the presence of us, who in his/her presence and at his/her request, and in the presence of each other, have hereunto subscribed our names as witnesses:

(1)_____of_____
                                        City   State

(2)_____of_____
                                        City   State

(3)_____of_____
                                        City   State

AFFIDAVIT

STATE OF_____ }

COUNTY OF_____ } **ss:**_____

Personally appeared (1)_____,

(2)_____and (3)_____,
who being duly sworn, depose and say that they attested the said Will and they subscribed the same at the request and in the presence of the said Testator and in the presence of each other, and the said Testator signed said Will in their presence and acknowledged that he/she had signed said Will and declared the same to be his/her LAST WILL AND TESTAMENT, and deponents further state that at the time of the execution of said Will the said Testator appeared to be of lawful age and sound mind and memory and there was no evidence of undue influence. The deponents make this affidavit at the request of the Testator.

(1)_____

(2)_____

(3)_____

Subscribed and sworn to before me this_____day of_____19____.

(Notary Seal)

_____
Notary Public

2

Last Will and Testament

KNOW ALL MEN BY THESE PRESENTS: That I_____

of the City/Town of_____, County of_____

and State of_____, being of sound and disposing mind and memory, do make, publish and declare the following to be my LAST WILL AND TESTAMENT, hereby revoking all Wills by me at any time heretofore made.

FIRST: I direct my Executor/Executrix, hereinafter named, to pay all my funeral expenses, administration expenses of my estate, including inheritance and succession taxes, state or federal, which may be occasioned by the passage of or succession to any interest in my estate under the terms of this instrument, and all my just debts, excepting mortgage notes secured by mortgages upon real estate.

SECOND: All the rest, residue and remainder of my estate, both real and personal, of whatsoever kind or character, and wheresoever situated, shall be divided into_____equal parts, and I give, devise and bequeath one such part to each of the following_____persons, to be his/hers absolutely and forever:

The share of any person above named who shall not survive me shall revert to such person's issue in equal shares, per stirpes; if such person has died leaving no issue, the part designated above as being for such person shall be divided among the other beneficiaries named above, in equal shares, per stirpes.

THIRD: I hereby appoint_____as Executor/Executrix of this my LAST WILL AND TESTAMENT and I direct that such person shall serve without bond.

IN WITNESS WHEREOF, I have hereunto set my hand and seal at_____,

this_____day of_____19____.

(sign here)_____L.S.

Signed, sealed, published and declared to be his/her LAST WILL AND TESTAMENT by the within named Testator in the presence of us, who in his/her presence and at his/her request, and in the presence of each other, have hereunto subscribed our names as witnesses:

(1)_____of_____
| | City | State |

(2)_____of_____
| | City | State |

(3)_____of_____
| | City | State |

1

AFFIDAVIT

STATE OF_____⎱

⎰ ss:_____

COUNTY OF_____⎰

Personally appeared (1)_____,

(2)_____and (3)_____,
who being duly sworn, depose and say that they attested the said Will and they subscribed the same at the request and in the presence of the said Testator and in the presence of each other, and the said Testator signed said Will in their presence and acknowledged that he/she had signed said Will and declared the same to be his/her LAST WILL AND TESTAMENT, and deponents further state that at the time of the execution of said Will the said Testator appeared to be of lawful age and sound mind and memory and there was no evidence of undue influence. The deponents make this affidavit at the request of the Testator.

(1)_____

(2)_____

(3)_____

Subscribed and sworn to before me this_____day of_____19____.

(Notary Seal)

_____
Notary Public

2

Last Will and Testament

KNOW ALL MEN BY THESE PRESENTS: That I,_____

of the City/Town of_____, County of_____

and State of_____, being of sound and disposing mind and memory, do make, publish and declare the following to be my LAST WILL AND TESTAMENT, hereby revoking all Wills by me at any time heretofore made.

FIRST: I direct my Executor/Executrix, hereinafter named, to pay all my funeral expenses, administration expenses of my estate, including inheritance and succession taxes, state or federal, which may be occasioned by the passage of or succession to any interest in my estate under the terms of this instrument, and all my just debts, excepting mortgage notes secured by mortgages upon real estate.

SECOND: All the rest, residue and remainder of my estate, both real and personal, of whatsoever kind or character, and wheresoever situated, shall be divided into_____equal parts, and I give, devise and bequeath one such part to each of the following_____persons, to be his/hers absolutely and forever:

The share of any person above named who shall not survive me shall be divided among the other beneficiaries named above, in equal shares.

THIRD: I hereby appoint_____as Executor/Executrix of this my LAST WILL AND TESTAMENT and I direct that such person shall serve without bond.

IN WITNESS WHEREOF, I have hereunto set my hand and seal at_____,

this_____day of_____19_____.

(sign here)_____L.S.

Signed, sealed, published and declared to be his/her LAST WILL AND TESTAMENT by the within named Testator in the presence of us, who in his/her presence and at his/her request, and in the presence of each other, have hereunto subscribed our names as witnesses:

(1)_____of_____
                                       City   State

(2)_____of_____
                                       City   State

(3)_____of_____
                                       City   State

1

AFFIDAVIT

STATE OF______________________ }
COUNTY OF_____________________ } ss:______________________

Personally appeared (1)____,

(2)______________________________and (3)______________________________,

who being duly sworn, depose and say that they attested the said Will and they subscribed the same at the request and in the presence of the said Testator and in the presence of each other, and the said Testator signed said Will in their presence and acknowledged that he/she had signed said Will and declared the same to be his/her LAST WILL AND TESTAMENT, and deponents further state that at the time of the execution of said Will the said Testator appeared to be of lawful age and sound mind and memory and there was no evidence of undue influence. The deponents make this affidavit at the request of the Testator.

(1)______________________________

(2)______________________________

(3)______________________________

Subscribed and sworn to before me this______________________day of______________________19______.

(Notary Seal)

____
Notary Public

Last Will and Testament

KNOW ALL MEN BY THESE PRESENTS: That I,_____

of the City/Town of_____, County of_____

and State of_____, being of sound and disposing mind and memory, do make, publish and declare the following to be my LAST WILL AND TESTAMENT, hereby revoking all Wills by me at any time heretofore made.

FIRST: I direct my Executor/Executrix, hereinafter named, to pay all my funeral expenses, administration expenses of my estate, including inheritance and succession taxes, state or federal, which may be occasioned by the passage of or succession to any interest in my estate under the terms of this instrument, and all my just debts, excepting mortgage notes secured by mortgages upon real estate.

SECOND: All the rest, residue and remainder of my estate, both real and personal, of whatsoever kind or character, and wheresoever situated, shall be divided into_____equal parts, and I give, devise and bequeath one such part to each of the following_____persons, to be his/hers absolutely and forever:

The share of any person above named who shall not survive me shall be divided among the other beneficiaries named above, in equal shares.

THIRD: I hereby appoint_____as Executor/Executrix of this my LAST WILL AND TESTAMENT and I direct that such person shall serve without bond.

IN WITNESS WHEREOF, I have hereunto set my hand and seal at_____,

this_____day of_____19____.

(sign here)_____L.S.

Signed, sealed, published and declared to be his/her LAST WILL AND TESTAMENT by the within named Testator in the presence of us, who in his/her presence and at his/her request, and in the presence of each other, have hereunto subscribed our names as witnesses:

(1)_____of_____
                                                       City   State

(2)_____of_____
  City   State

(3)_____of_____
  City   State

AFFIDAVIT

STATE OF_____ ⎫
                                   ⎬ ss:_____
COUNTY OF_____ ⎭

Personally appeared (1)_____,

(2)_____and (3)_____,

who being duly sworn, depose and say that they attested the said Will and they subscribed the same at the request and in the presence of the said Testator and in the presence of each other, and the said Testator signed said Will in their presence and acknowledged that he/she had signed said Will and declared the same to be his/her LAST WILL AND TESTAMENT, and deponents further state that at the time of the execution of said Will the said Testator appeared to be of lawful age and sound mind and memory and there was no evidence of undue influence. The deponents make this affidavit at the request of the Testator.

(1)_____

(2)_____

(3)_____

Subscribed and sworn to before me this_____day of_____19_____.

(Notary Seal)

_____
Notary Public

Last Will and Testament

KNOW ALL MEN BY THESE PRESENTS: That I,_____

of the City/Town of_____, County of_____

and State of_____, being of sound and disposing mind and memory, do make, publish and declare the following to be my LAST WILL AND TESTAMENT, hereby revoking all Wills by me at any time heretofore made.

FIRST: I direct my Executrix, hereinafter named, to pay all my funeral expenses, administration expenses of my estate, including inheritance and succession taxes, state or federal, which may be occasioned by the passage of or succession to any interest in my estate under the terms of this instrument, and all my just debts, excepting mortgage notes secured by mortgages upon real estate.

SECOND: All the rest, residue and remainder of my estate, both real and personal, of whatsoever kind or character, and wheresoever situated, I give, devise and bequeath to my beloved wife:

_____, to be hers absolutely and forever.

THIRD: If my said wife does not survive me, then I give, devise and bequeath such rest, residue and remainder of my estate to my beloved children, natural or adopted, in equal shares, per stirpes, to be theirs absolutely and forever; provided, that the share of any child of mine who has died leaving no issue shall be divided among my surviving children in equal shares, per stirpes.

FOURTH: If my beloved wife does not survive me, I hereby appoint

Name_____

Address_____
        Number   Street   City   State

as guardian of such of my children as shall then be minors.

FIFTH: I hereby appoint my wife,_____, as Executrix of this my LAST WILL AND TESTAMENT. If she does not survive me, then I appoint

Name_____

Address_____
        Number   Street   City   State

as Executor/Executrix of my estate. I direct that no Executor/Executrix serving hereunder shall be required to post bond.

IN WITNESS WHEREOF, I have hereunto set my hand and seal at_____

this_____day of_____19_____.

(sign here)_____L.S.

1

Signed, sealed, published and declared to be his **LAST WILL AND TESTAMENT** by the within named Testator in the presence of us, who in his presence and at his request, and in the presence of each other, have hereunto subscribed our names as witnesses:

(1)_____of_____
                                      City   State

(2)_____of_____
                                      City   State

(3)_____of_____
                                      City   State

AFFIDAVIT

STATE OF_____ ⎫
                                        ⎬ ss:_____
COUNTY OF_____ ⎭

Personally appeared (1)_____,

(2)_____and (3)_____,

who being duly sworn, depose and say that they attested the said Will and they subscribed the same at the request and in the presence of the said Testator and in the presence of each other, and the said Testator signed said Will in their presence and acknowledged that he had signed said Will and declared the same to be his **LAST WILL AND TESTAMENT**, and deponents further state that at the time of the execution of said Will the said Testator appeared to be of lawful age and sound mind and memory and there was no evidence of undue influence. The deponents make this affidavit at the request of the Testator.

(1)_____

(2)_____

(3)_____

Subscribed and sworn to before me this_____day of_____19_____.

(Notary Seal)   _____
                                           Notary Public

Last Will and Testament

KNOW ALL MEN BY THESE PRESENTS: That I,_____

of the City/Town of_____, County of_____

and State of_____, being of sound and disposing mind and memory, do make, publish and declare the following to be my LAST WILL AND TESTAMENT, hereby revoking all Wills by me at any time heretofore made.

FIRST: I direct my Executrix, hereinafter named, to pay all my funeral expenses, administration expenses of my estate, including inheritance and succession taxes, state or federal, which may be occasioned by the passage of or succession to any interest in my estate under the terms of this instrument, and all my just debts, excepting mortgage notes secured by mortgages upon real estate.

SECOND: All the rest, residue and remainder of my estate, both real and personal, of whatsoever kind or character, and wheresoever situated, I give, devise and bequeath to my beloved wife:

_____, to be hers absolutely and forever.

THIRD: If my said wife does not survive me, then I give, devise and bequeath such rest, residue and remainder of my estate to my beloved children, natural or adopted, in equal shares, per stirpes, to be theirs absolutely and forever; *provided,* that the share of any child of mine who has died leaving no issue shall be divided among my surviving children in equal shares, per stirpes.

FOURTH: If my beloved wife does not survive me, I hereby appoint

Name_____

Address_____

| Number | Street | City | State |

as guardian of such of my children as shall then be minors.

FIFTH: I hereby appoint my wife,_____, as Executrix of this my LAST WILL AND TESTAMENT. If she does not survive me, then I appoint

Name_____

Address_____

| Number | Street | City | State |

as Executor/Executrix of my estate. I direct that no Executor/Executrix serving hereunder shall be required to post bond.

IN WITNESS WHEREOF, I have hereunto set my hand and seal at_____

this_____day of_____19_____.

(sign here)_____ L.S.

1

Signed, sealed, published and declared to be his LAST WILL AND TESTAMENT by the within named Testator in the presence of us, who in his presence and at his request, and in the presence of each other, have hereunto subscribed our names as witnesses:

(1)_____of_____
                                                 City   State

(2)_____of_____
                                                 City   State

(3)_____of_____
                                                 City   State

AFFIDAVIT

STATE OF_____⎫
                                  ⎬ ss:_____
COUNTY OF_____⎭

Personally appeared (1)_____,

(2)_____and (3)_____,

who being duly sworn, depose and say that they attested the said Will and they subscribed the same at the request and in the presence of the said Testator and in the presence of each other, and the said Testator signed said Will in their presence and acknowledged that he had signed said Will and declared the same to be his LAST WILL AND TESTAMENT, and deponents further state that at the time of the execution of said Will the said Testator appeared to be of lawful age and sound mind and memory and there was no evidence of undue influence. The deponents make this affidavit at the request of the Testator.

(1)_____

(2)_____

(3)_____

Subscribed and sworn to before me this _____day of_____19_____.

(Notary Seal)

_____
                                   Notary Public

Last Will and Testament

KNOW ALL MEN BY THESE PRESENTS: That I,_____

of the City/Town of_____, County of_____

and State of_____, being of sound and disposing mind and memory, do make, publish and declare the following to be my LAST WILL AND TESTAMENT, hereby revoking all Wills by me at any time heretofore made.

FIRST: I direct my Executor, hereinafter named, to pay all my funeral expenses, administration expenses of my estate, including inheritance and succession taxes, state or federal, which may be occasioned by the passage of or succession to any interest in my estate under the terms of this instrument, and all my just debts, excepting mortgage notes secured by mortgages upon real estate.

SECOND: All the rest, residue and remainder of my estate, both real and personal, of whatsoever kind or character, and wheresoever situated, I give, devise and bequeath to my beloved husband:

_____, to be his absolutely and forever.

THIRD: If my said husband does not survive me, then I give, devise and bequeath such rest, residue and remainder of my estate to my beloved children, natural or adopted, in equal shares, per stirpes, to be theirs absolutely and forever; *provided,* that the share of any child of mine who has died leaving no issue shall be divided among my surviving children in equal shares, per stirpes.

FOURTH: If my beloved husband does not survive me, I hereby appoint

Name_____

Address_____
　　　　　Number　　　　　Street　　　　　City　　　　　State
as guardian of such of my children as shall then be minors.

FIFTH: I hereby appoint my husband,_____as Executor of this my

LAST WILL AND TESTAMENT. If he does not survive me, then I appoint

Name_____

Address_____
　　　　　Number　　　　　Street　　　　　City　　　　　State
as Executor/Executrix of my estate. I direct that no Executor/Executrix serving hereunder shall be required to post bond.

IN WITNESS WHEREOF, I have hereunto set my hand and seal at_____

this_____day of_____19____.

(sign here)_____L.S.

1

Signed, sealed, published and declared to be her **LAST WILL AND TESTAMENT** by the within named Testatrix in the presence of us, who in her presence and at her request, and in the presence of each other, have hereunto subscribed our names as witnesses:

(1)_____of_____
City   State

(2)_____of_____
City   State

(3)_____of_____
City   State

AFFIDAVIT

STATE OF_____⎫
                           ss:_____
COUNTY OF_____⎭

Personally appeared (1)_____,

(2)_____and (3)_____,

who being duly sworn, depose and say that they attested the said Will and they subscribed the same at the request and in the presence of the said Testatrix and in the presence of each other, and the said Testatrix signed said Will in their presence and acknowledged that she had signed said Will and declared the same to be her **LAST WILL AND TESTAMENT**, and deponents further state that at the time of the execution of said Will the said Testatrix appeared to be of lawful age and sound mind and memory and there was no evidence of undue influence. The deponents make this affidavit at the request of the Testatrix.

(1)_____

(2)_____

(3)_____

Subscribed and sworn to before me this_____day of_____19_____.

(Notary Seal)   _____
Notary Public

Last Will and Testament

KNOW ALL MEN BY THESE PRESENTS: That I,_____

of the City/Town of_____, County of_____

and State of_____, being of sound and disposing mind and memory, do make, publish and declare the following to be my LAST WILL AND TESTAMENT, hereby revoking all Wills by me at any time heretofore made.

FIRST: I direct my Executor, hereinafter named, to pay all my funeral expenses, administration expenses of my estate, including inheritance and succession taxes, state or federal, which may be occasioned by the passage of or succession to any interest in my estate under the terms of this instrument, and all my just debts, excepting mortgage notes secured by mortgages upon real estate.

SECOND: All the rest, residue and remainder of my estate, both real and personal, of whatsoever kind or character, and wheresoever situated, I give, devise and bequeath to my beloved husband:

_____, to be his absolutely and forever.

THIRD: If my said husband does not survive me, then I give, devise and bequeath such rest, residue and remainder of my estate to my beloved children, natural or adopted, in equal shares, per stirpes, to be theirs absolutely and forever; *provided,* that the share of any child of mine who has died leaving no issue shall be divided among my surviving children in equal shares, per stirpes.

FOURTH: If my beloved husband does not survive me, I hereby appoint

Name_____

Address_____
       Number   Street   City   State

as guardian of such of my children as shall then be minors.

FIFTH: I hereby appoint my husband,_____as Executor of this my

LAST WILL AND TESTAMENT. If he does not survive me, then I appoint

Name_____

Address_____
       Number   Street   City   State

as Executor/Executrix of my estate. I direct that no Executor/Executrix serving hereunder shall be required to post bond.

IN WITNESS WHEREOF, I have hereunto set my hand and seal at_____

this_____day of_____19_____.

(sign here)_____L.S.

Signed, sealed, published and declared to be her LAST WILL AND TESTAMENT by the within named Testatrix in the presence of us, who in her presence and at her request, and in the presence of each other, have hereunto subscribed our names as witnesses:

(1)_____of_____
City   State

(2)_____of_____
City   State

(3)_____of_____
City   State

AFFIDAVIT

STATE OF_____⎫
⎬ ss:_____
COUNTY OF_____⎭

Personally appeared (1)_____,

(2)_____and (3)_____,

who being duly sworn, depose and say that they attested the said Will and they subscribed the same at the request and in the presence of the said Testatrix and in the presence of each other, and the said Testatrix signed said Will in their presence and acknowledged that she had signed said Will and declared the same to be her LAST WILL AND TESTAMENT, and deponents further state that at the time of the execution of said Will the said Testatrix appeared to be of lawful age and sound mind and memory and there was no evidence of undue influence. The deponents make this affidavit at the request of the Testatrix.

(1)_____

(2)_____

(3)_____

Subscribed and sworn to before me this_____day of_____19_____.

(Notary Seal)   _____
Notary Public

Last Will and Testament

KNOW ALL MEN BY THESE PRESENTS: That I,_____

of the City/Town of_____, County of_____

and State of_____, being of sound and disposing mind and memory, do make, publish and declare the following to be my LAST WILL AND TESTAMENT, hereby revoking all former Wills by me made.

FIRST: I direct my Executor, hereinafter named, to pay all my funeral expenses, administration expenses of my estate, including inheritance taxes, state or federal, which may be occasioned by the passage of or succession to any interest in my estate under the terms of this instrument, and all my just debts, excepting mortgage notes secured by mortgages upon real estate.

SECOND: I give, devise and bequeath to my beloved wife,_____, to be hers absolutely and forever, all my personal effects, such as jewelry, mementos, clothing, furniture, automobiles and similar items of a like nature, excluding however, any stocks, bonds, cash or real estate.

THIRD: All the rest, residue and remainder of my estate, both real and personal, of whatsoever kind or character and wheresoever situated, I give, devise and bequeath to_____

of the City/Town of_____and State of_____as Trustee,

under the terms of a certain trust executed by me and by said_____

as of_____ 19____, and already in existence, and I specifically direct and provide that the property received by virtue of this bequest shall be held by said Trustee, to be administered by it in accordance with the provisions of Section B thereof, as an addition to the trust fund created by insurance proceeds therein and said Trustee shall dispose of said property as a part of said trust created by Section B in accordance with the provisions thereof.

FOURTH: In the event that my wife does not survive me, I request that

Name_____

Address_____
　　　　　　　Number　　　　　　Street　　　　　　　　　City　　　　　　　State
be appointed guardian of such of my children as shall then be minors.

FIFTH: This Will shall continue in full force and effect whether or not another child or children shall be born to me and my wife.

SIXTH: I make, constitute and appoint_____as Executor of this my LAST WILL AND TESTAMENT, to serve without bond.

IN WITNESS WHEREOF, I have hereunto set my hand and seal at_____,

this_____day of_____19____.

(sign here)_____L.S.

Signed, sealed, published and declared to be his LAST WILL AND TESTAMENT by the within named Testator in the presence of us, who in his presence and at his request, and in the presence of each other, have hereunto subscribed our names as witnesses:

(1)_____of_____
                                              City   State

(2)_____of_____
                                              City   State

(3)_____of_____
                                              City   State

AFFIDAVIT

STATE OF_____ }
                                          ss:_____
COUNTY OF_____

Personally appeared (1)_____,

(2)_____and (3)_____,

who being duly sworn, depose and say that they attested the said Will and they subscribed the same at the request and in the presence of the said Testator and in the presence of each other, and the said Testator signed said Will in their presence and acknowledged that he had signed said Will and declared the same to be his LAST WILL AND TESTAMENT, and deponents further state that at the time of the execution of said Will the said Testator appeared to be of lawful age and sound mind and memory and there was no evidence of undue influence. The deponents make this affidavit at the request of the Testator.

(1)_____

(2)_____

(3)_____

Subscribed and sworn to before me this_____day of_____, 19___.

                                                    Notary Public
(Notary Seal)   _____

2

Last Will and Testament

KNOW ALL MEN BY THESE PRESENTS: That I,_____

of the City/Town of_____, County of_____

and State of_____, being of sound and disposing mind and memory, do make, publish and declare the following to be my LAST WILL AND TESTAMENT, hereby revoking all former Wills by me made.

FIRST: I direct my Executor, hereinafter named, to pay all my funeral expenses, administration expenses of my estate, including inheritance taxes, state or federal, which may be occasioned by the passage of or succession to any interest in my estate under the terms of this instrument, and all my just debts, excepting mortgage notes secured by mortgages upon real estate.

SECOND: I give, devise and bequeath to my beloved wife,_____, to be hers absolutely and forever, all my personal effects, such as jewelry, mementos, clothing, furniture, automobiles and similar items of a like nature, excluding however, any stocks, bonds, cash or real estate.

THIRD: All the rest, residue and remainder of my estate, both real and personal, of whatsoever kind or character and wheresoever situated, I give, devise and bequeath to_____

of the City/Town of_____and State of_____as Trustee,

under the terms of a certain trust executed by me and by said_____

as of_____ 19____, and already in existence, and I specifically direct and provide that the property received by virtue of this bequest shall be held by said Trustee, to be administered by it in accordance with the provisions of Section B thereof, as an addition to the trust fund created by insurance proceeds therein and said Trustee shall dispose of said property as a part of said trust created by Section B in accordance with the provisions thereof.

FOURTH: In the event that my wife does not survive me, I request that

Name_____

Address_____
        Number   Street   City   State

be appointed guardian of such of my children as shall then be minors.

FIFTH: This Will shall continue in full force and effect whether or not another child or children shall be born to me and my wife.

SIXTH: I make, constitute and appoint_____as Executor of this my LAST WILL AND TESTAMENT, to serve without bond.

IN WITNESS WHEREOF, I have hereunto set my hand and seal at_____,

this_____day of_____19____.

(sign here)_____L.S.

1

Signed, sealed, published and declared to be his LAST WILL AND TESTAMENT by the within named Testator in the presence of us, who in his presence and at his request, and in the presence of each other, have hereunto subscribed our names as witnesses:

(1)_____of_____
City   State

(2)_____of_____
City   State

(3)_____of_____
City   State

AFFIDAVIT

STATE OF_____⎫
                                    ⎬ ss:_____
COUNTY OF_____⎭

Personally appeared (1)_____,

(2)_____and (3)_____,

who being duly sworn, depose and say that they attested the said Will and they subscribed the same at the request and in the presence of the said Testator and in the presence of each other, and the said Testator signed said Will in their presence and acknowledged that he had signed said Will and declared the same to be his LAST WILL AND TESTAMENT, and deponents further state that at the time of the execution of said Will the said Testator appeared to be of lawful age and sound mind and memory and there was no evidence of undue influence. The deponents make this affidavit at the request of the Testator.

(1)_____

(2)_____

(3)_____

Subscribed and sworn to before me this_____day of_____, 19____.

Notary Public

(Notary Seal)   _____

2

Last Will and Testament

KNOW ALL MEN BY THESE PRESENTS: That I,_____

of the City/Town of_____, County of_____

and State of_____, being of sound and disposing mind and memory, do make, publish and declare this as and for my LAST WILL AND TESTAMENT, hereby revoking all Wills by me at any time heretofore made.

FIRST: I direct my Executor, hereinafter named, to pay all my funeral expenses, administration expenses of my estate, including inheritance and succession taxes, state or federal, which may be occasioned by the passage of or succession to any interest in my estate under the terms of this instrument, and all my just debts, excepting mortgage notes secured by mortgages upon real estate.

SECOND: All of the rest, residue and remainder of my estate, both real and personal of whatsoever kind or character, and wheresoever situated, I give, devise and bequeath to my beloved husband:

_____, to be his absolutely and forever.

THIRD: In the event that my said husband shall predecease me, I give, devise and bequeath to my beloved children all of my personal effects, such as jewelry, mementos, clothing, furniture, automobiles and items of a like nature, excluding, however, any stocks, bonds, cash or real estate. All of the rest, residue and remainder of my estate, both real and personal, of whatsoever kind or character and wheresoever situated, I give, devise and bequeath to

_____of the City/Town of_____

and State of_____, as Trustee, under the terms of a certain deed of trust executed

by_____and by the said_____

as of_____and already in existence, and I specifically direct and provide that the property

received by virtue of this bequest shall be held by said_____, as such Trustee, to be administered by it in accordance with the provisions of Section B thereof, as an addition to the trust fund created by the insurance proceeds and securities therein and said Trustee shall dispose of said property as a part of said trust created by Section B in accordance with the provisions thereof.

FOURTH: I make, constitute and appoint my husband,_____ as Executor of this my LAST WILL AND TESTAMENT, and if he shall not have survived me, then I make,

constitue and appoint_____ of

_____, as Executor. The Executor shall serve without bond.

IN WITNESS WHEREOF, I have hereunto subscribed my name and affixed my seal this_____

day of_____, 19___.

(sign here)_____L.S.

1

Signed, sealed, published and declared to be her **LAST WILL AND TESTAMENT** by the within named Testatrix in the presence of us, who in her presence and at her request, and in the presence of each other, have hereunto subscribed our names as witnesses:

(1)_____ of _____

                                                                     City   State

(2)_____ of _____

                                                                     City   State

(3)_____ of _____

                                                                     City   State

AFFIDAVIT

STATE OF_____ ⎫
                                           ⎬ ss:_____

COUNTY OF_____ ⎭

Personally appeared (1)_____,

(2)_____ and (3)_____,

who being duly sworn, depose and say that they attested the said Will and they subscribed the same at the request and in the presence of the said Testatrix and in the presence of each other, and the said Testatrix signed said Will in their presence and acknowledged that she had signed said Will and declared the same to be her **LAST WILL AND TESTAMENT**; and deponents further state that at the time of the execution of said Will the said Testatrix appeared to be of lawful age and sound mind and memory and there was no evidence of undue influence. The deponents make this affidavit at the request of the Testatrix.

                                                    (1)_____

                                                    (2)_____

                                                    (3)_____

Subscribed and sworn to before me this_____ day of_____, 19____

(Notary Seal)   _____

                                                  Notary Public

Last Will and Testament

KNOW ALL MEN BY THESE PRESENTS: That I,_____

of the City/Town of_____, County of_____

and State of_____, being of sound and disposing mind and memory, do make, publish and declare this as and for my LAST WILL AND TESTAMENT, hereby revoking all Wills by me at any time heretofore made.

FIRST: I direct my Executor, hereinafter named, to pay all my funeral expenses, administration expenses of my estate, including inheritance and succession taxes, state or federal, which may be occasioned by the passage of or succession to any interest in my estate under the terms of this instrument, and all my just debts, excepting mortgage notes secured by mortgages upon real estate.

SECOND: All of the rest, residue and remainder of my estate, both real and personal of whatsoever kind or character, and wheresoever situated, I give, devise and bequeath to my beloved husband:

_____, to be his absolutely and forever.

THIRD: In the event that my said husband shall predecease me, I give, devise and bequeath to my beloved children all of my personal effects, such as jewelry, mementos, clothing, furniture, automobiles and items of a like nature, excluding, however, any stocks, bonds, cash or real estate. All of the rest, residue and remainder of my estate, both real and personal, of whatsoever kind or character and wheresoever situated, I give, devise and bequeath to

_____of the City/Town of_____

and State of_____, as Trustee, under the terms of a certain deed of trust executed

by_____and by the said_____

as of_____and already in existence, and I specifically direct and provide that the property

received by virtue of this bequest shall be held by said_____, as such Trustee, to be administered by it in accordance with the provisions of Section B thereof, as an addition to the trust fund created by the insurance proceeds and securities therein and said Trustee shall dispose of said property as a part of said trust created by Section B in accordance with the provisions thereof.

FOURTH: I make, constitute and appoint my husband,_____ as Executor of this my LAST WILL AND TESTAMENT, and if he shall not have survived me, then I make, constitue and appoint_____ of

_____, as Executor. The Executor shall serve without bond.

IN WITNESS WHEREOF, I have hereunto subscribed my name and affixed my seal this_____

day of_____, 19___.

(sign here)_____L.S.

Signed, sealed, published and declared to be her **LAST WILL AND TESTAMENT** by the within named Testatrix in the presence of us, who in her presence and at her request, and in the presence of each other, have hereunto subscribed our names as witnesses:

(1)_____ of _____
City   State

(2)_____ of _____
City   State

(3)_____ of _____
City   State

AFFIDAVIT

STATE OF_____ }

COUNTY OF_____ } ss:_____

Personally appeared (1)_____,

(2)_____ and (3)_____,
who being duly sworn, depose and say that they attested the said Will and they subscribed the same at the request and in the presence of the said Testatrix and in the presence of each other, and the said Testatrix signed said Will in their presence and acknowledged that she had signed said Will and declared the same to be her **LAST WILL AND TESTAMENT**; and deponents further state that at the time of the execution of said Will the said Testatrix appeared to be of lawful age and sound mind and memory and there was no evidence of undue influence. The deponents make this affidavit at the request of the Testatrix.

(1)_____

(2)_____

(3)_____

Subscribed and sworn to before me this_____ day of_____, 19____

(Notary Seal)

_____
Notary Public

2

EPILOGUE

During the past few years, there has been increasing controversy over the question of the unauthorized practice of law. At the root of the difficulty is the lawyer's insistence that only he has the right and the capacity to advise not only on the legal intricacies of the estate plan but also on a wide range of family planning decisions which must be made.

In estate planning, such questions as these may arise: To what extent should the marital deduction be utilized? Shall property be left outright or in trust? If in trust, what invasion rights shall be given? If in trust, at what ages shall principal be delivered to the children? Should a closely held business be held or liquidated at death? Who shall be the executors and trustees? Shall the entire estate be held for the benefit of the wife for life, with children's inheritance postponed until both parents are gone? Should gifts be made to reduce prospective death taxes? Should particular assets be allocated to particular beneficiaries?

While these questions do have legal implications, they are primarily matters of practical individual judgment. Lawyers have no monopoly on good judgment or on the experience necessary to guide people to sound decisions in this area. The professional estate planner accumulates every bit as much understanding and knowledge of what constitutes good family financial planning as does the lawyer—indeed, he probably accumulates more because his practice is concentrated in that field while the lawyer's is varied.

The Yale Law School's distinguished Professor Fred Rodell has written from a quarter-century's teaching experience these critical words about the profession and its pretensions in his classic volume, "Woe Unto You, Lawyers!":

"In tribal times, there were the medicine men. In the Middle Ages, there were the priests. Today there are the lawyers. For every age, a group of bright boys, learned in their trade and jealous of their learning, who blend technical competence with plain and fancy hocus-pocus to make themselves masters of their fellow men. For every age, a pseudo-intellectual autocracy, guarding the tricks of its trade from the uninitiated, and running, after its own pattern, the civilization of its day. It is the lawyers who run our civilization for us—our governments, our business, our private lives.

"We cannot die and leave our property to our children without calling on the lawyers to guide us through a maze of confusing gestures and formalities that lawyers have created. Why should not a man who wants to leave his property to his wife at his death say in his will, 'I want everything I own to go to my wife when I die', instead of having to hire a lawyer and go through a long rigamarole of legal language?

"It is through the medium of their weird and wordy mental gymnastics that the lawyers lay down the rules under which we live. And it is only because the average man cannot play their game, and so cannot see for himself how intrinsically empty-of-meaning their playthings are, that the lawyers continue to get away with it.

"The legal trade, in short, is nothing but a high-class racket. The lawyers—or at least 99 44/100 per cent of them—are not even aware that they are indulging in a racket, and would be shocked at the very mention of the idea. Once bitten by the legal bug, they lose all sense of perspective about what they are doing and how they are doing it. Like the medicine men of tribal times and the priests of the Middle Ages they actually believe in their own nonsense. This fact, of course, makes their racket all the more insidious. Consecrated fanatics are always more dangerous than conscious villains. And lawyers are fanatics indeed about the sacredness of the word-magic they call The Law.

"Yet the saddest and most insidious fact about the legal racket is that the general public doesn't realize it's a racket either. Scared, befuddled, impressed and ignorant, they take what is fed them, or rather what is sold them.

"If only the average man could be led to see and know the cold truth about the lawyers and their Law . . . if people could be made to realize how much of the vaunted majesty of The Law is a hoax and how many of the mighty processes of The Law are merely logical legerdemain, they would not long let the lawyers lead them around by the nose. And people have recently begun, bit by bit, to catch on. The great illusion of The Law has been leaking a little at the edges.

"If the ordinary man could see in black and white how silly and irrelevant and unnecessary it all is, he might be persuaded, in a peaceful way, to take the control of his civilization out of the hands of these modern purveyors of streamlined voodoo and chromium-plated theology, the lawyers.

"The Law, inexorably devoted to all its most ancient principles and precedents, makes a vice of innovation and a virtue of hoariness. Only The Law resists and resents the notion that it should ever change its antiquated ways to meet the challenge of a changing world.

"The Law not only stands still but is proud and determined to stand still. If a British barrister of two hundred years ago were suddenly to come alive in an American court-room, he would feel intellectually at home. The clothes would astonish him, the electric lights would astonish him, the architecture would astonish him. But as soon as the lawyers started talking legal talk, he would know that he was among friends. And given a couple of days with the law books, he could take the place of any lawyer present—or of the judge—and perform the whole legal mumbo-jumbo as well as they. Imagine, by contrast, a British surgeon of two hundred years ago plopped down into a modern hospital operating room. He would literally understand less of what was going on than would any passer-by brought in from the street at random.

"The Law, alone of all the sciences, just sits—aloof and practically motionless.

"Lawyers, with their advice and their principles and their strange language, no doubt increase, instead of decreasing, the number of transactions which end up in dispute and litigation. If they would let men carry on their affairs and make their agreements in simple, specific terms and in words intelligible to those involved, there would be fewer misunderstandings and fewer real or imagined causes for grievance."

Lawyers seize upon every opportunity to name themselves as trustee of the estates of their clients. A trustee does not perform a legal function and a legal education does not, in and of itself, qualify one to serve as a trustee. In dozens of actions in all parts of the country, the Bar has sought and obtained injunctions against trustee institutions on the grounds that they were engaging in the unauthorized practice of law. If the Bar is to raise a question of the unauthorized practice of law by trustees, it should be prepared to defend its equally "unauthorized" practice of trusteeship.

The Investment Advisors Act of 1940 regulates the giving of professional advice by investment counsellors. Other federal laws regulate the activities of brokers who may also be called upon to make investment recommendations. The Bar flouts these laws openly. I know lawyers who make it a regular practice to give their clients investment advice. In many instances, that advice has been disastrous.

The Bar periodically scolds public accountants for what it regards as instances of the unauthorized practice

of law. The scolding completed, the lawyers hustle back to their offices to make out a client's tax returns.

As might be expected, the injunctive actions which have been instituted by local and state bar groups against laymen on the grounds that the latter were practicing law have found full support in the courts. After all, when a bar association claims a man is practicing law, the judge who is hearing the evidence is himself a member of the Bar and therefore in the dual capacity of both plaintiff and judge. The mere fact that he has become a judge does not alter his thinking or his loyalty to his profession. A judge is, after all, simply a lawyer who knew a governor.

In Virginia, the lawyer-controlled legislature has actually made the state a laughing stock by passing a law making it a criminal offense for anyone other than a lawyer to describe what he does as "estate planning." The Old Dominion, which once led the fight against foreign despots, now has its own, home-grown variety.

In one historic case involving the Fairfield County (Connecticut) Bar Association, the complaining committee sought and obtained a temporary or "emergency" injunction secretly in the judge's chambers with no notice whatever to the individual against whom it was complaining. With full knowledge that the defendant knew nothing of the action and was not represented before him, the judge nevertheless granted the injunction on the strength of the Bar Association's sworn statement that it had "warned" the individual to desist from what he was doing and that his actions were causing "irreparable damage to the public interest". When the individual brought the Bar Association into court on a petition to dissolve the injunction, he drew from its representatives an admission that there had in fact been no such "warning" as was claimed. The Bar's counsel was asked: "About this 'irreparable damage'. Who, exactly, has been damaged?" The flustered man stammered: "Well, the Bar has been damaged." Faced with the evidence that the members of the Bar Committee had falsely sworn to the "facts" in their petition, did the judge take them to task? He did not. He sustained the injunction and went back to his chambers—and his conscience. It is this sort of thing which has brought the public image of both Bench and Bar to its present low estate.

However useful this volume may prove to the general public, it is hardly likely to be received with enthusiasm by members of the Bar who doubtless will view it as a blanket indictment of their "honorable profession"—and they will be right. It *is* an indictment of all of the members of the Bar—the bad ones who have been doing the looting of estates, and the good ones who have been standing silently by watching them.

Human nature being what it is, the most vociferous objections to the introduction of this layman's guide to estate planning will likely come from those who are profiting the most from the present unconscionable system of probate administration. They won't need to carry a sign; their howls of outrage will identify them. As Milton E. Meyer, Jr., distinguished member of the Colorado Bar, wrote in that state's Bar Journal:

> "There will be vague references to 'illegality', 'sham', 'fraud' and the like directed at efforts to by-pass probate through use of the living trust."

There will first be an outcry that this "do-it-yourself kit" for estate administration is a dangerous thing, that a carelessly-prepared instrument may have a harmful result. With this I am in complete agreement—a carelessly-drawn instrument can have *very* harmful results. I know this because my files are full of carelessly-drawn instruments prepared by members of the Bar. Once he passes his bar examination, the attorney is never again called upon to prove his skill. If he prepares an instrument badly, there is no one to take him to task. In the fraternity of the Bar it would be unthinkable for an attorney to initiate an action against another attorney on behalf of a client who had been badly served. Oh, if an attorney embezzles some money, the grievance committee will get after him, but if he simply botches job after job, the Bar will take no steps whatever to protect the public against his continued bungling.

The Bar maintains that the sole qualification for the preparation of instruments such as are contained in this volume is possession of a law degree. The countless examples of poor draftsmanship which I have collected testify to the fallacy of this line of reasoning. On the other hand the claim that the lack of a law degree automatically disqualifies one from drafting such instruments loses some of its force when one recalls that Roscoe Pound, late dean of the Harvard Law School and the greatest scholar in American legal history, had no law degree.

It is conceivable that among a thousand persons making use of the forms, one or two might execute them carelessly and end up with an imperfect instrument. On balance, though, the score is likely to be infinitely better than that of a like number of instruments individually drafted by attorneys of varying competence—or incompetence. The instructions supplied with each instrument are quite precise. Any sensible person who reads them thoughtfully several times and checks his understanding of them with another person should have no difficulty.

It will be said, too, that one cannot press the widely-varying needs of different people into a few standard forms. But attorneys do this regularly—in many law offices there are books of standard forms of wills and trusts of various types which have been prepared by experts. There is nothing wrong with the use of such forms. Indeed, if more such well-drawn stereotypes were used, we would find fewer instances of instruments clumsily contrived by inexperienced or incompetent draftsmen. A standard form, properly drawn by an expert, offers many advantages.

As to the forms provided in this volume, there will be a certain amount of nit-picking—something was omitted here, something else might have been expressed differently there, no provision was made for this or that contingency, etc. There are few things in this world which cannot be improved upon, and no claim is made that the instruments herein provided cannot be made more nearly perfect. They are legally correct, however, and may be employed with complete assurance that they will serve the readers' purposes well.

They are relatively brief—and deliberately so. Some attorneys write as if they were being paid by the pound, striving to make each instrument an encyclopedia of their personal knowledge of the mumbo-jumbo of the law and studiously avoiding saying anything in ten words which they can crowd into a hundred.

There are persons for whom the forms will not be suitable. Their special situations will call for more detailed drafting. This volume will, I trust, still prove valuable to them by pointing the way to probate exemption. Armed with that knowledge, they can instruct their attorneys what they want drawn. The law will become their servant, not their master.

A word of caution: Be punctilious in the execution of the instruments. Where witnesses are indicated, be certain that there are the required number, that they are adults, that they are disinterested persons so far as your estate is concerned, and that they sign their names correctly. However remote the relationship may be, whenever two persons in the family bear the same name, remove all doubt as to the person you intend to name by adding after the name some such parenthetical identification as "(my niece)" or "(my grandson)".

This volume is not intended as a text book, nor did I set out to explore exhaustively every aspect of the problems of estate administration in America. It is simply an estate planner's notebook in which I have tried to set down in reasonably simple language the basic facts which will enable your family and mine to avoid being exploited by the probate system. Whether or not I have succeeded I shall leave to the reader to decide.

N.F.D.

49 Plaza, Bridgeport, Connecticut

Appendix

AVOIDING PROBATE OF JOINTLY-OWNED REAL ESTATE

In Chapter 5, forms of inter vivos trust are provided by the use of which real estate held in the name of some one person may be conveyed to one or more persons upon the death of the owner without the necessity of going through probate.

We have already discussed the pitfalls of joint ownership and examined the possible disadvantages which may result from sharing title to property. The point was made that, with one exception, such joint tenancy should be avoided. The single exception was a family domicile jointly owned by husband and wife. This is the one type of asset which the Federal tax authorities will permit a husband to place in joint tenancy with his wife without the filing of a gift tax return, regardless of the amount of the "gift" to the wife represented by such joint tenancy. It is fortunate that such dispensation is granted, for joint ownership of the family domicile by husband and wife is common and frequent.

If such co-owners wished to obtain the probate exemption provided by the instruments in Chapter 5, it would be necessary for one or the other to relinquish the part-ownership enjoyed and permit the property to stand in one name alone. The person who thus became the sole owner would then execute an appropriate declaration of trust from among those provided in Chapter 5.

Recognizing that the decision as to which of the two parties should relinquish his share might be a difficult one in some instances, possibly provoking disagreement and an impasse which would effectively frustrate the effort to achieve probate avoidance, I have prepared three additional forms of declaration of trust which may be used by joint owners of real estate to avoid probate of their holdings without disturbing the joint ownership. These will be found on the pages which follow. A special form of joint quit claim deed for execution by the two joint owners is also provided. It is extremely important that this special form of quit claim deed be used *only* in conjunction with Declarations of Trust DT-1J, DT-2J, and DT-3J. It is not to be used with the forms numbered DT-1, DT-2, DT-3 and DT-4 provided in the Appendix to Chapter 5.

A P P E N D I X   **A**

DECLARATION OF TRUST
FOR NAMING
ONE BENEFICIARY
TO RECEIVE
JOINTLY-OWNED REAL ESTATE

Instructions:

On the following pages will be found duplicate copies of a declaration of trust (DT-1J) which will be suitable for use where it is desired simply to name some one person to receive real estate upon the death of the surviving joint owner.

Enter the names of the two co-owners on the first line.

Cross out *"city"* or *"town"*, leaving the appropriate designation of your community. If your house has no street number, cross out *"(and known as)"*.

Enter the description of your property as it appears in the warranty deed or quit claim deed under which you acquired it.

Note that under this instrument, not only your house but also its entire contents—including your personal effects—will pass to the beneficiary named without going through probate. If you do not wish to include your furniture and personal effects in the trust, cross out *"and all furniture, fixtures and real and personal property situated therein"* and initial it.

Enter the name of the beneficiary in the appropriate place in Paragraph 1.

Whenever there is any possibility of a minor child receiving the property, make certain that you name an adult who can act as trustee for the child. The name of that adult should be inserted in Paragraph 5 of the instrument shown here. Avoid naming as trustee a person not likely to survive until the child has reached age 21.

When completed in the manner shown on the reverse side hereof, one copy of the declaration of trust and one copy of the joint quit claim deed (see Page 353) should be filed with the town clerk's or other municipal office where real estate transfers in your community are customarily recorded. The remaining copies of both instruments may be retained for reference purposes.

WHEREVER THE INSTRUCTION *"INITIAL IT"* APPEARS ABOVE, IT MEANS THAT *BOTH* CO-OWNERS SHOULD INITIAL IT.

Declaration of Trust

WHEREAS, WE, **John J. Smith** and **Mary Smith**, of the City/Town of **Jonesville**, County of **Fairfax**, State of **Connecticut**, are the owners as joint tenants of certain real property located at (and known as) **525 Main Street** in the City/Town of **Jonesville**, State of **Connecticut**, which property is described more fully in the Deed conveying it from **Henry B. Green** to **John J. Smith and Mary Smith**, as "that certain piece or parcel of land with buildings thereon standing. located in said **Jonesville**, being

the rear portions of Lots #34 and 35, on Map of Building Lots of George Spooner, said map being dated May 3, 1952, and filed for record in the office of the Town Clerk, Jonesville, Connecticut, in Book 5, Page 16, of said Maps. Said parcel of land is more particularly described as:

Beginning at a point on the south line of Lot #34, on said map, 73.5 feet East of the East line of Park Avenue --- running thence North along land of James E. Beach, 100 feet to a point on the North line of Lot #35 on said map, 70.44 feet East of the East line of Cornwall Street, thence East along land of the said James E. Beach (being Lot #51 on said map) 55 feet --- thence South along land of Thomas Cook (being Lot #56 on said map) 100 feet to the aforesaid North line of Bartram Street --- thence West to the point of beginning.

NOW. THEREFORE, KNOW ALL MEN BY THESE PRESENTS, that we do hereby acknowledge and declare that we hold and will hold said real property and all right, title and interest in and to said property and all furniture, fixtures and real and personal property situated therein, IN TRUST

1. For the use and benefit of

(Name) **Mary A. Smith (our niece)** **Jonesville** **Connecticut**
   City   State

(Address) **750 Porter Street**
   Number   Street

Upon the death of the survivor of us, unless the beneficiary shall predecease us or unless we all shall die as a result of a common accident or disaster, our Successor Trustee is hereby directed forthwith to transfer said property and all right, title and interest in and to said property unto the beneficiary absolutely and thereby terminate this trust; provided, however, that if the beneficiary hereunder shall the trust assets in continuing

5. Upon the death or legal incapacity of one of us, the survivor shall continue as sole Trustee. Upon the death of the survivor of us, or if we both shall die in a common accident, we hereby nominate and appoint as Successor Trustee hereunder whosoever shall at that time be beneficiary hereunder, unless such beneficiary be a minor or legally incapacitated, in which event we hereby nominate and appoint

(Name) **Henry P. Adams** **Jonesville** **Connecticut**
   City   State

(Address) **125 Barnum Street**
   Number   Street

to be Successor Trustee.

6. This Declaration of Trust shall extend to and be binding upon the heirs, executors, administrators and assigns of the undersigned and upon the Successors to the Trustee.

7. We as Trustees and our Successor Trustee shall serve without bond.

8. This Declaration of Trust shall be construed and enforced in accordance with the laws of the State of **Connecticut**

Declaration of Trust

WHEREAS, WE,_____and_____, of the

City/Town of_____, County of_____, State of_____,

are the owners as joint tenants of certain real property located at (and known as)_____

_____ in the said City/Town of_____, State of

_____, which property is described more fully in the Deed conveying it

from_____ to_____, as "that

certain piece or parcel of land with buildings thereon standing, located in said_____

_____, being

NOW, THEREFORE, KNOW ALL MEN BY THESE PRESENTS, that we do hereby acknowledge and declare that we hold and will hold said real property and all right, title and interest in and to said property and all furniture, fixtures and real and personal property situated therein, IN TRUST

1. For the use and benefit of

(Name)_____

(Address)_____

      Number   Street   City   State

Upon the death of the survivor of us, unless the beneficiary shall predecease us or unless we all shall die as a result of a common accident or disaster, our Successor Trustee is hereby directed forthwith to transfer said property and all right, title and interest in and to said property unto the beneficiary absolutely and thereby terminate this trust; provided, however, that if the beneficiary hereunder shall then be a minor, the Successor Trustee shall hold the trust assets in continuing trust until such beneficiary attains the age of twenty-one years. During such period of continuing trust the Successor Trustee, in his absolute discretion, may retain the specific trust property herein described if he believes it in the best interest of the beneficiary so to do, or he may sell or otherwise dispose of such specific trust property, investing and reinvesting the proceeds as he may deem appropriate. If the specific trust property shall be productive of income or if it be sold or otherwise disposed of, the Successor Trustee may apply or expend any or all of the income or principal directly for the maintenance, education and support of the minor beneficiary without the intervention of any guardian and without application to any court. Such payments of income or principal may be made to the parents of such minor or to the person with whom the minor is living without any liability upon the Successor Trustee to see to the application thereof. If such minor survives us but dies before attaining the age of twenty-one years, at his or her death the Successor Trustee shall deliver, pay over, transfer and distribute the trust property to such minor's personal representatives, absolutely.

2. We reserve unto ourselves the power and right (a) to place a mortgage or other lien upon the property, and (b) to collect any rental or other income which may accrue from the trust property and, in our sole discretion as trustees, either to accumulate such income as an addition to the trust assets being held hereunder or pay such income to ourselves as individuals.

3. We reserve unto ourselves the power and right at any time during our lifetime to amend or revoke in whole or in part the trust hereby created without the necessity of obtaining the consent of the beneficiary and without giving notice to the beneficiary. The sale or other disposition by us of the whole or any part of the property held hereunder shall constitute as to such whole or part a revocation of this trust.

4. The death during our lifetime, or in a common accident or disaster with us, of the beneficiary designated hereunder shall revoke such designation, and in the former event, we reserve the right to designate a new beneficiary. Should we for any reason fail to designate such new beneficiary, this trust shall terminate upon the death of the survivor of us and the trust property shall revert to the estate of such survivor.

5. Upon the death or legal incapacity of one of us, the survivor shall continue as sole Trustee. Upon the death of the survivor of us, or if we both shall die in a common accident, we hereby nominate and appoint as Successor Trustee hereunder whosoever shall at that time be beneficiary hereunder, unless such beneficiary be a minor or legally incapacitated, in which event we hereby nominate and appoint

(Name)_____

(Address)_____

| Number | Street | City | State |

to be Successor Trustee.

6. This Declaration of Trust shall extend to and be binding upon the heirs, executors, administrators and assigns of the undersigned and upon the Successors to the Trustee.

7. We as Trustees and our Successor Trustee shall serve without bond.

8. This Declaration of Trust shall be construed and enforced in accordance with the laws of the State of

_____.

IN WITNESS WHEREOF we have hereunto set our hands and seals this_____

day of_____ 19____.

(First co-owner sign here)_____L.S.

(Second co-owner sign here)_____L.S.

Witness: (1)_____ Witness: (2)_____

State of_____ }

County of_____ } ss:_____

On the_____day of_____, nineteen hundred and_____

before me came_____and_____,

known to me to be the individuals described in, and who executed the foregoing instrument, and they acknowledged that they executed the same, and in due form of law acknowledged the foregoing instrument to be their free act and deed and desired the same might be recorded as such.

(Notary Seal)   _____

                                            Notary Public

Declaration of Trust

DT-1J
Duplicate

WHEREAS, WE,_____and_____, of the

City/Town of_____, County of_____, State of_____,

are the owners as joint tenants of certain real property located at (and known as)_____

_____ in the City/Town of_____, State of

_____, which property is described more fully in the Deed conveying it

from_____ to_____, as "that

certain piece or parcel of land with buildings thereon standing, located in said_____

_____, being

NOW, THEREFORE, KNOW ALL MEN BY THESE PRESENTS, that we do hereby acknowledge and declare that we hold and will hold said real property and all right, title and interest in and to said property and all furniture, fixtures and real and personal property situated therein, IN TRUST

1. For the use and benefit of

(Name)_____

(Address)_____

<table>
<tr><td>Number</td><td>Street</td><td>City</td><td>State</td></tr>
</table>

Upon the death of the survivor of us, unless the beneficiary shall predecease us or unless we all shall die as a result of a common accident or disaster, our Successor Trustee is hereby directed forthwith to transfer said property and all right, title and interest in and to said property unto the beneficiary absolutely and thereby terminate this trust; provided, however, that if the beneficiary hereunder shall then be a minor, the Successor Trustee shall hold the trust assets in continuing trust until such beneficiary attains the age of twenty-one years. During such period of continuing trust the Successor Trustee, in his absolute discretion, may retain the specific trust property herein described if he believes it in the best interest of the beneficiary so to do, or he may sell or otherwise dispose of such specific trust property, investing and reinvesting the proceeds as he may deem appropriate. If the specific trust property shall be productive of income or if it be sold or otherwise disposed of, the Successor Trustee may apply or expend any or all of the income or principal directly for the maintenance, education and support of the minor beneficiary without the intervention of any guardian and without application to any court. Such payments of income or principal may be made to the parents of such minor or to the person with whom the minor is living without any liability upon the Successor Trustee to see to the application thereof. If such minor survives us but dies before attaining the age of twenty-one years, at his or her death the Successor Trustee shall deliver, pay over, transfer and distribute the trust property to such minor's personal representatives, absolutely.

2. We reserve unto ourselves the power and right (a) to place a mortgage or other lien upon the property, and (b) to collect any rental or other income which may accrue from the trust property and, in our sole discretion as trustees, either to accumulate such income as an addition to the trust assets being held hereunder or pay such income to ourselves as individuals.

3. We reserve unto ourselves the power and right at any time during our lifetime to amend or revoke in whole or in part the trust hereby created without the necessity of obtaining the consent of the beneficiary and without giving notice to the beneficiary. The sale or other disposition by us of the whole or any part of the property held hereunder shall constitute as to such whole or part a revocation of this trust.

4. The death during our lifetime, or in a common accident or disaster with us, of the beneficiary designated hereunder shall revoke such designation, and in the former event, we reserve the right to designate a new beneficiary. Should we for any reason fail to designate such new beneficiary, this trust shall terminate upon the death of the survivor of us and the trust property shall revert to the estate of such survivor.

5. Upon the death or legal incapacity of one of us, the survivor shall continue as sole Trustee. Upon the death of the survivor of us, or if we both shall die in a common accident, we hereby nominate and appoint as Successor Trustee hereunder whosoever shall at that time be beneficiary hereunder, unless such beneficiary be a minor or legally incapacitated, in which event we hereby nominate and appoint

(Name)_____

(Address)_____
          Number   Street   City   State
to be Successor Trustee.

6. This Declaration of Trust shall extend to and be binding upon the heirs, executors, administrators and assigns of the undersigned and upon the Successors to the Trustee.

7. We as Trustees and our Successor Trustee shall serve without bond.

8. This Declaration of Trust shall be construed and enforced in accordance with the laws of the State of

_____.

IN WITNESS WHEREOF we have hereunto set our hands and seals this_____

day of_____ 19____.

(First co-owner sign here)_____L.S.

(Second co-owner sign here)_____L.S.

Witness: (1)_____ Witness: (2)_____

State of_____)

County of_____ } ss:_____

On the_____day of_____, nineteen hundred and_____

before me came_____and_____,

known to me to be the individuals described in, and who executed the foregoing instrument, and they acknowledged that they executed the same, and in due form of law acknowledged the foregoing instrument to be their free act and deed and desired the same might be recorded as such.

(Notary Seal)   _____
                                      Notary Public

> ## DECLARATION OF TRUST
> FOR NAMING
> ## ONE PRIMARY BENEFICIARY
> AND
> ## ONE CONTINGENT BENEFICIARY
> TO RECEIVE
> ## JOINTLY-OWNED REAL ESTATE

Instructions:

On the following pages will be found duplicate copies of a declaration of trust (DT-2J) which will be suitable for use where it is desired to name *one* person as primary beneficiary to receive jointly-owned real estate, with some *one* other person as contingent beneficiary to receive the property if the primary beneficiary does not outlive the surviving co-owner.

Enter the names of the two co-owners on the first line.

Cross out *"city" or "town"*, leaving the appropriate designation of your community. If your house has no street number, cross out *"(and known as)"*.

Enter the description of your property as it appears in the warranty deed or quit claim deed under which you acquired it.

Note that under this instrument, not only your house but also its entire contents—including your personal effects—will pass to the beneficiary named without going through probate. If you do not wish to include your furniture and personal effects in the trust, cross out *"and all furniture, fixtures and real and personal property situated therein"* and initial it.

Enter the names of the beneficiaries in the appropriate places in Paragraph 1.

Whenever there is any possibility of a minor child receiving the property, make certain that you name an adult who can act as trustee for him. The name of that adult should be inserted in Paragraph 5 of the instrument shown here. Avoid naming as trustee a person not likely to survive until the child has reached age 21.

When completed in the manner shown on the reverse side hereof, one copy of the declaration of trust and one copy of the quit claim deed (see Page 353) should be filed in the town clerk's or other municipal office where real estate transfers in your community are customarily recorded. The remaining copies of both instruments may be retained for reference.

> WHEREVER THE INSTRUCTION *"INITIAL IT"* APPEARS ABOVE, IT MEANS THAT *BOTH* CO-OWNERS SHOULD INITIAL IT.

Declaration of Trust

WHEREAS, WE ___John J. Smith___ and ___Mary Smith___ , of the City/Town of ___Jonesville___ , County of ___Fairfax___ , State of ___Connecticut___ , are the owners as joint tenants of certain real property located at (and known as) ___525 Main Street___ in the City/Town of ___Jonesville___ , State of ___Connecticut___ , which property is described more fully in the Deed conveying it

from ___Henry B. Green___ to ___John J. Smith and Mary Smith___ as "that certain piece or parcel of land with buildings thereon standing, located in said ___Jonesville___ , being

the rear portions of Lots #34 and 35, on Map of Building Lots of George Spooner, said map being dated May 3, 1952, and filed for record in the office of the Town Clerk, Jonesville, Connecticut, in Book 5, Page 16, of said Maps. Said parcel of land is more particularly described as:

Beginning at a point on the south line of Lot #34, on said map, 73.5 feet East of the East line of Park Avenue --- running thence North along land of James E. Beach, 100 feet to a point on the North line of Lot #35 on said map, 70.44 feet East of the East line of Cornwall Street, thence East along land of the said James E. Beach (being Lot #51 on said map) 55 feet --- thence South along land of Thomas Cook (being Lot #56 on said map) 100 feet to the aforesaid North line of Bartram Street --- thence West to the point of beginning.

NOW, THEREFORE, KNOW ALL MEN BY THESE PRESENTS, that we do hereby acknowledge and declare that we hold and will hold said real property and all right, title and interest in and to said property and all furniture, fixtures and real and personal property situated therein IN TRUST

1. For the use and benefit of

(Name) ___Mary A. Smith (our niece)___ ___Jonesville___ ___Connecticut___
City   State

(Address) ___750___ ___Porter Street___
Number   Street

or, if such beneficiary be not surviving, for the use and benefit of

(Name) ___William B. Connors (our nephew)___ ___Jonesville___ ___Connecticut___
City   State

(Address) ___250___ ___County Street___
Number   Street

Upon the death of the survivor of us, unless the beneficiaries shall predecease us or unless we all shall die as a result of a common accident, our Successor Trustee is hereby directed forthwith to transfer said property and all right, title and interest in and to said

5. Upon the death or legal incapacity of one of us, the survivor shall continue as sole Trustee. Upon the death of the survivor of us, or if we both shall die in a common accident, we hereby nominate and appoint as Successor Trustee hereunder whosoever shall at that time be beneficiary hereunder, unless such beneficiary be a minor or legally incapacitated, in which event we hereby nominate and appoint

(Name) ___Henry P. Adams___ ___Jonesville___ ___Connecticut___
City   State

(Address) ___125___ ___Barnum Street___
Number   Street

to be Successor Trustee.

6. This Declaration of Trust shall extend to and be binding upon the heirs, executors, administrators and assigns of the undersigned and upon the Successors to the Trustee.

7. We as Trustees and our Successor Trustee shall serve without bond.

8. This Declaration of Trust shall be construed and enforced in accordance with the laws of the State of ___Connecticut___

WHEREAS, WE,_____ and _____, of the

City/Town of_____, County of_____, State of_____,

are the owners as joint tenants of certain real property located at (and known as)_____

_____ in the City/Town of_____, State of

_____, which property is described more fully in the Deed conveying it

from_____ to_____ as "that

certain piece or parcel of land with buildings thereon standing, located in said_____

_____, being

NOW, THEREFORE, KNOW ALL MEN BY THESE PRESENTS, that we do hereby acknowledge and declare that we hold and will hold said real property and all right, title and interest in and to said property and all furniture, fixtures and real and personal property situated therein IN TRUST

1. For the use and benefit of

(Name)_____

(Address)_____

       Number   Street   City   State

or, if such beneficiary be not surviving, for the use and benefit of

(Name)_____

(Address)_____

       Number   Street   City   State

Upon the death of the survivor of us, unless the beneficiaries shall predecease us or unless we all shall die as a result of a common accident, our Successor Trustee is hereby directed forthwith to transfer said property and all right, title and interest in and to said property unto the beneficiary absolutely and thereby terminate this trust; provided, however, that if the beneficiary hereunder shall then be a minor, the Successor Trustee shall hold the trust assets in continuing trust until such beneficiary attains the age of twenty-one years. During such period of continuing trust the Successor Trustee, in his absolute discretion, may retain the specific trust property herein described if he believes it in the best interest of the beneficiary so to do, or he may sell or otherwise dispose of such specific trust property, investing and reinvesting the proceeds as he may deem appropriate. If the specific trust property shall be productive of income or if it be sold or otherwise disposed of, the Successor Trustee may apply or expend any or all of the income or principal directly for the maintenance, education, and support of the minor beneficiary without the intervention of any guardian and without application to any court. Such payments of income or principal may be made to the parents of such minor or to the person with whom the minor is living without any liability upon the Successor Trustee to see to the application thereof. If any such minor survives us but dies before attaining the age of twenty-one years, at his or her death the Successor Trustee shall deliver, pay over, transfer and distribute the trust property to such minor's personal representatives, absolutely.

2. We reserve unto ourselves the power and right (a) to place a mortgage or other lien upon the property, and (b) to collect any rental or other income which may accrue from the trust property and, in our sole discretion as trustees, either to accumulate such income as an addition to the trust assets being held hereunder or pay such income to ourselves as individuals.

3. We reserve unto ourselves the power and right at any time during our lifetime to amend or revoke in whole or in part the trust hereby created without the necessity of obtaining the consent of the beneficiaries and without giving notice to the beneficiaries. The sale or other disposition by us of the whole or any part of the property held hereunder shall constitute as to such whole or part a revocation of this trust.

4. The death during our lifetime, or in a common accident or disaster with us, of both of the beneficiaries designated hereunder shall revoke such designation, and in the former event, we reserve the right to designate a new beneficiary. Should we for any reason fail to designate such new beneficiary, this trust shall terminate upon the death of the survivor of us and the trust property shall revert to the estate of such survivor.

5. Upon the death or legal incapacity of one of us, the survivor shall continue as sole Trustee. Upon the death of the survivor of us, or if we both shall die in a common accident, we hereby nominate and appoint as Successor Trustee hereunder whosoever shall at that time be beneficiary hereunder, unless such beneficiary be a minor or legally incapacitated, in which event we hereby nominate and appoint

(Name)_____

(Address)_____
                    Number   Street   City   State
to be Successor Trustee.

6. This Declaration of Trust shall extend to and be binding upon the heirs, executors, administrators and assigns of the undersigned and upon the Successors to the Trustee.

7. We as Trustees and our Successor Trustee shall serve without bond.

8. This Declaration of Trust shall be construed and enforced in accordance with the laws of the State of

_____.

IN WITNESS WHEREOF we have hereunto set our hands and seals this_____day of

_____ 19____.

                    (First co-owner sign here)_____L.S.

                    (Second co-owner sign here)_____L.S.

Witness: (1)_____   Witness: (2)_____

State of_____
                                                                    } ss: _____
County of_____

On the_____day of_____, nineteen hundred and_____,

before me came_____and_____,
known to me to be the individuals described in, and who executed the foregoing instrument, and they acknowledged that they executed the same, and in due form of law acknowledged the foregoing instrument to be their free act and deed and desired the same might be recorded as such.

        (Notary Seal)   _____
                                                                            Notary Public

Declaration of Trust

Duplicate

WHEREAS, WE,_____ and _____, of the

City/Town of_____, County of_____, State of_____,

are the owners as joint tenants of certain real property located at (and known as)_____

_____ in the said City/Town of_____, State of

_____, which property is described more fully in the Deed conveying it

from_____ to_____ as "that

certain piece or parcel of land with buildings thereon standing, located in said_____

_____, being

NOW, THEREFORE, KNOW ALL MEN BY THESE PRESENTS, that we do hereby acknowledge and declare that we hold and will hold said real property and all right, title and interest in and to said property and all furniture, fixtures and real and personal property situated therein IN TRUST

1. For the use and benefit of

(Name)_____

(Address)_____
          Number   Street   City   State

or, if such beneficiary be not surviving, for the use and benefit of

(Name)_____

(Address)_____
          Number   Street   City   State

Upon the death of the survivor of us, unless the beneficiaries shall predecease us or unless we all shall die as a result of a common accident, our Successor Trustee is hereby directed forthwith to transfer said property and all right, title and interest in and to said property unto the beneficiary absolutely and thereby terminate this trust; <u>provided</u>, however, that if the beneficiary hereunder shall then be a minor, the Successor Trustee shall hold the trust assets in continuing trust until such beneficiary attains the age of twenty-one years. During such period of continuing trust the Successor Trustee, in his absolute discretion, may retain the specific trust property herein described if he believes it in the best interest of the beneficiary so to do, or he may sell or otherwise dispose of such specific trust property, investing and reinvesting the proceeds as he may deem appropriate. If the specific trust property shall be productive of income or if it be sold or otherwise disposed of, the Successor Trustee may apply or expend any or all of the income or principal directly for the maintenance, education, and support of the minor beneficiary without the intervention of any guardian and without application to any court. Such payments of income or principal may be made to the parents of such minor or to the person with whom the minor is living without any liability upon the Successor Trustee to see to the application thereof. If any such minor survives us but dies before attaining the age of twenty-one years, at his or her death the Successor Trustee shall deliver, pay over, transfer and distribute the trust property to such minor's personal representatives, absolutely.

2. We reserve unto ourselves the power and right (a) to place a mortgage or other lien upon the property, and (b) to collect any rental or other income which may accrue from the trust property and, in our sole discretion as trustees, either to accumulate such income as an addition to the trust assets being held hereunder or pay such income to ourselves as individuals.

3. We reserve unto ourselves the power and right at any time during our lifetime to amend or revoke in whole or in part the trust hereby created without the necessity of obtaining the consent of the beneficiaries and without giving notice to the beneficiaries. The sale or other disposition by us of the whole or any part of the property held hereunder shall constitute as to such whole or part a revocation of this trust.

4. The death during our lifetime, or in a common accident or disaster with us, of both of the beneficiaries designated hereunder shall revoke such designation, and in the former event, we reserve the right to designate a new beneficiary. Should we for any reason fail to designate such new beneficiary, this trust shall terminate upon the death of the survivor of us and the trust property shall revert to the estate of such survivor.

5. Upon the death or legal incapacity of one of us, the survivor shall continue as sole Trustee. Upon the death of the survivor of us, or if we both shall die in a common accident, we hereby nominate and appoint as Successor Trustee hereunder whosoever shall at that time be beneficiary hereunder, unless such beneficiary be a minor or legally incapacitated, in which event we hereby nominate and appoint

(Name)_____

(Address)_____

           Number   Street   City   State

to be Successor Trustee.

6. This Declaration of Trust shall extend to and be binding upon the heirs, executors, administrators and assigns of the undersigned and upon the Successors to the Trustee.

7. We as Trustees and our Successor Trustee shall serve without bond.

8. This Declaration of Trust shall be construed and enforced in accordance with the laws of the State of

_____.

IN WITNESS WHEREOF we have hereunto set our hands and seals this_____day of

_____ 19_____.

               *(First co-owner sign here)*_____L.S.

               *(Second co-owner sign here)*_____L.S.

Witness: (1)_____   Witness: (2)_____

State of_____}
                         ss: _____
County of_____}

On the_____day of_____, nineteen hundred and_____,

before me came_____and_____,
known to me to be the individuals described in, and who executed the foregoing instrument, and they acknowledged that they executed the same, and in due form of law acknowledged the foregoing instrument to be their free act and deed and desired the same might be recorded as such.

    (Notary Seal)   _____
                                           Notary Public

APPENDIX C

DECLARATION OF TRUST
FOR NAMING
TWO OR MORE BENEFICIARIES, SHARING EQUALLY
TO RECEIVE
JOINTLY-OWNED REAL ESTATE

Instructions:

On the following pages will be found duplicate copies of a declaration of trust (DT-3J) which will be suitable for use where it is desired to name two or more persons to share jointly-owned real estate equally upon the death of the surviving joint owner.

Enter the names of the two co-owners on the first line.

Cross out *"city"* or *"town",* leaving the appropriate designation of your community. If your house has no street number, cross out *"(and known as)".*

Enter the description of your property as it appears in the warranty deed or quit claim deed under which you acquired it.

Note that under this instrument, not only your house but also its entire contents—including your personal effects—will pass to the beneficiaries named without going through probate. If you do not wish to include your furniture and personal effects in the trust, cross out *"and all furniture, fixtures and real and personal property situated therein"* and initial it.

Note that the instrument specifies that the named beneficiaries are to receive *"in equal shares, or the survivor of them/per stirpes".*

Now, think carefully: If you as joint owners have named three persons to share the property equally upon the death of the survivor of you with the understanding that if one of them predeceases you, *his* children are to receive *his* share, cross out *"or the survivor of them"* and initial it. If that is not what you want—if, for example, you prefer that the share of the deceased beneficiary be divided by the two surviving beneficiaries, cross out *"per stirpes"* and initial it. Remember, you *must* cross out *"or the survivor of them"* or *"per stirpes"*—one or the other.

In Paragraph 1, enter the *number* of *persons* you are naming (to discourage unauthorized additions to the list) and then insert their names. The one whose name appears *first* will be the successor trustee responsible for seeing to the distribution of the trust property.

Whenever there is any possibility of a minor child receiving any portion of the property, make certain that you name an adult who can act as trustee for him. The name of that adult should be inserted in Paragraph 5 of the instrument shown here. Avoid naming as trustee a person not likely to survive until the child has reached age 21.

When completed in the manner shown on the reverse side hereof, one copy of the declaration of trust and one copy of the quit claim deed (see Page 353) should be filed with the town clerk's or other municipal office where real estate transactions in your community are customarily recorded. The remaining copies of both instruments may be retained for reference.

| WHEREVER THE INSTRUCTION *"INITIAL IT"* APPEARS ABOVE, IT MEANS THAT *BOTH* CO-OWNERS SHOULD INITIAL IT.

Declaration of Trust

WHEREAS, WE, __John J. Smith__ and __Mary Smith__, of the ~~City~~/Town of __Jonesville__, County of __Fairfax__, State of __Connecticut__, are the owners as joint tenants of certain real property located at (and known as) __525 Main Street__,

in the ~~City~~/Town of __Jonesville__, State of __Connecticut__, which property is described more fully in the Deed conveying it from __Henry B. Green__

to __John J. Smith and Mary Smith__, as "that certain piece or parcel of land with buildings thereon standing, located in said __Jonesville__, being

the rear portion of Lots #34 and 35, on Map of Building Lots of George Spooner, said map being dated May 3, 1952, and filed for record in the office of the Town Clerk, Jonesville, Connecticut, in Book 5, Page 16, of said Maps. Said parcel of land is more particularly described as:

Beginning at a point on the south line of Lot #34, on said map, 73.5 feet East of the East line of Park Avenue --- running thence North along land of James E. Beach, 100 feet to a point on the North line of Lot #35 on said map, 70.44 feet East of the East line of Cornwall Street, thence East along land of the said James E. Beach (being Lot #51 on said map) 55 feet --- thence South along land of Thomas Cook (being Lot #56 on said map) 100 feet to the aforesaid North line of Bartram Street --- thence West to the point of beginning.

NOW, THEREFORE, KNOW ALL MEN BY THESE PRESENTS, that we do hereby acknowledge and declare that we hold and will hold said real property and all right, title and interest in and to said property and all furniture, fixtures and real and personal property situated therein IN TRUST

1. For the use and benefit of the following __three__ persons, in equal shares, or the survivor of them/per stirpes:

> __Thomas B. Smith (our nephew)__
> __William R. Smith (our nephew)__
> __Charles M. Smith (our nephew)__

Upon the death of the survivor of us, unless all the beneficiaries shall predecease us or unless we all shall die as a result of a common accident or disaster, our Successor Trustee is hereby directed forthwith to transfer said property and all right, title and interest in and to said property unto the beneficiaries absolutely and thereby terminate this trust; provided, however, that if any bene-

5. Upon the death or legal incapacity of one of us, the survivor shall continue as sole Trustee. Upon the death of the survivor of us, or if we both shall die in a common accident, we hereby nominate and appoint as Successor Trustee hereunder the beneficiary first above named, unless such beneficiary be a minor or legally incompetent, in which event we hereby nominate and appoint as Successor Trustee hereunder the beneficiary whose name appears second above. If such beneficiary named second above shall be a minor or legally incompetent, then we nominate and appoint as Successor Trustee hereunder:

(Name) __Henry P. Adams__   __Jonesville__   __Connecticut__
                               City   State

(Address) __125__ __Barnum Street__
          Number   Street

6. This Declaration of Trust shall extend to and be binding upon the heirs, executors, administrators and assigns of the undersigned and upon the Successors to the Trustee.

7. We as Trustees and our Successor Trustee shall serve without bond.

8. This Declaration of Trust shall be construed and enforced in accordance with the laws of the State of __Connecticut__

WHEREAS, WE,_____and_____, of the

City/Town of_____, County of_____, State of_____,

are the owners as joint tenants of certain real property located at (and known as)_____

in the City/Town of_____, State of_____,

which property is described more fully in the Deed conveying it from_____

to_____, as "that certain piece or parcel of land with buildings thereon

standing, located in said_____, being

NOW, THEREFORE, KNOW ALL MEN BY THESE PRESENTS, that we do hereby acknowledge and declare that we hold and will hold said real property and all right, title and interest in and to said property and all furniture, fixtures and real and personal property situated therein IN TRUST

1. For the use and benefit of the following_____persons, in equal shares, or the survivor of them/per stirpes:

Upon the death of the survivor of us, unless all the beneficiaries shall predecease us or unless we all shall die as a result of a common accident or disaster, our Successor Trustee is hereby directed forthwith to transfer said property and all right, title and interest in and to said property unto the beneficiaries absolutely and thereby terminate this trust; provided, however, that if any beneficiary hereunder shall then be a minor, the Successor Trustee shall hold the trust assets in continuing trust until such beneficiary attains the age of twenty-one years. During such period of continuing trust the Successor Trustee, in his absolute discretion, may retain the specific trust property herein described if he believes it in the best interest of the beneficiary so to do, or he may sell or otherwise dispose of such specific trust property, investing and reinvesting the proceeds as he may deem appropriate. If the specific trust property shall be productive of income or if it be sold or otherwise disposed of, the Successor Trustee may apply or expend any or all of the income or principal directly for the maintenance, education and support of the minor beneficiary without the intervention of any guardian and without application to any court. Such payments of income or principal may be made to the parents of such minor or to the person with whom the minor is living without any liability upon the Successor Trustee to see to the application thereof. If any such minor survives us but dies before the age of twenty-one years, at his or her death the Successor Trustee shall deliver, pay over, transfer and distribute the trust property being held for such minor to said minor's personal representatives, absolutely.

2. We reserve unto ourselves the power and right (a) to place a mortgage or other lien upon the property, and (b) to collect any rental or other income which may accrue from the trust property and, in our sole discretion as Trustees, either to accumulate such income as an addition to the trust assets being held hereunder or pay such income to ourselves as individuals.

3. We reserve unto ourselves the power and right at any time during our lifetime to amend or revoke in whole or in part the trust hereby created without the necessity of obtaining the consent of any beneficiary and without giving notice to any beneficiary. The sale or other disposition by us of the whole or any part of the property held hereunder shall constitute as to such whole or part a revocation of this trust.

4. The death during our lifetime, or in a common accident or disaster with us, of all of the beneficiaries designated hereunder shall revoke such designation, and in the former event, we reserve the right to designate new beneficiaries. Should we for any reason fail to designate such new beneficiaries, this trust shall terminate upon the death of the survivor of us and the trust property shall revert to the estate of such survivor.

5. Upon the death or legal incapacity of one of us, the survivor shall continue as sole Trustee. Upon the death of the survivor of us, or if we both shall die in a common accident, we hereby nominate and appoint as Successor Trustee hereunder the beneficiary first above named, unless such beneficiary be a minor or legally incompetent, in which event we hereby nominate and appoint as Successor Trustee hereunder the beneficiary whose name appears second above. If such beneficiary named second above shall be a minor or legally incompetent, then we nominate and appoint as Successor Trustee hereunder:

(Name) _____

(Address) _____
      Number   Street   City   State

6. This Declaration of Trust shall extend to and be binding upon the heirs, executors, administrators and assigns of the undersigned and upon the Successors to the Trustee.

7. We as Trustees and our Successor Trustee shall serve without bond.

8. This Declaration of Trust shall be construed and enforced in accordance with the laws of the State of _____ _____.

IN WITNESS WHEREOF we have hereunto set our hands and seals this _____ day of

_____, 19____.

(First co-owner sign here) _____ L.S.

(Second co-owner sign here) _____ L.S.

Witness: (1) _____

Witness: (2) _____

State of _____ ⎫
                    ⎬ ss: _____
County of _____ ⎭

On the _____ day of _____, nineteen hundred and _____,

before me came _____ and _____,
known to me to be the individuals described in, and who executed the foregoing instrument, and they acknowledged that they executed the same, and in due form of law acknowledged the foregoing instrument to be their free act and deed and desired the same might be recorded as such.

(Notary Seal)   _____
                                      Notary Public

WHEREAS, WE,_____and_____, of the

City/Town of_____, County of_____, State of_____,

are the owners as joint tenants of certain real property located at (and known as)_____

in the City/Town of_____, State of_____,

which property is described more fully in the Deed conveying it from_____

to_____, as "that certain piece or parcel of land with buildings thereon

standing, located in said_____, being

NOW, THEREFORE, KNOW ALL MEN BY THESE PRESENTS, that we do hereby acknowledge and declare that we hold and will hold said real property and all right, title and interest in and to said property and all furniture, fixtures and real and personal property situated therein IN TRUST

1. For the use and benefit of the following_____persons, in equal shares, or the survivor of them/per stirpes:

Upon the death of the survivor of us, unless all the beneficiaries shall predecease us or unless we all shall die as a result of a common accident or disaster, our Successor Trustee is hereby directed forthwith to transfer said property and all right, title and interest in and to said property unto the beneficiaries absolutely and thereby terminate this trust; provided, however, that if any beneficiary hereunder shall then be a minor, the Successor Trustee shall hold the trust assets in continuing trust until such beneficiary attains the age of twenty-one years. During such period of continuing trust the Successor Trustee, in his absolute discretion, may retain the specific trust property herein described if he believes it in the best interest of the beneficiary so to do, or he may sell or otherwise dispose of such specific trust property, investing and reinvesting the proceeds as he may deem appropriate. If the specific trust property shall be productive of income or if it be sold or otherwise disposed of, the Successor Trustee may apply or expend any or all of the income or principal directly for the maintenance, education and support of the minor beneficiary without the intervention of any guardian and without application to any court. Such payments of income or principal may be made to the parents of such minor or to the person with whom the minor is living without any liability upon the Successor Trustee to see to the application thereof. If any such minor survives us but dies before the age of twenty-one years, at his or her death the Successor Trustee shall deliver, pay over, transfer and distribute the trust property being held for such minor to said minor's personal representatives, absolutely.

2. We reserve unto ourselves the power and right (a) to place a mortgage or other lien upon the property, and (b) to collect any rental or other income which may accrue from the trust property and, in our sole discretion as Trustees, either to accumulate such income as an addition to the trust assets being held hereunder or pay such income to ourselves as individuals.

3. We reserve unto ourselves the power and right at any time during our lifetime to amend or revoke in whole or in part the trust hereby created without the necessity of obtaining the consent of any beneficiary and without giving notice to any beneficiary. The sale or other disposition by us of the whole or any part of the property held hereunder shall constitute as to such whole or part a revocation of this trust.

4. The death during our lifetime, or in a common accident or disaster with us, of all of the beneficiaries designated hereunder shall revoke such designation, and in the former event, we reserve the right to designate new beneficiaries. Should we for any reason fail to designate such new beneficiaries, this trust shall terminate upon the death of the survivor of us and the trust property shall revert to the estate of such survivor.

5. Upon the death or legal incapacity of one of us, the survivor shall continue as sole Trustee. Upon the death of the survivor of us, or if we both shall die in a common accident, we hereby nominate and appoint as Successor Trustee hereunder the beneficiary first above named, unless such beneficiary be a minor or legally incompetent, in which event we hereby nominate and appoint as Successor Trustee hereunder the beneficiary whose name appears second above. If such beneficiary named second above shall be a minor or legally incompetent, then we nominate and appoint as Successor Trustee hereunder:

(Name)_____

(Address)_____
          Number   Street   City   State

6. This Declaration of Trust shall extend to and be binding upon the heirs, executors, administrators and assigns of the undersigned and upon the Successors to the Trustee.

7. We as Trustees and our Successor Trustee shall serve without bond.

8. This Declaration of Trust shall be construed and enforced in accordance with the laws of the State of_____

_____

IN WITNESS WHEREOF we have hereunto set our hands and seals this_____day of

_____, 19_____.

          *(First co-owner sign here)*_____L.S.

          *(Second co-owner sign here)*_____L.S.

Witness: (1)_____

Witness: (2)_____

State of_____ ⎫
                              ⎬ ss: _____
County of_____ ⎭

On the_____day of_____, nineteen hundred and_____,

before me came_____and_____,
known to me to be the individuals described in, and who executed the foregoing instrument, and they acknowledged that they executed the same, and in due form of law acknowledged the foregoing instrument to be their free act and deed and desired the same might be recorded as such.

(Notary Seal)   _____
                                               Notary Public

APPENDIX D

QUIT CLAIM DEED—JOINT

Instructions:

One or the other of two legal documents is ordinarily used to transfer title to real estate—a warranty deed or a quit claim deed.

When you buy a house, the owner gives you a warranty deed by which he "warrants" or guarantees that the house is his to sell. With that deed, you can hold him responsible if someone else turns up with a valid claim to ownership of the property.

If he gave you a quit claim deed, he would be providing no guarantee at all that he actually owned the property. He'd be saying: "Whatever title or claim I may have to this property I am turning over to you."

When you buy a house, then, you're not satisfied with a quit claim deed; you insist upon being given a warranty deed. The quit claim deed is used when property is being transferred from one member of a family to another, with no financial consideration being involved, or when one of two co-owners, not necessarily related, wishes to transfer his interest in the property to the other co-owner with or without a financial consideration being involved. They know each other and they know that they own the property between them, and there is no need for the retiring co-owner to "warrant" to the other that he owns one-half of the property.

In connection with the transfer of the title to your real estate from yourselves as individuals to yourselves as trustees, as explained in the Appendix, a quit claim deed will be found on Page 353 which will adequately serve your purpose.

Enter your names and the date of the Declaration of Trust (DT-1J, DT-2J or DT-3J) which you have executed. In the large space provided, enter the description of the property as it appears in the Declaration of Trust. Finally, sign the instrument in the presence of two witnesses and before a notary, and file it with the town clerk's or other office where property transfers in your community are customarily recorded. After it is recorded, it will be returned to you.

351

QUIT CLAIM DEED (JOINT)

To all People to whom these Presents shall come, Greetings;

KNOW YE, THAT WE,

(Name) __John J. Smith__   and (Name) __Mary Smith__

in conformity with the terms of a certain Declaration of Trust executed by us under date of _____
__June 20, 1965__, do by these presents release and forever Quit-Claim to ourselves as Trustees under the terms of such Declaration of Trust, and to our successors as Trustee under the terms of such Declaration of Trust, all right, title, interest, claim and demand whatsoever which we as Releasors have or ought to have in or to the property located at:

102 Bartram Street, Jonesville, Connecticut, being the rear portions of Lots #34 and 35, on Map of Building Lots of George Spooner, said map being dated May 3, 1952, and filed for record in the office of the Town Clerk, Jonesville, Connecticut, in Book 5, Page 16, of said Maps. Said parcel of land is more particularly described as:

Beginning at a point on the south line of Lot #34, on said map, 73.5 feet East of the East line of Park Avenue --- running thence North along land of James E. Beach, 100 feet to a point on the North line of Lot #35 on said map, 70.44 feet East of the East line of Cornwall Street, thence East along land of the said James E. Beach (being Lot #51 on said map) 55 feet --- thence South along land of Thomas Cook (being Lot #56 on said map) 100 feet to the aforesaid North line of Bartram Street - thence West to the point of beginning.

To Have and to Hold the premises, with all the appurtenances, as such Trustees forever; and we declare and agree that neither we as individuals nor our heirs or assigns shall have or make any claim or demand upon such property.

In Witness Whereof,

Signed, sealed and delivered in presence of two witnesses:

Witness _Arthur Jones_

Witness _Helen Woodruff_

John J. Smith L.S.
Releasor (First co-owner)

Mary Smith L.S.
Releasor (Second-co-owner)

STATE OF _Connecticut_ } ss. _Jonesville_
COUNTY OF _Fairfield_

Personally appeared before me this _tenth_ _____ day of _February_, 1966, _John J. Smith_ and _Mary Smith_ known to me to be the signers and sealers of the foregoing instrument, and acknowledged the same to be their free act and deed.

George P. Brown
Notary Public

(Notary Seal)

Received for record_____ Date _____ at _____ Time _____ Attest:_____ Clerk

The consideration for this transfer is less than One Dollar.

QUIT CLAIM DEED (JOINT)

To all People to whom these Presents shall come, Greetings;

KNOW YE, THAT WE,

(Name) _____ and (Name) _____

in conformity with the terms of a certain Declaration of Trust executed by us under date of_____

_____, do by these presents release and forever Quit-Claim to ourselves as Trustees under the terms of such Declaration of Trust, and to our successors as Trustee under the terms of such Declaration of Trust, all right, title, interest, claim and demand whatsoever which we as Releasors have or ought to have in or to the property located at:

To Have and to Hold the premises, with all the appurtenances, as such Trustees forever; and we declare and agree that neither we as individuals nor our heirs or assigns shall have or make any claim or demand upon such property.

In Witness Whereof,

Signed, sealed and delivered in presence of two witnesses:

_____   _____ L.S.
            Witness   Releasor (First co-owner)

_____   _____ L.S.
            Witness   Releasor (Second-co-owner)

STATE OF_____ } ss. _____
COUNTY OF_____ }

   Personally appeared before me this_____day of _____,
19____, _____and_____, known to me to be the
signers and sealers of the foregoing instrument, and acknowledged the same to be their free act and deed.

(Notary Seal)   _____
                                          Notary Public

_____

Received for record_____at_____Attest:_____
                          Date   Time   Clerk

The consideration for this transfer is less than One Dollar.

353

Quit Claim Deed

From

_____

_____ and

_____

To

_____

_____ and

_____, Trustees

Received for record _____ 19_____.

At _____
Time

and recorded in Vol._____

on Page_____of the

Land Records by

_____
Authorized Official

QUIT CLAIM DEED (JOINT)

𝕿𝖔 𝖆𝖑𝖑 𝕻𝖊𝖔𝖕𝖑𝖊 𝖙𝖔 𝖜𝖍𝖔𝖒 𝖙𝖍𝖊𝖘𝖊 𝕻𝖗𝖊𝖘𝖊𝖓𝖙𝖘 𝖘𝖍𝖆𝖑𝖑 𝖈𝖔𝖒𝖊, 𝕲𝖗𝖊𝖊𝖙𝖎𝖓𝖌𝖘;

KNOW YE, THAT WE,

(Name) _____ and (Name) _____

in conformity with the terms of a certain Declaration of Trust executed by us under date of_____

_____, do by these presents release and forever Quit-Claim to ourselves as Trustees under the terms of such Declaration of Trust, and to our successors as Trustee under the terms of such Declaration of Trust, all right, title, interest, claim and demand whatsoever which we as Releasors have or ought to have in or to the property located at:

To Have and to Hold the premises, with all the appurtenances, as such Trustees forever; and we declare and agree that neither we as individuals nor our heirs or assigns shall have or make any claim or demand upon such property.

In Witness Whereof,

Signed, sealed and delivered in presence of two witnesses:

_____   _____L.S.

   Witness   Releasor (First co-owner)

_____   _____L.S.

   Witness   Releasor (Second-co-owner)

STATE OF_____⎱ ss. _____
COUNTY OF_____⎰

   Personally appeared before me this_____day of _____,

19____, _____and_____, known to me to be the signers and sealers of the foregoing instrument, and acknowledged the same to be their free act and deed.

(Notary Seal)   _____

                                        Notary Public

Received for record_____at_____Attest:_____

                  Date   Time   Clerk

The consideration for this transfer is less than One Dollar.

5

Quit Claim Deed

From

_____, and

_____

To

_____ and

_____, Trustees

Received for record _____ 19_____.

At _____ Time

and recorded in Vol._____

on Page_____ of the

Land Records by

_____

Authorized Official

GLOSSARY OF LEGAL TERMS
USED IN FINANCIAL PLANNING

To assist the reader who may be unfamiliar with the usage of certain terms in trusts, estates and taxation, this glossary attempts a non-technical definition of such terms.

1. Disposition of Property at Death

A WILL is a document with which a person may dispose of his property at his death. A CODICIL is a document which amends or changes a will. An IN-VALID WILL is a document which, as a matter of law, is not effective to dispose of the property of a dead person (a DECEDENT). The EXECUTION of a will is the signing of a will (not to be confused with the duties of an Executor; see below) with the formalities required by law. The PROBATE of a will is the process of filing a will in a court and proving to the court that the will was signed by the decedent with all the formalities required by law, that the decedent signed of his own free will and understood what he was doing. A TESTAMENT or a LAST WILL AND TESTAMENT is a will. A TESTAMENTARY DIS-POSITION is a disposition of property by will. A TESTAMENTARY TRUST is a trust set up in a will. A TESTATOR (female-TESTATRIX) is a person who made a will. A decedent who made a will is said to have died TESTATE.

LETTERS TESTAMENTARY: a document issued by a court naming the person who is to carry out the terms of a will. An EXECUTOR (female-EXECU-TRIX) is the person named in a will to carry out its provisions. An ADMINISTRATOR WITH WILL AN-NEXED (female-ADMINISTRATRIX) is the person designated by a court to carry out the terms of a will where the will fails to name an executor, or the executor named is unable to act as such. REPRESENTATIVE, LEGAL REPRESENTATIVE or PERSONAL REP-RESENTATIVE are general terms referring to an ex-ecutor or administrator. An ESTATE is the property left by a decedent. (An additional meaning is given in section 4.)

A LEGACY or BEQUEST is a gift made by will. A DEVISE is a gift of real property (land, buildings, etc.) made by will. To BEQUEATH or DEVISE is to make a gift by will. A LEGATEE or DEVISEE is a person named in a will to receive a legacy, bequest or devise. A RESIDUARY LEGATEE is one who is given the balance of an estate after payment of claims, expenses, taxes and all specified legacies.

INTESTACY refers to a decedent who left no will; he is said to have died INTESTATE. INTESTATE SUCCESSION is the disposition of the property of a decedent who left no will in accordance with the LAWS OF INTESTACY (also called LAWS OF DESCENT AND DISTRIBUTION) to persons who bear certain relationships to the decedent and who are variously referred to as HEIRS, HEIRS-AT-LAW, LEGAL HEIRS, NEXT-OF-KIN and DISTRIBUTEES. An ADMINISTRATOR (female-ADMINISTRATRIX) is a person appointed by a court to take charge of the estate of an intestate decedent. LETTERS OF AD-MINISTRATION: a document issued by a court which designates the person to act as administrator.

EXPENSES OF ADMINISTRATION are the expenses incurred by an executor or administrator in carrying out the terms of a will or in administering an estate in accordance with provisions of law. These include the fees of a probate or surrogate's court and of the execu-tors or administrators, attorneys' fees, accountants' fees and appraisers fees.

2. Lifetime Disposition of Property

A DONOR is a person who makes a gift. A DONEE is a person who receives a gift. An INCOMPLETE gift is no gift at all because the donor did not complete the gift by delivery of the property or a document of transfer to the donee. An INTER VIVOS gift is one made by the donor during his lifetime. A TESTA-MENTARY gift is one made by will. A gift IN CON-TEMPLATION OF DEATH is a gift made by the donor shortly before his death (a period of three years before death, for tax purposes) because he believes he will die shortly. A gift IN TRUST is a gift of property to a trustee to hold for the benefit of someone else. A GIFT TAX is a tax imposed on the making of gifts.

3. Transfers of Property in Trust

A TRUST is a relationship of confidence or trust in which one person assumes an obligation to hold and manage property for the benefit of another person. If the parties express their intention to create a trust, usually in writing, it is called an EXPRESS trust. A TRUST AGREEMENT or TRUST INDENTURE is the document which expresses the terms of the trust; it is an agreement between the person who is transferring property, called the SETTLOR (sometimes DONOR or GRANTOR), and the person receiving and agreeing to manage the property, called the TRUSTEE, for the benefit of another person, called the BENEFICIARY. If the settlor names himself as trustee, the trust document is called a DECLARATION OF TRUST.

If the interest of a beneficiary does not begin unless some event (such as surviving someone else) occurs, he is a CONTINGENT beneficiary; if his interest is limited to income earned, he is an INCOME beneficiary; if his interest is solely in distributions of principal, he is a PRINCIPAL beneficiary; a beneficiary who is to receive distributions as long as he lives is said to have a LIFE INTEREST (sometimes incorrectly referred to as a LIFE ESTATE) and is referred to as a LIFE BENEFICIARY; the beneficiary who is to receive the property upon the termination of the trust is loosely referred to as a REMAINDERMAN, and his interest is generally called a REMAINDER. The property transferred in trust is variously called the RES, CORPUS or PRINCIPAL.

Various Types of Trusts

If the trust is set up to operate during the lifetime of the settlor, it is called an INTER VIVOS, LIVING or LIFETIME trust; if it is set up in his will, it is called a TESTAMENTARY TRUST.

Special names are sometimes used to identify trusts which contain special features: if the settlor retains the power to revoke a trust, the trust is called REVOCABLE; if he does not retain power to revoke a trust, the trust is called IRREVOCABLE; if the trustee has the power to terminate the trust, it is called TERMINABLE; if the trust property is to be returned to the set-

tlor upon termination, it is called REVERSIONARY; trusts, which for income tax reasons are set up for a fixed number of years, are referred to as SHORT-TERM TRUSTS—such as a TWO YEAR TRUST (sometimes called a CHARITABLE INCOME TRUST) or a TEN YEAR TRUST (sometimes referred to as a REVERSIONARY TRUST); if the trust property is to be given to a charity upon the termination of the trust, it is loosely called a CHARITABLE REMAINDER TRUST; a trust which prohibits a beneficiary from selling his interest or pledging it to secure a loan and prevents his creditors from seizing his interest is called a SPENDTHRIFT TRUST; a trust which gives the trustee the power, in his discretion, to distribute or to withhold distribution or to determine the distributive shares of various beneficiaries is called a DISCRETIONARY TRUST; SPRINKLE TRUSTS give the trustee discretion to determine the amounts of income or principal to be distributed to various beneficiaries; an ACCUMULATION TRUST requires the trustee to accumulate the income earned over a period for some future distribution or other purpose; a POUR-OVER TRUST is a living trust which receives or is to receive a legacy under the terms of a will, as distinguished from a TESTAMENTARY TRUST which is set up in the will.

A POWER OF APPOINTMENT is a power given to a beneficiary to designate persons to receive certain distributions from a trust. A LIMITED or SPECIAL POWER OF APPOINTMENT limits the persons who may be chosen to receive distributions. A GENERAL POWER OF APPOINTMENT does not limit the persons who may be chosen to receive distributions. A POWER OF INVASION is a power given to either a beneficiary or the trustee to make distributions from principal if the income distributions are for some reason inadequate.

A CUSTODIAN FOR A MINOR is akin to a trustee whose duties and powers are set forth in a state statute which provides for gifts of securities or money to minors by registration of the securities or the deposit account in the name of the CUSTODIAN.

LEGALS or INVESTMENTS LEGAL FOR TRUSTEES are the investments which a trustee is permitted to make by state law where the trust agreement fails to set forth the trustees' investment powers. In some states, a LEGAL LIST is provided, that is, a statutory list of securities legal for trustees to invest in. In some states, however, where the trust agreement fails to set forth the trustees' investment powers, the trustee may invest under the PRUDENT MAN RULE, that is to say, in any security, such as a mutual fund, in which a prudent man considering the permanent disposition of his funds would invest with due regard to the income as well as the probable safety of the capital to be invested.

4. Property Terms

An ESTATE is an interest in property. (An additional meaning is given in section 1.) A TENANT is a person who holds an interest in property. A LIFE ESTATE or LEGAL LIFE ESTATE is an interest in the use of, or income from, property for someone's life. The holder of such interest is called a LIFE TENANT. A RE-MAINDER is an interest in property which is to be enjoyed after the expiration of a LIFE ESTATE. The holder of such interest is called a REMAINDERMAN. A REVERSION is the right to the return of property after a life estate or a fixed number of years. A FU-TURE INTEREST is loosely used to mean any interest which cannot be enjoyed until some future time.

A TENANCY IN COMMON is the holding of frac-tional undivided interests by several persons in the same property. A JOINT TENANCY WITH RIGHT OF SURVIVORSHIP is the holding of fractional un-divided interests of two persons, each of whom has the right to the entire property if and when he sur-vives the other. A JOINT TENANCY is loosely used to mean a joint tenancy with right of survivorship but in most states its legal meaning is a tenancy in com-mon. A TENANCY BY THE ENTIRETY describes a joint tenancy with right of survivorship for a hus-band and wife.

COMMUNITY PROPERTY (as used in a few of the states with a French or Spanish law tradition) refers to a partnership interest of a husband and wife in the property of both accumulated during the marriage by the efforts of either of them.

5. Corporate Terms

A CORPORATION is a business organization created in accordance with statute (STOCK CORPORATION LAW or BUSINESS CORPORATION LAW) to per-mit its owners to limit their liability for its debts to their investment in the corporation. Ownership of a corporation is referred to as ownership of its STOCK or SHARES of stock which are represented by CER-TIFICATES of ownership of shares of stock, also called STOCK CERTIFICATES; the owners of the corporation are therefore referred to as STOCKHOLD-ERS or SHAREHOLDERS. When an investor makes an investment in a corporation, it is said to ISSUE its stock to him; the stock is REGISTERED in his name on the books of the corporation and certificates representing the shares of stock purchased are delivered to him.

The stock of a corporation may be divided into COM-MON stock and PREFERRED stock, which has special rights, such as a prior right to dividends.

When an investor lends money to a corporation, it is said to issue a DEBT SECURITY to him. The debt securities of a corporation may be issued in many forms; thus BONDS, which are usually secured by mortgages, DEBENTURES, which are usually un-secured, NOTES, which are commercial paper usually used in borrowing from banks or for evidencing trade debts, and CONVERTIBLE BONDS or DEBEN-TURES, which give the holder the right to surrender the security in exchange for stock.

AUTHORIZED stock refers to the amount of stock which a corporation is authorized by law to issue. OUT-STANDING stock refers to the amount of stock in the hands of the stockholders. TREASURY stock re-fers to previously issued stock reacquired by the cor-poration from its stockholders and held for future dis-position. STOCK RIGHTS or WARRANTS are rights of stockholders to purchase more stock of a corpora-tion; sometimes referred to as a right to SUBSCRIBE to more stock.

The stockholders elect a BOARD OF DIRECTORS who set corporate policy and appoint the executive of-ficers (PRESIDENT, VICE-PRESIDENT, TREAS-URER and SECRETARY) to execute the board poli-cies in operating the corporation.

A DIVIDEND is a distribution of money or property or stock made by a corporation to its stockholders; if the dividend is a return of part of the stockholders in-vestment, it is called a CAPITAL dividend and some-times a LIQUIDATING dividend; if it is paid out of the earnings of a corporation, it is called an ORDI-NARY INCOME dividend; if it is paid by a registered open-end investment company (a mutual fund) out of the profits from the sale of securities, it is called a CAPITAL GAIN or SECURITY PROFITS distribu-tion; if the dividend is paid in the stock of the corpora-tion paying the dividend, it is called a STOCK divi-dend; and if the stockholder has the option to take a cash or a stock dividend, it is called an OPTIONAL dividend or an OPTIONAL STOCK dividend.

6. Federal Income Tax Terms

The dictionary defines INCOME as the gain or bene-fit from labor, business or property. In general, it means the same thing in law, but, specifically, whether or not any given item is treated as income may vary under the many tax and related statutes.

GROSS INCOME, for an individual, is the aggregate of his incomes from all sources without deduction for the expenses of producing such incomes. GROSS RE-CEIPTS are the receipts of a business without any de-ductions whatsoever. NET INCOME is basically an accounting term which means the business revenues minus the business expenses. ADJUSTED GROSS IN-COME is a tax term which, for an individual, means the sum of his salary, his interest income, his dividend income, his net income from a business or profession, his net income from rents, etc. TAXABLE INCOME is the amount on which the tax is computed; it is the result of subtracting from adjusted gross income all allowable DEDUCTIONS and EXEMPTIONS.

The allowable deductions may be the STANDARD DEDUCTION, that is a specified 10% of adjusted gross income but not in excess of $1000 on a joint return (or $500 on a separate return of a married person), or the ITEMIZED DEDUCTIONS, that is deductions for charitable contributions, medical and dental expenses, interest, casualty losses, etc. TAX CREDITS are amounts which the taxpayer may deduct from the tax itself.

TAX-FREE or TAX-EXEMPT income is income which for statutory or constitutional law reasons is not subject to income taxation. In reporting dividend income, the taxpayer may deduct from his gross income, $50 of dividends received from certain U. S. business corporations. This deduction is called the DIVIDEND EXCLUSION. From his tax, he may subtract 4% of the balance of his dividends from U. S. business corporations. This deduction is called the DIVIDEND TAX CREDIT.

A CAPITAL ASSET is basically an investment; it may be a share of stock, a bond, an interest in real estate or a mine, etc. A CAPITAL GAIN or LOSS is a gain or loss from the sale of an investment. A LONG-TERM capital gain or loss is a gain or loss on the sale of an investment which had been owned for more than six months prior to the sale. A SHORT-TERM capital gain or loss is a gain or loss on the sale of an investment which had been owned for six months or less prior to the sale. Security profits (capital gain) distributions from mutual funds are considered long-term gains no matter how long the fund shares have been owned prior to the distribution.

7. Federal Estate Tax Terms

The term ESTATE TAX, in general, refers to a tax on the property and interests in property left by a decedent or on the transfer of such property as a result of death; it is also referred to as an INHERITANCE tax, or a DEATH tax.

The GROSS ESTATE of a decedent is the aggregate of the property and interests in property which he leaves, property which he gave away within three years of his death IN CONTEMPLATION OF DEATH, the face amount of insurance on his life owned by

him, property which he had the power to give away even though not owned by him, property which he had transferred to trusts which he could revoke during his lifetime or over which he retained certain kinds of controls or which were really substitutes for a will. The TAXABLE ESTATE, the amount on which the tax is computed, is the result of subtracting from the value of the gross estate certain allowable DEDUCTIONS (such as debts, taxes, losses, and charitable bequests) and EXEMPTIONS. The GROSS ESTATE TAX is the amount of tax computed on the taxable estate. From the gross estate tax may be subtracted certain CREDITS to arrive at the NET ESTATE TAX, which is the amount payable.

Where there is no provision in a will for the source of the funds from which the estate taxes are to be paid, the law provides for the APPORTIONMENT of the tax among the legatees.

Each estate is permitted a $60,000 EXEMPTION from the gross estate. Each estate is permitted a MARITAL DEDUCTION, that is a deduction of the value of property left to a spouse. The maximum marital deduction is 50% of the ADJUSTED GROSS ESTATE (the gross estate minus expenses, debts, certain taxes and certain losses). No marital deduction is allowed for the value of property left to the wife for a limited period or until the occurrence or non-occurrence of some event. Such interests are called TERMINABLE.

8. Federal Gift Tax Terms

A GIFT TAX is a tax on the gift of property by the DONOR to the DONEE. Each donor is allowed to make gifts worth up to $3000 to each donee each year free of gift tax. This $3000 allowance is called the ANNUAL EXCLUSION. In addition to the annual exclusion, each donor may claim a SPECIFIC or LIFETIME EXEMPTION of $30,000—that is to say, that by filing gift tax returns, he may deduct amounts up to $30,000 during his lifetime for gifts made by him in addition to the annual exclusions. By filing a joint gift tax return with his spouse, the donor can increase the annual exclusion to $6000 for each donee and the lifetime exemption to $60,000. This is spoken of as GIFT SPLITTING because for tax purposes the gift is treated as having been given half by the husband and half by the wife. DEDUCTIONS are allowed for gifts to a spouse (MARITAL DEDUCTION) and to charitable institutions (CHARITABLE DEDUCTION). The maximum marital deduction is 50% of the value of the gifts made to a spouse in any one year but no marital deduction is allowed for TERMINABLE INTERESTS (interests for a limited period).

The National Estate Planning Council
49 Plaza
Bridgeport, Conn. 06603

Gentlemen:

Enclosed find check or money order for $_____.

(a) Please send me additional sets of the instruments circled below. It is my understanding that the cost of each "set" (consisting of an original and a duplicate copy of the instrument), sent postpaid, is $1.00 (with the exception of DT-17, which is $4.00 per set, and DT-18, which is $3.00).

FOR REAL ESTATE

Declarations of Trust for *Individually Held* Real Estate

DT-1   For naming one beneficiary.

DT-2   For naming one primary beneficiary and one contingent beneficiary to receive if the primary beneficiary is not surviving.

DT-3   For naming two or more persons to share equally.

DT-4   For naming one primary beneficiary, with one's children sharing equally as contingent beneficiaries.

QCD   Quit claim deed for use with any of the above.

Declarations of Trust for *Jointly Held* Real Estate

DT-1-J For naming one beneficiary to receive real estate upon the death of the surviving joint-owner.

DT-2-J For naming one primary beneficiary and one contingent beneficiary to receive real estate upon the death of the surviving joint-owner.

DT-3-J For naming two or more persons sharing equally to receive real estate upon the death of the surviving joint-owner.

QCD-J Quit claim deed for use with any of the above.

FOR SAVINGS OR CHECKING ACCOUNTS (ACCOUNTS IN INDIVIDUAL NAMES ONLY; NOT FOR JOINT ACCOUNTS)

DT-5   For naming one beneficiary.

DT-6   For naming one primary beneficiary and one contingent beneficiary to receive if the primary beneficiary is not surviving.

DT-7   For naming two or more persons to share equally.

DT-8   For naming one primary beneficiary, with one's children sharing equally as contingent beneficiaries.

FOR MUTUAL FUNDS (SHARES IN INDIVIDUAL NAMES ONLY; NOT FOR JOINTLY HELD SHARES)

DT-9   For naming one beneficiary.

DT-10   For naming one primary beneficiary and one contingent beneficiary to receive if the primary beneficiary is not surviving.

DT-11   For naming two or more persons to share equally.

DT-12   For naming one primary beneficiary, with one's children sharing equally as contingent beneficiaries.

FOR STOCKS (SHARES IN INDIVIDUAL NAMES ONLY; NOT FOR JOINTLY HELD SHARES)

DT-13   For naming one beneficiary.

DT-14   For naming one primary beneficiary and one contingent beneficiary to receive if the primary beneficiary is not surviving.

DT-15   For naming two or more persons to share equally.

DT-16   For naming one primary beneficiary, with one's children sharing equally as contingent beneficiaries.

FOR A DACEY TRUST
DT-17

FOR A WIFE'S TRUST
DT-18

FOR A CHARITABLE TRUST
DT-19

FOR A REVERSIONARY TRUST
DT-20

FOR MAKING A GIFT TO A MINOR
DT-21

FOR PERSONAL EFFECTS
DT-22

FOR AN UNINCORPORATED BUSINESS
DT-23

FOR A BROKERAGE ACCOUNT (ACCOUNTS IN INDIVIDUAL NAMES ONLY; NOT FOR JOINTLY OWNED ACCOUNTS)

DT-24   For naming one beneficiary.

DT-25   For naming one primary beneficiary and one contingent beneficiary to receive if the primary beneficiary is not surviving.

DT-26   For naming two or more persons to share equally.

DT-27   For naming one primary beneficiary, with one's children sharing equally as contingent beneficiaries.

FOR A SAFE DEPOSIT BOX (BOXES IN INDIVIDUAL NAMES ONLY; NOT FOR JOINTLY HELD BOXES)

DT-28   For naming one beneficiary.

DT-29   For naming one primary beneficiary and one contingent beneficiary to receive if the primary beneficiary is not surviving.

DT-30   For naming two or more persons to share equally.

DT-31   For naming one primary beneficiary, with one's children sharing equally as contingent beneficiaries.

FOR U.S. SAVINGS BONDS (BONDS IN INDIVIDUAL NAMES ONLY; NOT FOR JOINTLY HELD BONDS)

DT-32   For naming one beneficiary.

DT-33   For naming one primary beneficiary and one contingent beneficiary to receive if the primary beneficiary is not surviving.

DT-34   For naming two or more persons to share equally.

DT-35   For naming one primary beneficiary, with one's children sharing equally as contingent beneficiaries.

REVOCATIONS

REV-1-2-3-4   To revoke either DT-1, DT-2, DT-3 or DT-4.

REV-1-2-3-J   To revoke either DT-1-J, DT-2-J or DT-3-J.

REV-9-10-11-12   To revoke either DT-9, DT-10, DT-11 or DT-12.

REV-13-14-15-16   To revoke either DT-13, DT-14, DT-15 or DT-16.

REV-22   To revoke DT-22.

REV-23   To revoke DT-23.

REV-24-25-26-27   To revoke either DT-24, DT-25, DT-26 or DT-27.

REV-28-29-30-31   To revoke either DT-28, DT-29, DT-30 or DT-31.

REV-32-33-34-35   To revoke either DT-32, DT-33, DT-34 or DT-35.

WILLS

W-1   Husband's will leaving everything to wife, or to some *one* other person if his wife does not survive him.

W-2   Wife's will leaving everything to husband, or to some *one* other person if her husband does not survive her.

W-3   Husband's will leaving everything to wife, or, if she does not survive him, to two or more other persons whose children will take their share if they are not living.

W-4   Wife's will leaving everything to husband, or, if he does not survive her, to two or more other persons whose children will take their share if they are not living.

W-5   Husband's will leaving everything to wife, or, if she does not survive him, to two or more other persons sharing equally; if one of such persons dies, the surviving persons will divide his share.

W-6   Wife's will leaving everything to husband, or, if he does not survive her, to two or more other persons sharing equally; if one of such persons dies, the surviving persons will divide his share.

W-7   Will leaving everything to two or more persons to share equally; if one of such persons dies, his children will take his share.

W-8   Will leaving everything to the two or more persons to share equally; if one of such persons dies, the surviving persons will divide his share.

W-9   Will of husband and father leaving everything to his wife, and to his children if his wife does not survive him.

W-10   Will of wife and mother leaving everything to her husband, and to her children if her husband does not survive her.

W-11   Will for individual who has established a Dacey Trust. Incorporates the balance of his estate into the trust.

W-12   Will for wife of individual who has established a Dacey Trust. Leaves everything to her husband if he survives her. If he does not survive her, incorporates her estate into his Dacey Trust.

W-13   Will leaving everything to some *one* person, or some *one* other person if the first beneficiary be not surviving.

W-14   Will leaving everything to some *one* person, or to two or more other persons in equal shares if the first beneficiary be not surviving.

POWER OF ATTORNEY

POA   General Power of Attorney permitting another person to act for you. (Effective only during your lifetime; expires automatically at your death.)

(b)   Please send me_____additional copies of HOW TO AVOID PROBATE at $4.95 per copy, postpaid.

(c)   Please send me_____copies of WHAT'S WRONG WITH YOUR LIFE INSURANCE, a 445-page buyer's guide to life insurance, at $4.95 per copy, postpaid.

Name_____

Street_____

City_____State_____

GIFT ORDER

Send the book(s) noted above to the following person(s) with a note indicating that it is a gift from me:

Name_____

Street_____

City_____State_____

Name_____

Street_____

City_____State_____